CERES™
Celestial Legend
Volume 8: Miori
Shôjo Edition

STORY & ART BY YÛ WATASE

English Adaptation/Gary Leach

Translation/Lillian Olsen
Touch-Up Art & Lettering/Melanie Lewis
Cover & Graphic Design/Hidemi Sahara
Editor/Avery Gotoh
Supervising Editor/Frances E. Wall

Managing Editor/Annette Roman
Editor-in-Chief/Alvin Lu
Sr. Director of Licensing & Acquisitions/Rika Inouye
Production Manager/Noboru Watanabe
Vice President of Sales/Joe Morici
Vice President of Marketing/Liza Coppola
Executive Vice President/Hyoe Narita
Publisher/Seiji Horibuchi

Printed in Canada

Published by VIZ, LLC
P.O. Box 77010 • San Francisco CA 94107

Shôjo Edition

10 9 8 7 6 5 4 3 2 1

First printing, July 2004

VIZ GRAPHIC NOVEL

CERES

Celestial Legend

Vol. 8: Miori

Story and Art by
YÛ WATASE

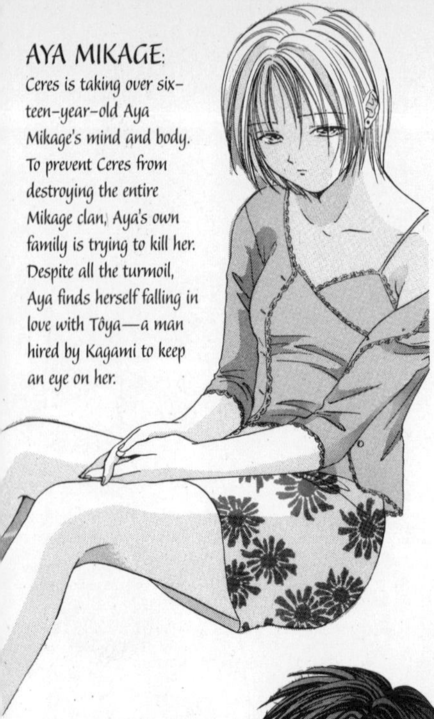

AYA MIKAGE:

Ceres is taking over sixteen-year-old Aya Mikage's mind and body. To prevent Ceres from destroying the entire Mikage clan, Aya's own family is trying to kill her. Despite all the turmoil, Aya finds herself falling in love with Tôya—a man hired by Kagami to keep an eye on her.

AKI MIKAGE:

Aya's twin brother. While the consciousness of Ceres is taking over Aya, Aki is showing signs of bearing the consciousness of the founder (progenitor) of the Mikage family line. Placed under confinement by the Mikage family to keep him separated from Aya, still nothing will keep him from her....

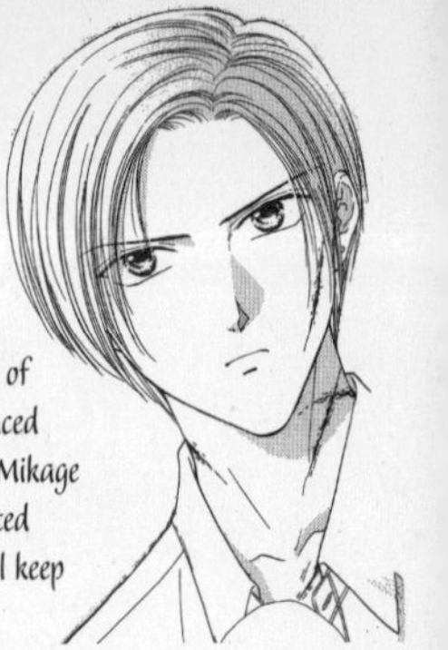

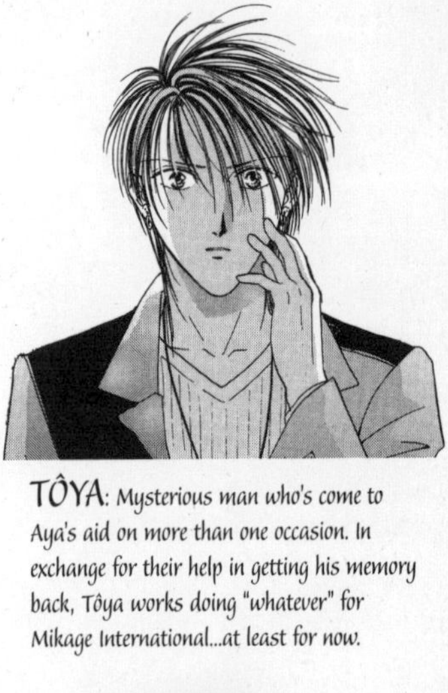

TÔYA: Mysterious man who's come to Aya's aid on more than one occasion. In exchange for their help in getting his memory back, Tôya works doing "whatever" for Mikage International...at least for now.

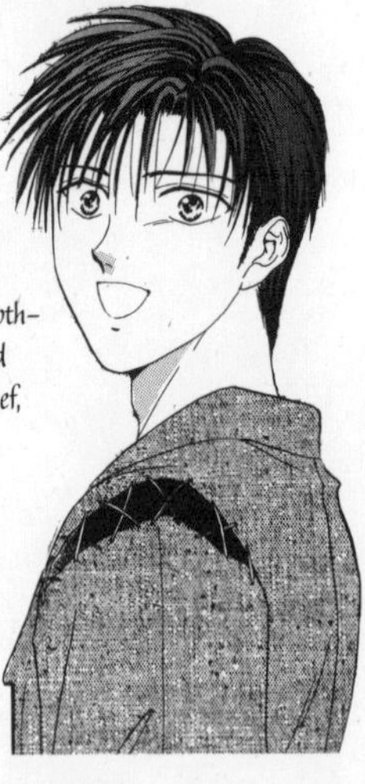

YÛHI: Sixteen-year-old brother-in-law to Suzumi. A skilled martial artist and aspiring chef, Yûhi has been asked (ordered, more like) to serve as Aya's watchful protector and guardian...his own feelings for her notwithstanding.

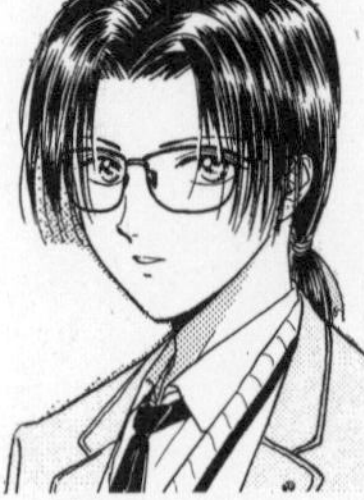

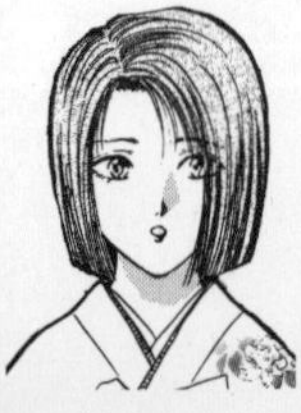

SUZUMI: Instructor of traditional Japanese dance and descendant of ten'nyo or "celestial maidens" herself. A big sister figure, Suzumi has welcomed Aya into her household, and is more than happy to provide her with all the protection, assistance and support that she can.

SHURO: Surviving member of the beautiful, androgynous Japan pop duo, GeSANG. A woman (with ten'nyo ancestry) passing as a man, her agent's urging prompts Shuro to consider a return to the pop-music scene, this time as a solo act.

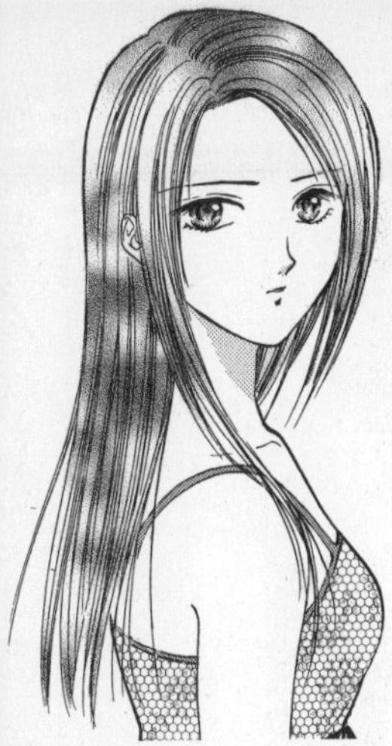

CERES: Once upon a time...long, long ago...a ten'nyo named Ceres descended to Earth. Her hagoromo or "feathered robes" stolen, Ceres—unable to return to the heavens—was forced by the human thief to become his wife and bear his children...thus beginning the Mikage family line. Awakened after aeons of waiting—and anger—Ceres wants her hagoromo back and vows to use all her celestial powers to avenge herself against the descendants of the man who wronged her.

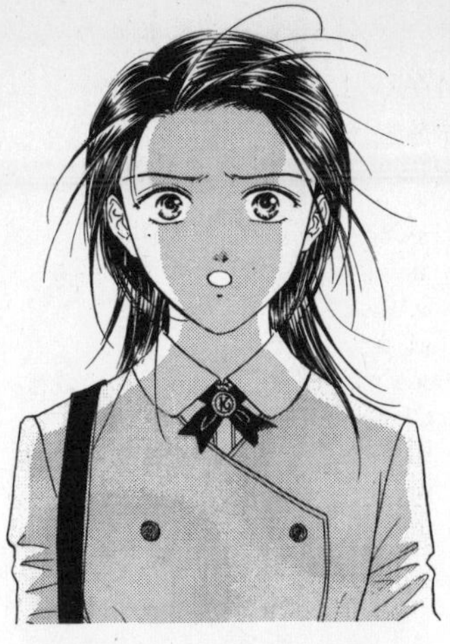

MIORI SAHARA: Pretty, slightly mysterious girl at Aya and Yûhi's new high school in Shizuoka. She not only looks a little like Aya—she looks a lot like her. A lot.

KAGAMI: Although the Mikage family wants to kill off Ceres through Aya, Kagami—head of Mikage International's research and development department—has put into motion his own agenda: C-Project, a plan to gather descendants of ten'nyo and use their power.

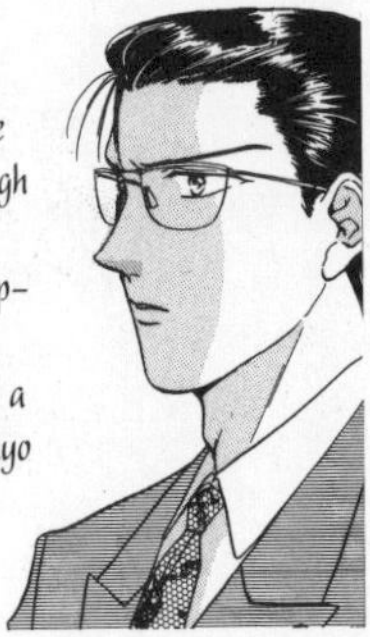

CHIDORI: Awakened to her own, unsuspected celestial powers only after her younger brother was put in mortal danger, Chidori Kuruma was at first another target of Kagami's, but was spared by the compassion of Tôya. Deceptively young in appearance (she looks like a grade-schooler but is actually in high school, just like Aya), Chidori has since decided to help Aya and the others in the search for Ceres' missing hagoromo.

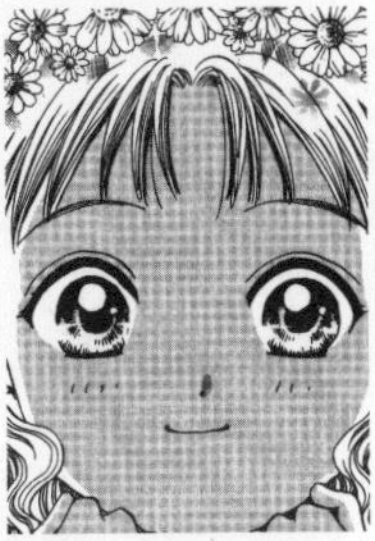

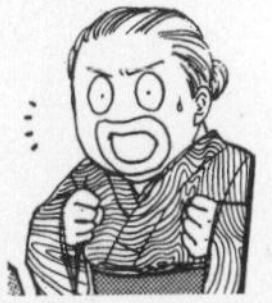

MRS. Q (ODA-KYÛ): Eccentric yet loyal-to-a-fault servant of the Aogiri household.

You may have noticed some unfamiliar people and things mentioned in CERES. VIZ left these Japanese pop-culture references as they originally appeared in the manga series. Here's an explanation for those who may not be so J-Pop savvy:

Page 06: "Print Club": As mentioned last volume, "Puri-kura" or "Print Club" machines are like the usual photo booths found at airports, arcades, etc., except the neat thing about Print Club machines is, they print the photos on handy, variable-sized stickers. Great for plastering all over everything...like cell phones!

Page 12: "Statue of Hakuryô": Located at the entrance to Miho no Matsubara Beach, in Shizuoka, this actual statue of a fisherman holding a celestial robe represents a character from the play of actor, playwright and drama theorist Zeami (1363–1443).

BIRTHDAY March 2 🐟∴˚

BLOOD TYPE B

After transformation → T: 5'5" B: 33" W: 22" H: 33"

T. 4'11"   **B.** 30"   **W.** 22"   **H.** 31"

HOBBY Taking pics ✌ Print club ✌ Collecting cute jewelry and stickers

SPECIALTY Loudmouth (?). Pretending to be a grade-schooler

CHIDORI KURUMA

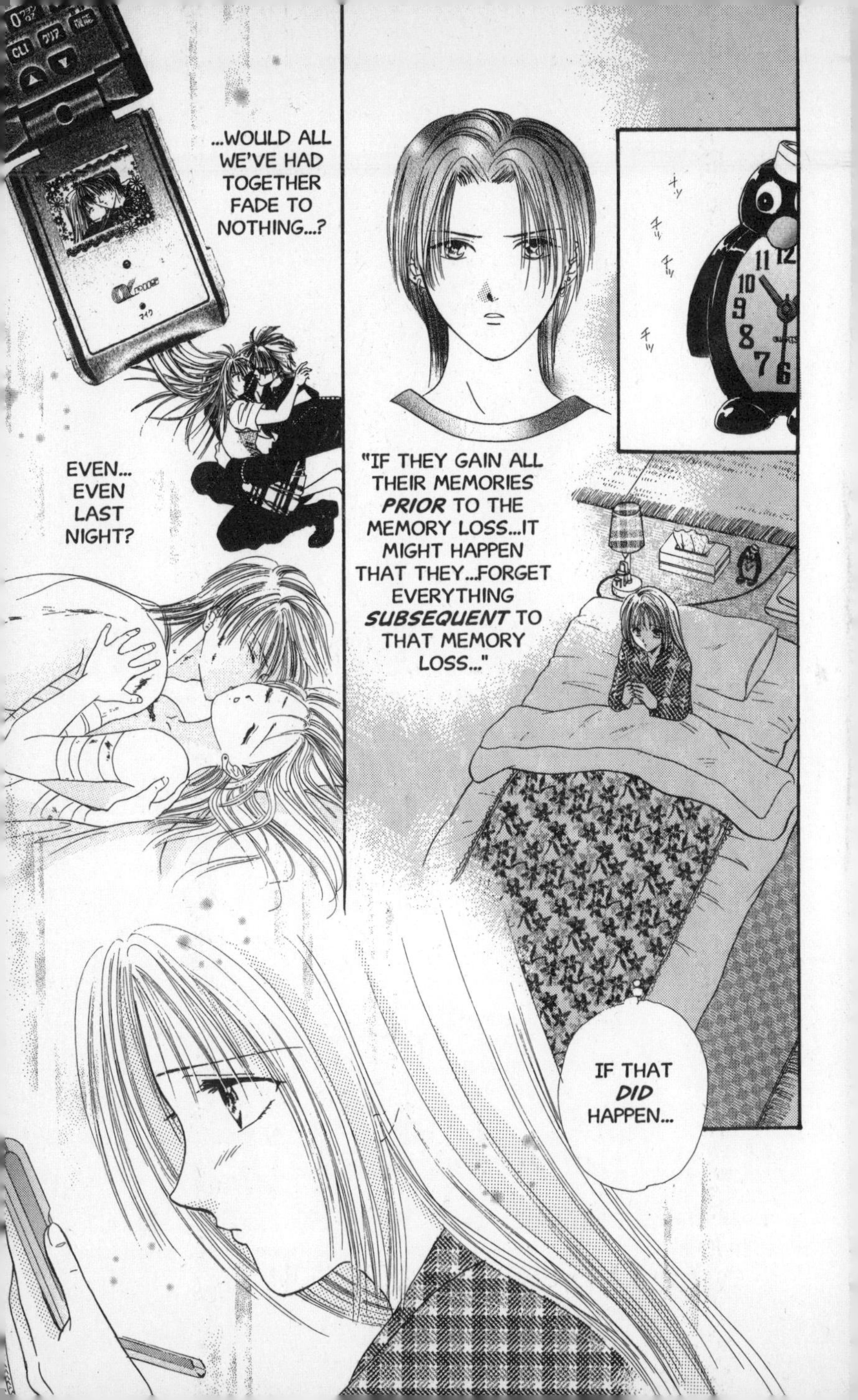

"IF THEY GAIN ALL THEIR MEMORIES *PRIOR* TO THE MEMORY LOSS...IT MIGHT HAPPEN THAT THEY...FORGET EVERYTHING *SUBSEQUENT* TO THAT MEMORY LOSS..."
IF THAT *DID* HAPPEN...
...WOULD ALL WE'VE HAD TOGETHER FADE TO NOTHING...?
EVEN... EVEN LAST NIGHT?

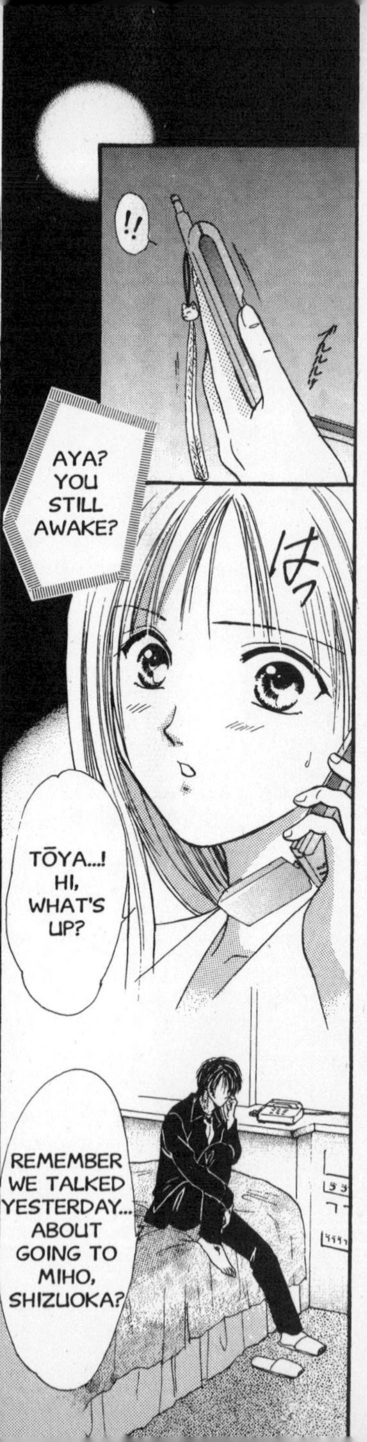
!!
AYA? YOU STILL AWAKE?
はっ
TŌYA...! HI, WHAT'S UP?
REMEMBER WE TALKED YESTERDAY... ABOUT GOING TO MIHO, SHIZUOKA?

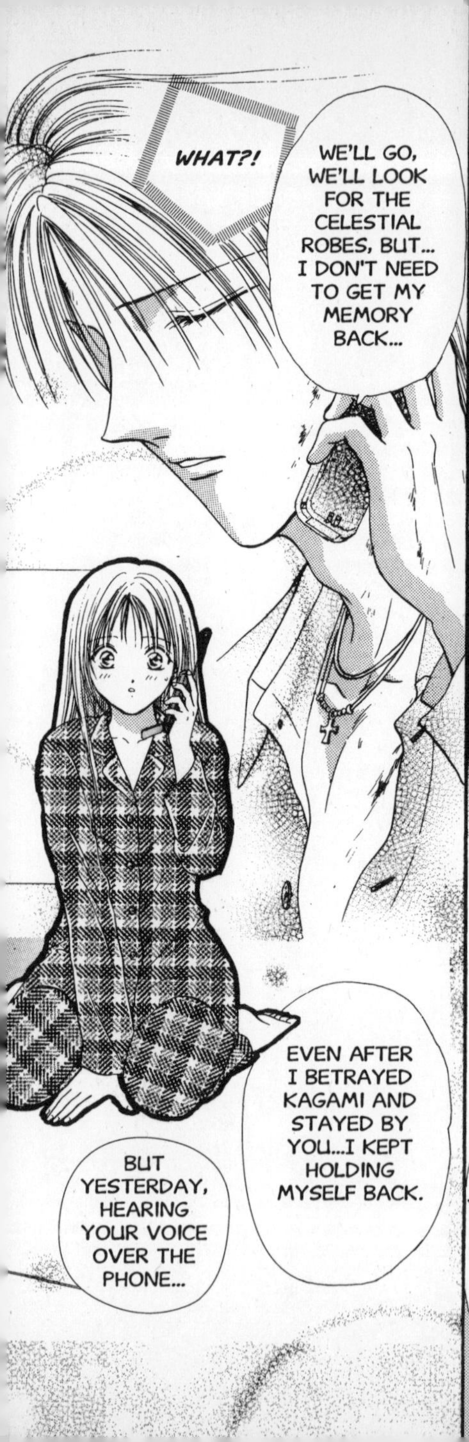
WE'LL GO, WE'LL LOOK FOR THE CELESTIAL ROBES, BUT... I DON'T NEED TO GET MY MEMORY BACK...
WHAT?!
EVEN AFTER I BETRAYED KAGAMI AND STAYED BY YOU...I KEPT HOLDING MYSELF BACK.
BUT YESTERDAY, HEARING YOUR VOICE OVER THE PHONE...

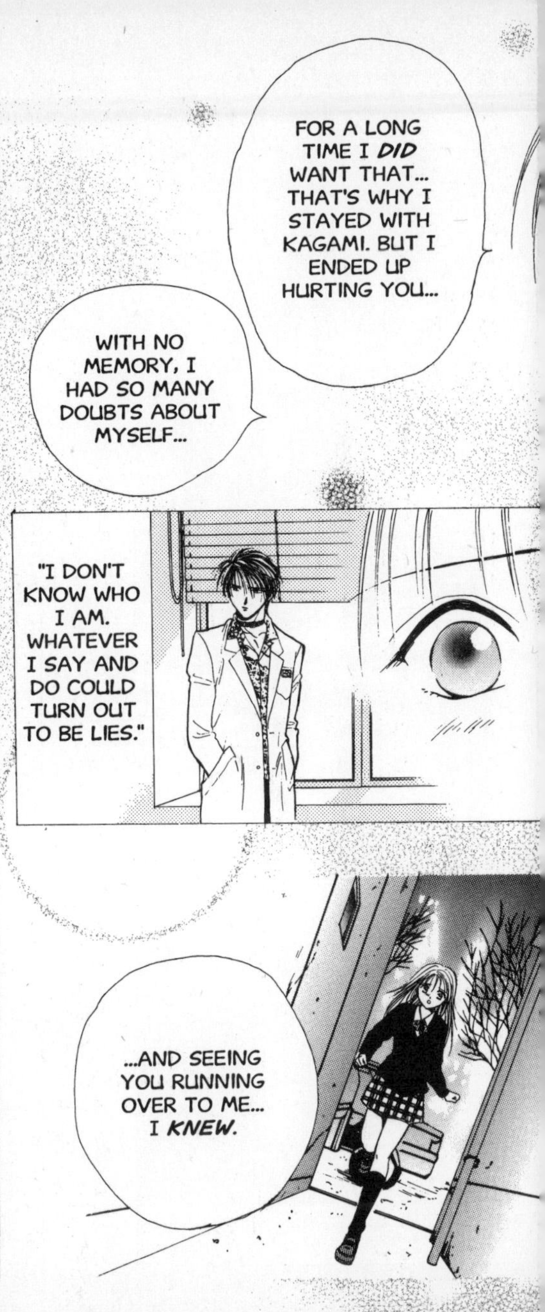
FOR A LONG TIME I *DID* WANT THAT... THAT'S WHY I STAYED WITH KAGAMI. BUT I ENDED UP HURTING YOU...
WITH NO MEMORY, I HAD SO MANY DOUBTS ABOUT MYSELF...
"I DON'T KNOW WHO I AM. WHATEVER I SAY AND DO COULD TURN OUT TO BE LIES."
...AND SEEING YOU RUNNING OVER TO ME... I *KNEW*.

Ceres: 8

It's me. It is I. It's Watase. Maybe you kinda figured that by now. (?) Anyway, hi there.

Hmm, there's so much to write about this time, I don't know where to start.

Shuro's pretty popular, and a few have asked, "Is GeSANG modeled after Lazy Knack...?!" Actually, I didn't really model them after anyone specific. When I conceived of Shuro, I imagined him as "the modern cool kid," so I made Kei be a different type...and that's how they came about. I pulled out tapes of the group access, which I used to like, and wondered if there were other duos that sang in that style of pop. Then my assistant brought over tapes of Lazy Knack. So I was listening to their music, at least, while I drew. GeSANG is "song" in German. I like the word. The "e" in lower case is on purpose, just for variety.

At first, I wondered if I should make them into a band, or maybe a group of 4-6 like V6 (...and then Da Pump came out—I was surprised that they were from Okinawa, too). Then my editor told me that a group would get too confusing, so I focused it down to two.

The character of Shuro actually existed soon after the serialization started. I also deliberated whether to make her into a real guy or not, but I settled on female because she's a celestial maiden, after all. A lot of people were disappointed, including my assistants. ◡̈ But she's still popular, so there you go. ◡̈

Oh, speaking of Shuro—the readers in Okinawa taught me a lot of regional slang...

...To be continued!

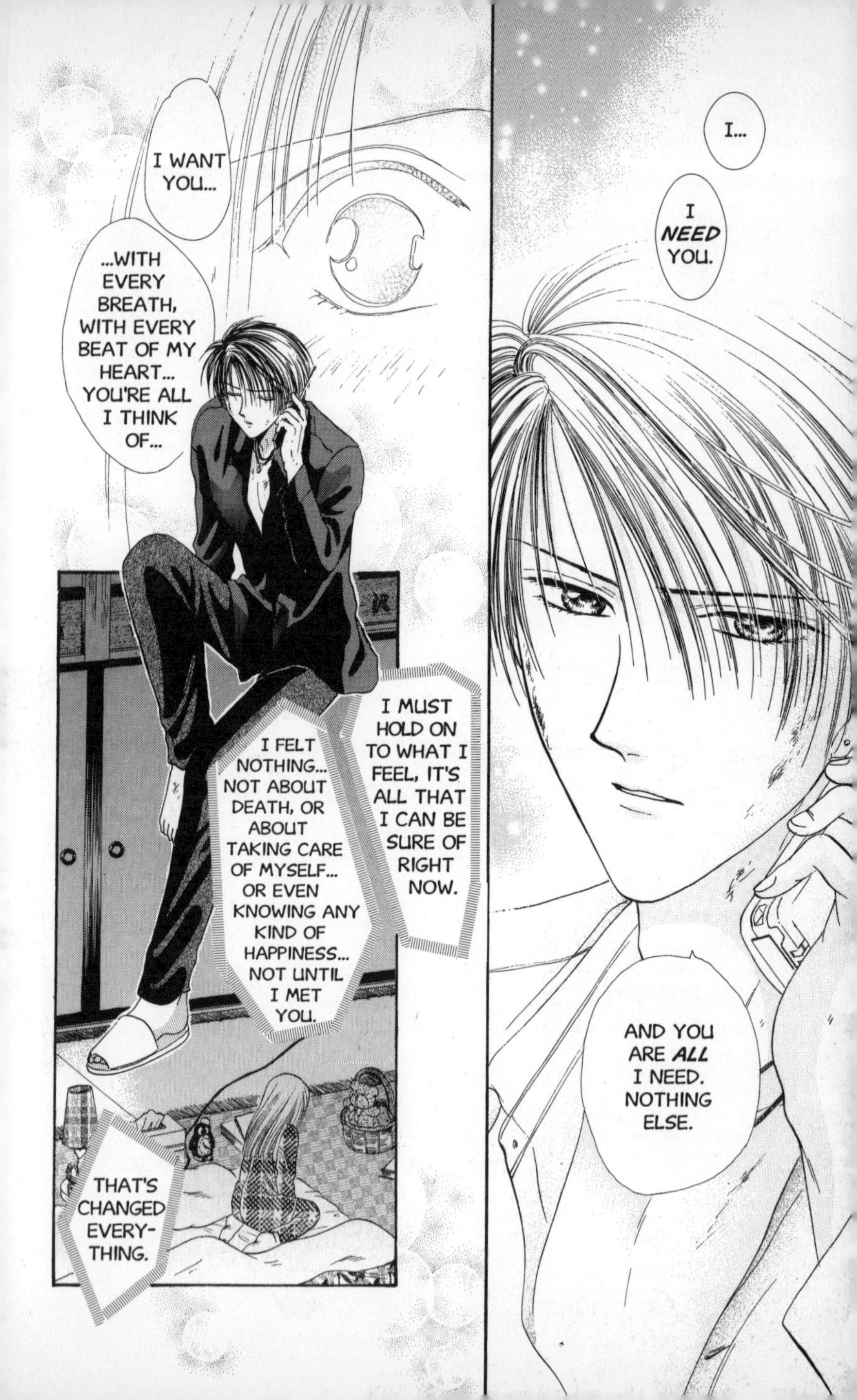
I...
I *NEED* YOU.
AND YOU ARE *ALL* I NEED. NOTHING ELSE.
I WANT YOU...
...WITH EVERY BREATH, WITH EVERY BEAT OF MY HEART... YOU'RE ALL I THINK OF...
I MUST HOLD ON TO WHAT I FEEL, IT'S ALL THAT I CAN BE SURE OF RIGHT NOW.
I FELT NOTHING... NOT ABOUT DEATH, OR ABOUT TAKING CARE OF MYSELF... OR EVEN KNOWING ANY KIND OF HAPPINESS... NOT UNTIL I MET YOU.
THAT'S CHANGED EVERY-THING.

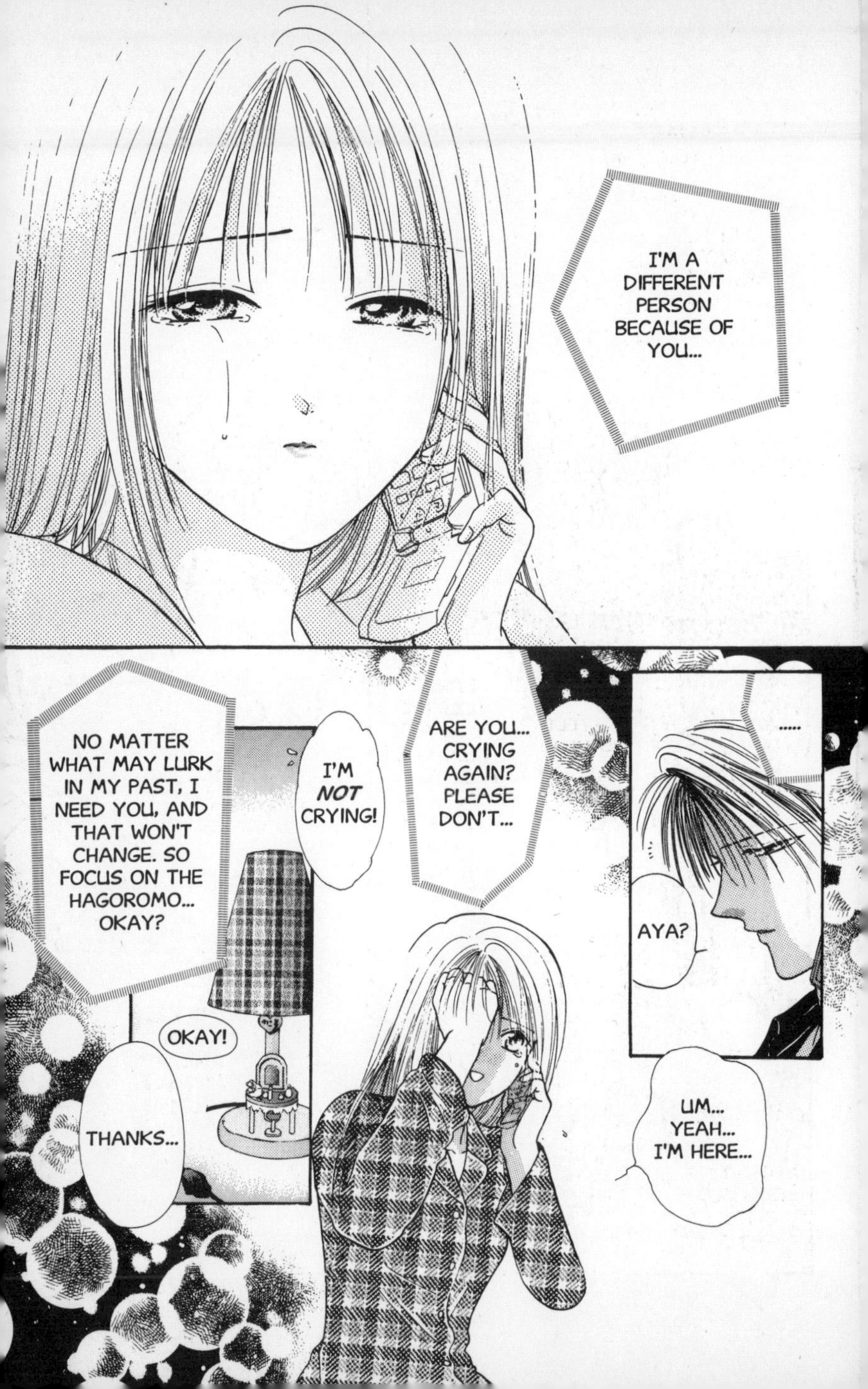
I'M A DIFFERENT PERSON BECAUSE OF YOU...
.....
AYA?
UM... YEAH... I'M HERE...
ARE YOU... CRYING AGAIN? PLEASE DON'T...
I'M *NOT* CRYING!
NO MATTER WHAT MAY LURK IN MY PAST, I NEED YOU, AND THAT WON'T CHANGE. SO FOCUS ON THE HAGOROMO... OKAY?
OKAY!
THANKS...

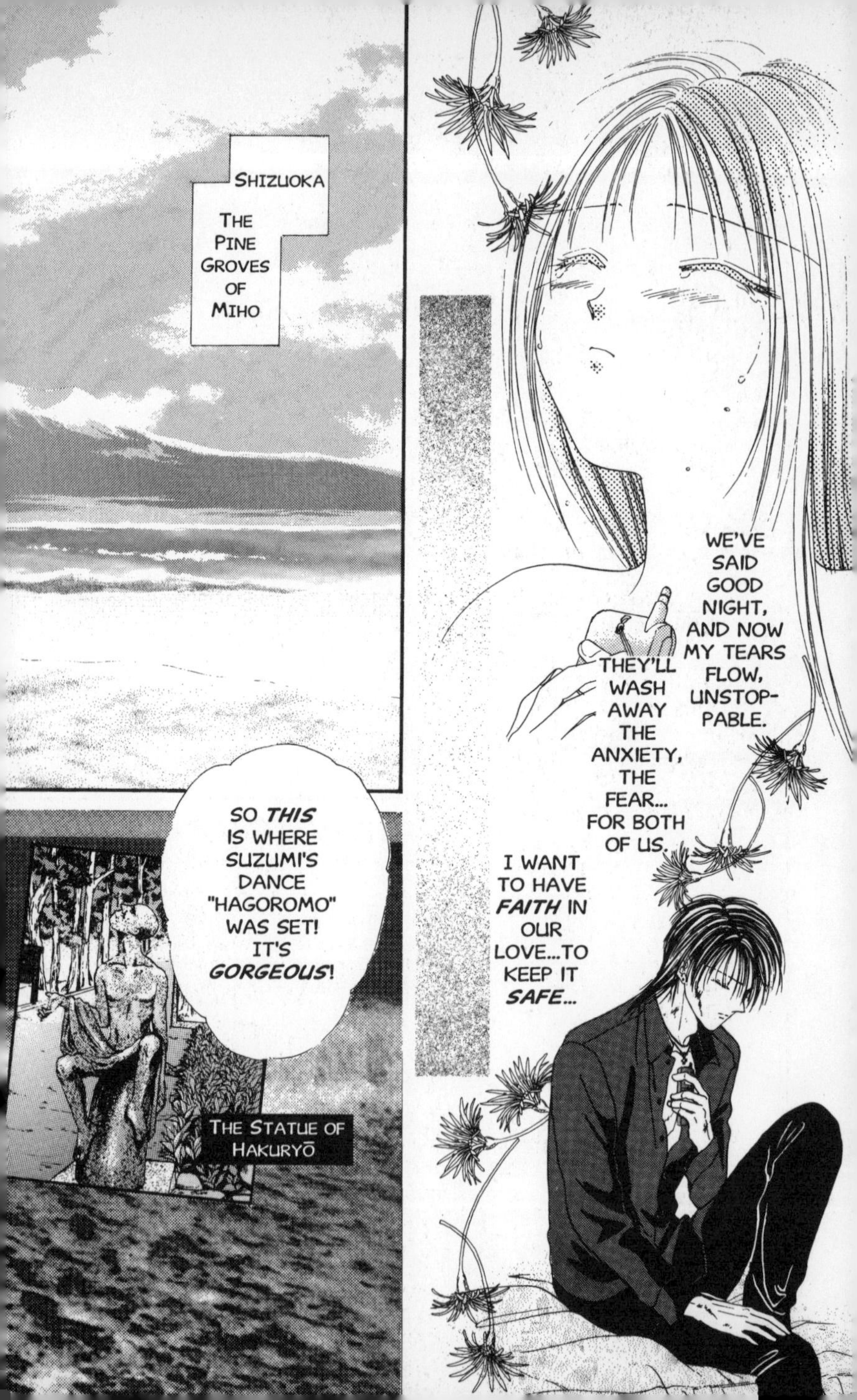
WE'VE SAID GOOD NIGHT, AND NOW MY TEARS FLOW, UNSTOP-PABLE.
THEY'LL WASH AWAY THE ANXIETY, THE FEAR... FOR BOTH OF US.
I WANT TO HAVE *FAITH* IN OUR LOVE...TO KEEP IT *SAFE*...
SHIZUOKA
THE PINE GROVES OF MIHO
SO *THIS* IS WHERE SUZUMI'S DANCE "HAGOROMO" WAS SET! IT'S *GORGEOUS*!
THE STATUE OF HAKURYŌ

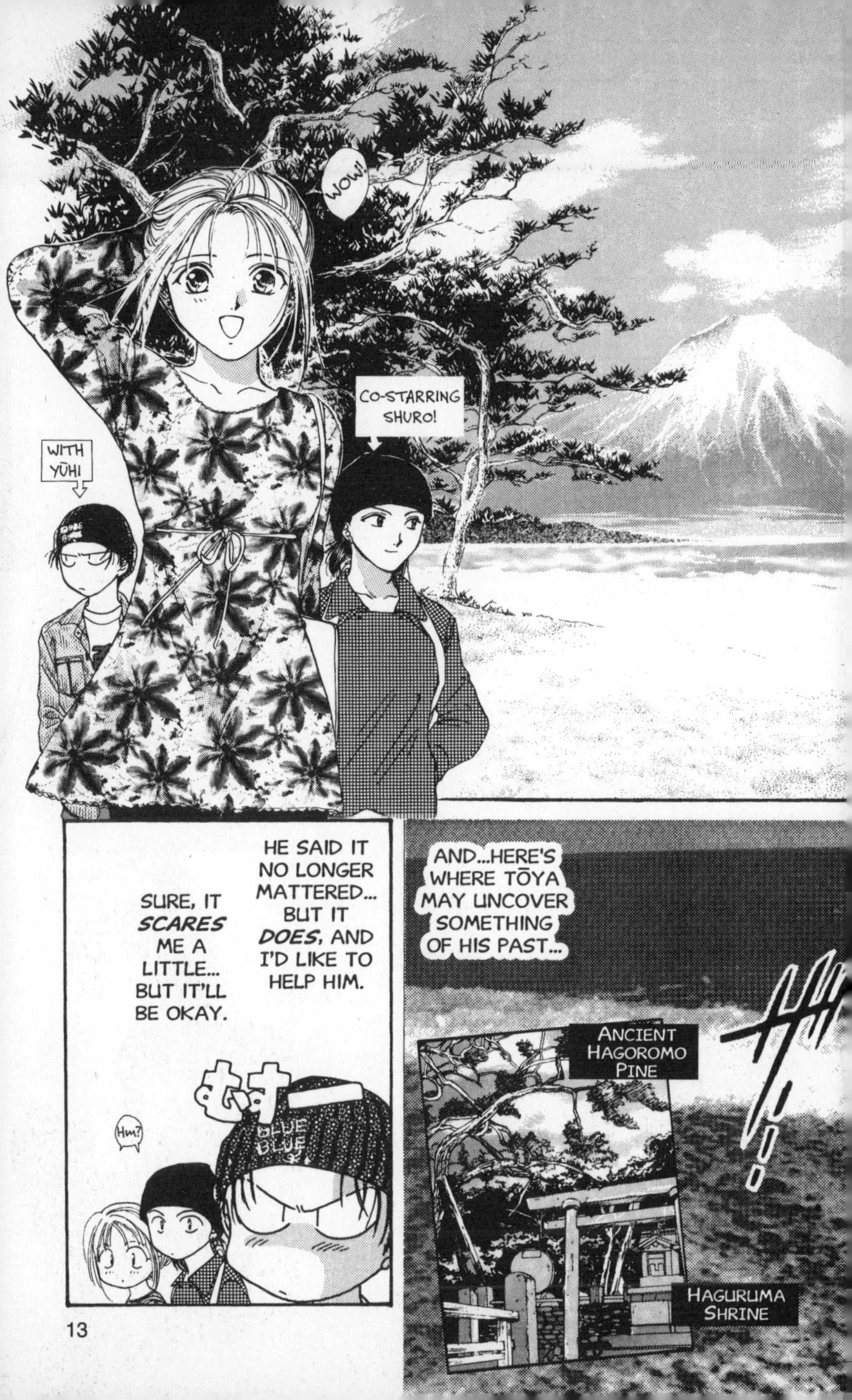
WOW!
CO-STARRING SHURO!
WITH YŪHI
AND...HERE'S WHERE TŌYA MAY UNCOVER SOMETHING OF HIS PAST...
ANCIENT HAGOROMO PINE
HAGURUMA SHRINE
HE SAID IT NO LONGER MATTERED... BUT IT *DOES*, AND I'D LIKE TO HELP HIM.
SURE, IT *SCARES* ME A LITTLE... BUT IT'LL BE OKAY.
むすー
Hm?

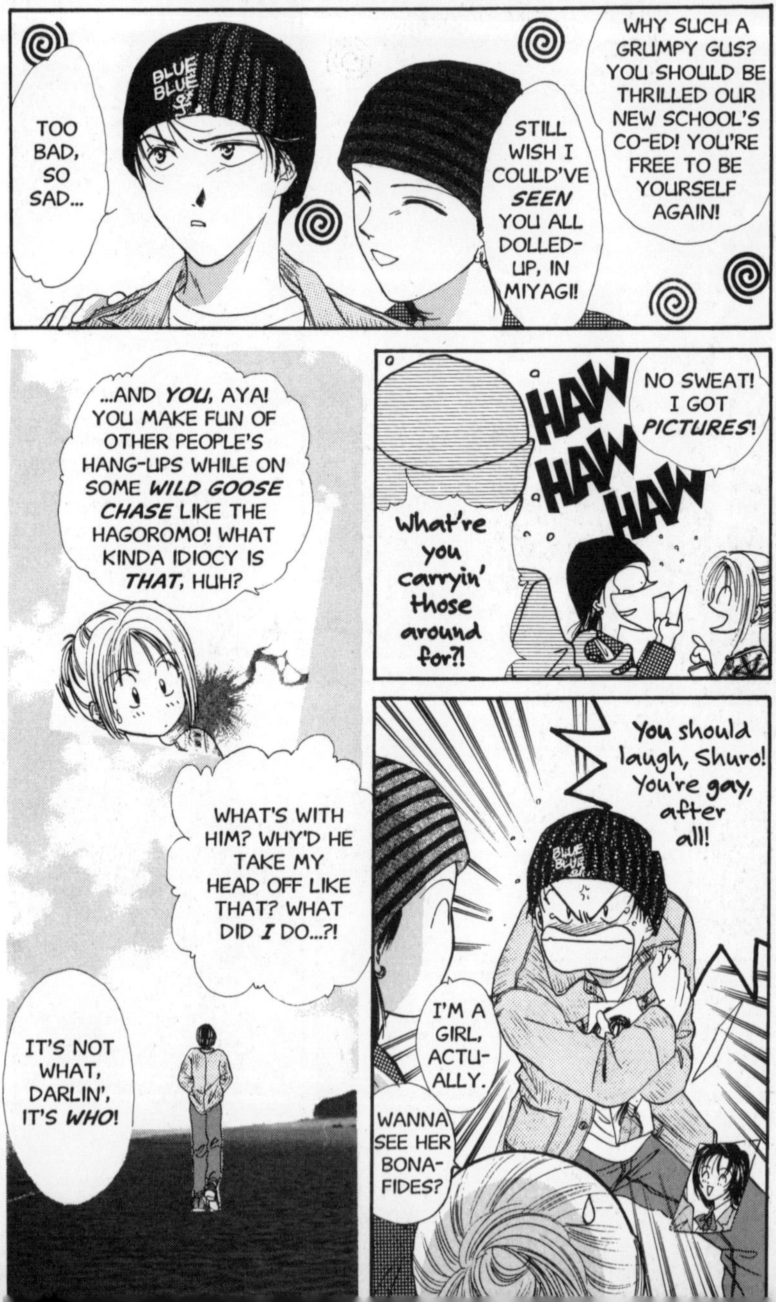
WHY SUCH A GRUMPY GUS? YOU SHOULD BE THRILLED OUR NEW SCHOOL'S CO-ED! YOU'RE FREE TO BE YOURSELF AGAIN!
STILL WISH I COULD'VE SEEN YOU ALL DOLLED-UP, IN MIYAGI!
TOO BAD, SO SAD...
NO SWEAT! I GOT PICTURES!
HAW HAW HAW
What're you carryin' those around for?!
You should laugh, Shuro! You're gay, after all!
I'M A GIRL, ACTUALLY.
WANNA SEE HER BONA-FIDES?
...AND YOU, AYA! YOU MAKE FUN OF OTHER PEOPLE'S HANG-UPS WHILE ON SOME WILD GOOSE CHASE LIKE THE HAGOROMO! WHAT KINDA IDIOCY IS THAT, HUH?
WHAT'S WITH HIM? WHY'D HE TAKE MY HEAD OFF LIKE THAT? WHAT DID I DO...?!
IT'S NOT WHAT, DARLIN', IT'S WHO!

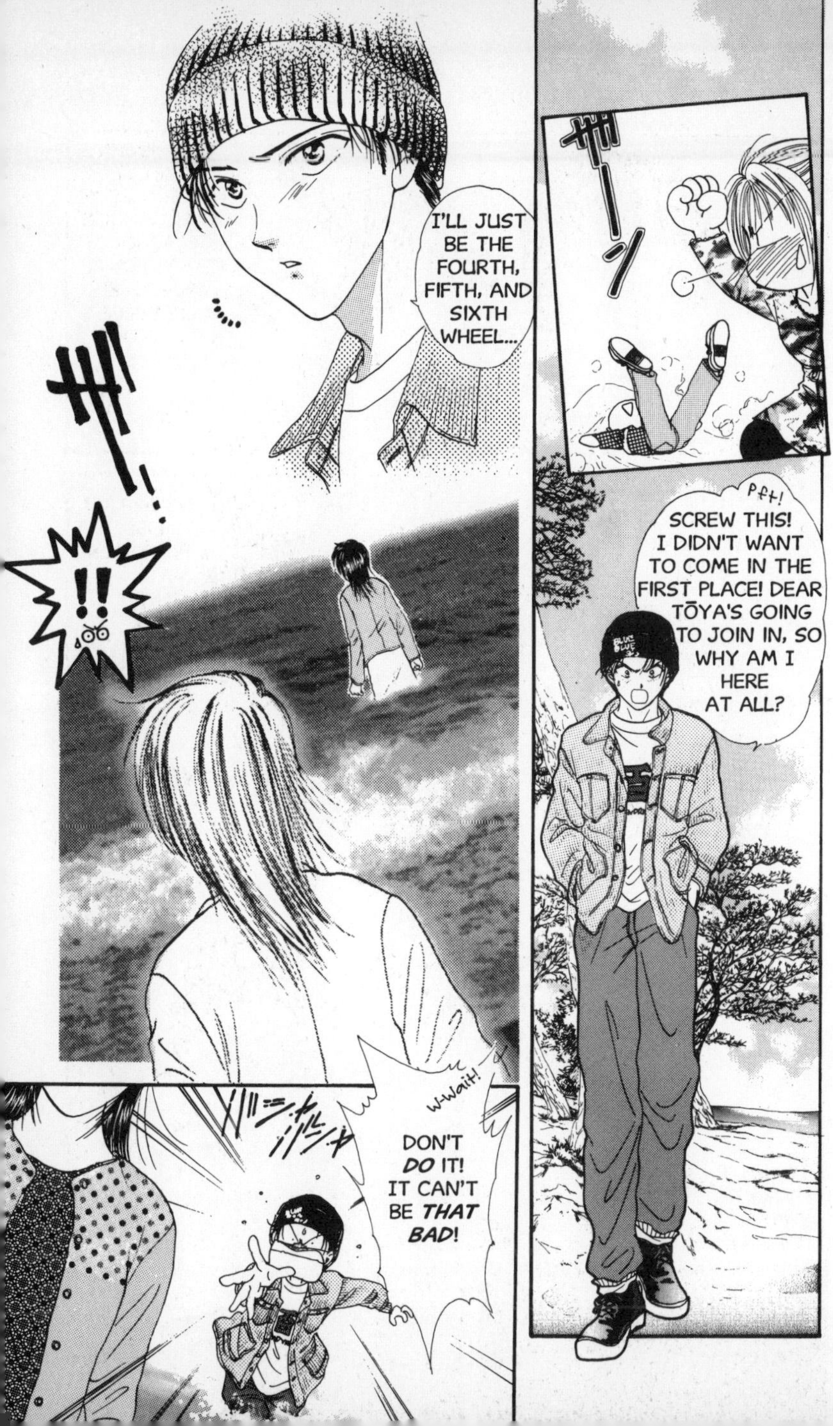
Pft!
SCREW THIS! I DIDN'T WANT TO COME IN THE FIRST PLACE! DEAR TŌYA'S GOING TO JOIN IN, SO WHY AM I HERE AT ALL?
I'LL JUST BE THE FOURTH, FIFTH, AND SIXTH WHEEL...
!!
W-wait!
DON'T *DO* IT! IT CAN'T BE ***THAT BAD***!

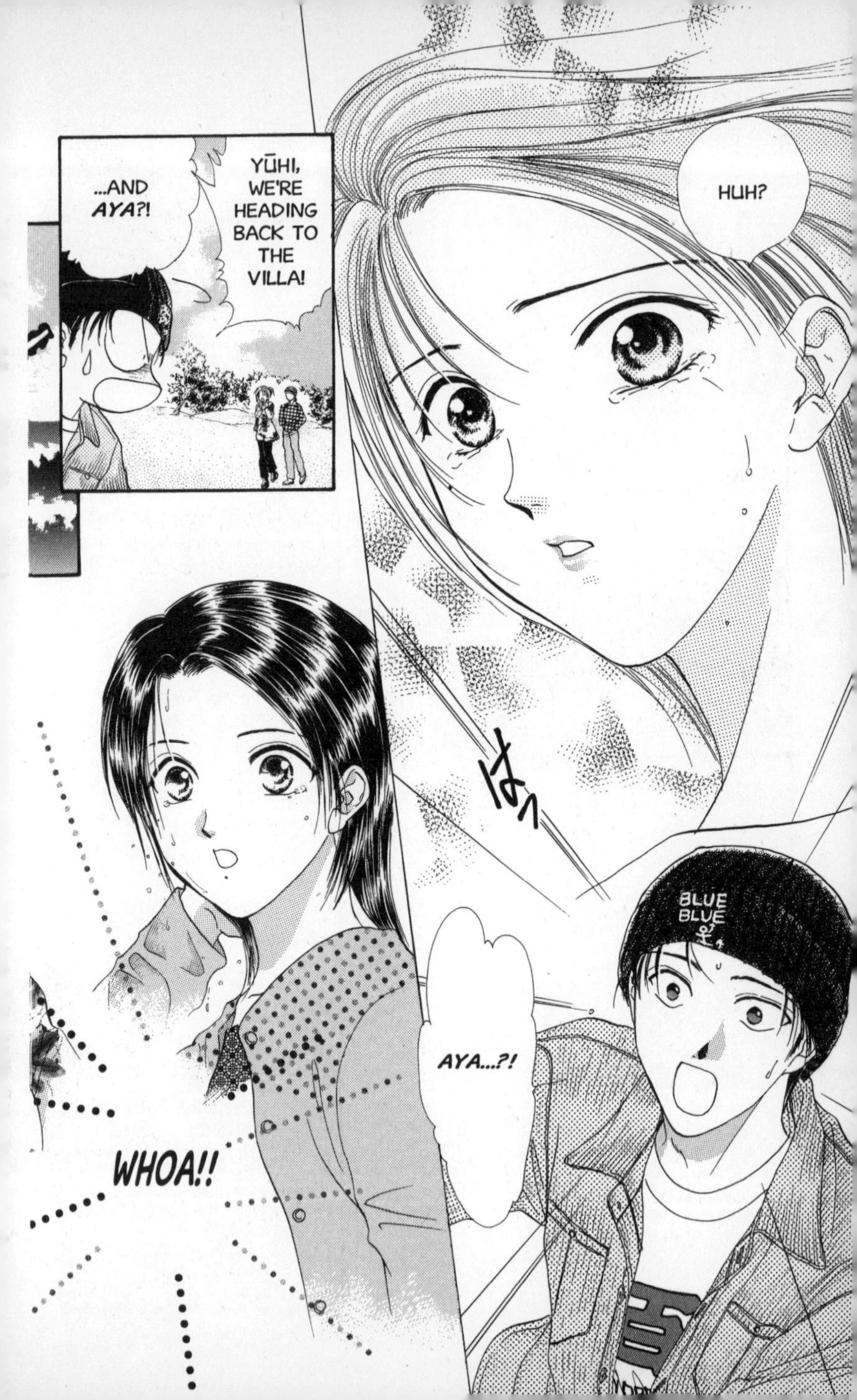
HUH?
はっ
YŪHI, WE'RE HEADING BACK TO THE VILLA!
...AND AYA?!
AYA...?!
WHOA!!

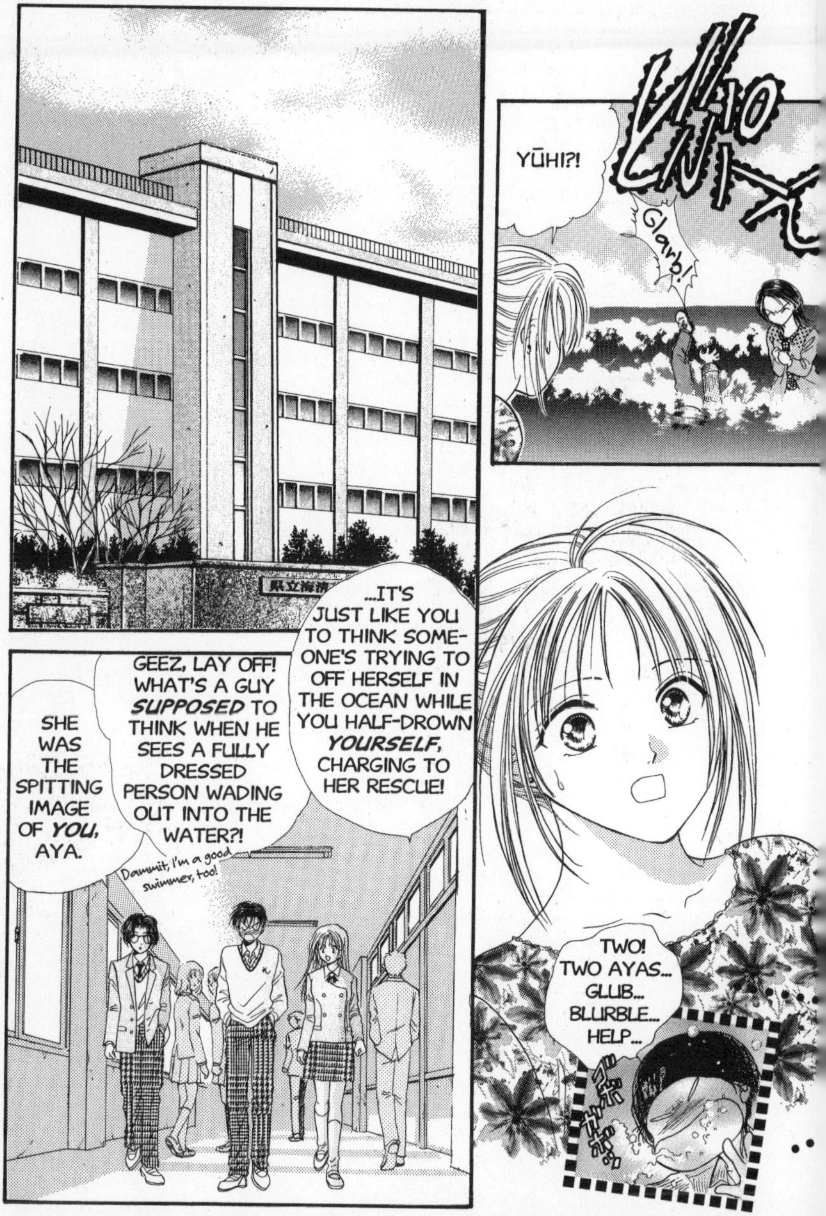
YŪHI?!
Glarb!
TWO! TWO AYAS... GLUB... BLURBLE... HELP...
...IT'S JUST LIKE YOU TO THINK SOME-ONE'S TRYING TO OFF HERSELF IN THE OCEAN WHILE YOU HALF-DROWN *YOURSELF*, CHARGING TO HER RESCUE!
GEEZ, LAY OFF! WHAT'S A GUY *SUPPOSED* TO THINK WHEN HE SEES A FULLY DRESSED PERSON WADING OUT INTO THE WATER?!
SHE WAS THE SPITTING IMAGE OF *YOU*, AYA.
Dammit, I'm a good swimmer, too!

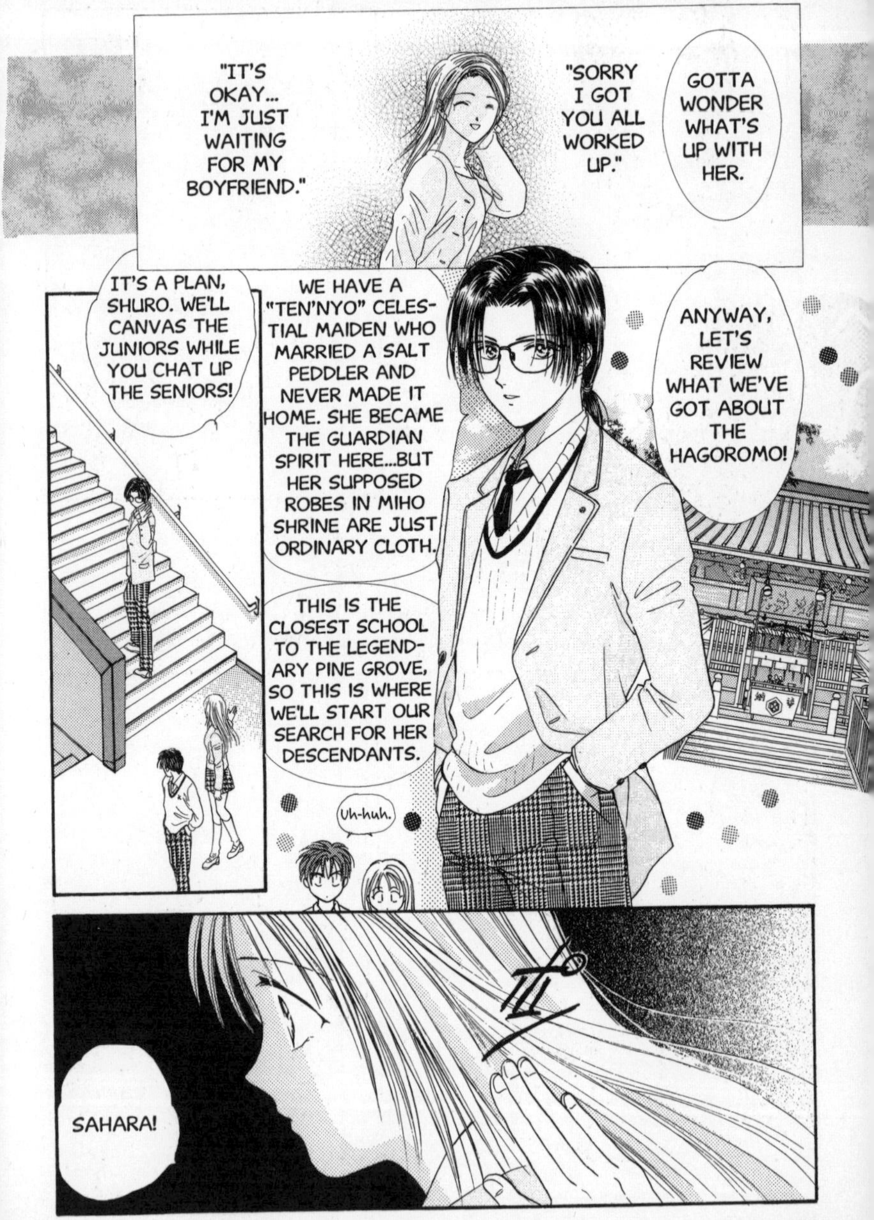
GOTTA WONDER WHAT'S UP WITH HER.
"SORRY I GOT YOU ALL WORKED UP."
"IT'S OKAY... I'M JUST WAITING FOR MY BOYFRIEND."
ANYWAY, LET'S REVIEW WHAT WE'VE GOT ABOUT THE HAGOROMO!
WE HAVE A "TEN'NYO" CELES-TIAL MAIDEN WHO MARRIED A SALT PEDDLER AND NEVER MADE IT HOME. SHE BECAME THE GUARDIAN SPIRIT HERE...BUT HER SUPPOSED ROBES IN MIHO SHRINE ARE JUST ORDINARY CLOTH.
THIS IS THE CLOSEST SCHOOL TO THE LEGEND-ARY PINE GROVE, SO THIS IS WHERE WE'LL START OUR SEARCH FOR HER DESCENDANTS.
Uh-huh.
IT'S A PLAN, SHURO. WE'LL CANVAS THE JUNIORS WHILE YOU CHAT UP THE SENIORS!
SAHARA!

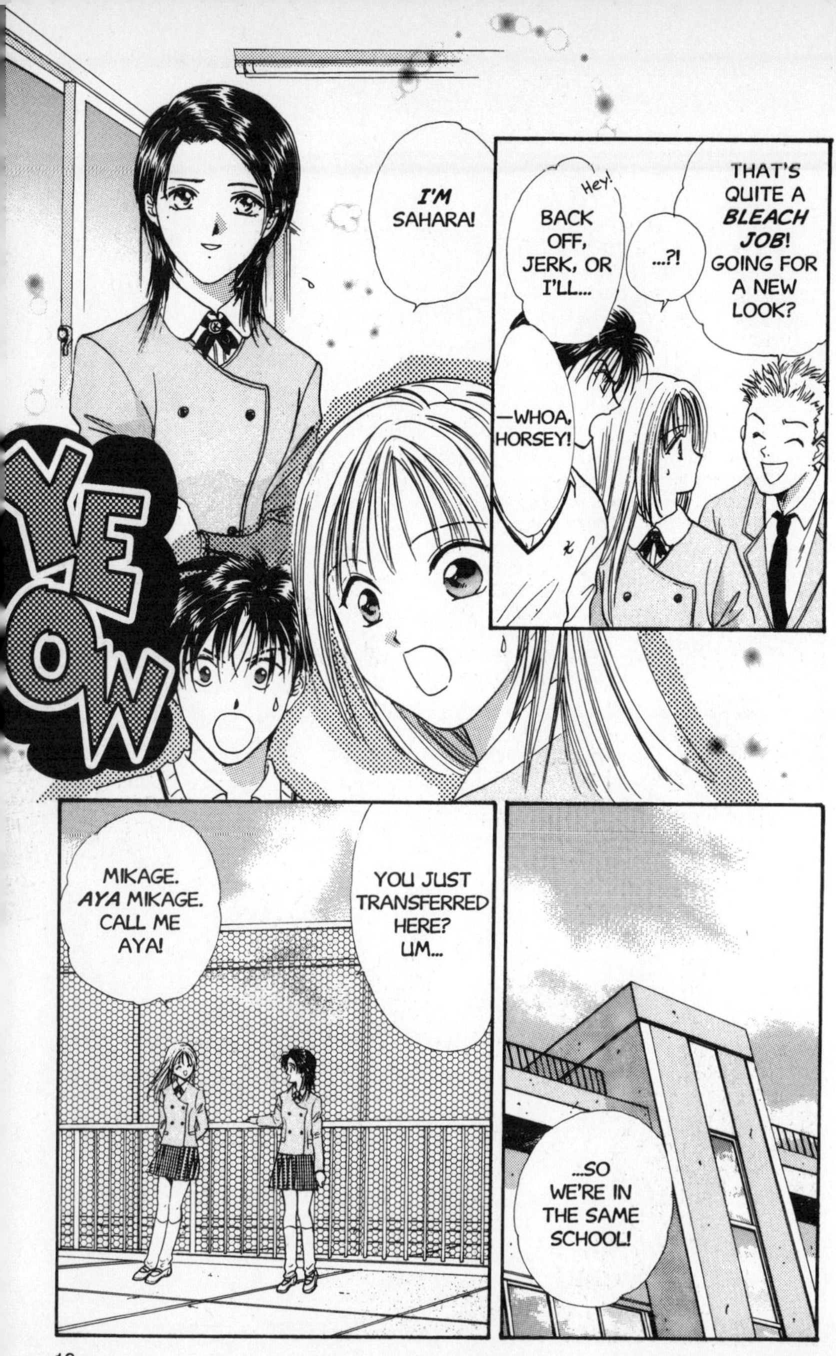
THAT'S QUITE A *BLEACH JOB*! GOING FOR A NEW LOOK?
...?!
Hey!
BACK OFF, JERK, OR I'LL...
—WHOA, HORSEY!
I'M SAHARA!
YEOW
...SO WE'RE IN THE SAME SCHOOL!
YOU JUST TRANSFERRED HERE? UM...
MIKAGE. *AYA* MIKAGE. CALL ME AYA!

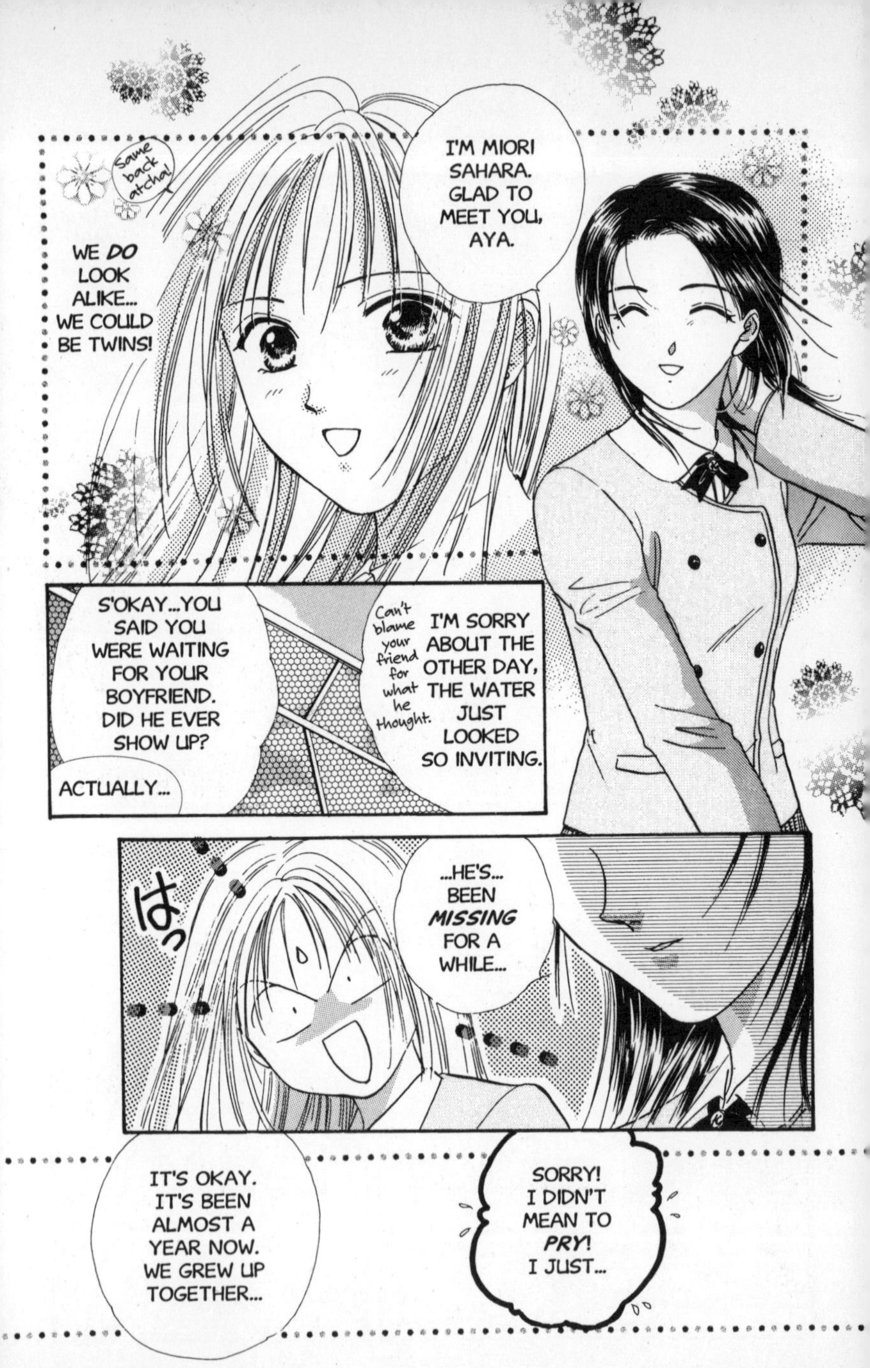
I'M MIORI SAHARA. GLAD TO MEET YOU, AYA.
WE *DO* LOOK ALIKE... WE COULD BE TWINS!
Same back atcha!
I'M SORRY ABOUT THE OTHER DAY, THE WATER JUST LOOKED SO INVITING.
Can't blame your friend for what he thought.
S'OKAY...YOU SAID YOU WERE WAITING FOR YOUR BOYFRIEND. DID HE EVER SHOW UP?
ACTUALLY...
...HE'S... BEEN ***MISSING*** FOR A WHILE...
はっ
SORRY! I DIDN'T MEAN TO ***PRY***! I JUST...
IT'S OKAY. IT'S BEEN ALMOST A YEAR NOW. WE GREW UP TOGETHER...

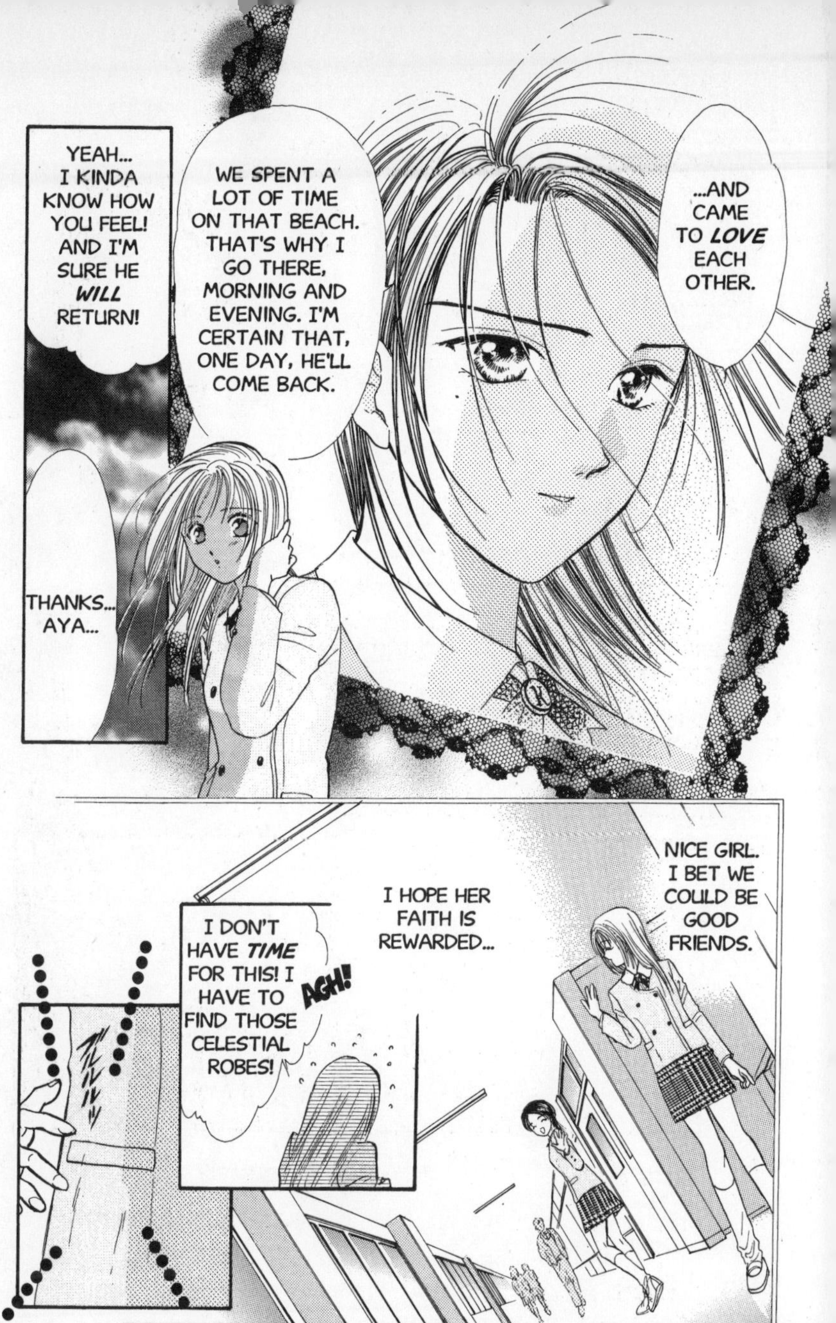
...AND CAME TO *LOVE* EACH OTHER.
WE SPENT A LOT OF TIME ON THAT BEACH. THAT'S WHY I GO THERE, MORNING AND EVENING. I'M CERTAIN THAT, ONE DAY, HE'LL COME BACK.
YEAH... I KINDA KNOW HOW YOU FEEL! AND I'M SURE HE *WILL* RETURN!
THANKS... AYA...
NICE GIRL. I BET WE COULD BE GOOD FRIENDS.
I HOPE HER FAITH IS REWARDED...
I DON'T HAVE *TIME* FOR THIS! I HAVE TO FIND THOSE CELESTIAL ROBES!
AGH!

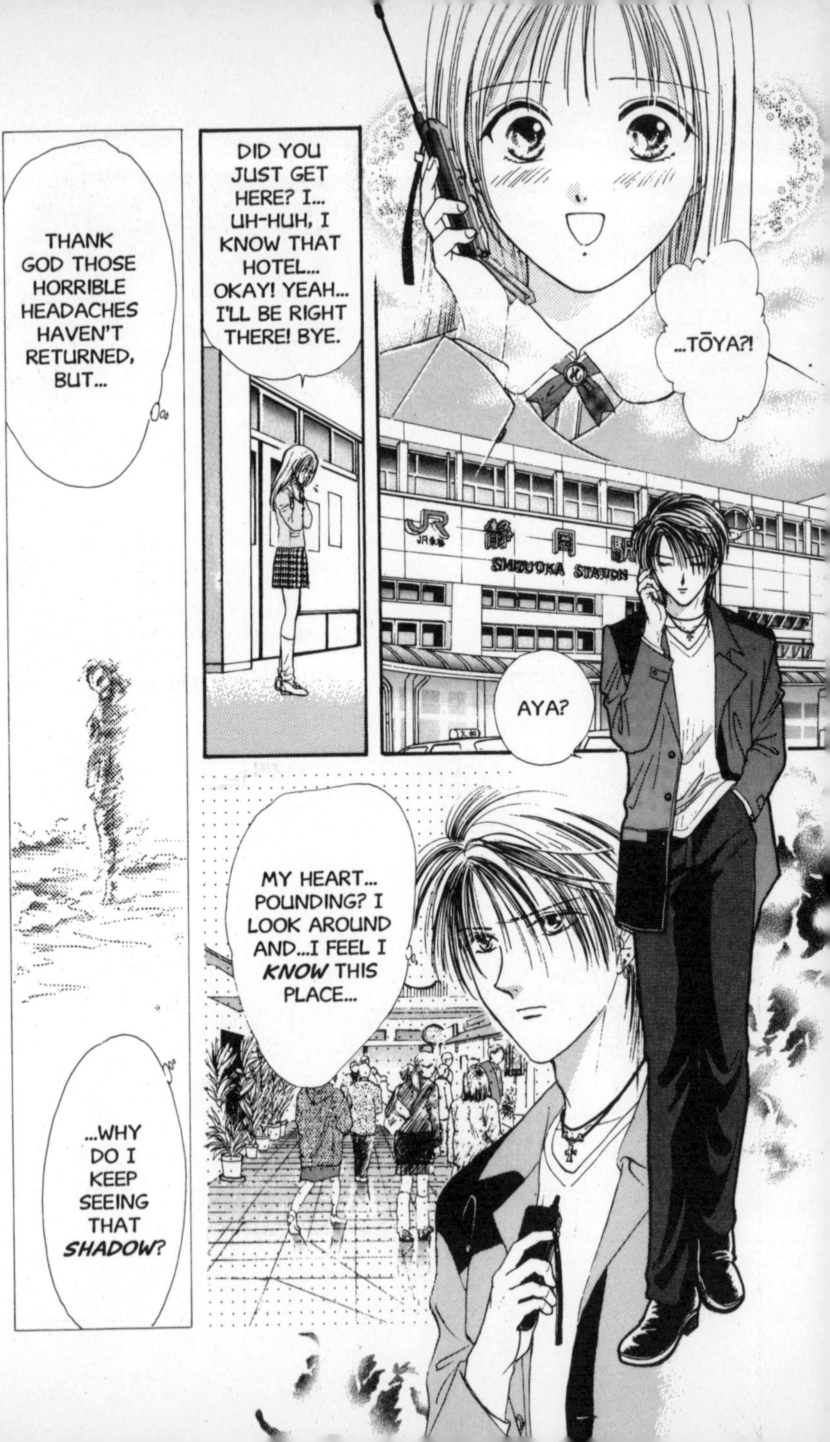
...TŌYA?!
AYA?
DID YOU JUST GET HERE? I... UH-HUH, I KNOW THAT HOTEL... OKAY! YEAH... I'LL BE RIGHT THERE! BYE.
SHIZUOKA STATION
MY HEART... POUNDING? I LOOK AROUND AND...I FEEL I *KNOW* THIS PLACE...
THANK GOD THOSE HORRIBLE HEADACHES HAVEN'T RETURNED, BUT...
...WHY DO I KEEP SEEING THAT *SHADOW*?

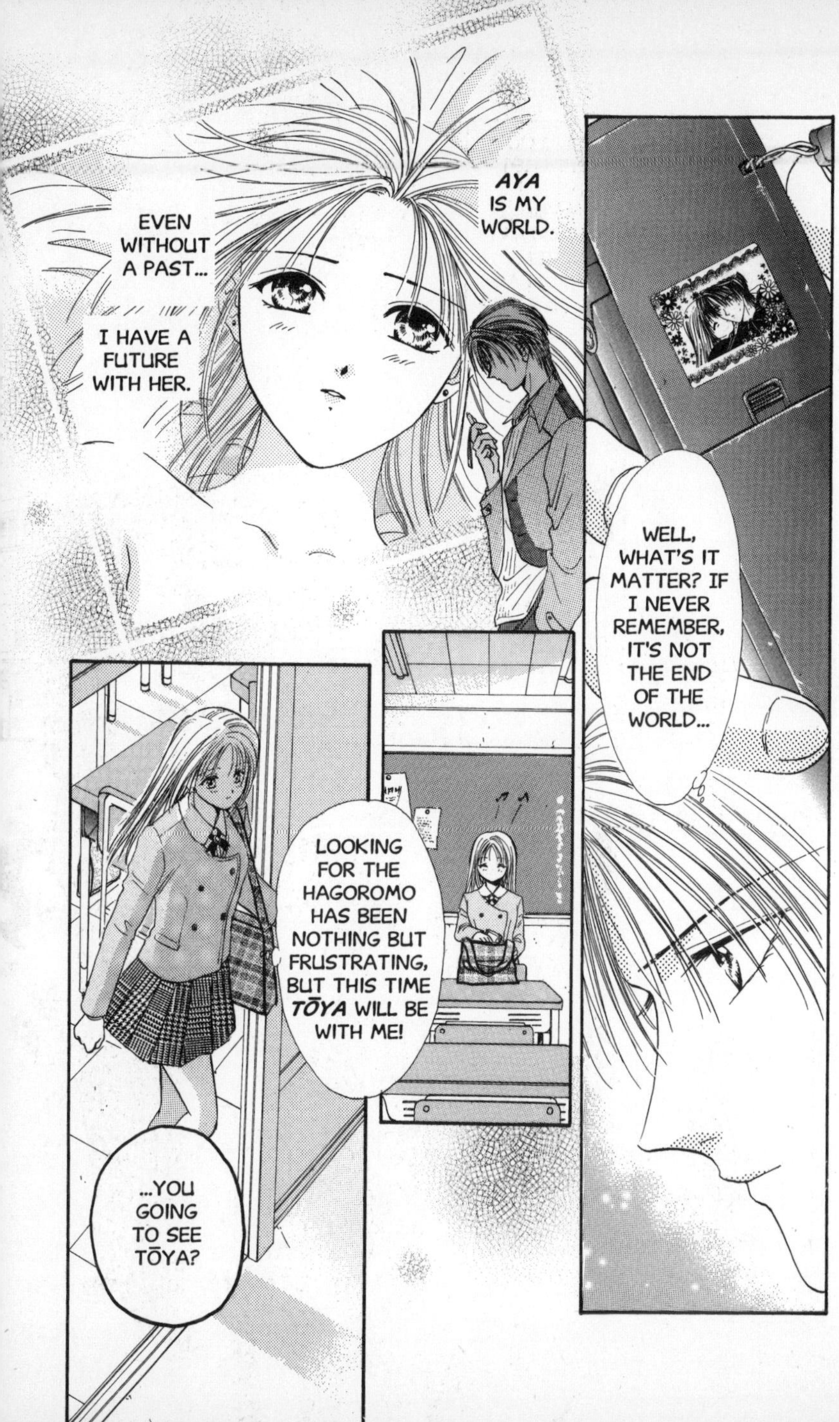
WELL, WHAT'S IT MATTER? IF I NEVER REMEMBER, IT'S NOT THE END OF THE WORLD...
AYA IS MY WORLD.
EVEN WITHOUT A PAST...
I HAVE A FUTURE WITH HER.
LOOKING FOR THE HAGOROMO HAS BEEN NOTHING BUT FRUSTRATING, BUT THIS TIME TŌYA WILL BE WITH ME!
...YOU GOING TO SEE TŌYA?

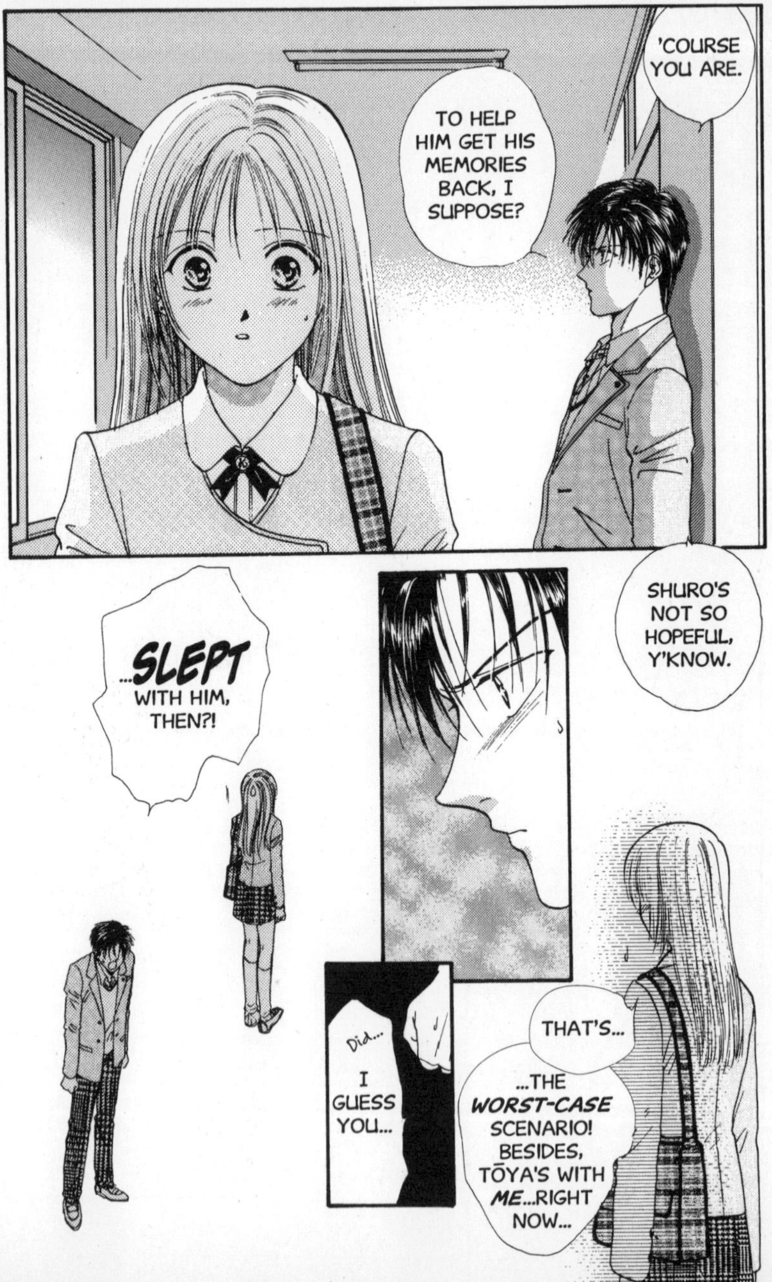
'COURSE YOU ARE.
TO HELP HIM GET HIS MEMORIES BACK, I SUPPOSE?
SHURO'S NOT SO HOPEFUL, Y'KNOW.
THAT'S...
...THE WORST-CASE SCENARIO! BESIDES, TŌYA'S WITH ME...RIGHT NOW...
Did...
I GUESS YOU...
...SLEPT WITH HIM, THEN?!

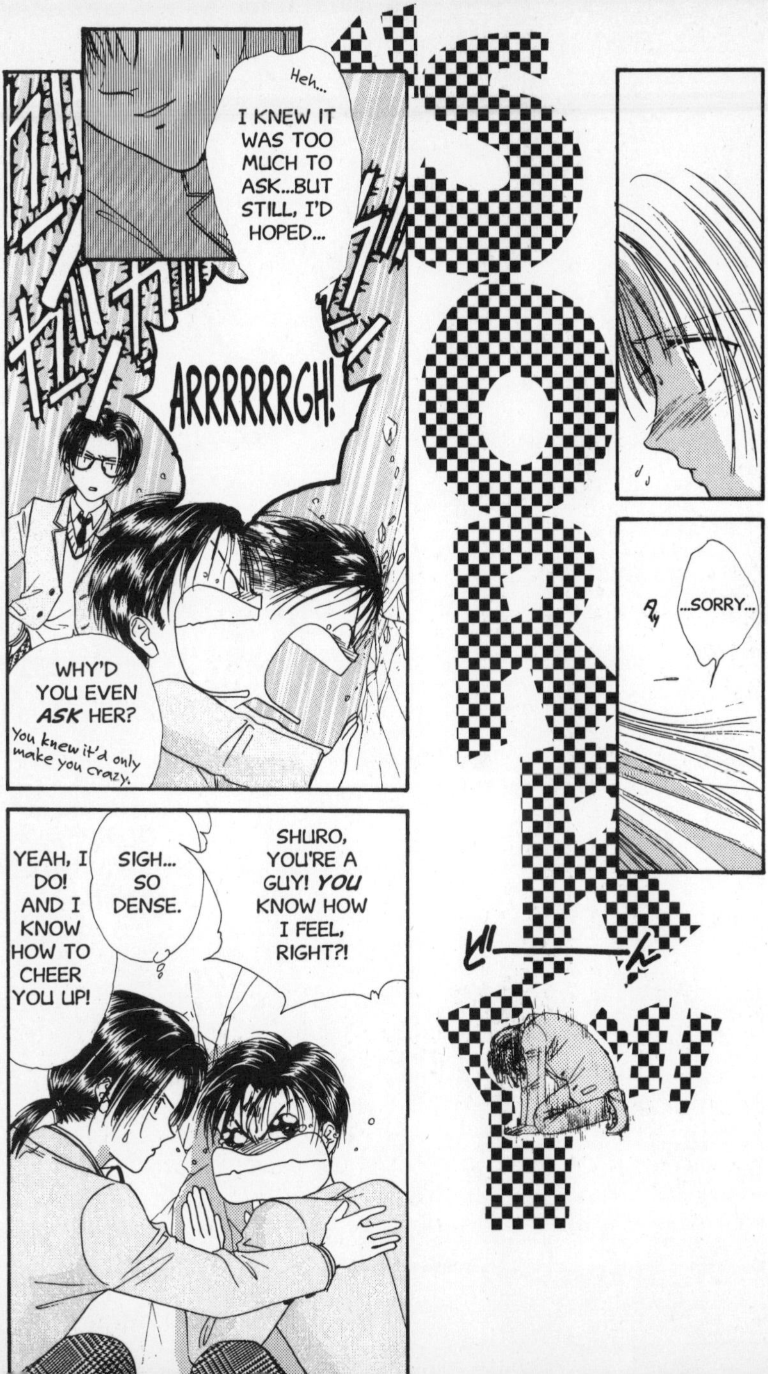
Ah
...SORRY...
SORRY!
Heh...
I KNEW IT WAS TOO MUCH TO ASK...BUT STILL, I'D HOPED...
ARRRRRRGH!
WHY'D YOU EVEN ASK HER?
You knew it'd only make you crazy.
SHURO, YOU'RE A GUY! YOU KNOW HOW I FEEL, RIGHT?!
SIGH... SO DENSE.
YEAH, I DO! AND I KNOW HOW TO CHEER YOU UP!

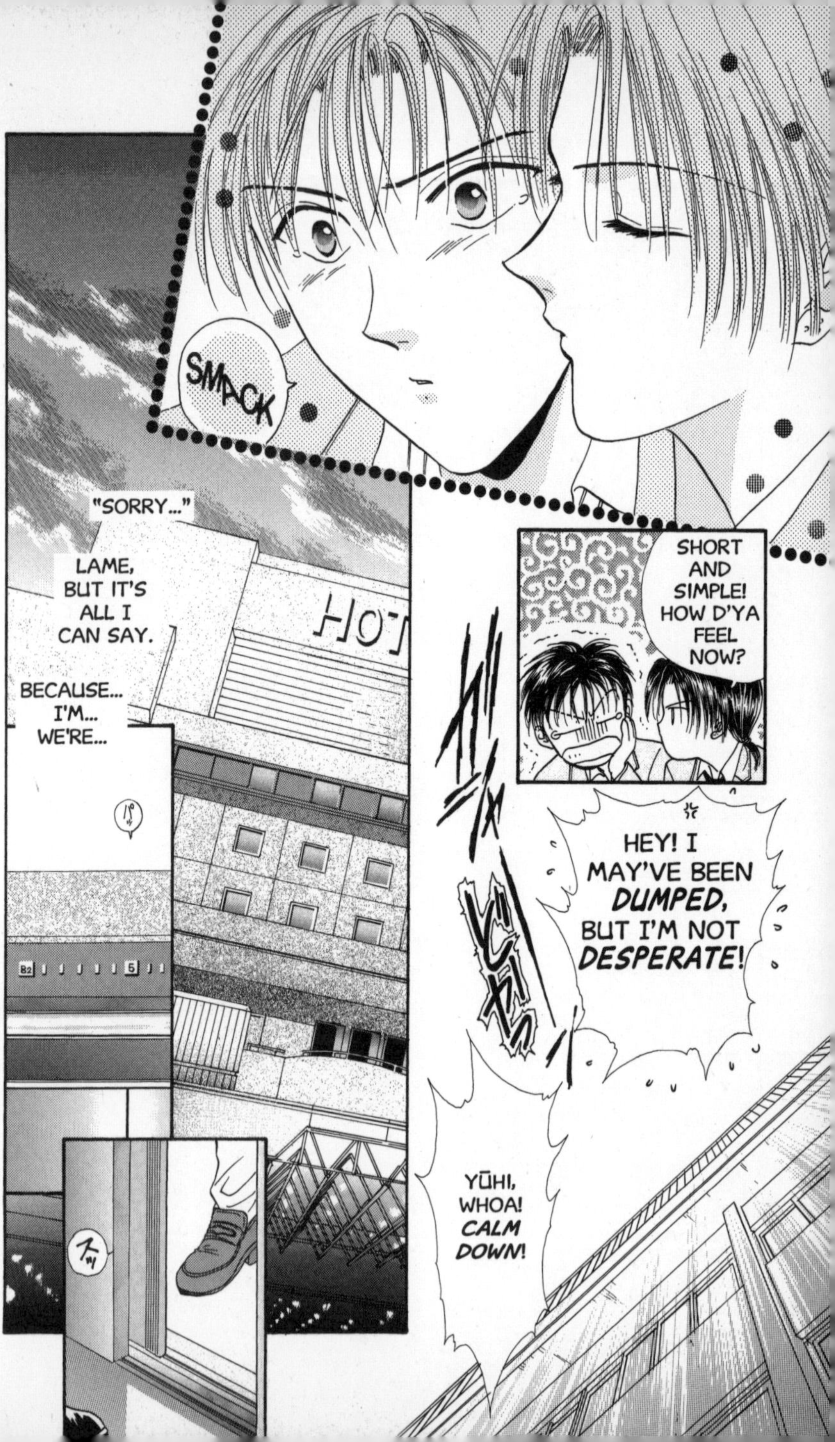

SMACK
SHORT AND SIMPLE! HOW D'YA FEEL NOW?
HEY! I MAY'VE BEEN *DUMPED*, BUT I'M NOT *DESPERATE*!
YŪHI, WHOA! *CALM DOWN*!
"SORRY..."
LAME, BUT IT'S ALL I CAN SAY.
BECAUSE... I'M... WE'RE...
HOT

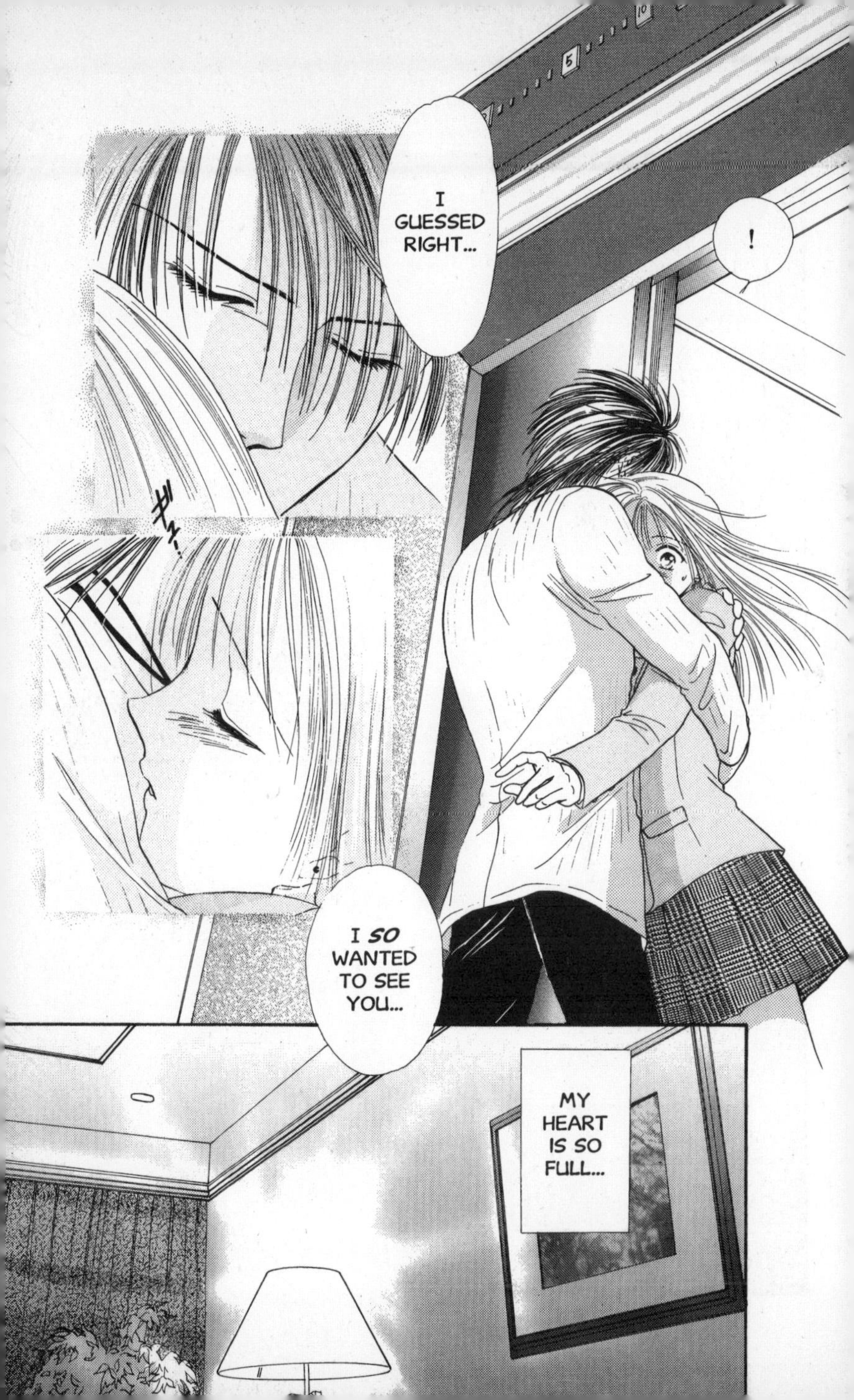
!
I GUESSED RIGHT...
I *SO* WANTED TO SEE YOU...
MY HEART IS SO FULL...

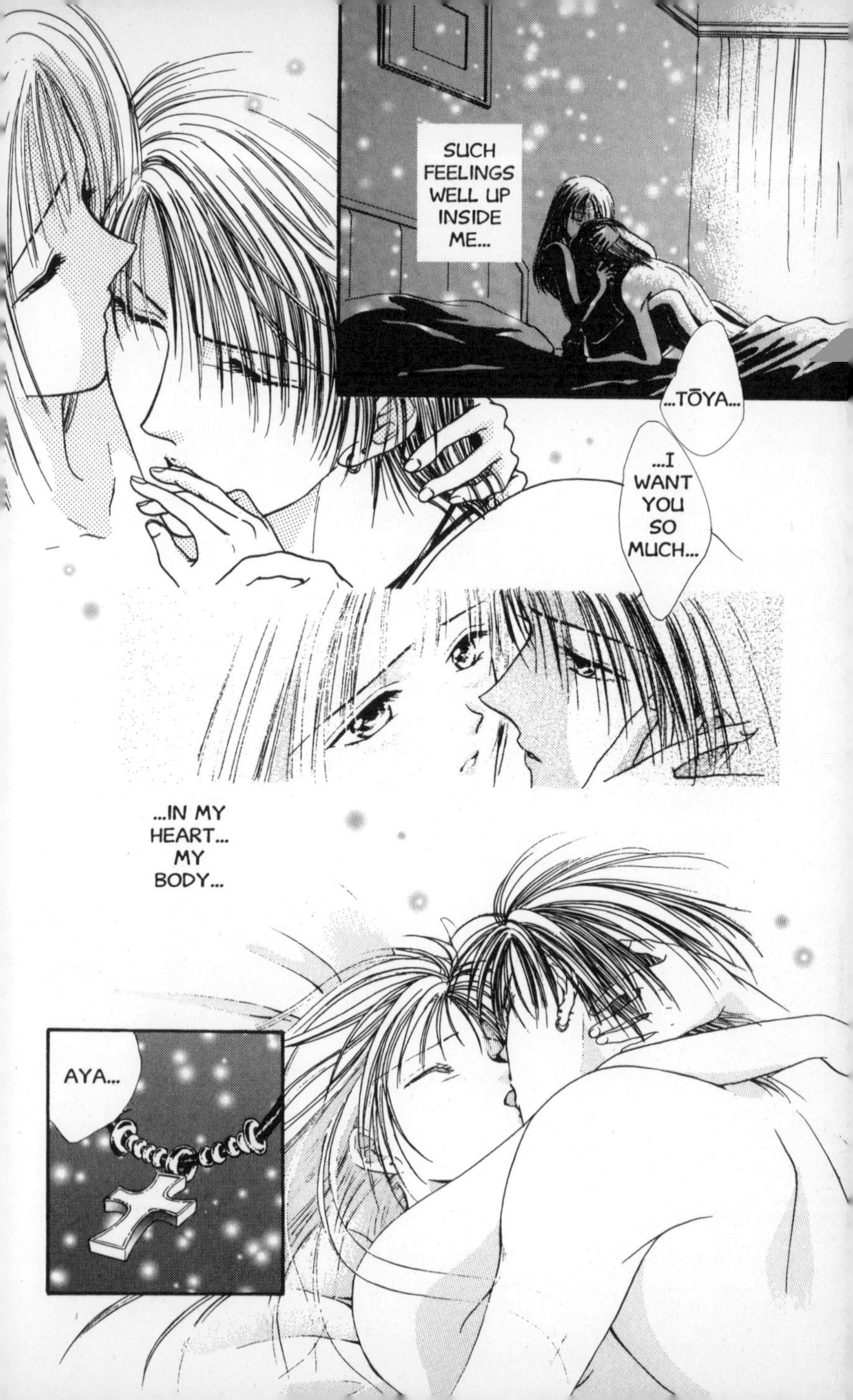
SUCH FEELINGS WELL UP INSIDE ME...
...TŌYA...
...I WANT YOU SO MUCH...
...IN MY HEART... MY BODY...
AYA...

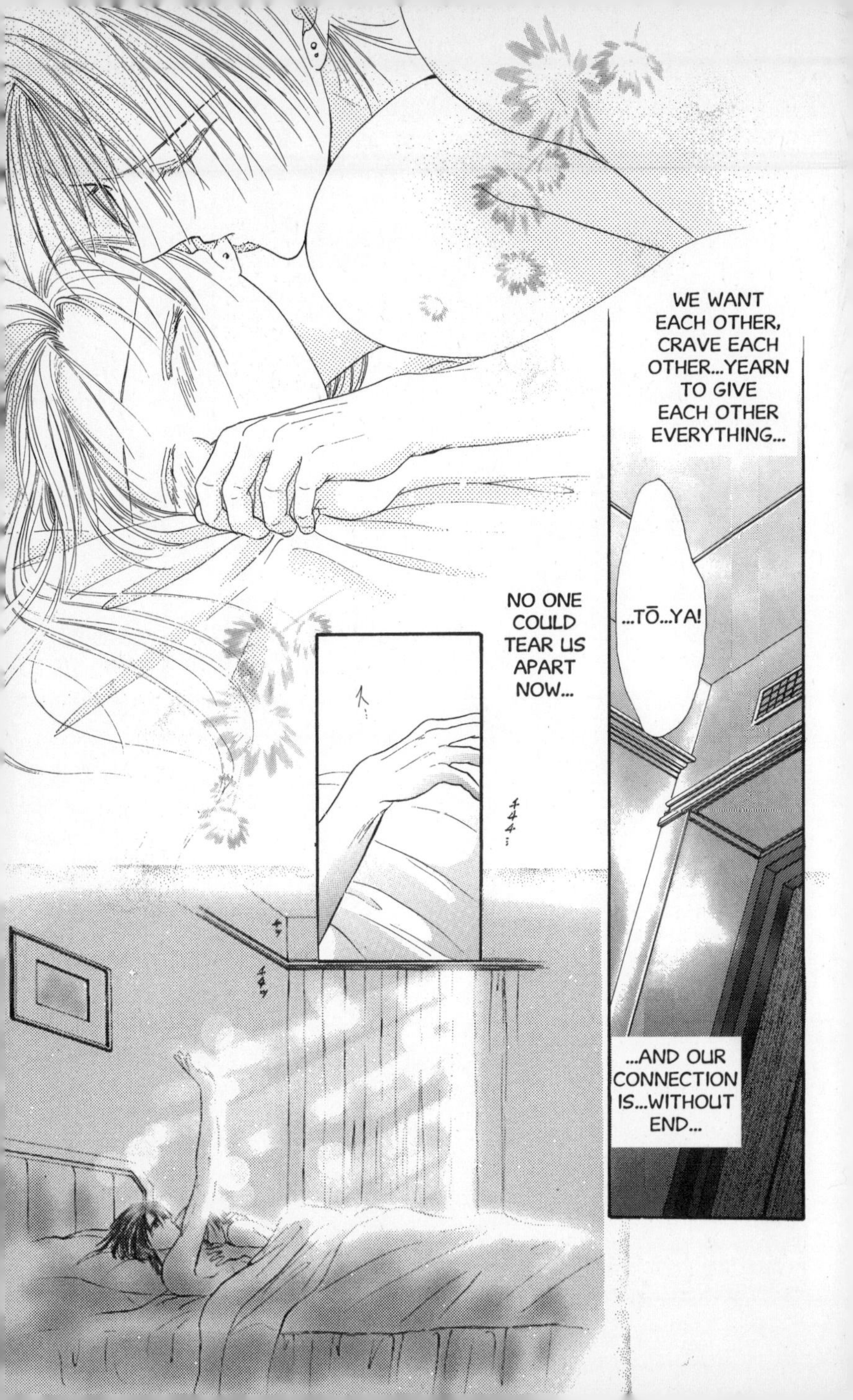
WE WANT EACH OTHER, CRAVE EACH OTHER...YEARN TO GIVE EACH OTHER EVERYTHING...
...TŌ...YA!
...AND OUR CONNECTION IS...WITHOUT END...
NO ONE COULD TEAR US APART NOW...

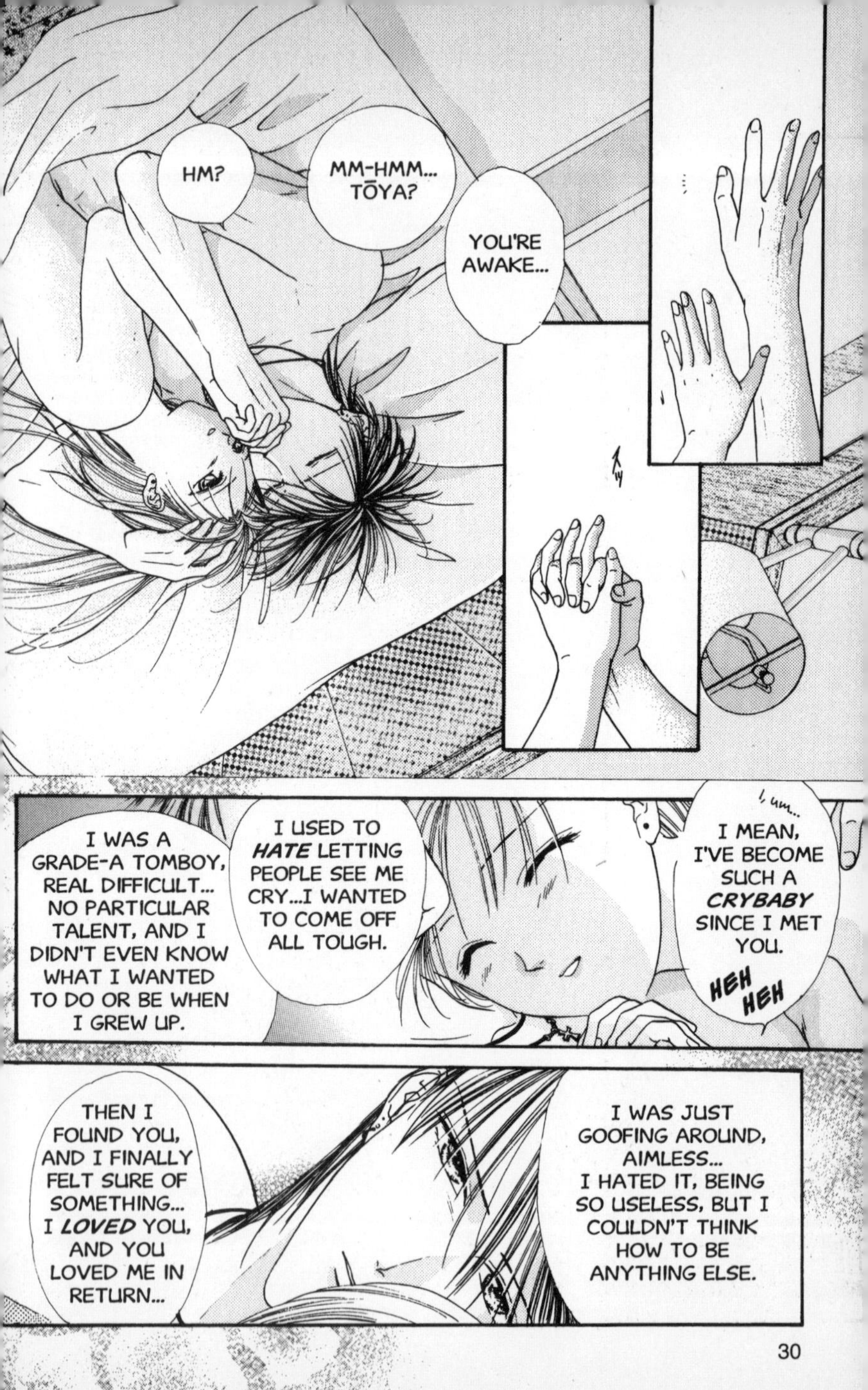
...
YOU'RE AWAKE...
MM-HMM... TŌYA?
HM?
I, um...
I MEAN, I'VE BECOME SUCH A *CRYBABY* SINCE I MET YOU.
HEH HEH
I USED TO *HATE* LETTING PEOPLE SEE ME CRY...I WANTED TO COME OFF ALL TOUGH.
I WAS A GRADE-A TOMBOY, REAL DIFFICULT... NO PARTICULAR TALENT, AND I DIDN'T EVEN KNOW WHAT I WANTED TO DO OR BE WHEN I GREW UP.
I WAS JUST GOOFING AROUND, AIMLESS... I HATED IT, BEING SO USELESS, BUT I COULDN'T THINK HOW TO BE ANYTHING ELSE.
THEN I FOUND YOU, AND I FINALLY FELT SURE OF SOMETHING... I *LOVED* YOU, AND YOU LOVED ME IN RETURN...

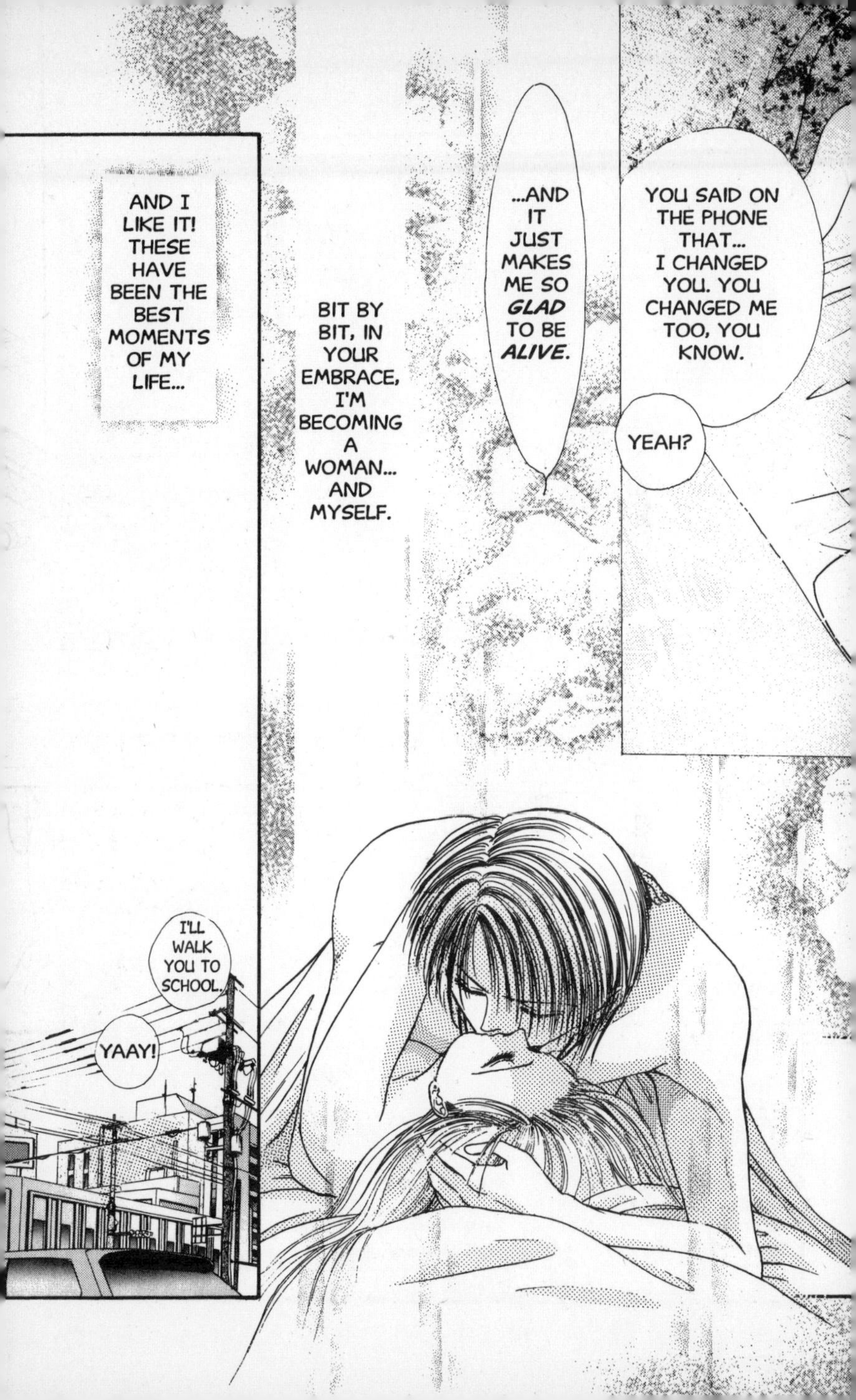
YOU SAID ON THE PHONE THAT... I CHANGED YOU. YOU CHANGED ME TOO, YOU KNOW.
YEAH?
...AND IT JUST MAKES ME SO *GLAD* TO BE *ALIVE*.
BIT BY BIT, IN YOUR EMBRACE, I'M BECOMING A WOMAN... AND MYSELF.
AND I LIKE IT! THESE HAVE BEEN THE BEST MOMENTS OF MY LIFE...
I'LL WALK YOU TO SCHOOL.
YAAY!

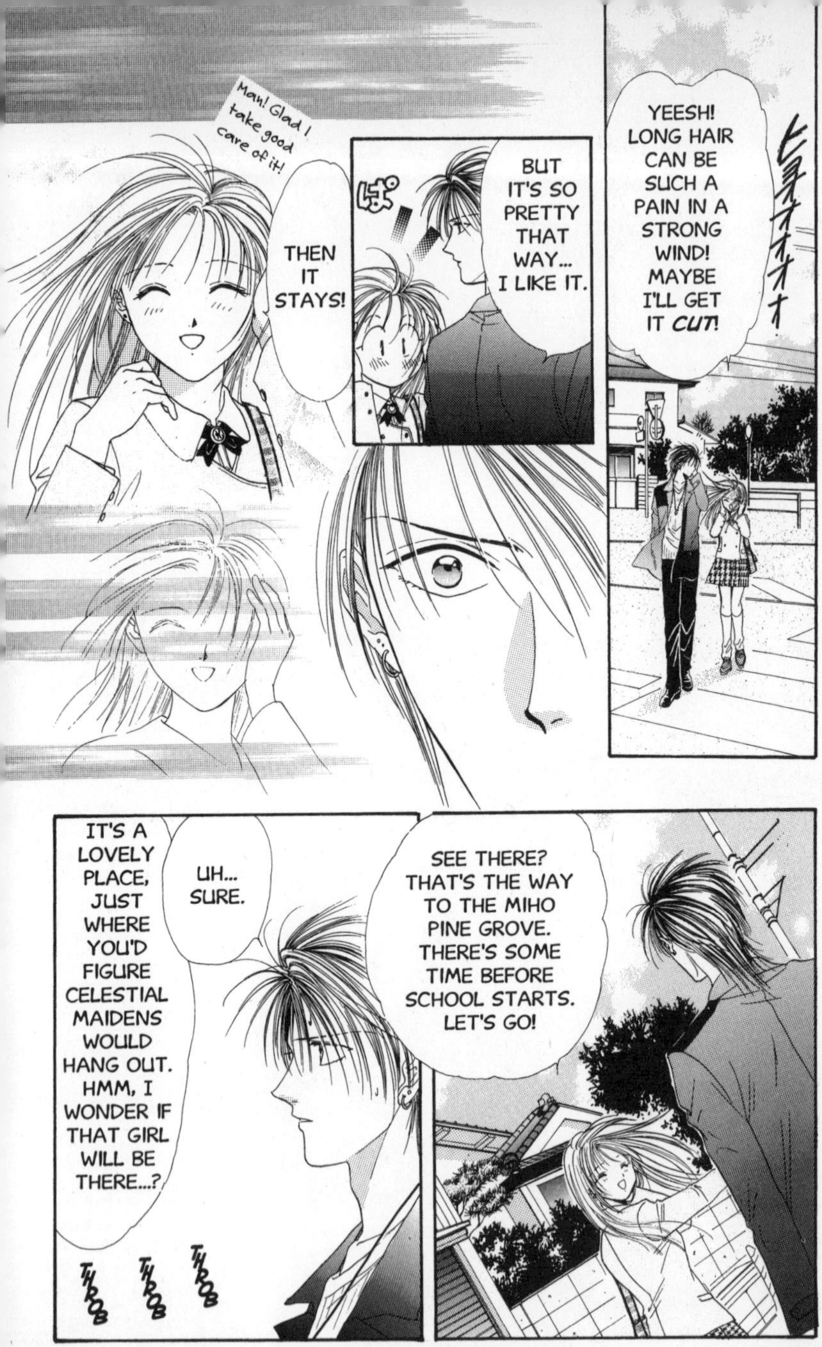
YEESH! LONG HAIR CAN BE SUCH A PAIN IN A STRONG WIND! MAYBE I'LL GET IT *CUT*!
ヒュオオオオオ
BUT IT'S SO PRETTY THAT WAY... I LIKE IT.
ぱ
Man! Glad I take good care of it!
THEN IT STAYS!
SEE THERE? THAT'S THE WAY TO THE MIHO PINE GROVE. THERE'S SOME TIME BEFORE SCHOOL STARTS. LET'S GO!
UH... SURE.
IT'S A LOVELY PLACE, JUST WHERE YOU'D FIGURE CELESTIAL MAIDENS WOULD HANG OUT. HMM, I WONDER IF THAT GIRL WILL BE THERE...?
THROB
THROB
THROB

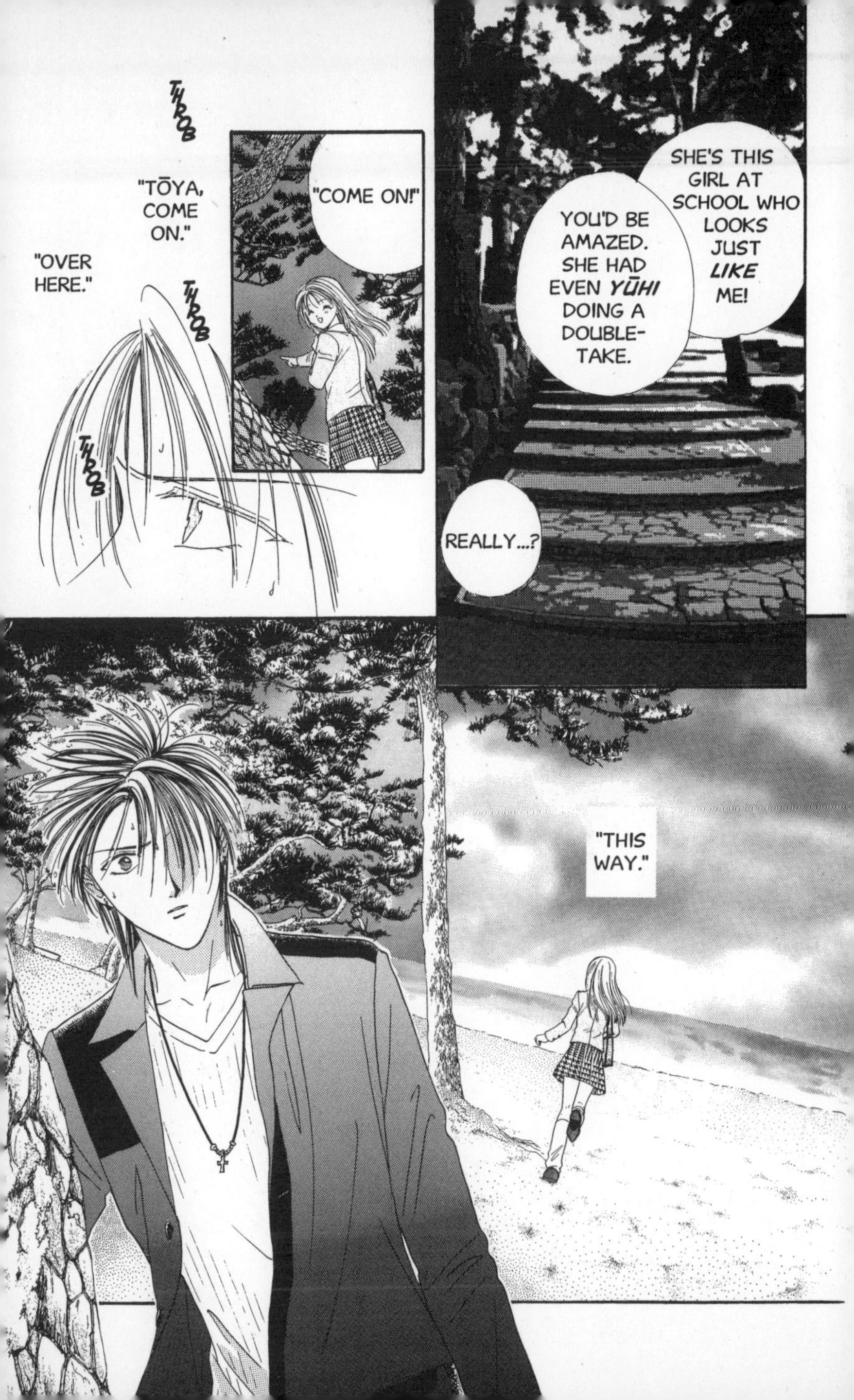
SHE'S THIS GIRL AT SCHOOL WHO LOOKS JUST LIKE ME!
YOU'D BE AMAZED. SHE HAD EVEN YŪHI DOING A DOUBLE-TAKE.
REALLY...?
"COME ON!"
THROB
"TŌYA, COME ON."
"OVER HERE."
THROB
THROB
"THIS WAY."

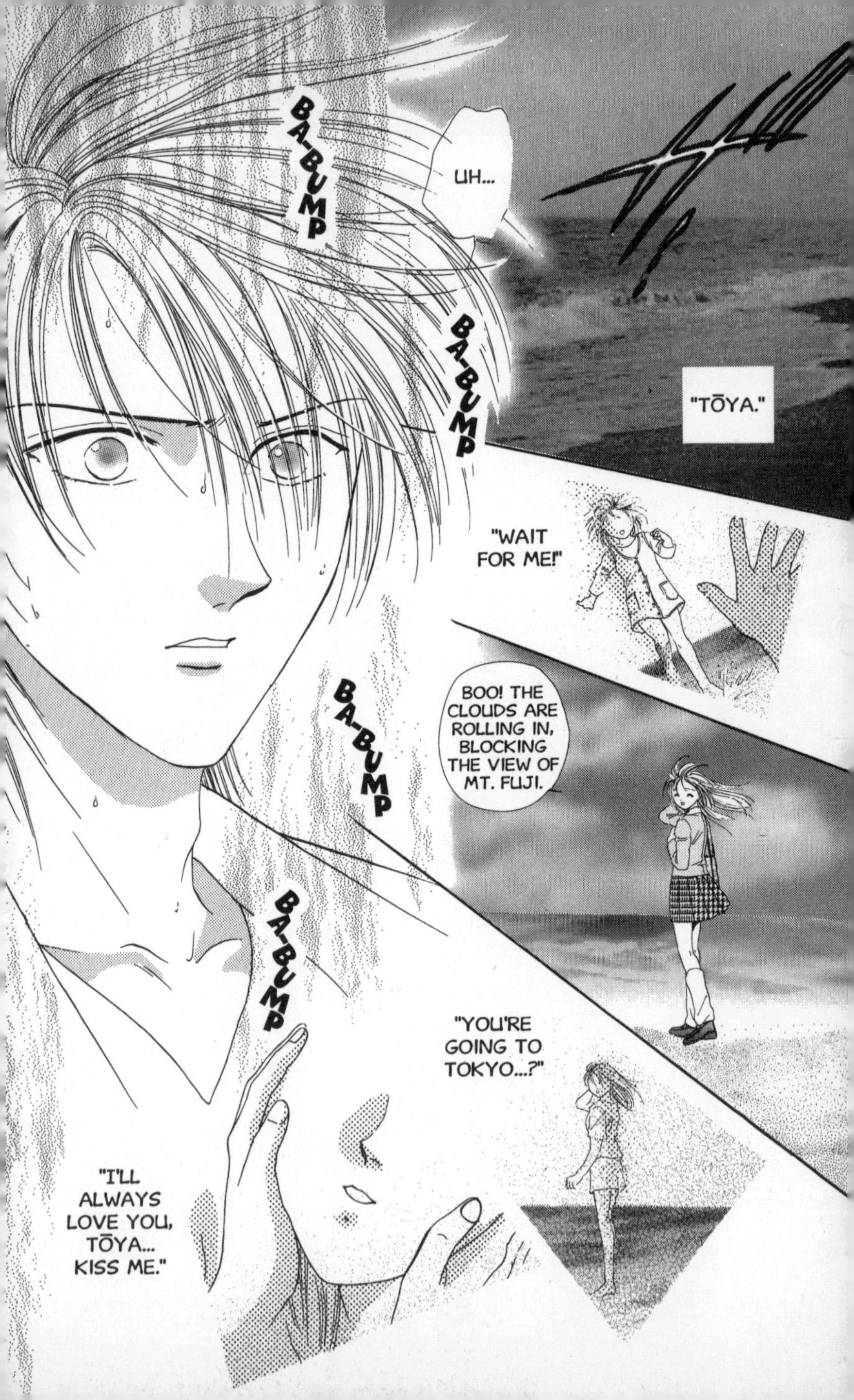
UH...
BA-BUMP
"TŌYA."
BA-BUMP
"WAIT FOR ME!"
BOO! THE CLOUDS ARE ROLLING IN, BLOCKING THE VIEW OF MT. FUJI.
BA-BUMP
"YOU'RE GOING TO TOKYO...?"
BA-BUMP
"I'LL ALWAYS LOVE YOU, TŌYA... KISS ME."

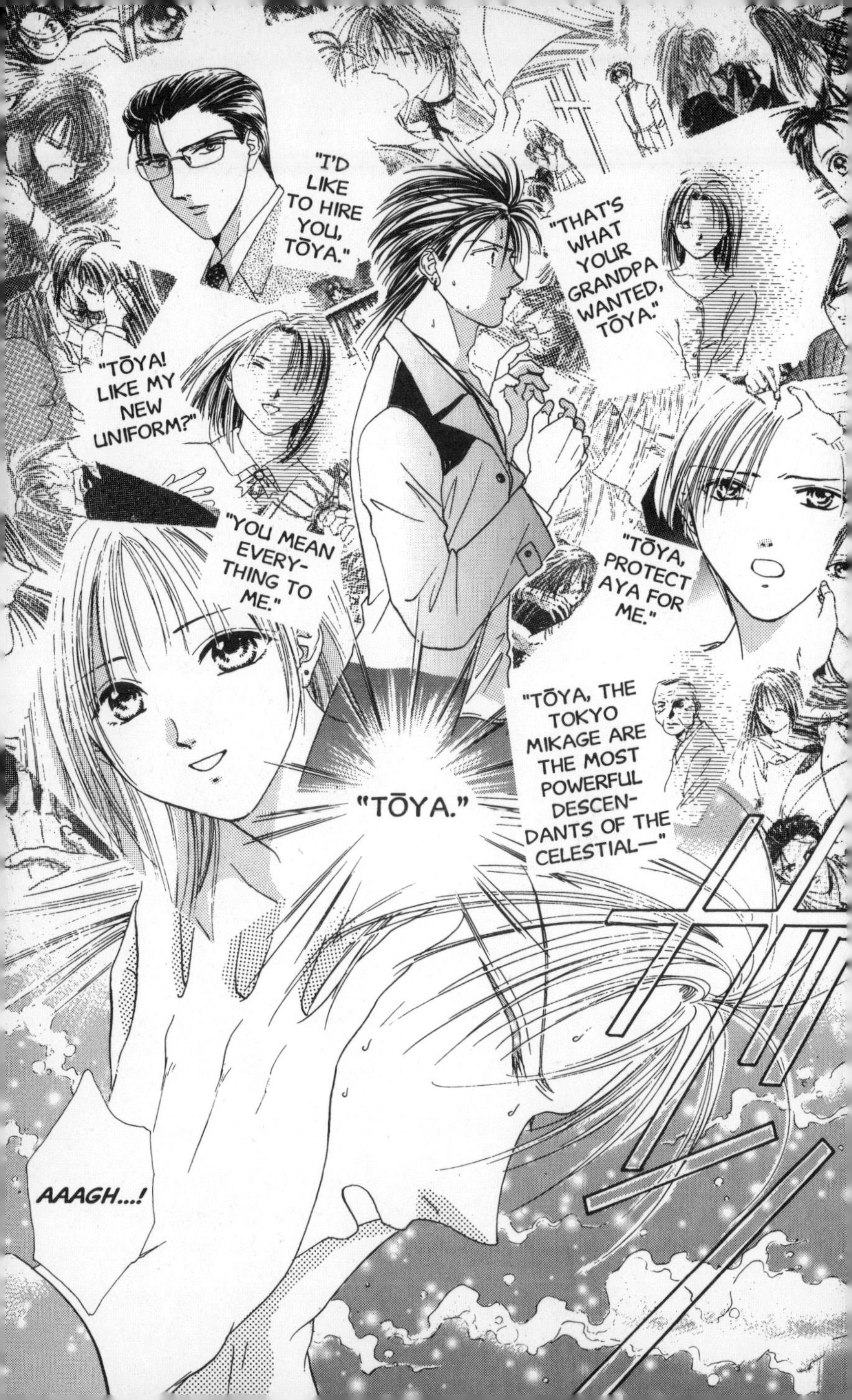
"THAT'S WHAT YOUR GRANDPA WANTED, TŌYA."
"I'D LIKE TO HIRE YOU, TŌYA."
"TŌYA! LIKE MY NEW UNIFORM?"
"TŌYA, PROTECT AYA FOR ME."
"YOU MEAN EVERY-THING TO ME."
"TŌYA, THE TOKYO MIKAGE ARE THE MOST POWERFUL DESCEN-DANTS OF THE CELESTIAL—"
"TŌYA."
AAAGH...!

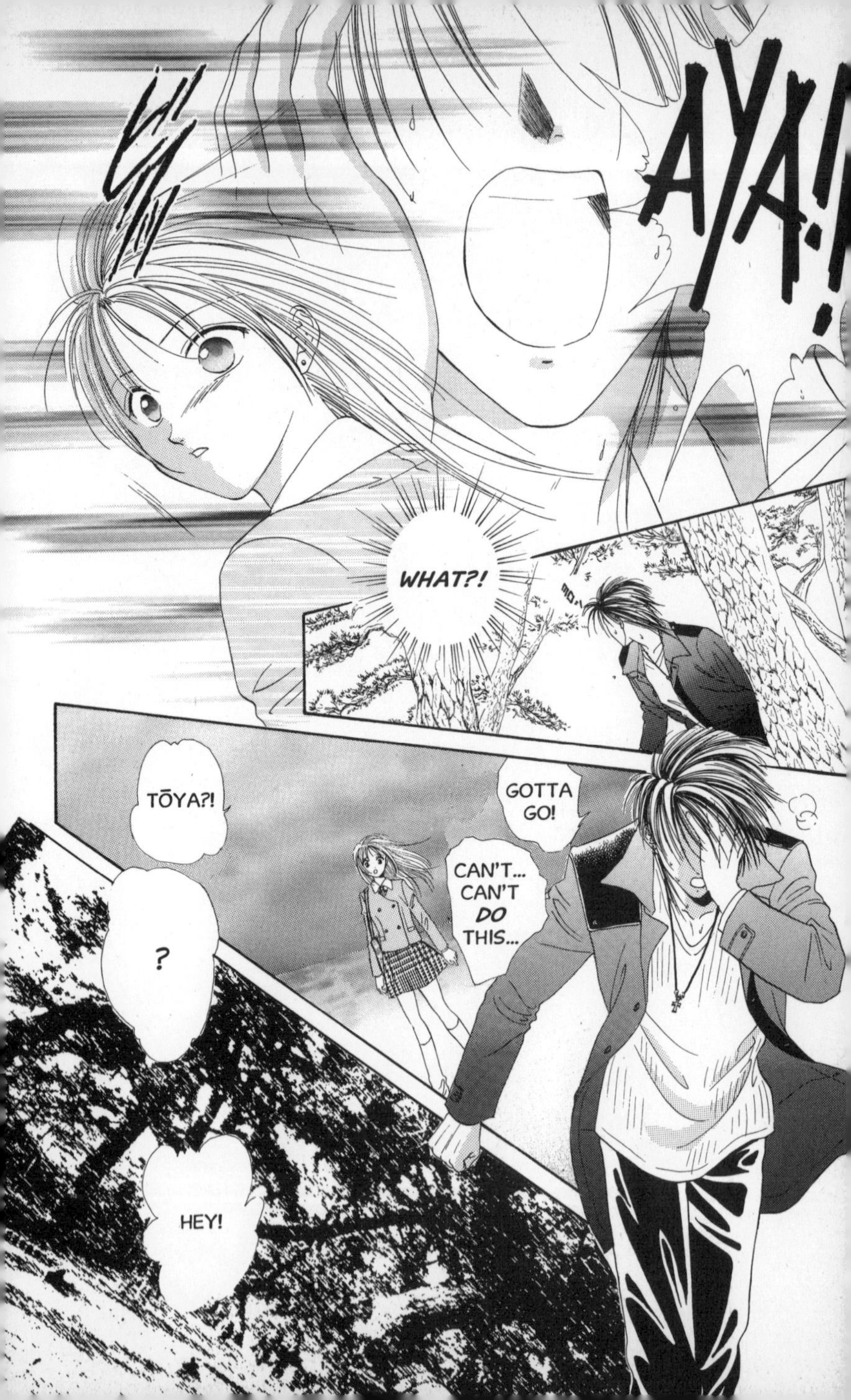
AYA!!
WHAT?!
GOTTA GO!
CAN'T... CAN'T *DO* THIS...
TŌYA?!
?
HEY!

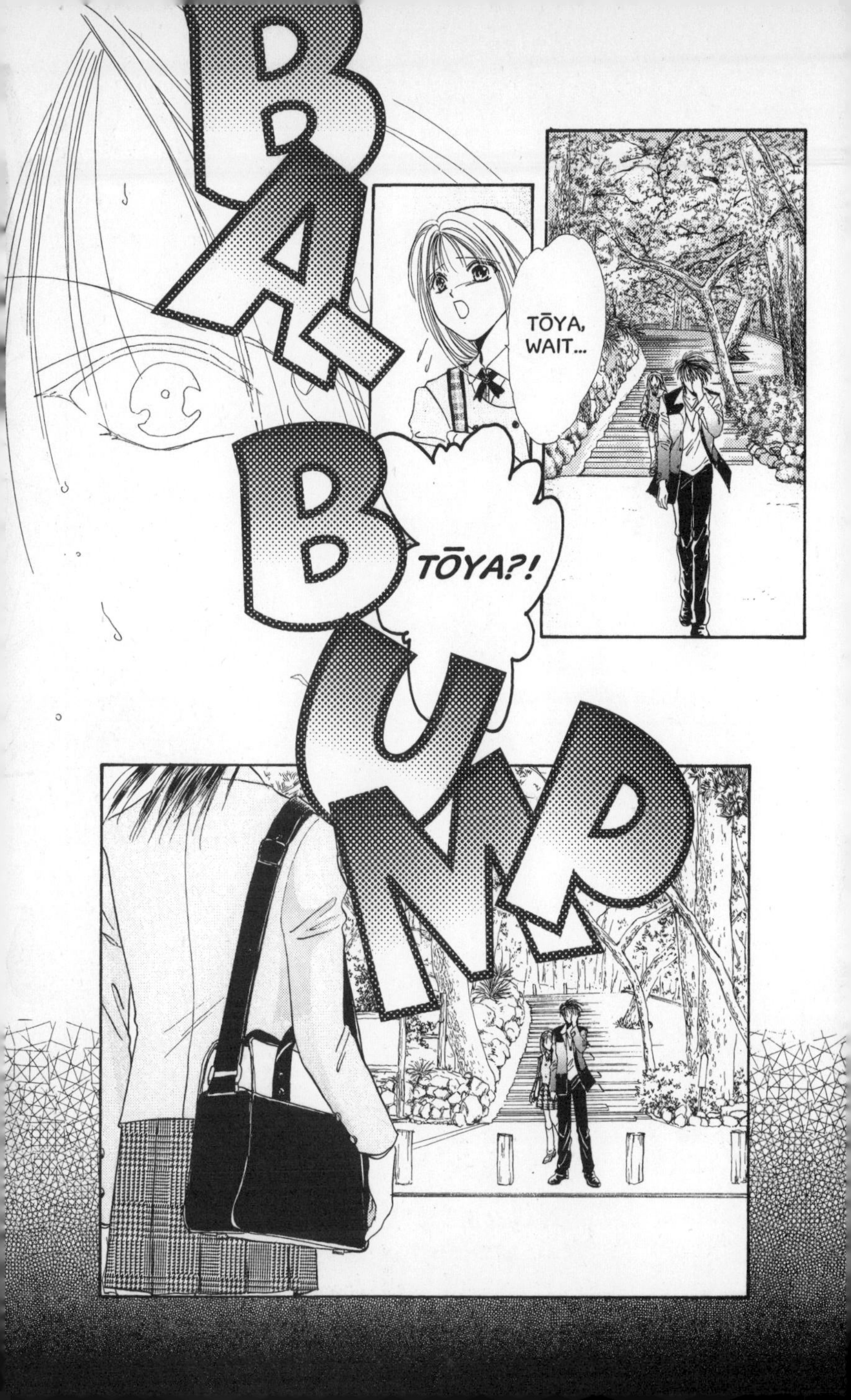
TŌYA, WAIT...
TŌYA?!
BA-BUMP

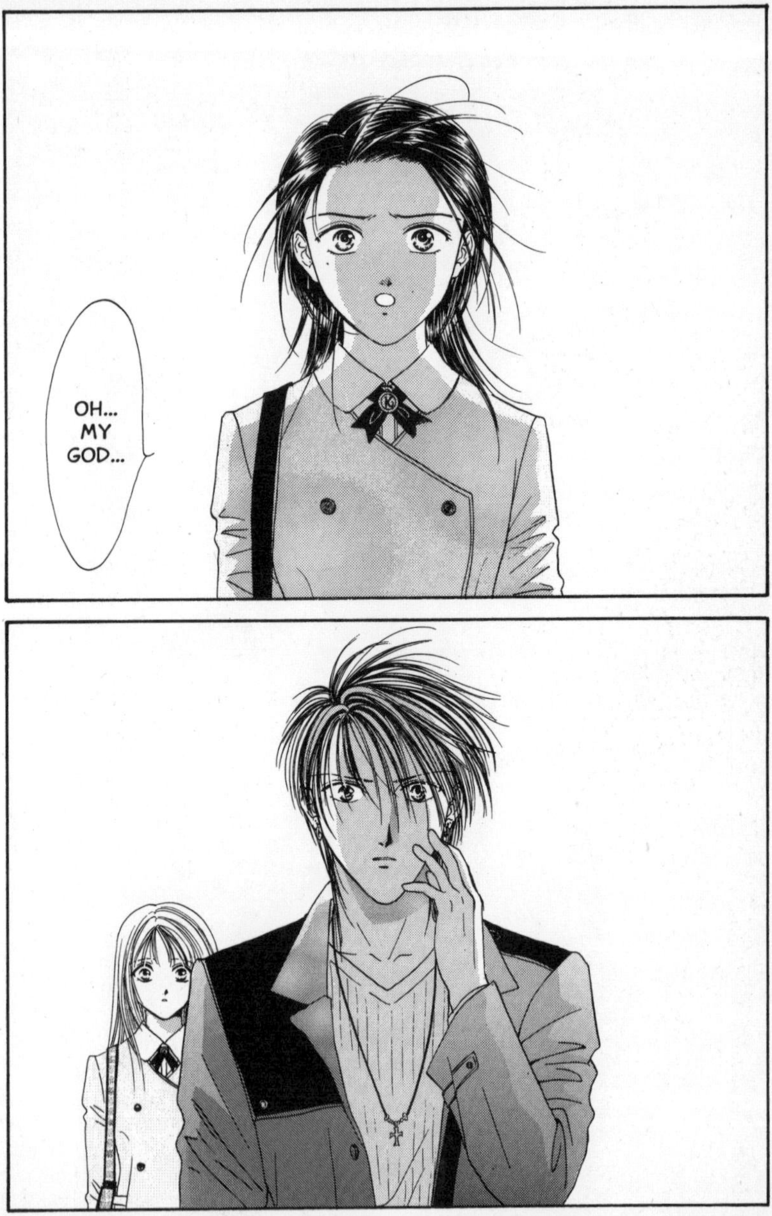
OH... MY GOD...

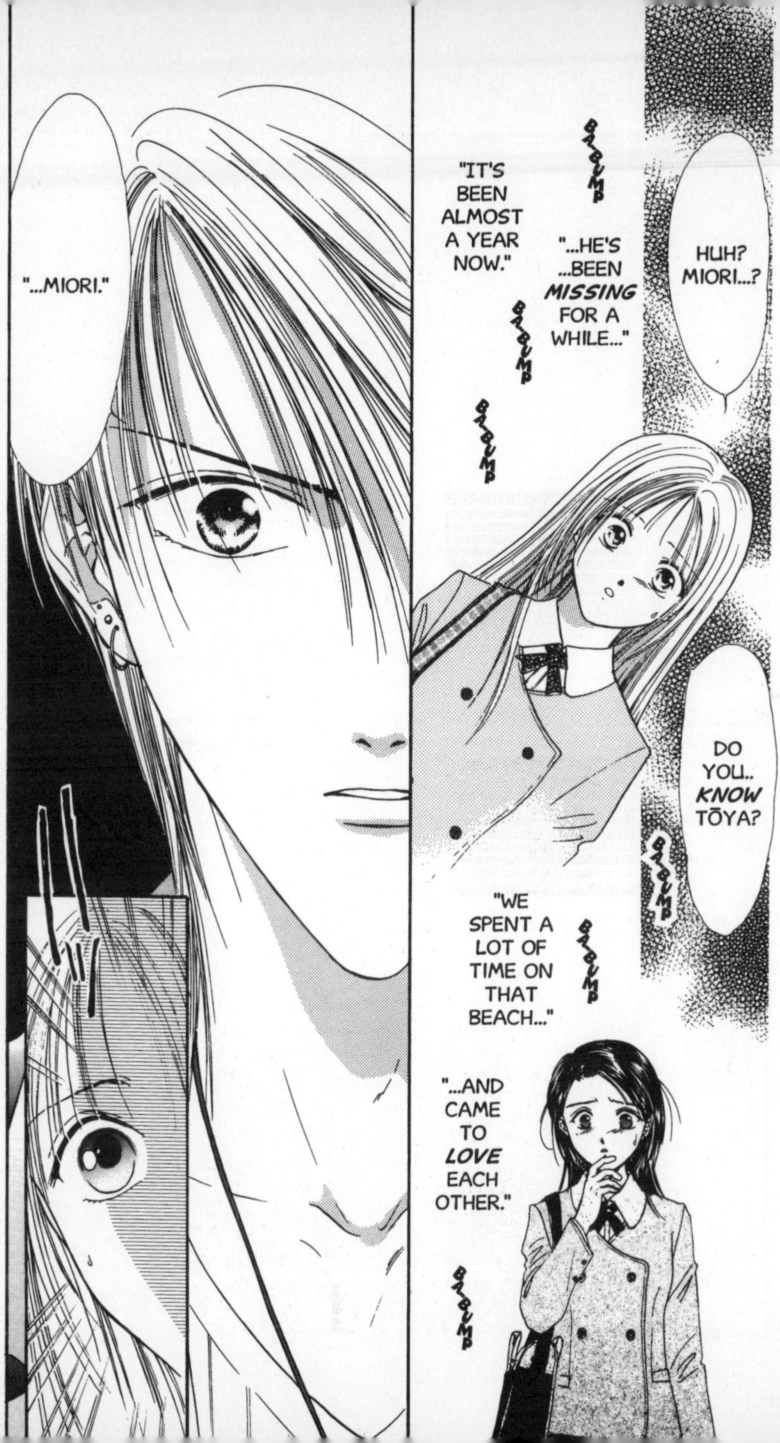
HUH? MIORI...?
"IT'S BEEN ALMOST A YEAR NOW."
BA-BUMP
"...HE'S ...BEEN *MISSING* FOR A WHILE..."
BA-BUMP
BA-BUMP
DO YOU.. *KNOW* TŌYA?
BA-BUMP
"WE SPENT A LOT OF TIME ON THAT BEACH..."
BA-BUMP
"...AND CAME TO *LOVE* EACH OTHER."
BA-BUMP
"...MIORI."

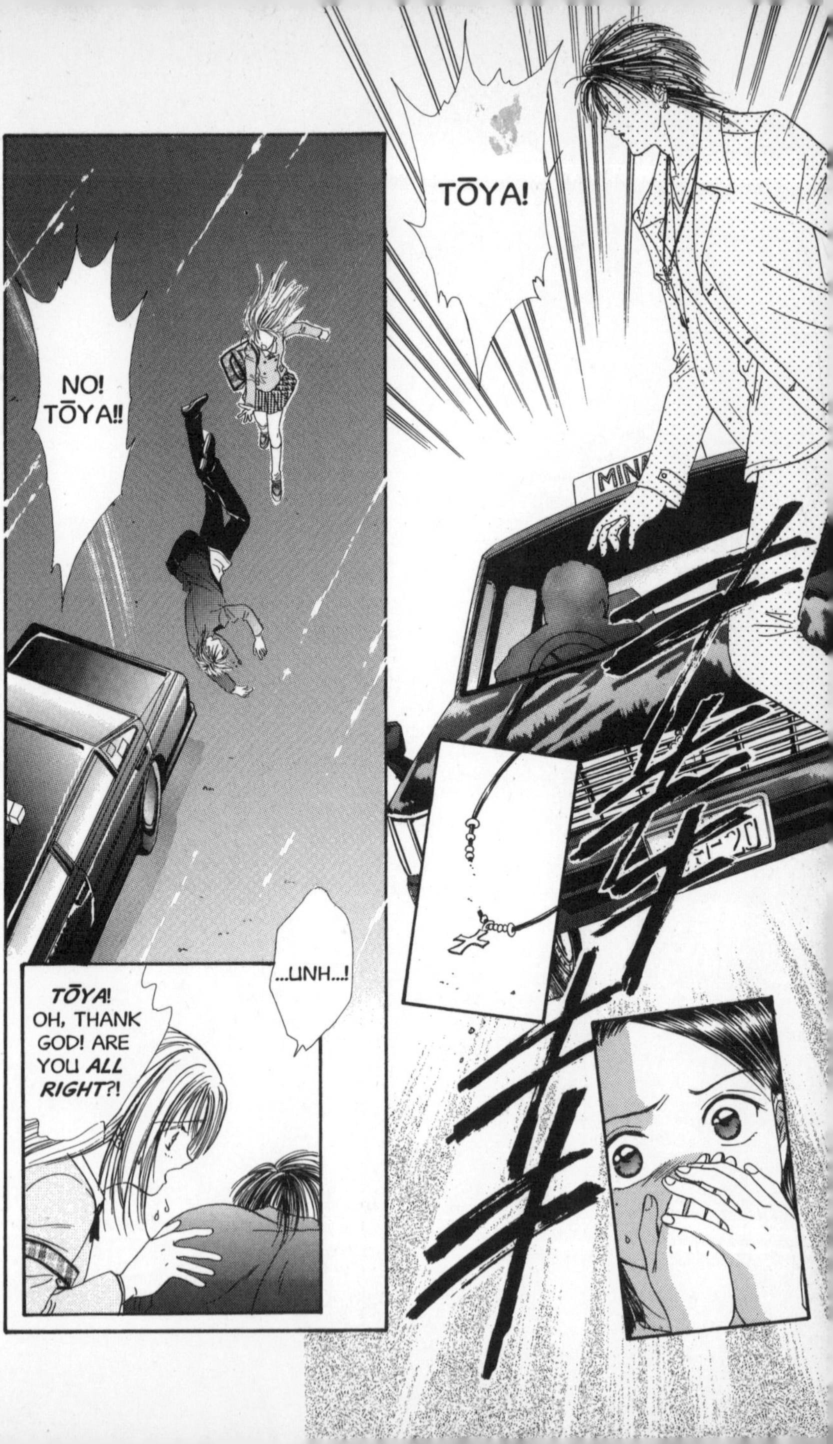
TŌYA!
NO! TŌYA!!
...UNH...!
TŌYA! OH, THANK GOD! ARE YOU ALL RIGHT?!

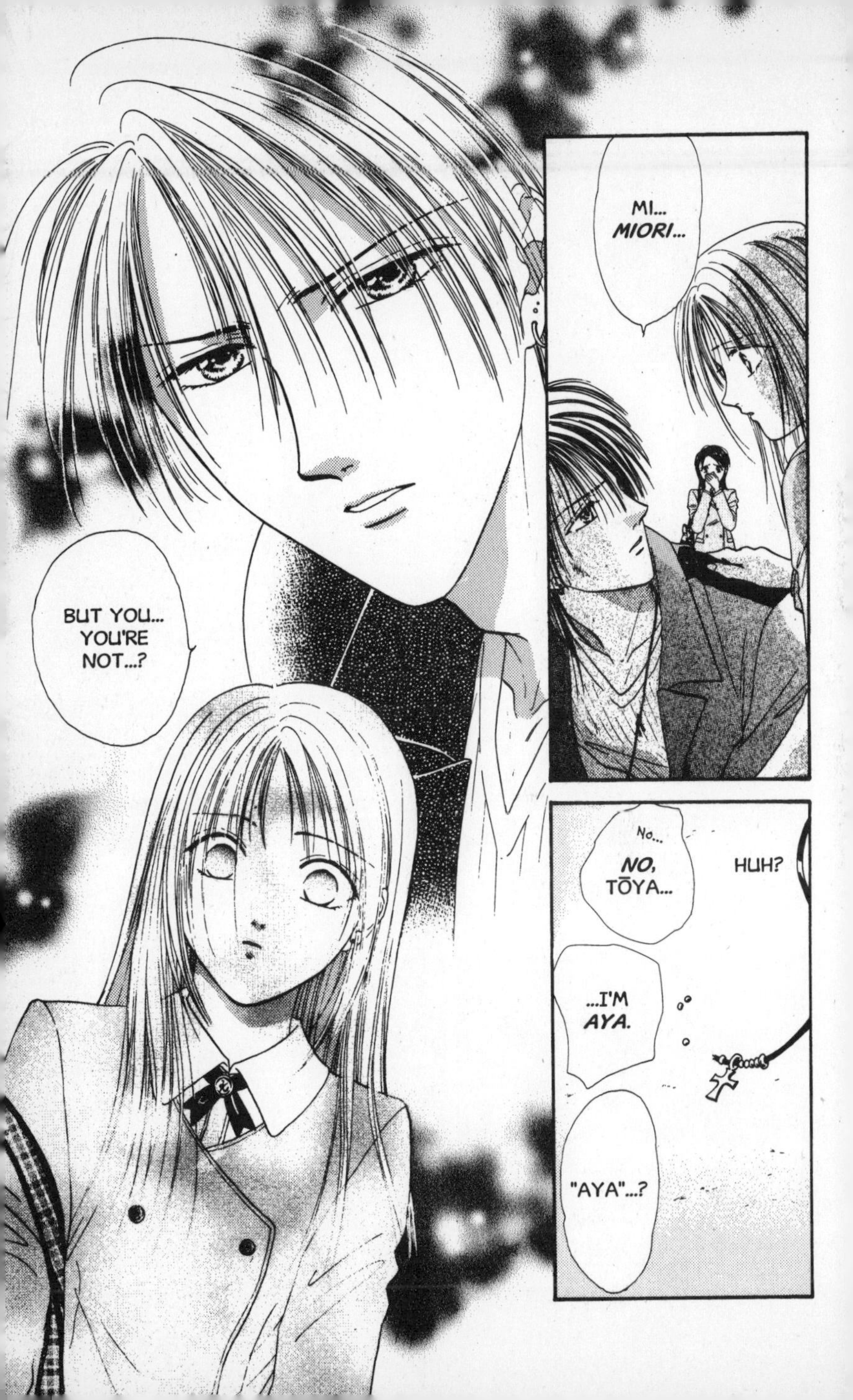
MI... MIORI...
HUH?
No... NO, TŌYA...
...I'M AYA.
"AYA"...?
BUT YOU... YOU'RE NOT...?

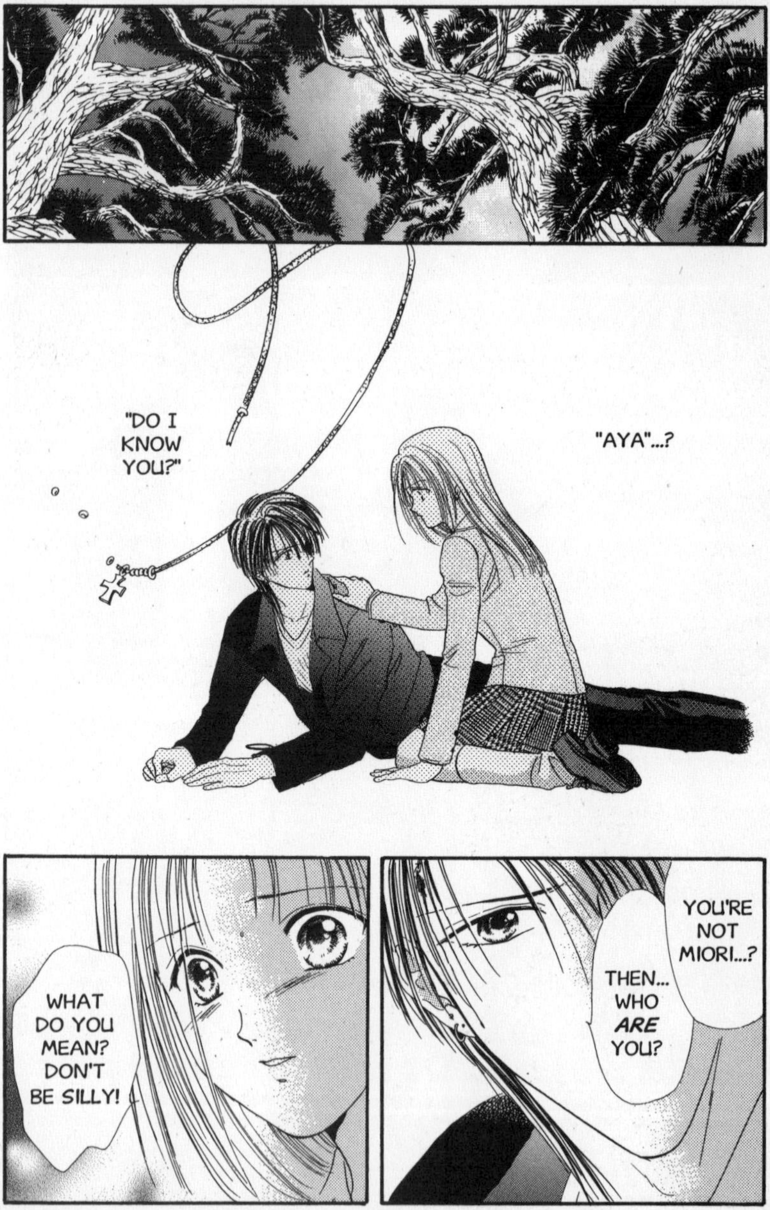
"AYA"...?
"DO I KNOW YOU?"
YOU'RE NOT MIORI...?
THEN... WHO *ARE* YOU?
WHAT DO YOU MEAN? DON'T BE SILLY!

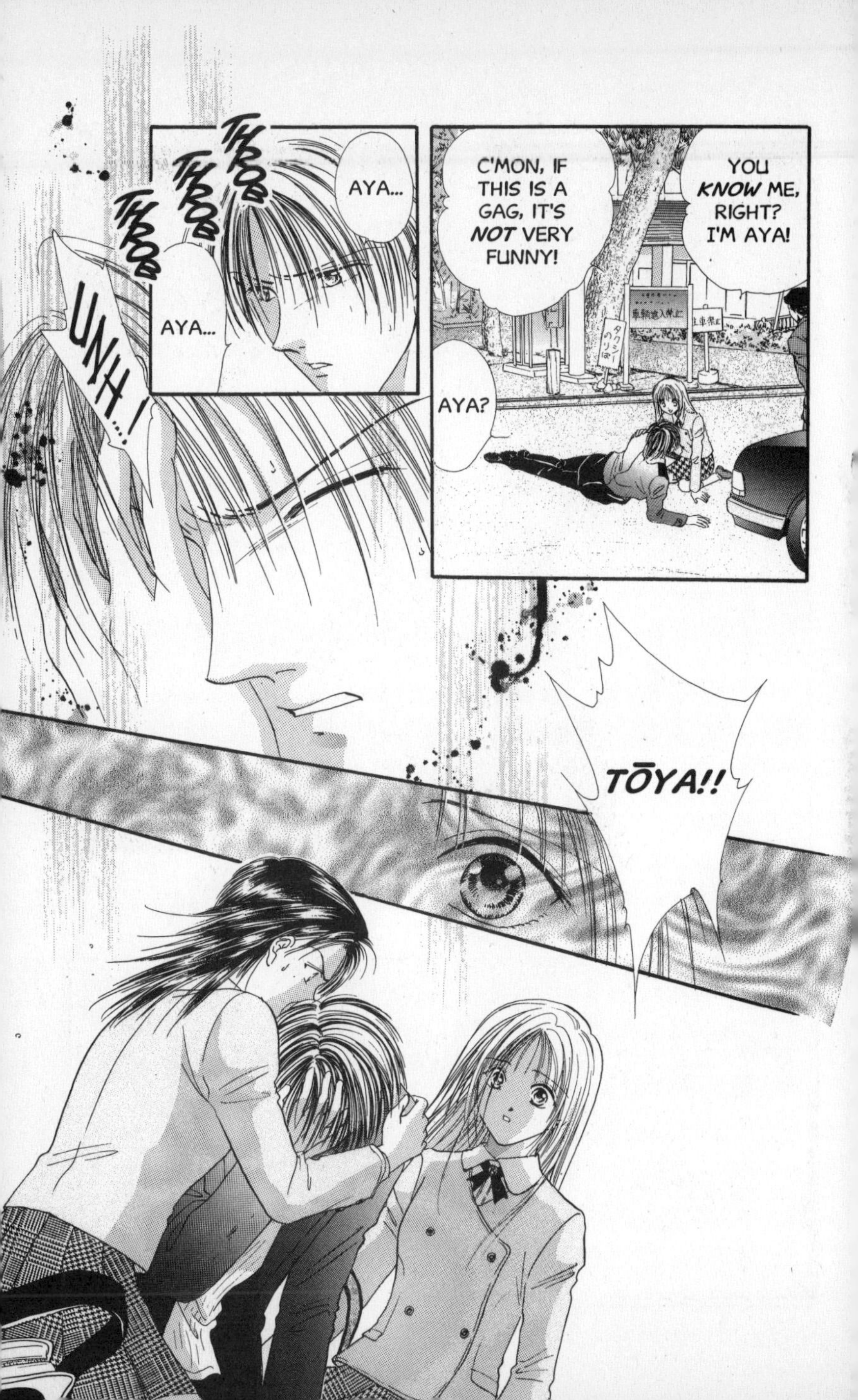
YOU *KNOW* ME, RIGHT? I'M AYA!
C'MON, IF THIS IS A GAG, IT'S *NOT* VERY FUNNY!
AYA?
AYA...
THROB THROB THROB
AYA...
UNH...!
TŌYA!!

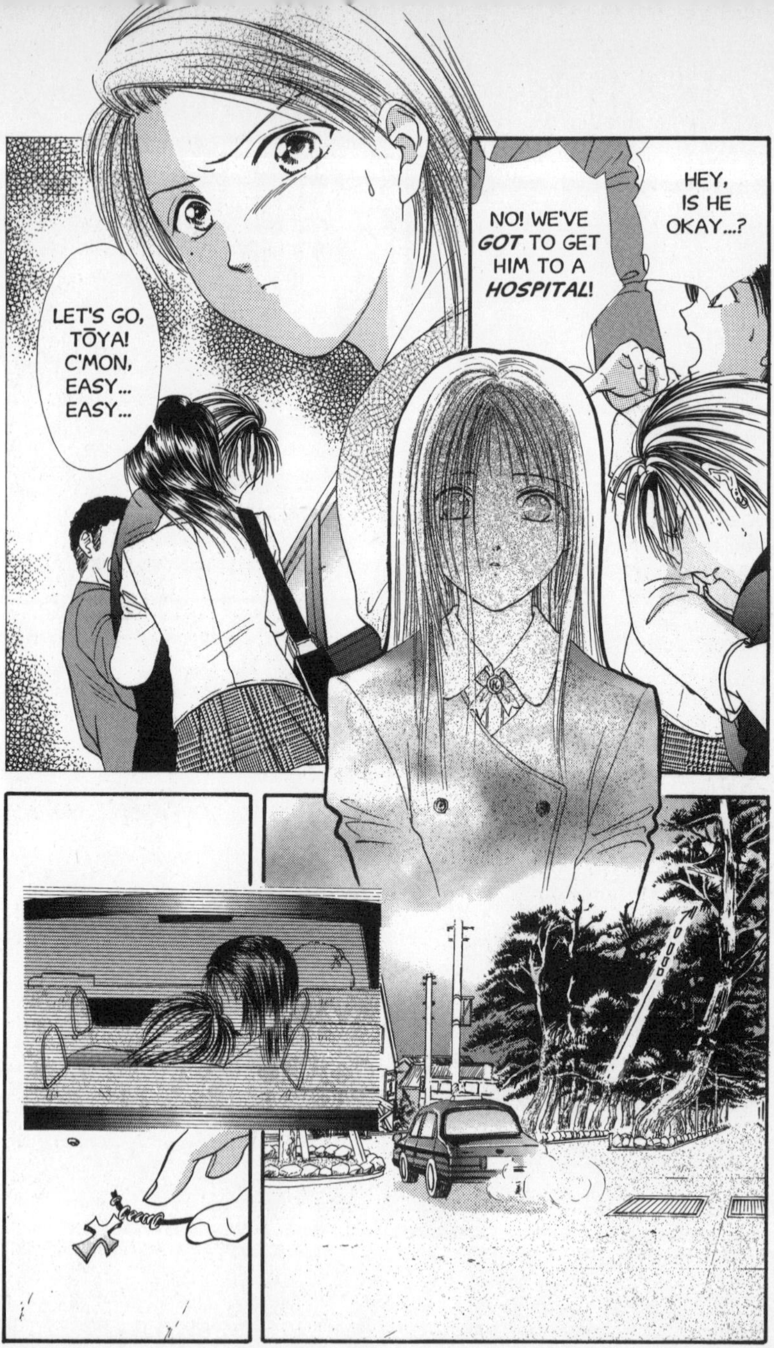
HEY, IS HE OKAY...?
NO! WE'VE ***GOT*** TO GET HIM TO A ***HOSPITAL***!
LET'S GO, TŌYA! C'MON, EASY... EASY...

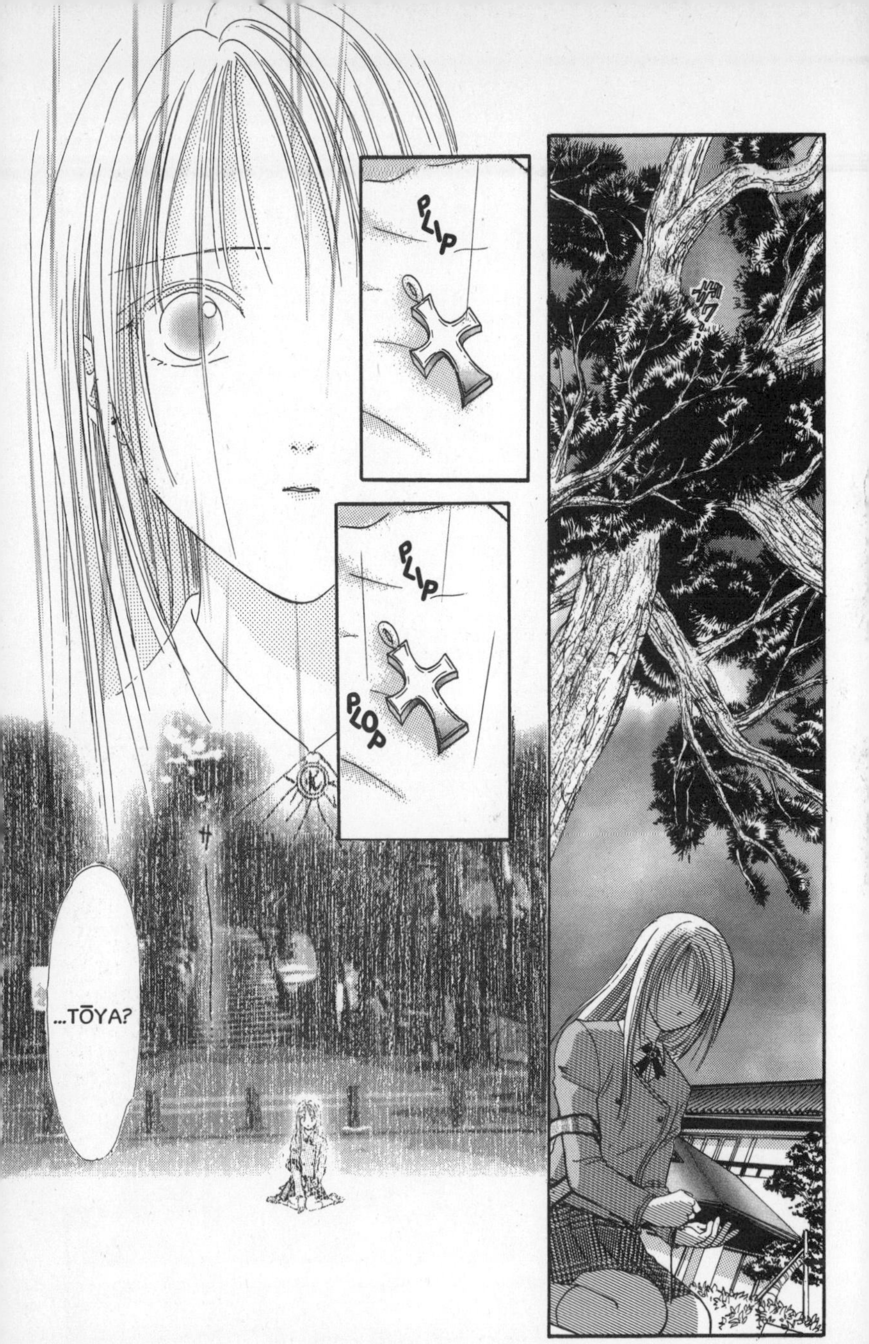
ザワ…
PLIP
PLIP
PLOP
...TŌYA?

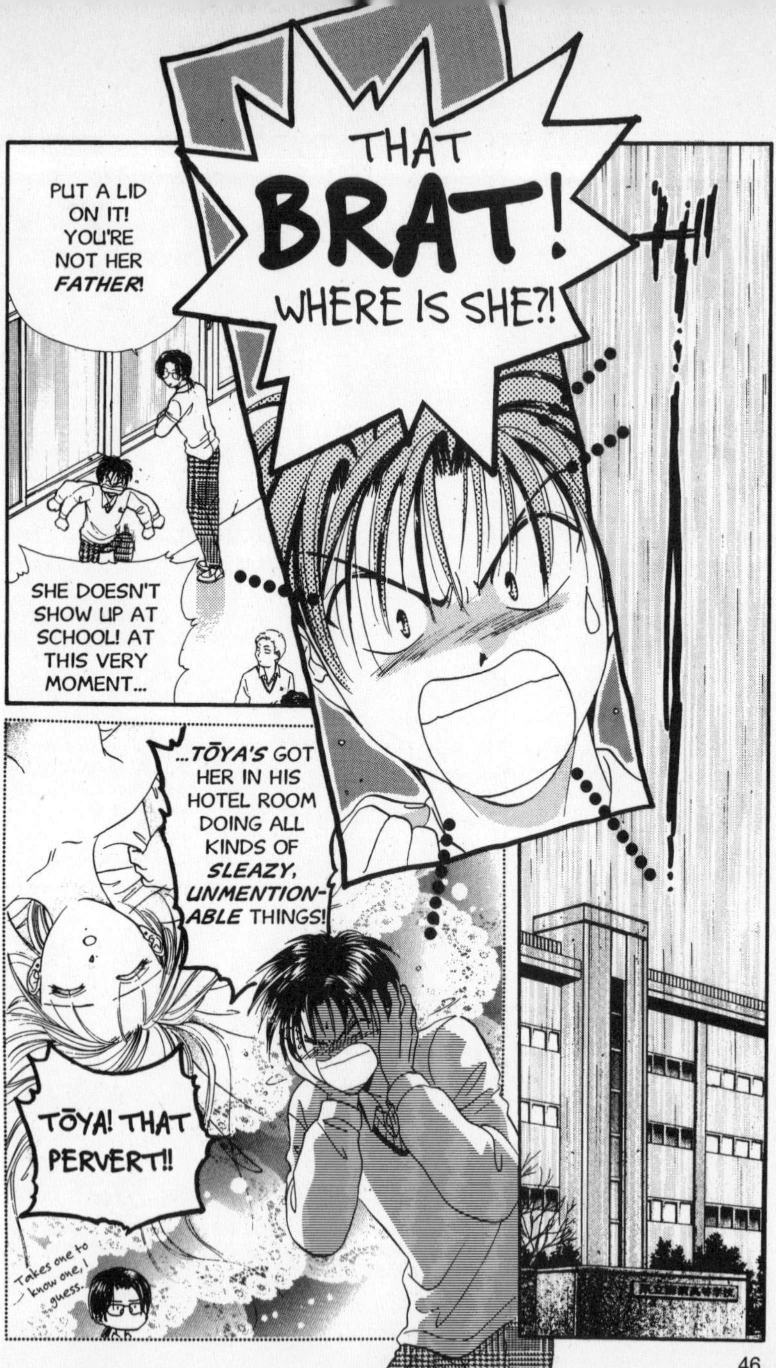
THAT BRAT! WHERE IS SHE?!
PUT A LID ON IT! YOU'RE NOT HER FATHER!
SHE DOESN'T SHOW UP AT SCHOOL! AT THIS VERY MOMENT...
...TŌYA'S GOT HER IN HIS HOTEL ROOM DOING ALL KINDS OF SLEAZY, UNMENTION-ABLE THINGS!
TŌYA! THAT PERVERT!!
Takes one to know one, I guess.

Ceres: 8

The local slang in **Ceres** gets looked over by editors who came from those regions. We even got a writer from Okinawa to take a look at that story arc. I had read in a book that there was Okinawan dialect for "Wow," but the writer had never heard of it, so I didn't use it because I thought it might be confusing. I did get a couple letters about the Kumamoto slang in Vol. 6. But! Those were given the green light by an editor from Kumamoto. Some people still said they wouldn't speak that way, so I asked someone else I knew from there (who's in her early 20's) and she said, "What? Sure they do." What's going on???

...I was thinking, even in the "Kansai" dialect, there are regional differences for Osaka, Kobe, Nara, or Kyoto...etc. Furthermore, it makes a difference if you're from "Osaka, the city," or "Osaka, the prefecture," so there are different dialects even within Osaka. (When I went to high school around Sakai, Osaka, I used my local dialect and they told me I sounded freaky. So I stopped. D) Suzumi is from Hyogo, but I'm using the generalized Kansai dialect. There probably is a separate dialect, though.

Dialects can be different a couple towns over, even within the same region. (Really, only people who live there are bothered by it; nobody else notices. D) I do hope people will understand.

AYA, YOU IDIOT! YOU MORON!
IT'S OKAY, FOLKS. IT'S JUST A LITTLE EMOTIONAL MELTDOWN.
THIS WON'T GET ME DOWN! I'VE PICKED UP THE CUISINES OF TOCHIGI! OKINAWA! MIYAGI! AND NOW SHIZUOKA! I'LL BE THE MOST VERSATILE CHEF IN JAPAN, AND...
Are you Shuro of GeSANG?
Naw, wish I was. Who wouldn't?
LISTEN.
YOU'RE GETTIN' DOWNRIGHT PATHETIC, YŪHI, YOU KNOW THAT?
WHADDYA MEAN? HAVE YOU NO SYMPATHY AT ALL?!

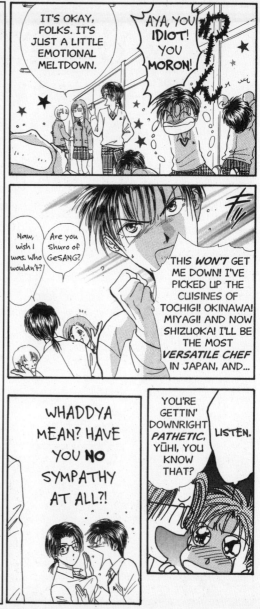

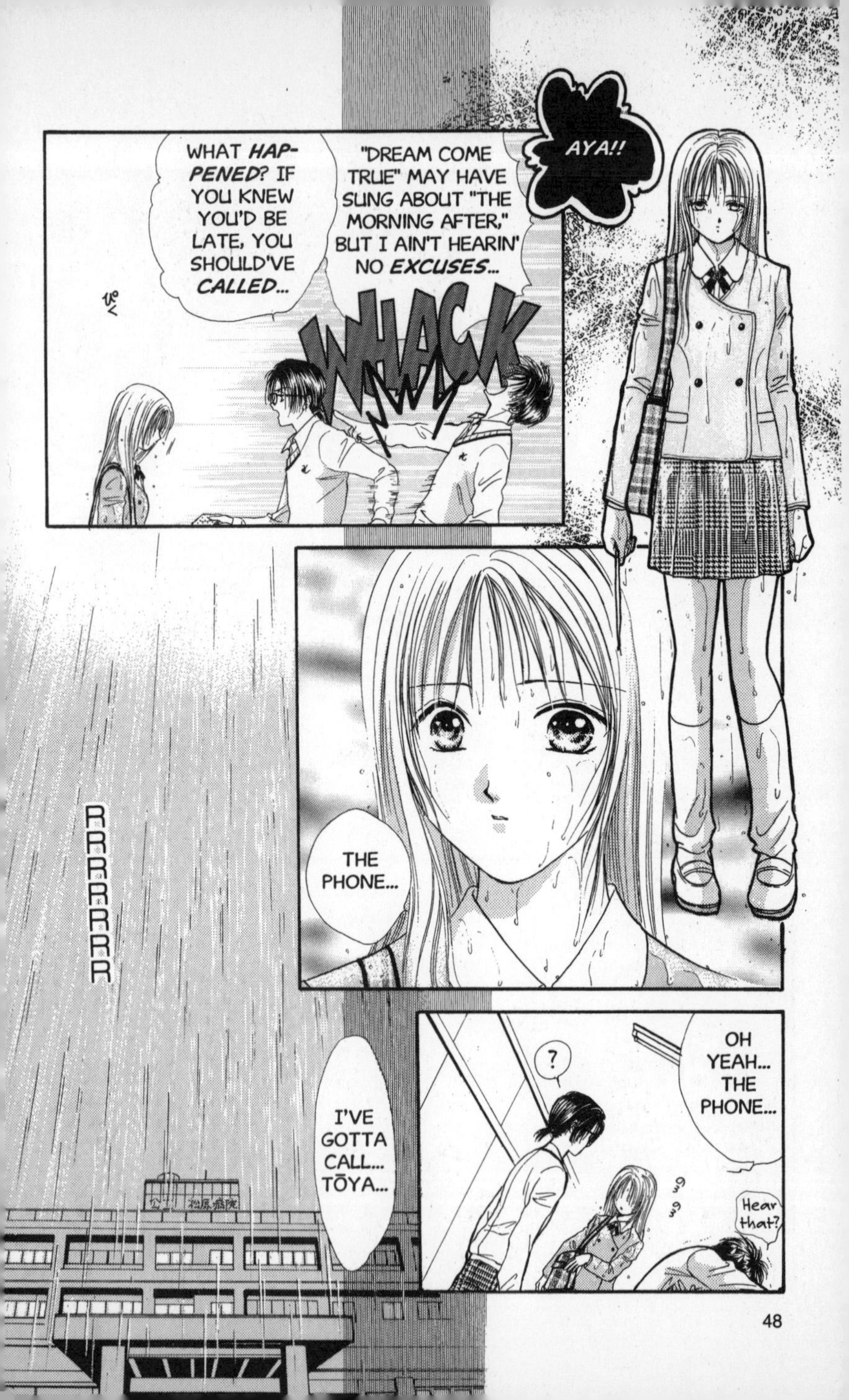
AYA!!
"DREAM COME TRUE" MAY HAVE SUNG ABOUT "THE MORNING AFTER," BUT I AIN'T HEARIN' NO *EXCUSES*...
WHAT *HAP-PENED*? IF YOU KNEW YOU'D BE LATE, YOU SHOULD'VE *CALLED*...
WHACK
ぴく
THE PHONE...
RRRRRRRR
OH YEAH... THE PHONE...
?
Hear that?
I'VE GOTTA CALL... TŌYA...

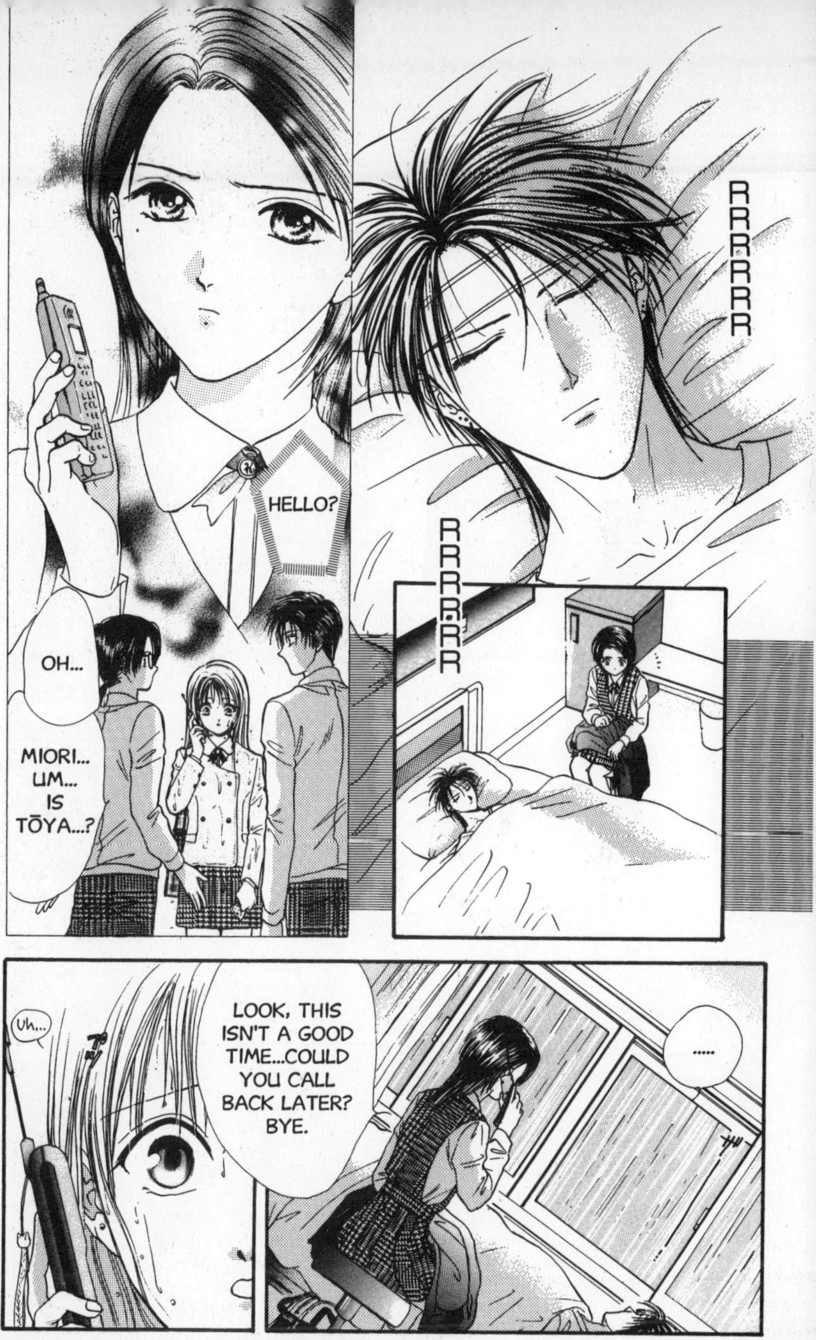
RRRRRR
RRRRRR
HELLO?
OH...
MIORI... UM... IS TŌYA...?
.....
LOOK, THIS ISN'T A GOOD TIME...COULD YOU CALL BACK LATER? BYE.
Uh...

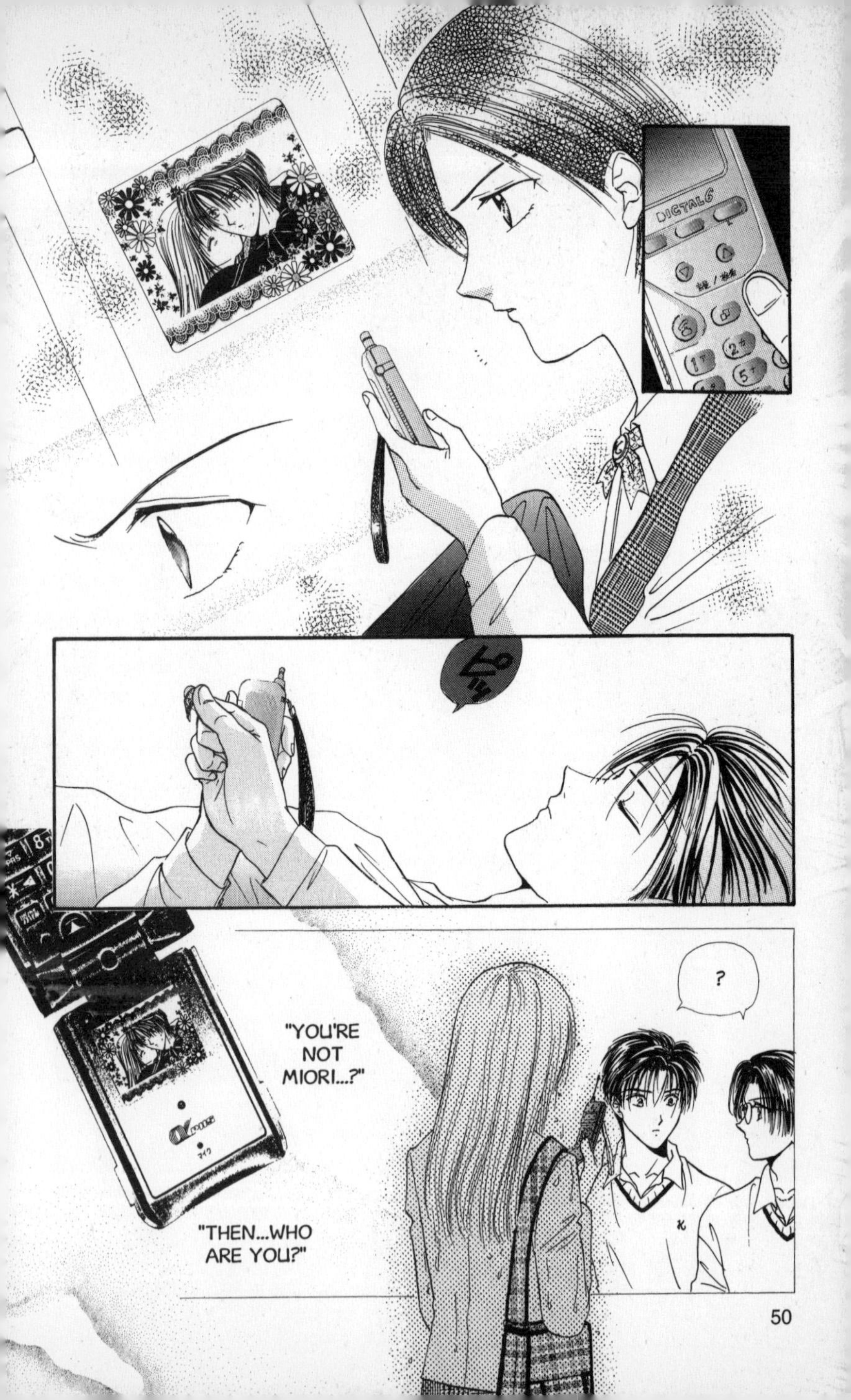
?
"YOU'RE NOT MIORI...?"
"THEN...WHO ARE YOU?"

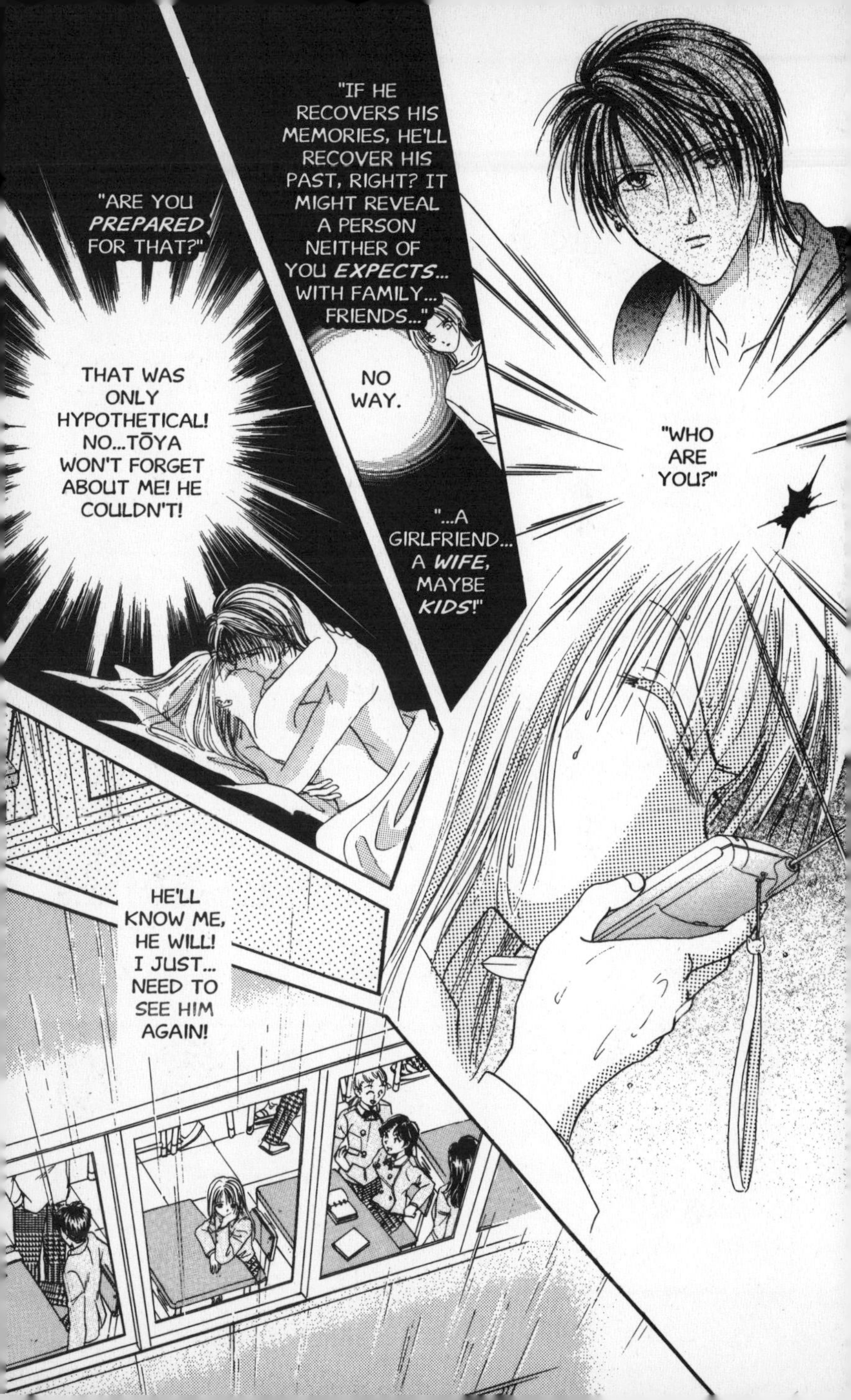
"WHO ARE YOU?"
"IF HE RECOVERS HIS MEMORIES, HE'LL RECOVER HIS PAST, RIGHT? IT MIGHT REVEAL A PERSON NEITHER OF YOU *EXPECTS*... WITH FAMILY... FRIENDS..."
NO WAY.
"...A GIRLFRIEND... A *WIFE*, MAYBE *KIDS*!"
"ARE YOU *PREPARED* FOR THAT?"
THAT WAS ONLY HYPOTHETICAL! NO...TŌYA WON'T FORGET ABOUT ME! HE COULDN'T!
HE'LL KNOW ME, HE WILL! I JUST... NEED TO SEE HIM AGAIN!

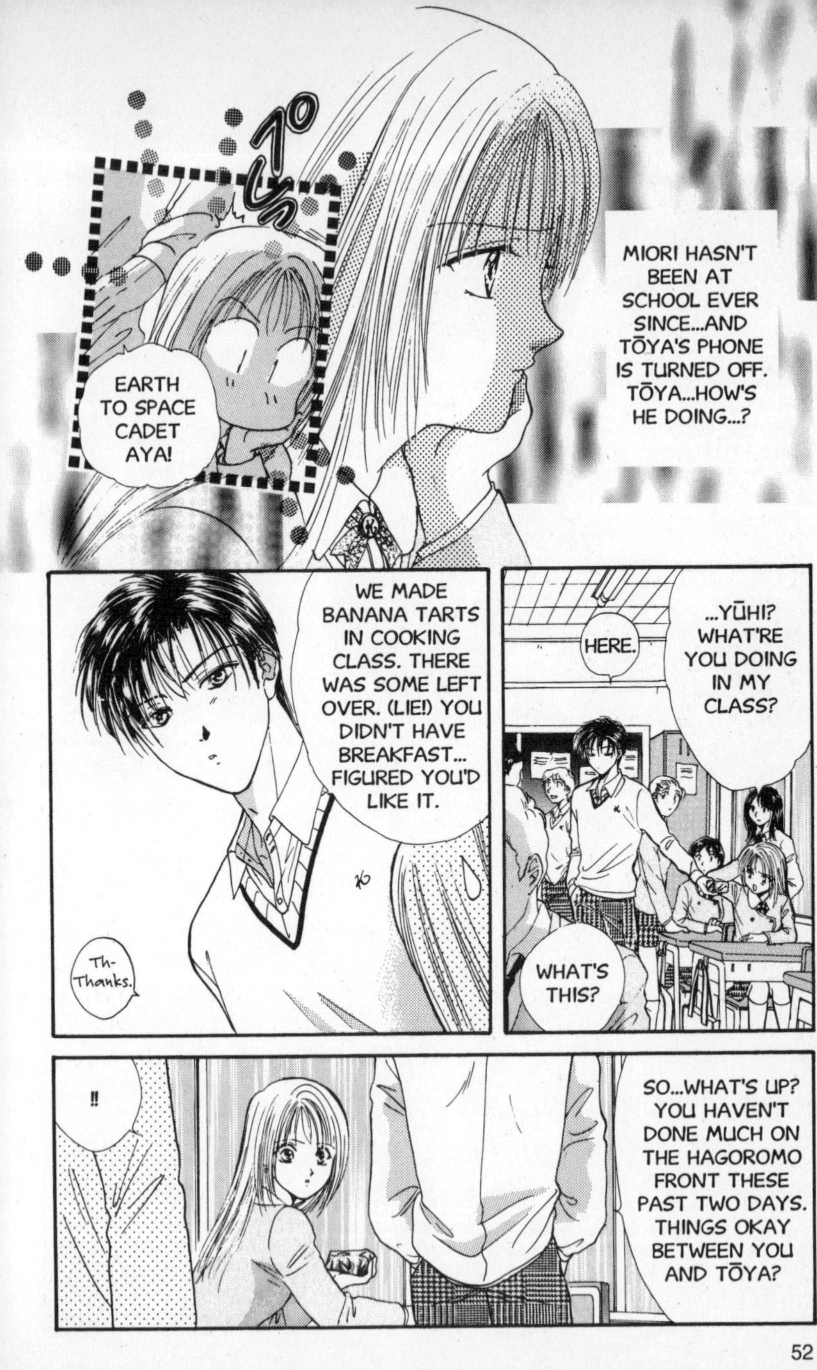
MIORI HASN'T BEEN AT SCHOOL EVER SINCE...AND TŌYA'S PHONE IS TURNED OFF. TŌYA...HOW'S HE DOING...?
EARTH TO SPACE CADET AYA!
...YŪHI? WHAT'RE YOU DOING IN MY CLASS?
HERE.
WHAT'S THIS?
WE MADE BANANA TARTS IN COOKING CLASS. THERE WAS SOME LEFT OVER. (LIE!) YOU DIDN'T HAVE BREAKFAST... FIGURED YOU'D LIKE IT.
Th-Thanks.
SO...WHAT'S UP? YOU HAVEN'T DONE MUCH ON THE HAGOROMO FRONT THESE PAST TWO DAYS. THINGS OKAY BETWEEN YOU AND TŌYA?
!!

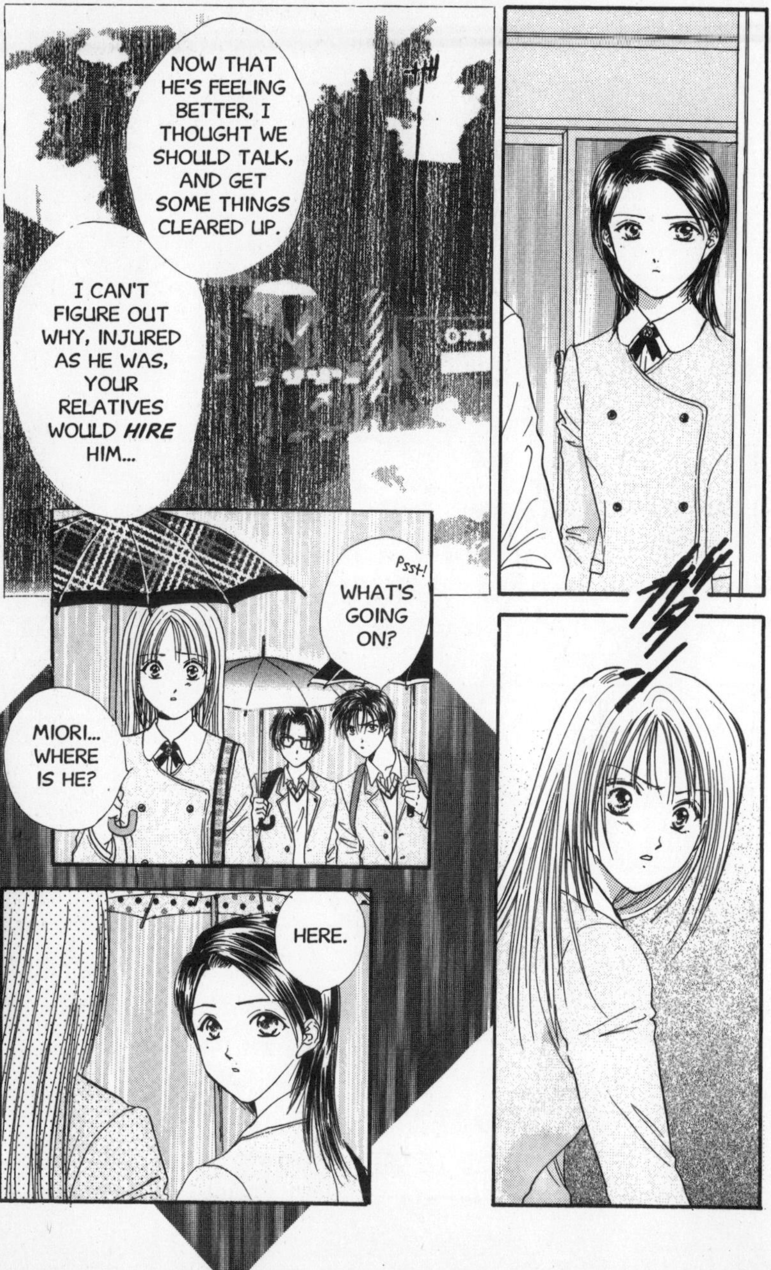
NOW THAT HE'S FEELING BETTER, I THOUGHT WE SHOULD TALK, AND GET SOME THINGS CLEARED UP.
I CAN'T FIGURE OUT WHY, INJURED AS HE WAS, YOUR RELATIVES WOULD *HIRE* HIM...
Psst!
WHAT'S GOING ON?
MIORI... WHERE IS HE?
HERE.

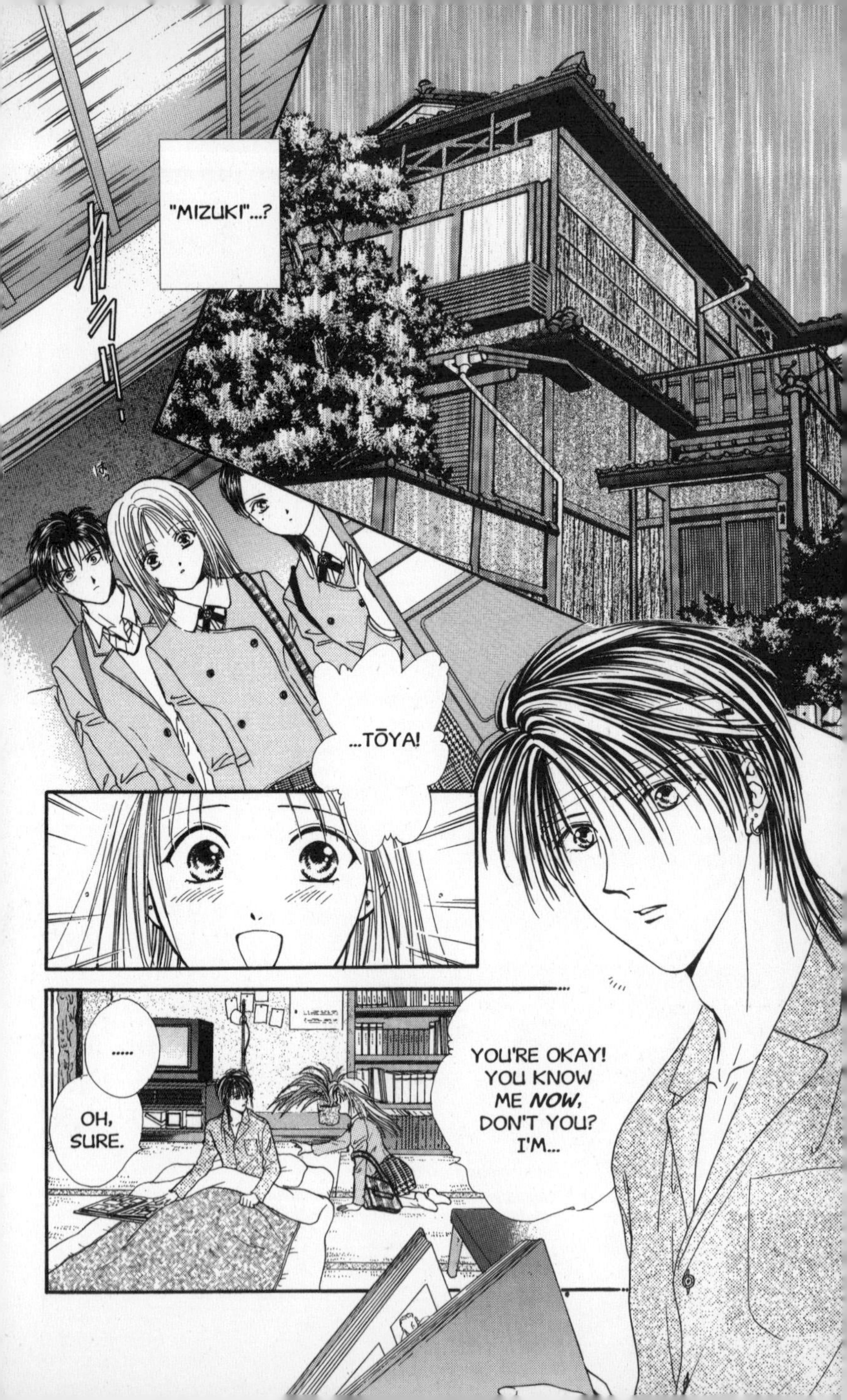
"MIZUKI"...?
...TŌYA!
YOU'RE OKAY! YOU KNOW ME *NOW*, DON'T YOU? I'M...
.....
OH, SURE.

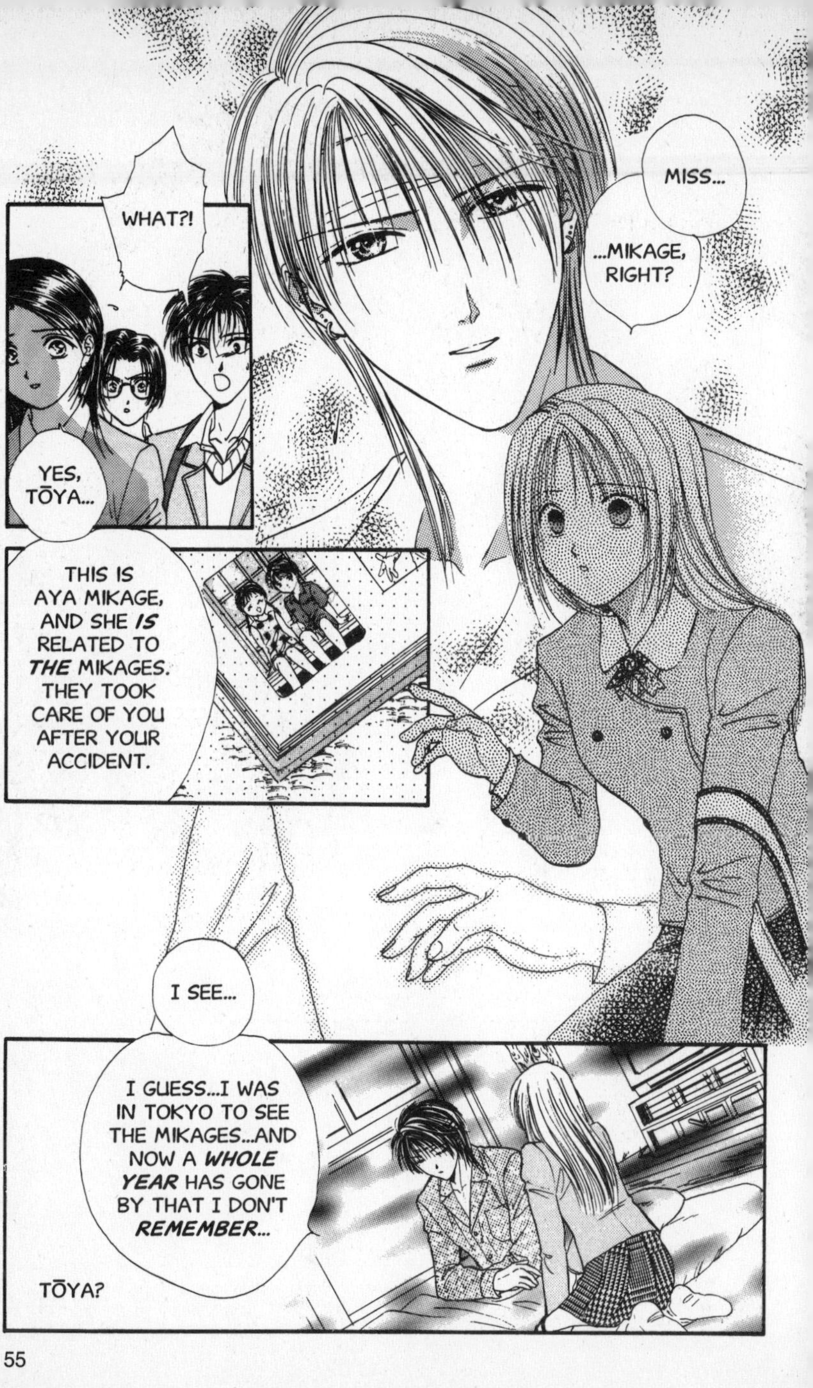
MISS...
...MIKAGE, RIGHT?
WHAT?!
YES, TŌYA...
THIS IS AYA MIKAGE, AND SHE *IS* RELATED TO *THE* MIKAGES. THEY TOOK CARE OF YOU AFTER YOUR ACCIDENT.
I SEE...
I GUESS...I WAS IN TOKYO TO SEE THE MIKAGES...AND NOW A *WHOLE YEAR* HAS GONE BY THAT I DON'T *REMEMBER*...
TŌYA?

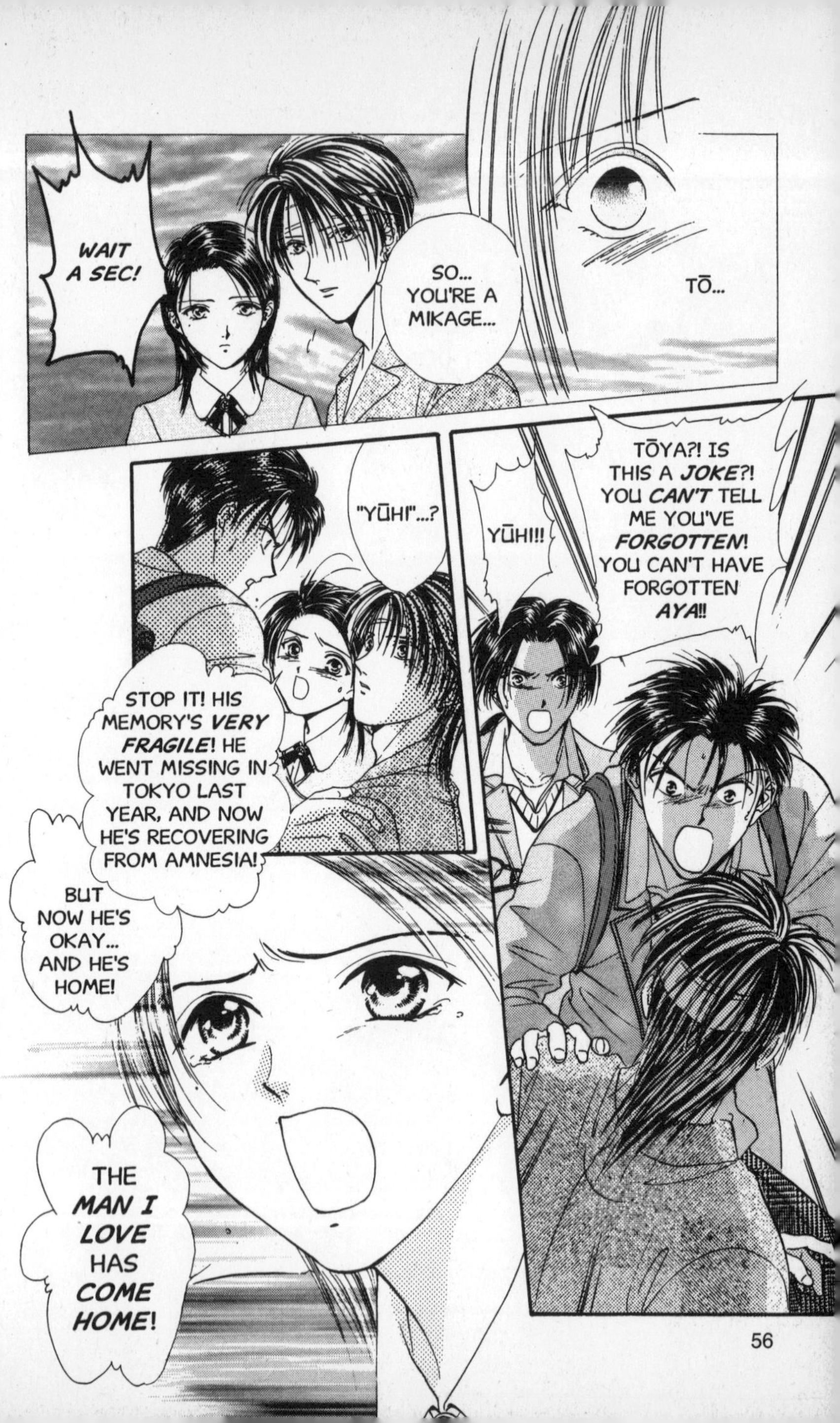

TŌ...
SO... YOU'RE A MIKAGE...
WAIT A SEC!
TŌYA?! IS THIS A *JOKE*?! YOU *CAN'T* TELL ME YOU'VE *FORGOTTEN*! YOU CAN'T HAVE FORGOTTEN *AYA*!!
YŪHI!!
"YŪHI"...?
STOP IT! HIS MEMORY'S *VERY FRAGILE*! HE WENT MISSING IN TOKYO LAST YEAR, AND NOW HE'S RECOVERING FROM AMNESIA!
BUT NOW HE'S OKAY... AND HE'S HOME!
THE *MAN I LOVE* HAS *COME HOME*!

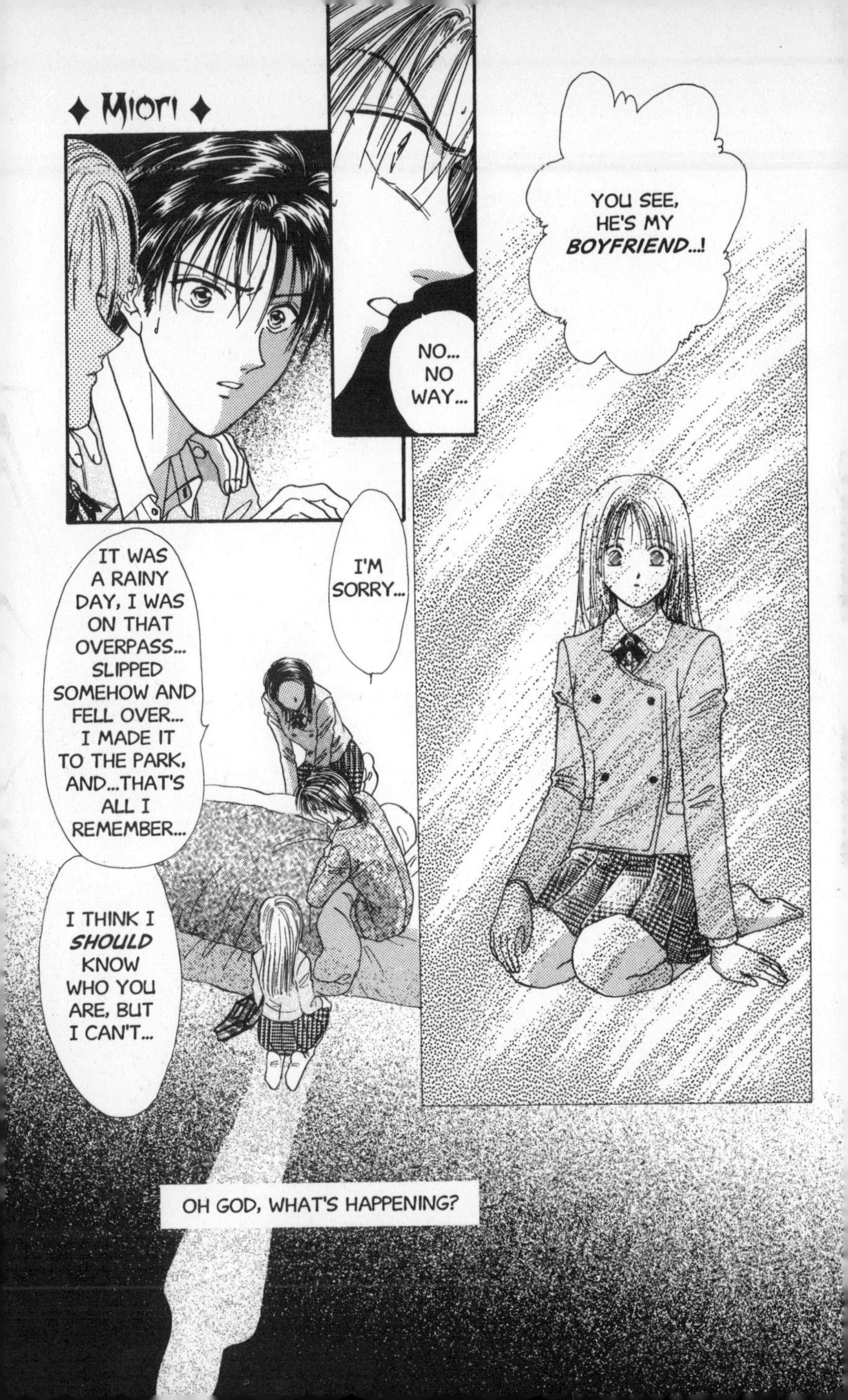
YOU SEE, HE'S MY BOYFRIEND...!
♦ Miori ♦
NO... NO WAY...
I'M SORRY...
IT WAS A RAINY DAY, I WAS ON THAT OVERPASS... SLIPPED SOMEHOW AND FELL OVER... I MADE IT TO THE PARK, AND...THAT'S ALL I REMEMBER...
I THINK I SHOULD KNOW WHO YOU ARE, BUT I CAN'T...
OH GOD, WHAT'S HAPPENING?

JUST THE OTHER NIGHT...

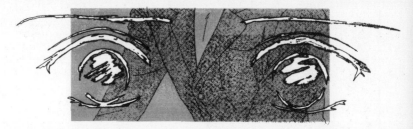

...HE PUT THOSE ARMS AROUND ME, HELD ME SO CLOSE.

DON'T, TŌYA! YOU'RE *TRYING* TOO HARD! YOU'LL GET ANOTHER HEADACHE!

THROB

NO, THIS ISN'T...DO I EVEN KNOW THIS PERSON?

TŌYA WOULDN'T...

...OR LOOKED AT ME LIKE... LIKE HE DOES NOW.

I'm fine, Miori.

TŌYA NEVER SMILED SO EASILY...

MIORI...

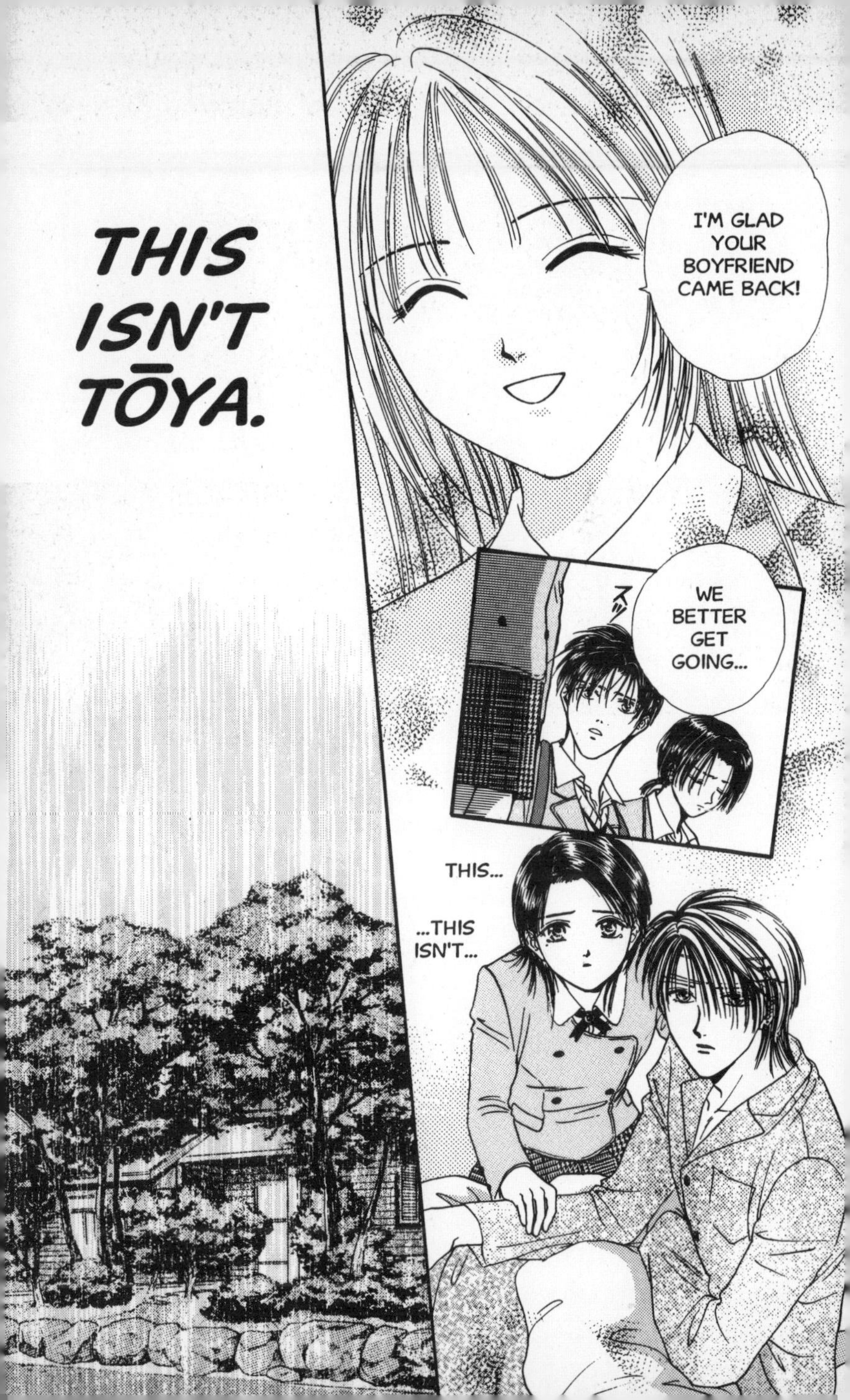
I'M GLAD YOUR BOYFRIEND CAME BACK!
WE BETTER GET GOING...
THIS...
...THIS ISN'T...
THIS ISN'T TŌYA.

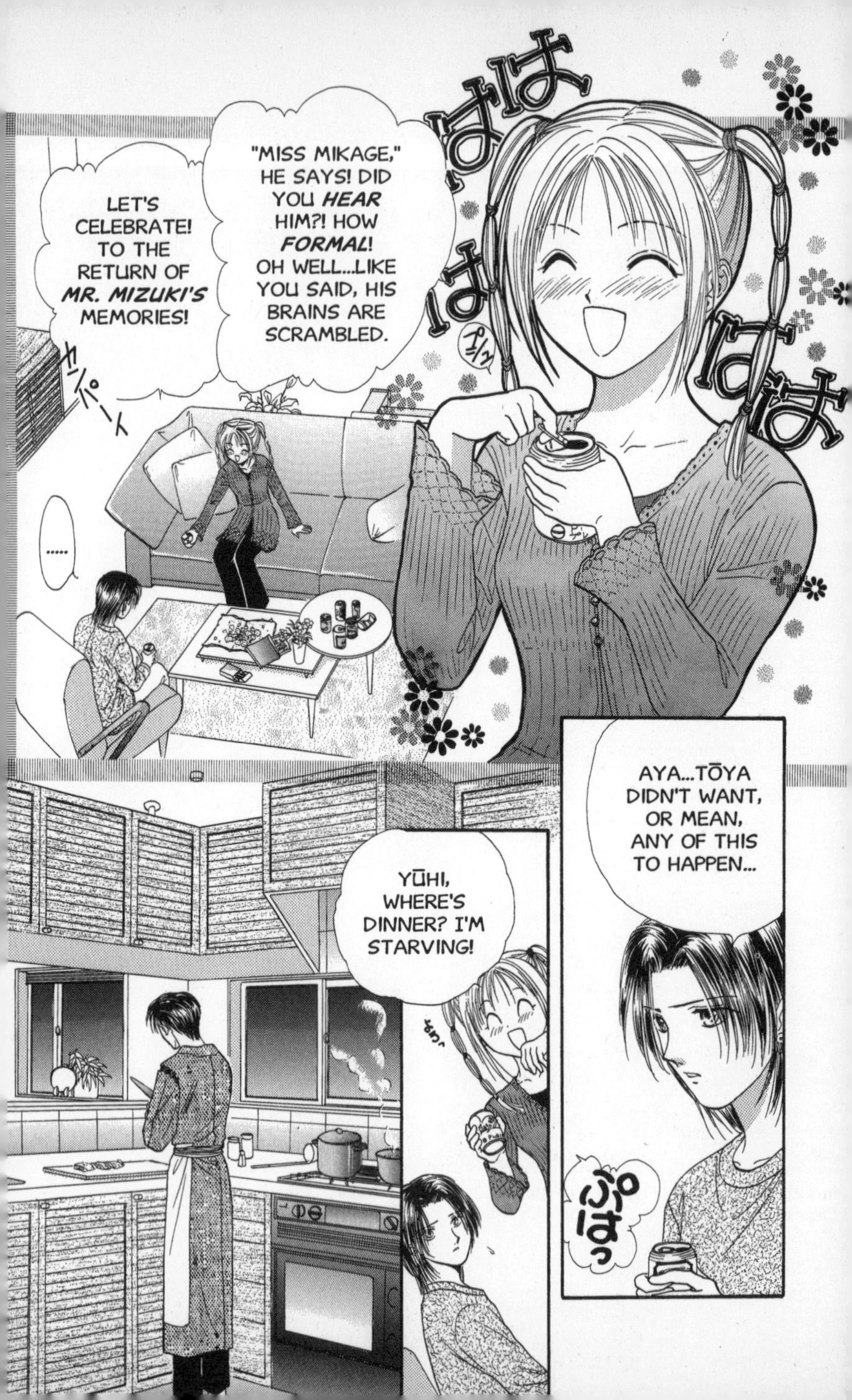
"MISS MIKAGE," HE SAYS! DID YOU *HEAR* HIM?! HOW *FORMAL*! OH WELL...LIKE YOU SAID, HIS BRAINS ARE SCRAMBLED.
LET'S CELEBRATE! TO THE RETURN OF *MR. MIZUKI'S* MEMORIES!
......
AYA...TŌYA DIDN'T WANT, OR MEAN, ANY OF THIS TO HAPPEN...
ぷはっ
YŪHI, WHERE'S DINNER? I'M STARVING!

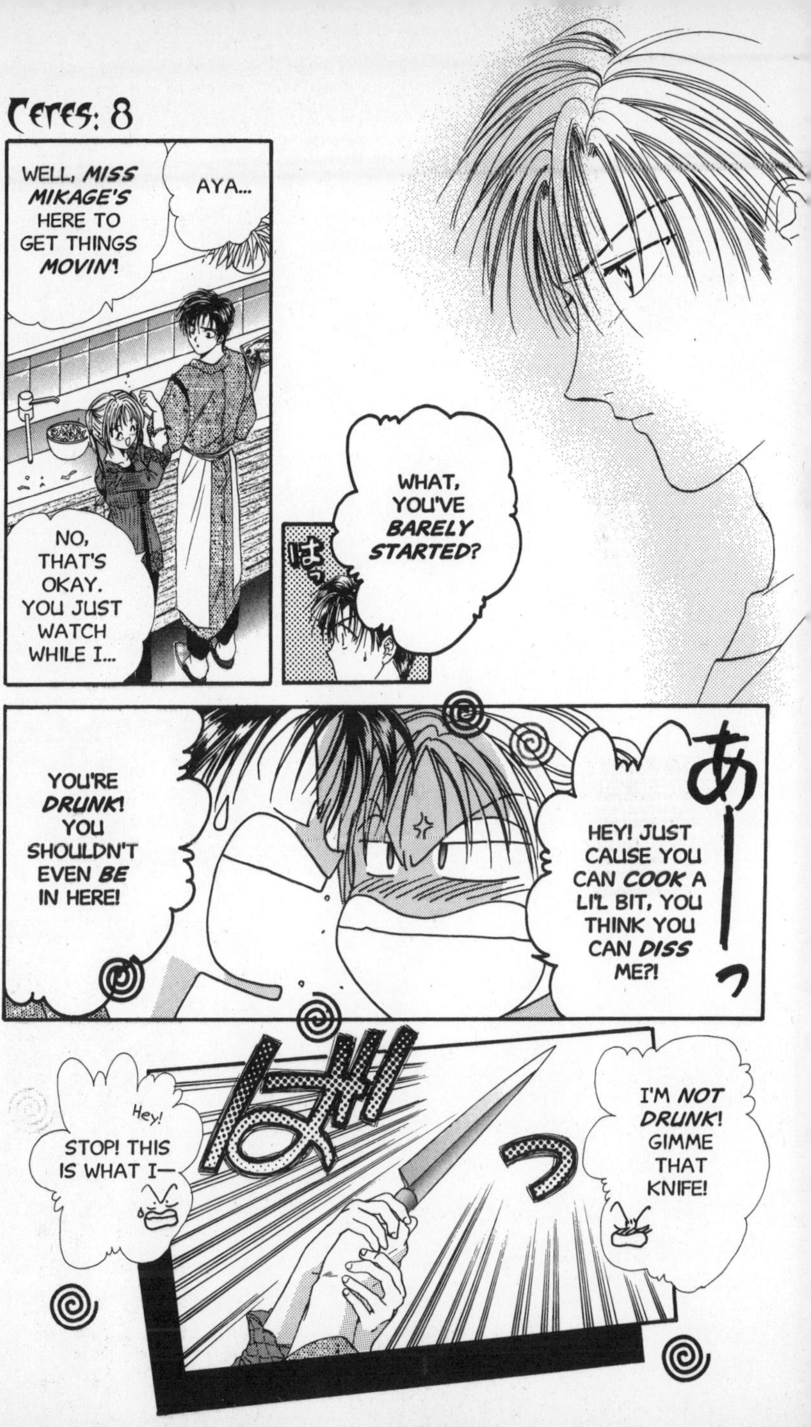
AYA...
WELL, *MISS MIKAGE'S* HERE TO GET THINGS *MOVIN'*!
NO, THAT'S OKAY. YOU JUST WATCH WHILE I...
はっ
WHAT, YOU'VE *BARELY STARTED*?
あーっ
HEY! JUST CAUSE YOU CAN *COOK* A LI'L BIT, YOU THINK YOU CAN *DISS* ME?!
YOU'RE *DRUNK*! YOU SHOULDN'T EVEN *BE* IN HERE!
I'M *NOT DRUNK*! GIMME THAT KNIFE!
ばっ
Hey!
STOP! THIS IS WHAT I—

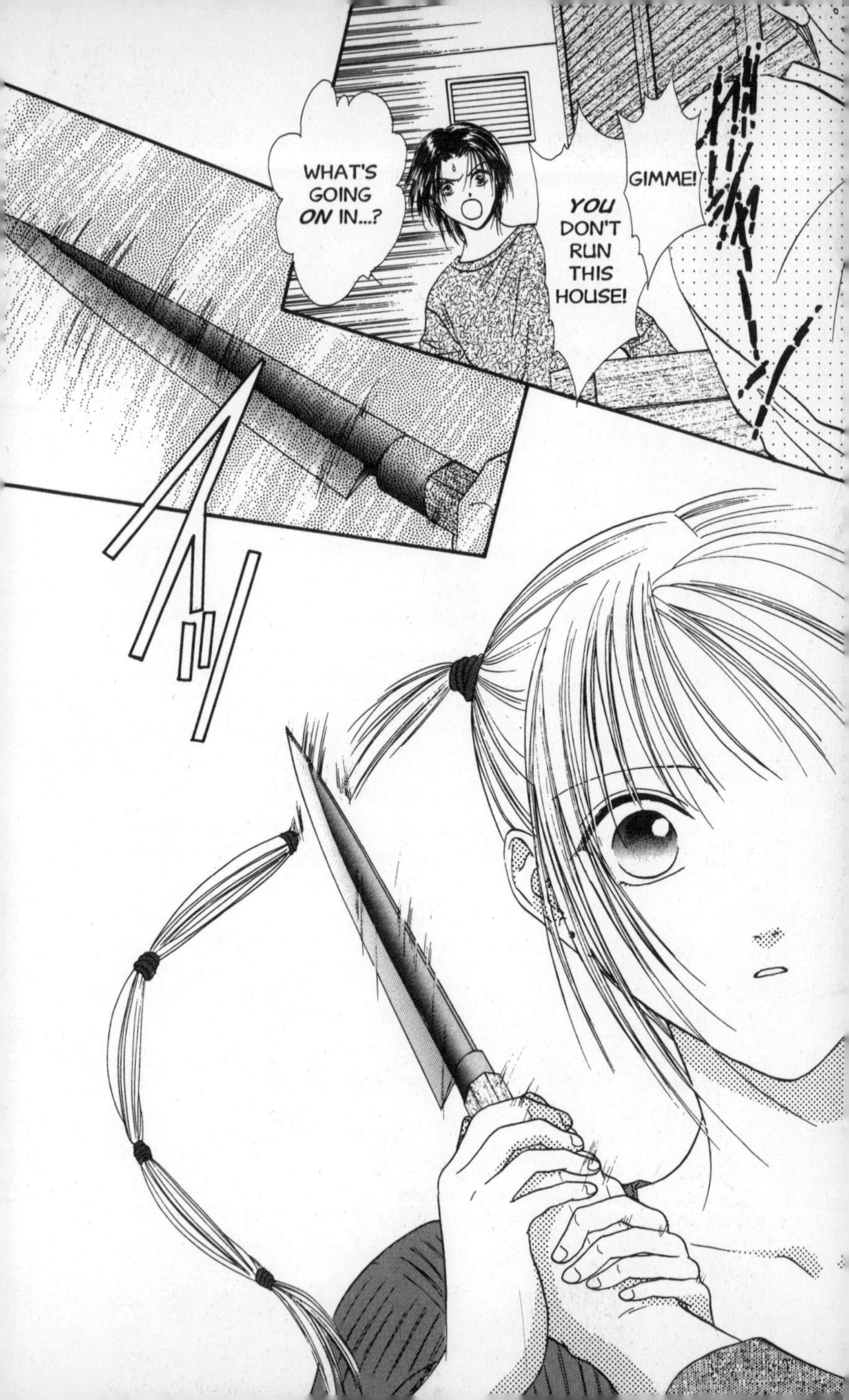
GIMME!
YOU DON'T RUN THIS HOUSE!
WHAT'S GOING ON IN...?

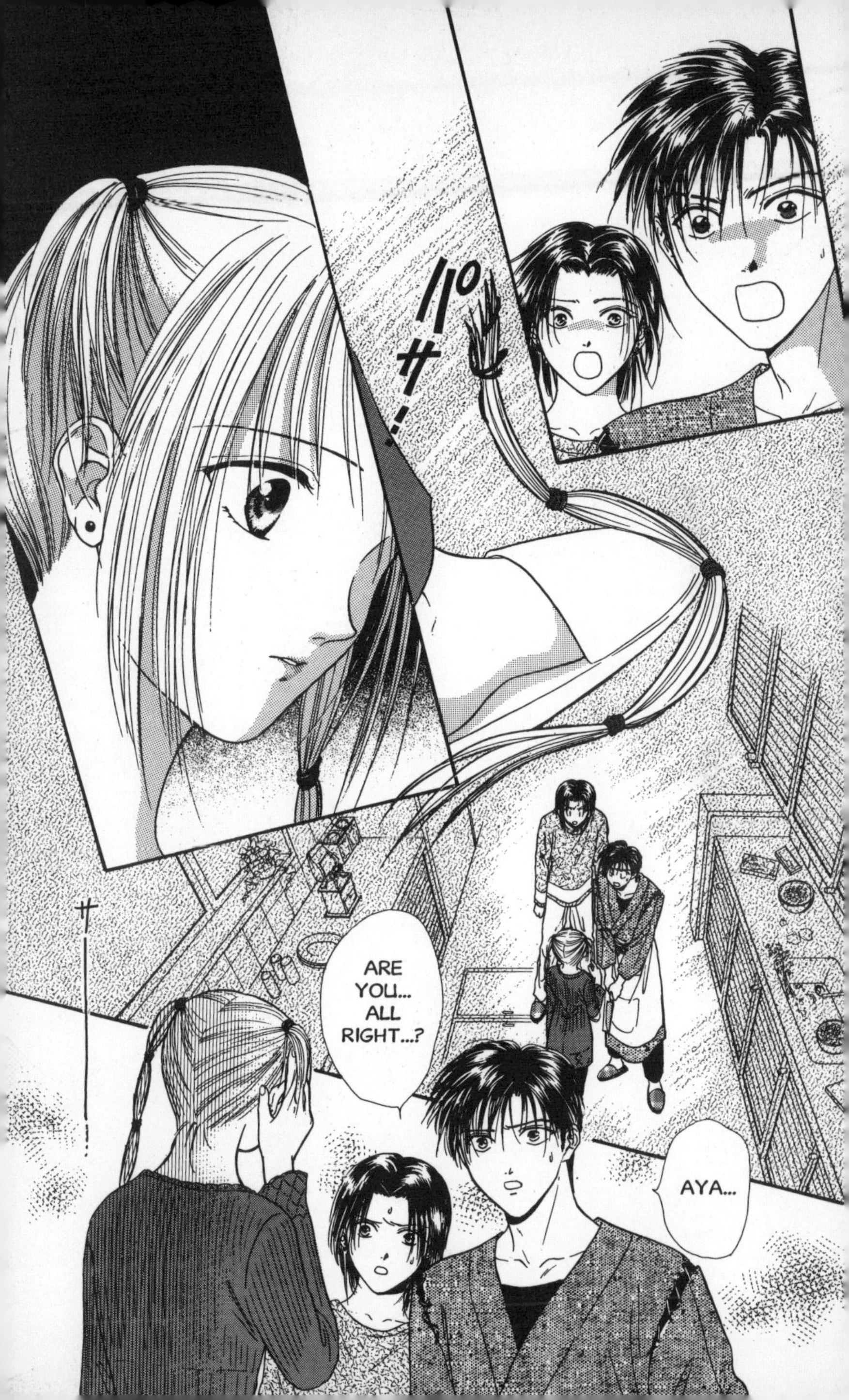
パサ!
ARE YOU... ALL RIGHT...?
AYA...
サー

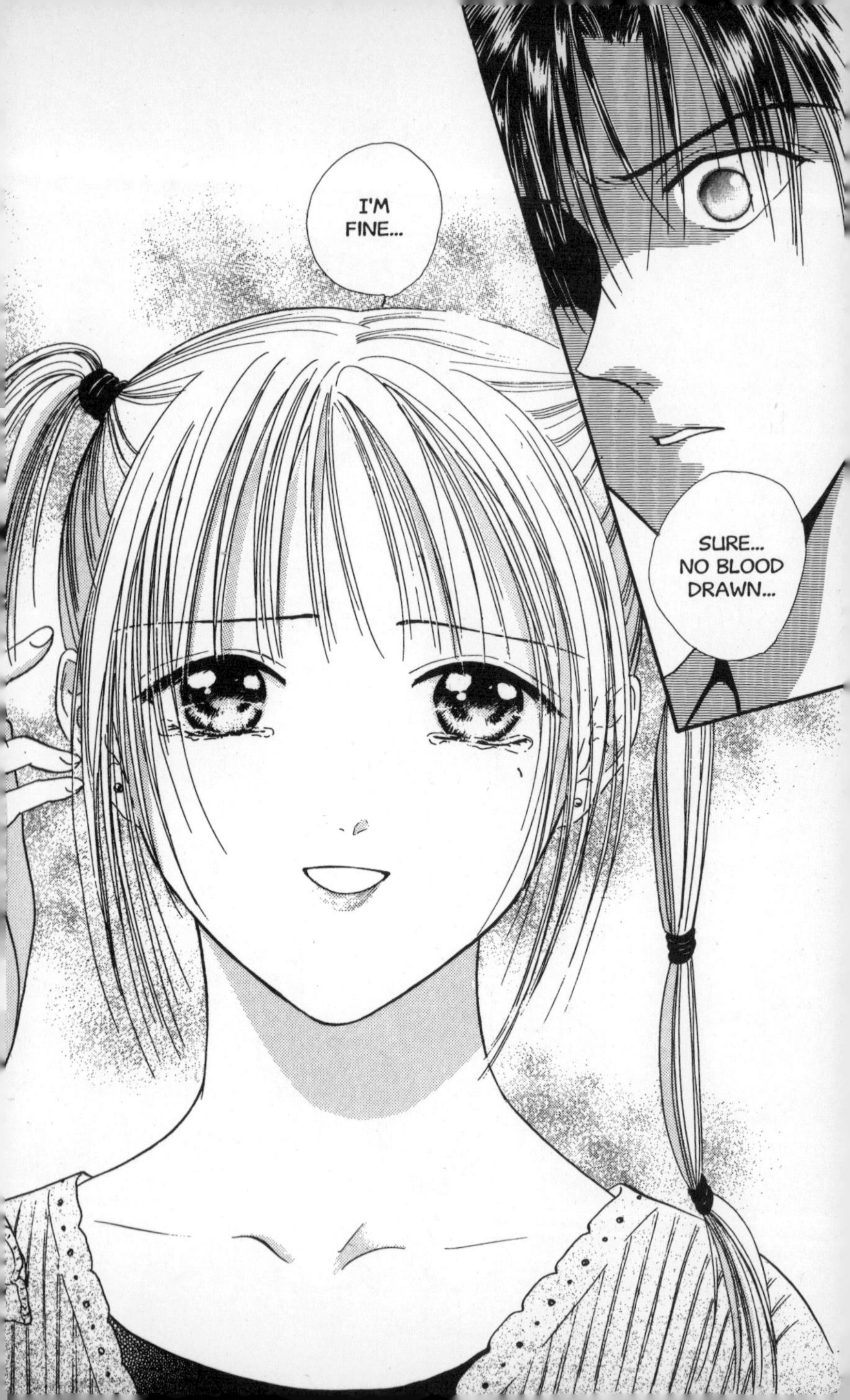
I'M FINE...
SURE... NO BLOOD DRAWN...

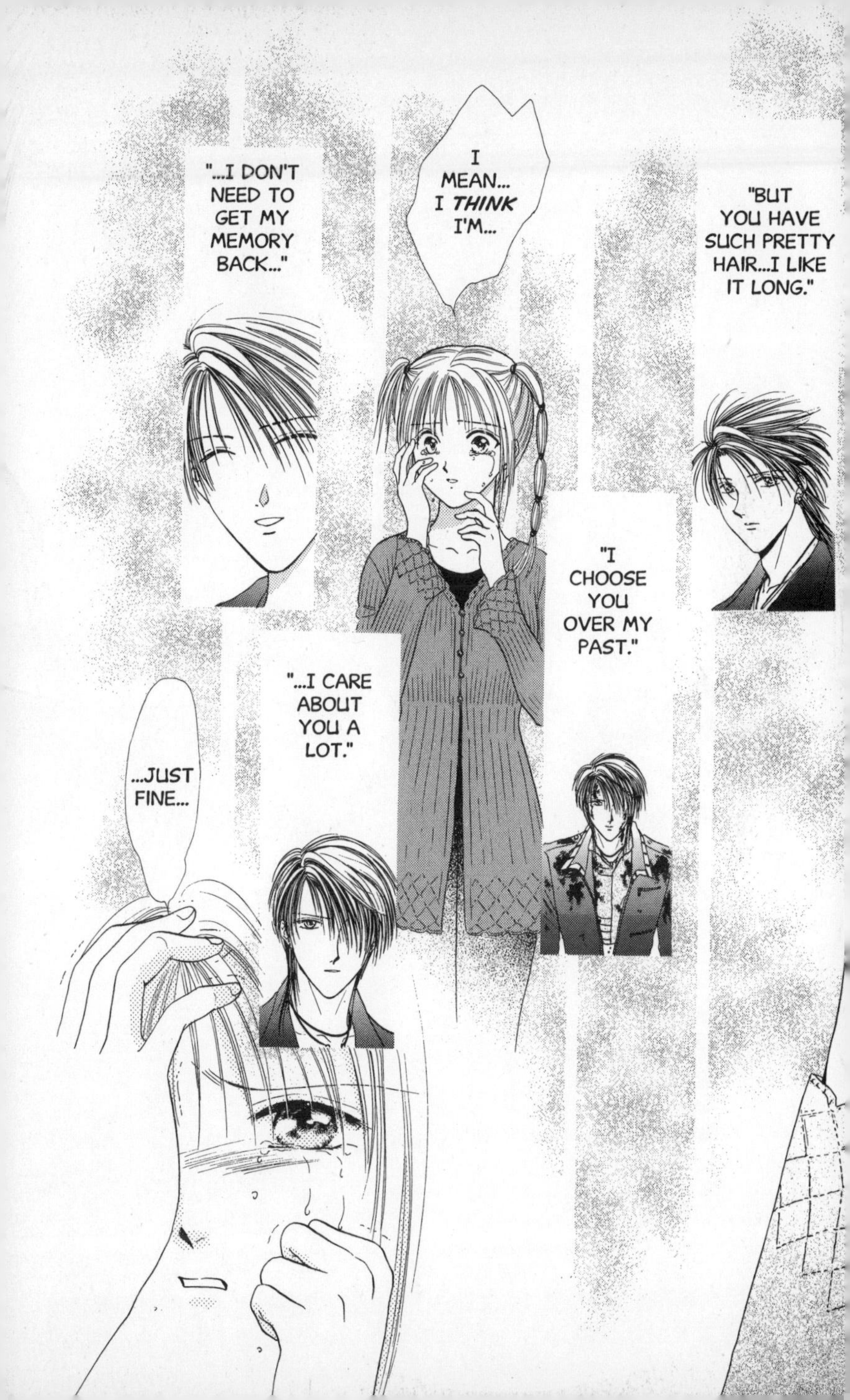
"BUT YOU HAVE SUCH PRETTY HAIR...I LIKE IT LONG."
I MEAN... I *THINK* I'M...
"...I DON'T NEED TO GET MY MEMORY BACK..."
"I CHOOSE YOU OVER MY PAST."
"...I CARE ABOUT YOU A LOT."
...JUST FINE...

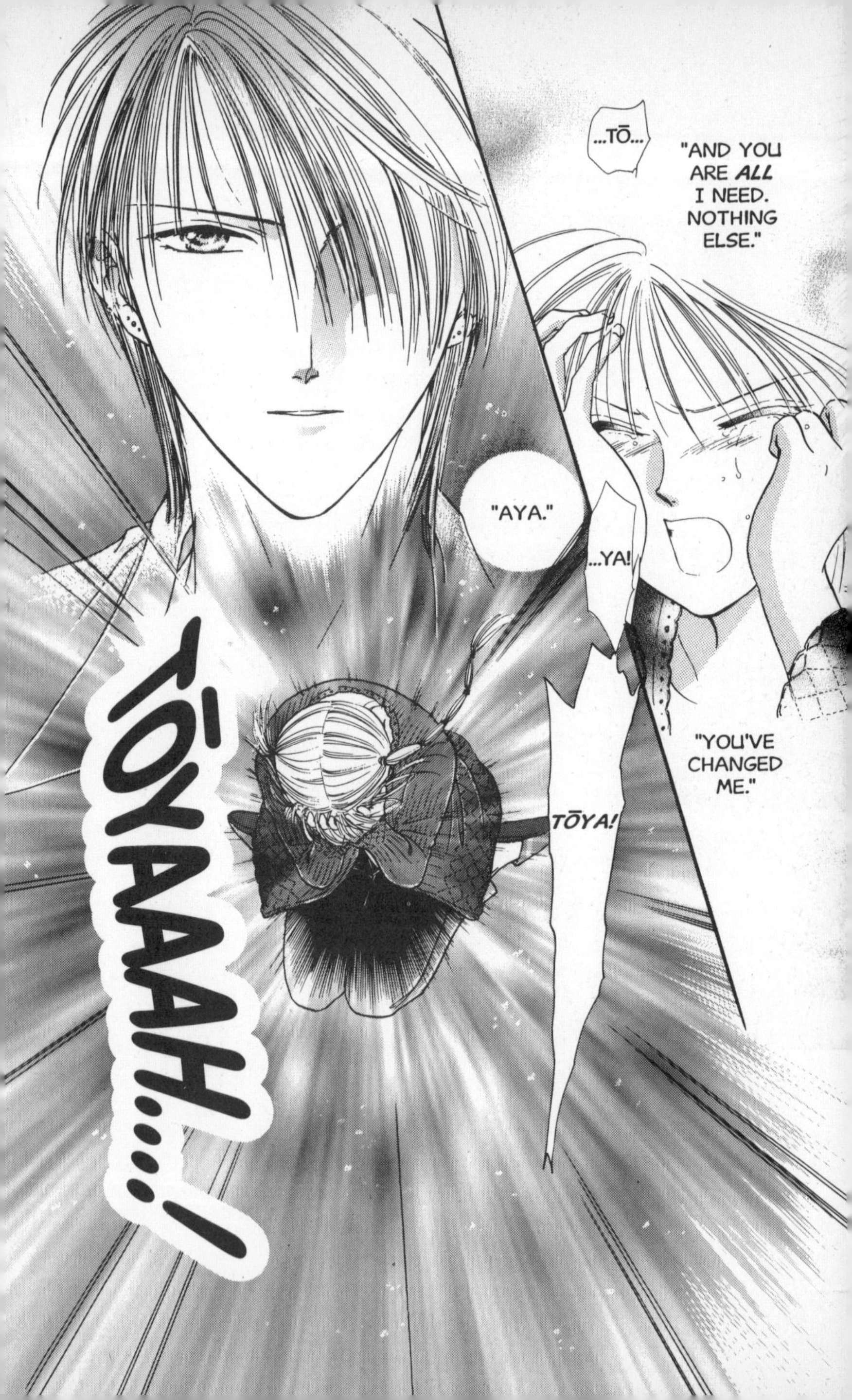
"AND YOU ARE ALL I NEED. NOTHING ELSE."
...TŌ...
"AYA."
...YA!
"YOU'VE CHANGED ME."
TŌYA!
TŌYAAAH...!

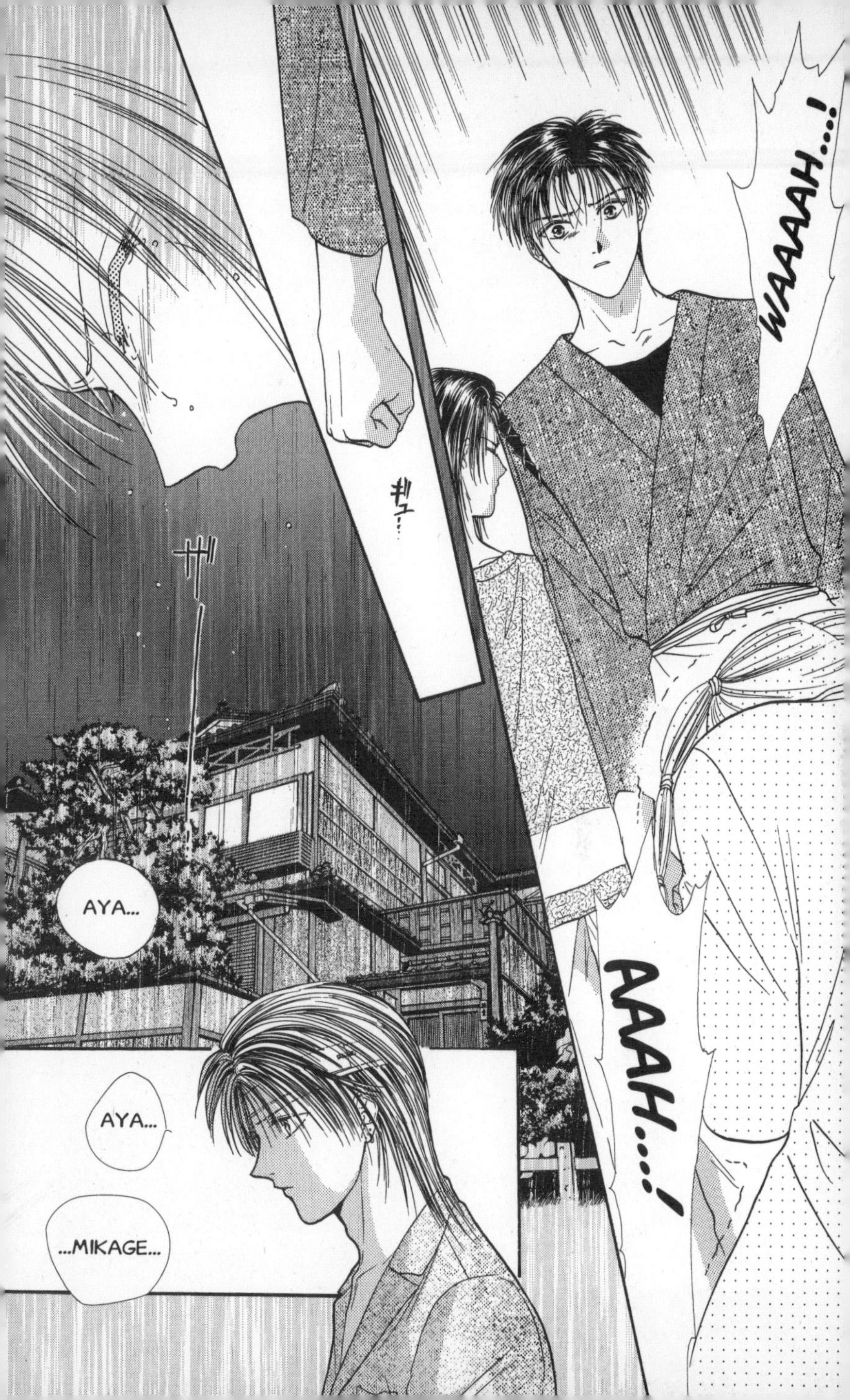
WAAAAAH...!
AAAH....!
ギュ…
ザ
AYA...
AYA...
...MIKAGE...

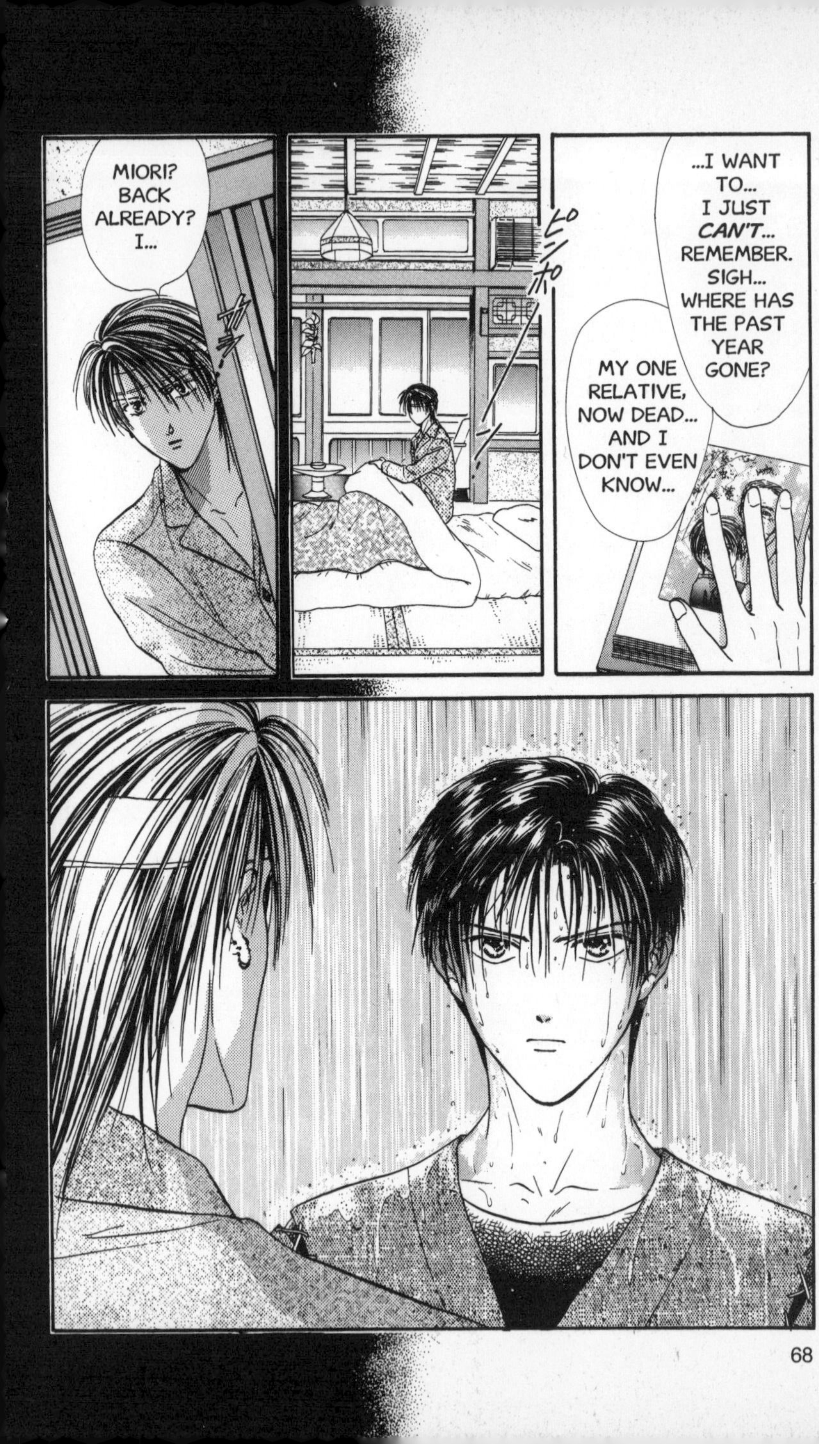
...I WANT TO... I JUST *CAN'T*... REMEMBER. SIGH... WHERE HAS THE PAST YEAR GONE?
MY ONE RELATIVE, NOW DEAD... AND I DON'T EVEN KNOW...
ピンポーン
MIORI? BACK ALREADY? I...

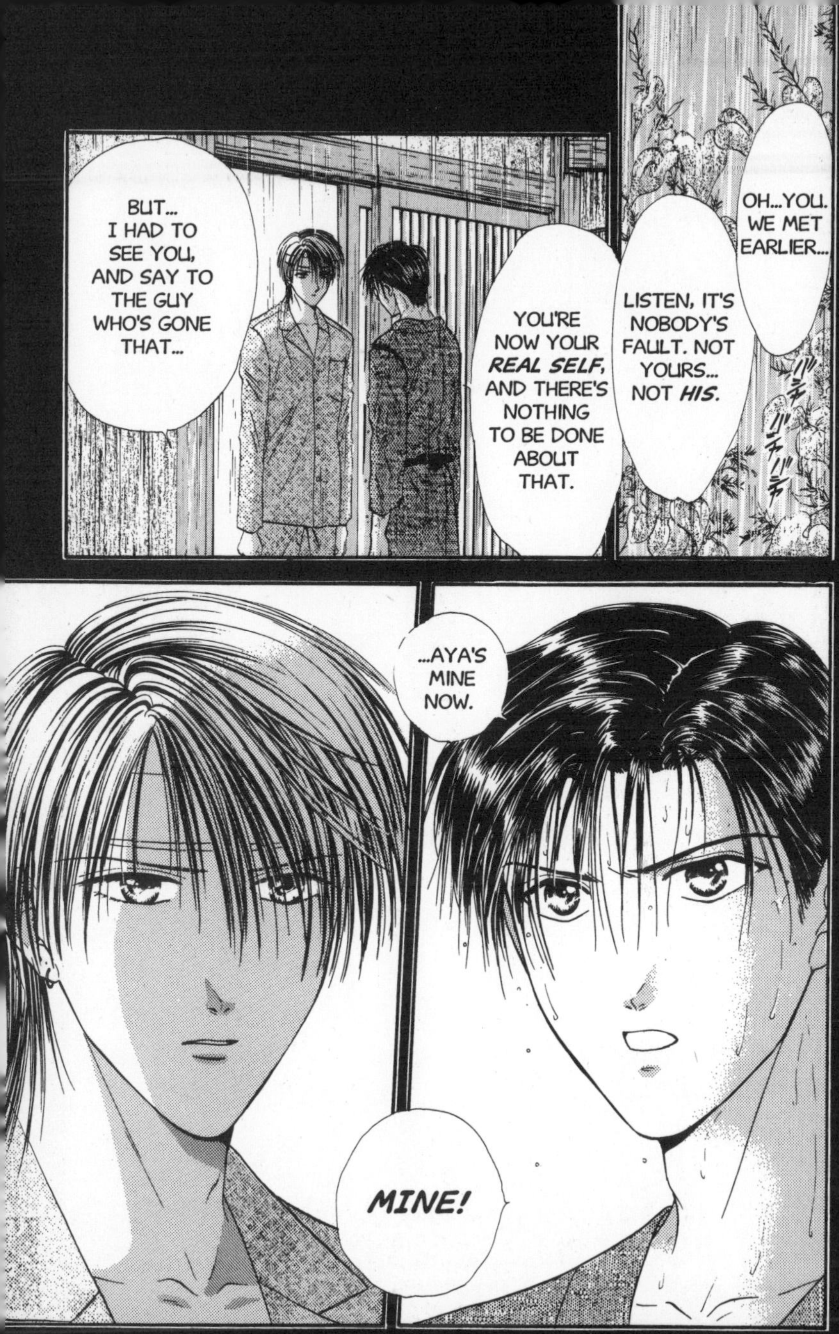
OH...YOU. WE MET EARLIER...
LISTEN, IT'S NOBODY'S FAULT. NOT YOURS... NOT *HIS*.
BUT... I HAD TO SEE YOU, AND SAY TO THE GUY WHO'S GONE THAT...
YOU'RE NOW YOUR *REAL SELF*, AND THERE'S NOTHING TO BE DONE ABOUT THAT.
...AYA'S MINE NOW.
MINE!

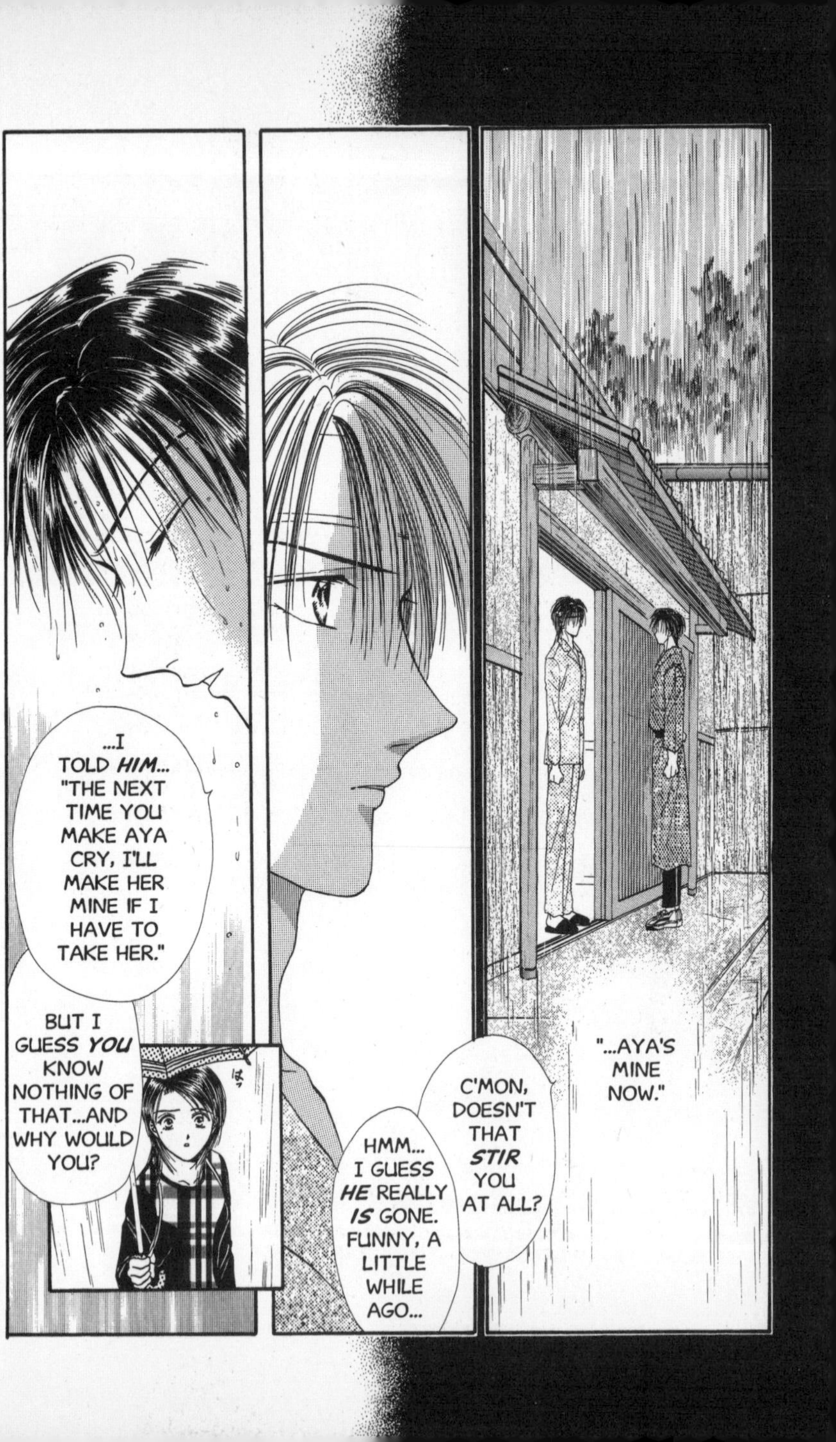
"...AYA'S MINE NOW."
C'MON, DOESN'T THAT *STIR* YOU AT ALL?
HMM... I GUESS *HE* REALLY *IS* GONE. FUNNY, A LITTLE WHILE AGO...
...I TOLD *HIM*... "THE NEXT TIME YOU MAKE AYA CRY, I'LL MAKE HER MINE IF I HAVE TO TAKE HER."
BUT I GUESS *YOU* KNOW NOTHING OF THAT...AND WHY WOULD YOU?

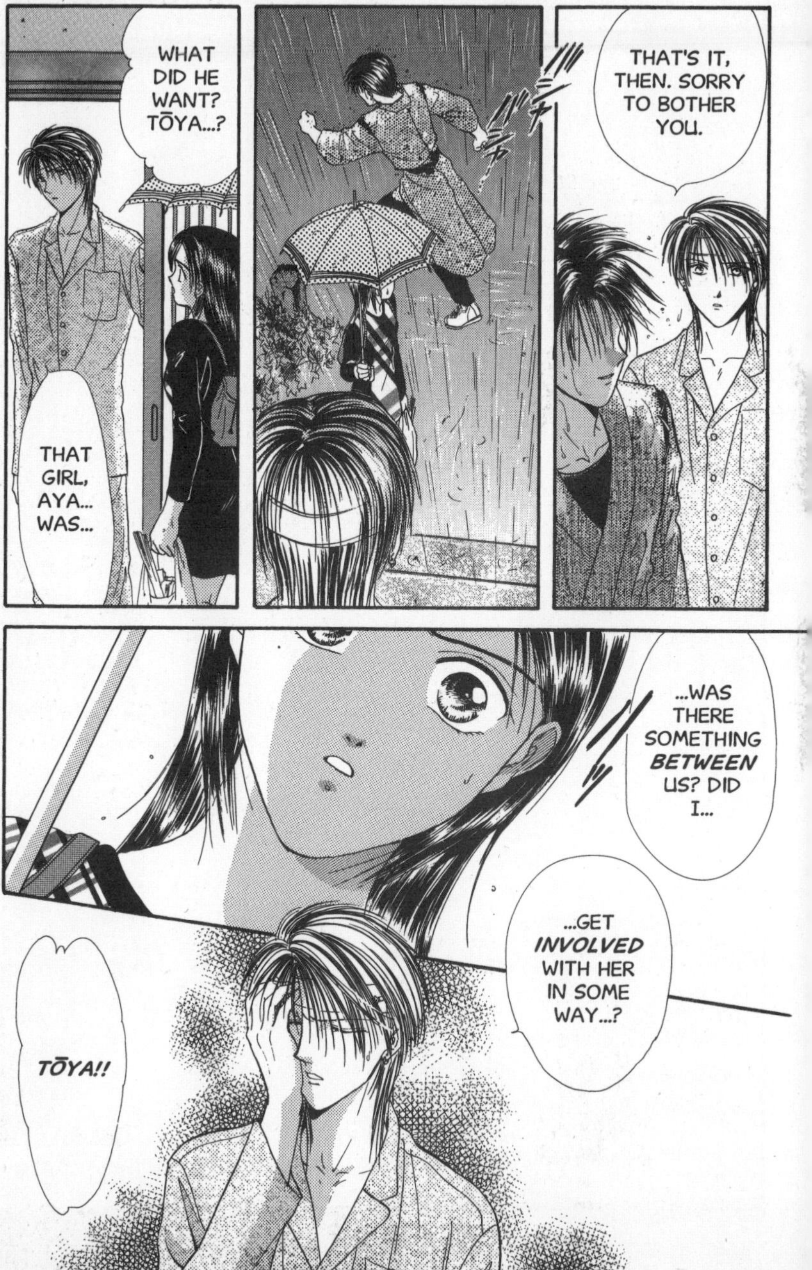
THAT'S IT, THEN. SORRY TO BOTHER YOU.
WHAT DID HE WANT? TŌYA...?
THAT GIRL, AYA... WAS...
...WAS THERE SOMETHING *BETWEEN* US? DID I...
...GET *INVOLVED* WITH HER IN SOME WAY...?
TŌYA!!

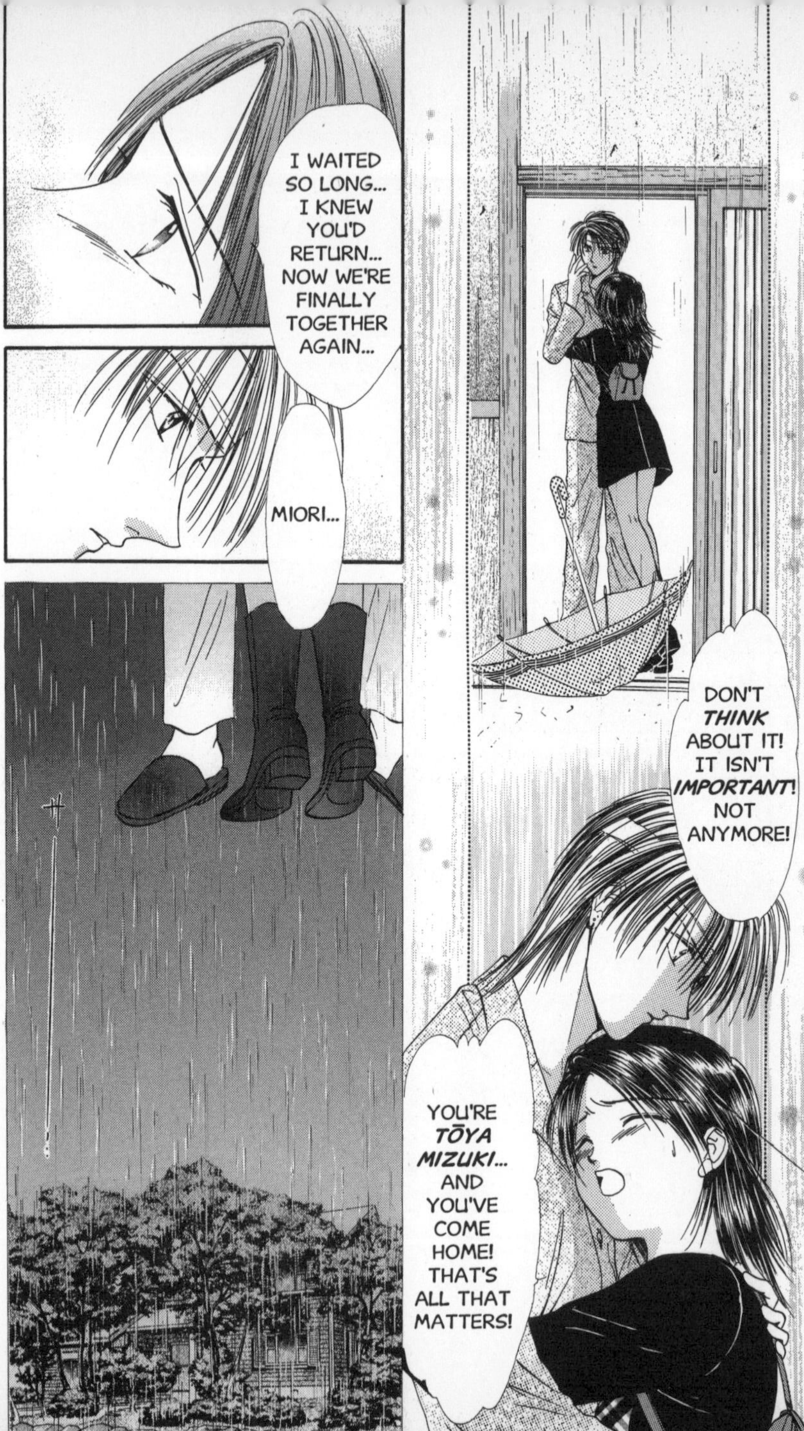
DON'T *THINK* ABOUT IT! IT ISN'T *IMPORTANT*! NOT ANYMORE!
YOU'RE *TŌYA MIZUKI*... AND YOU'VE COME HOME! THAT'S ALL THAT MATTERS!
I WAITED SO LONG... I KNEW YOU'D RETURN... NOW WE'RE FINALLY TOGETHER AGAIN...
MIORI...

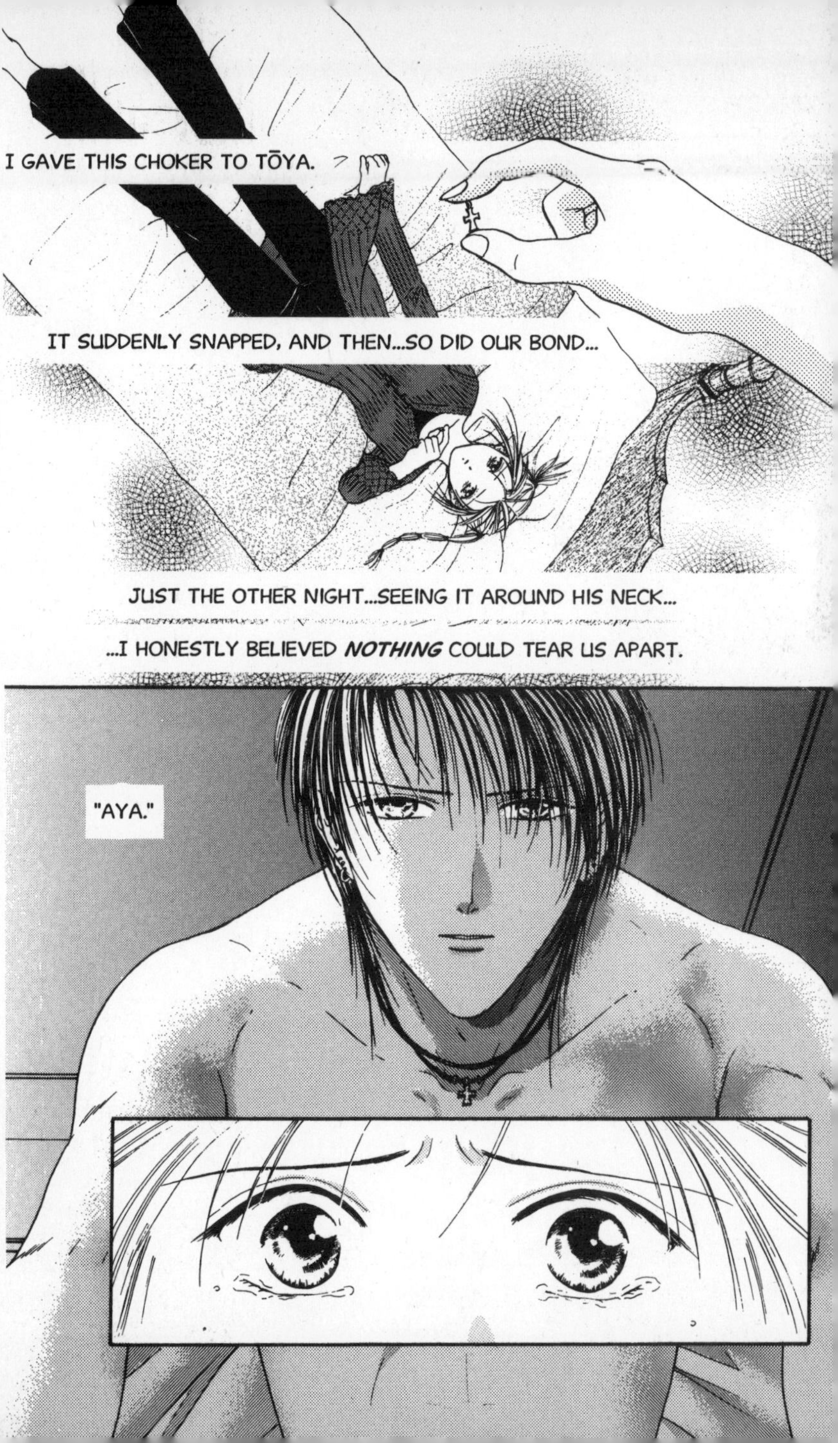
I GAVE THIS CHOKER TO TŌYA.
IT SUDDENLY SNAPPED, AND THEN...SO DID OUR BOND...
JUST THE OTHER NIGHT...SEEING IT AROUND HIS NECK...
...I HONESTLY BELIEVED *NOTHING* COULD TEAR US APART.
"AYA."

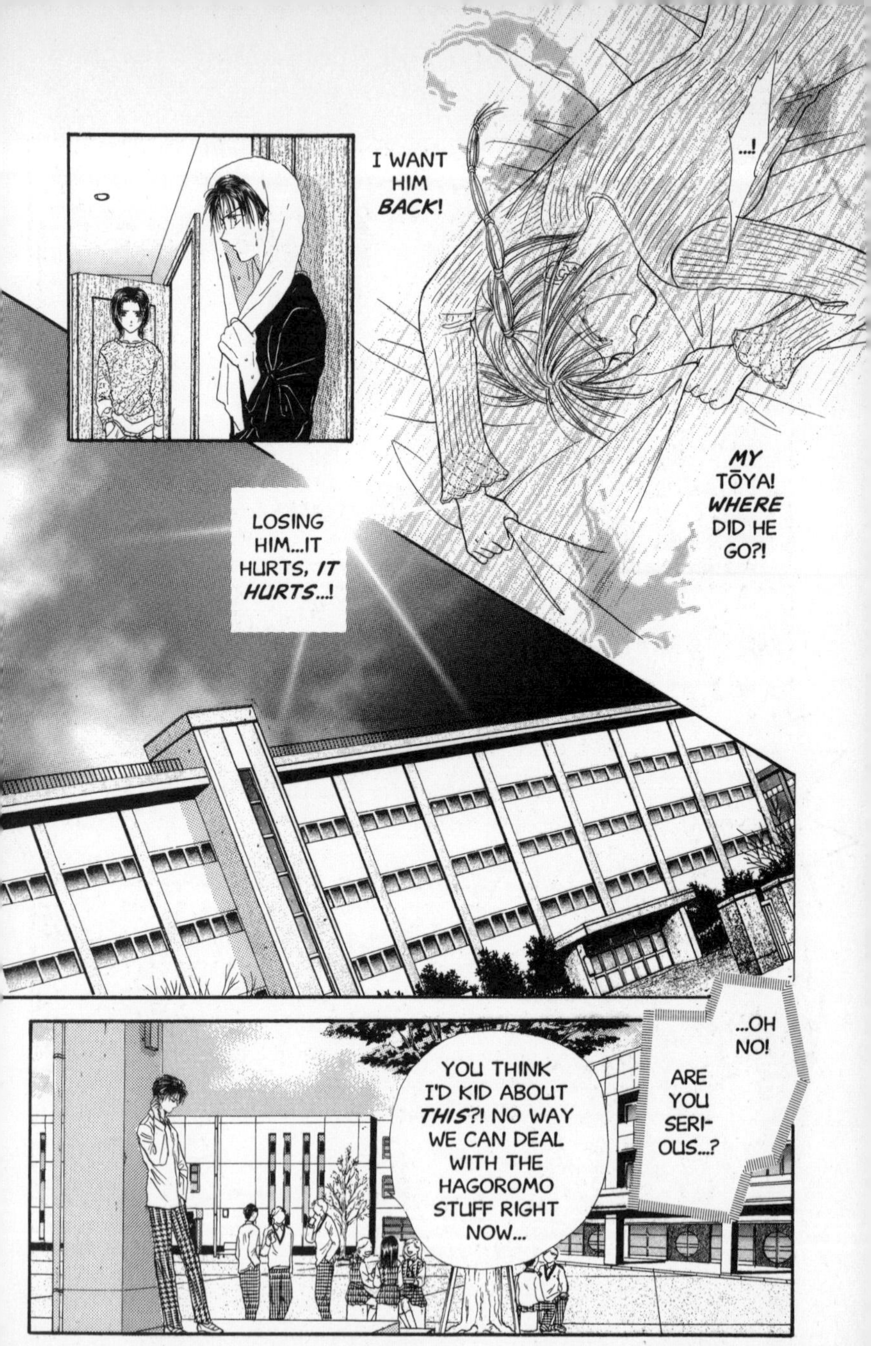
...!
I WANT HIM BACK!
MY TŌYA! WHERE DID HE GO?!
LOSING HIM...IT HURTS, IT HURTS...!
...OH NO!
ARE YOU SERIOUS...?
YOU THINK I'D KID ABOUT THIS?! NO WAY WE CAN DEAL WITH THE HAGOROMO STUFF RIGHT NOW...

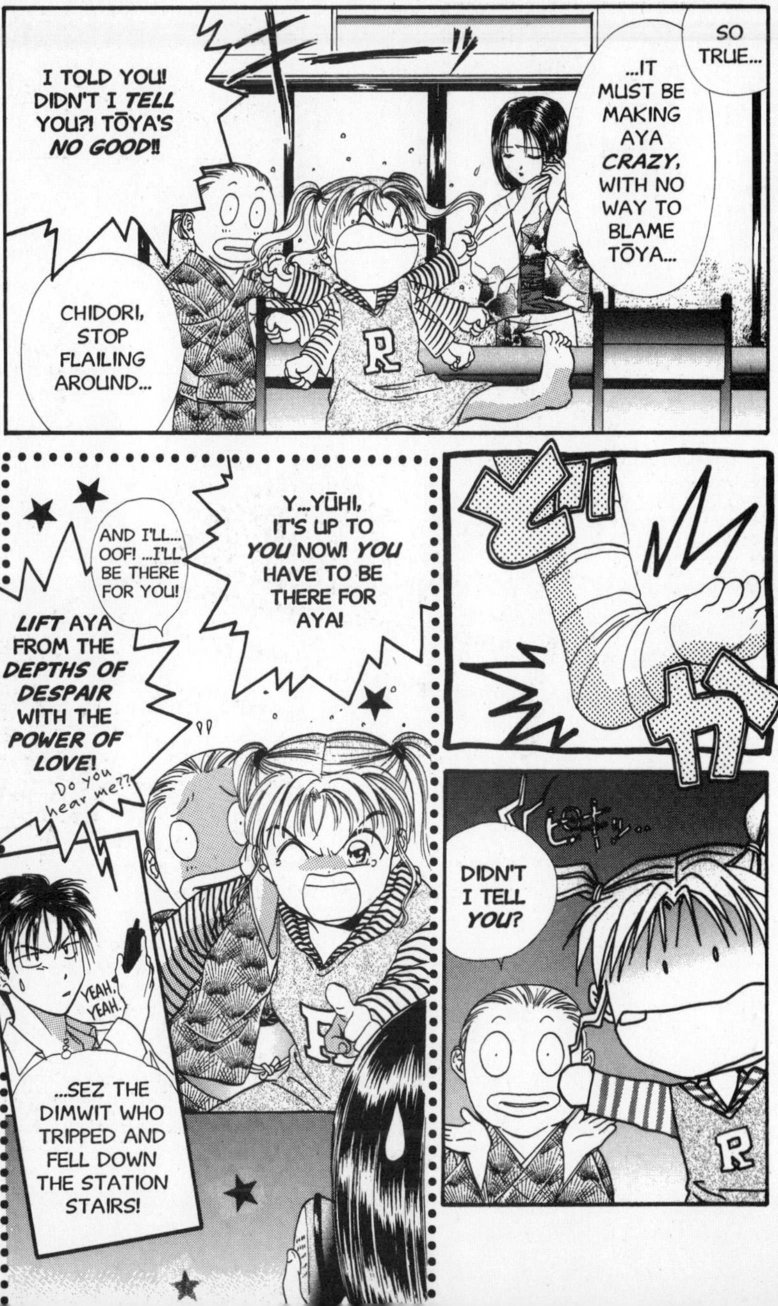
SO TRUE...
...IT MUST BE MAKING AYA *CRAZY*, WITH NO WAY TO BLAME TŌYA...
I TOLD YOU! DIDN'T I *TELL* YOU?! TŌYA'S *NO GOOD*!!
CHIDORI, STOP FLAILING AROUND...
DIDN'T I TELL *YOU*?
Y...YŪHI, IT'S UP TO *YOU* NOW! *YOU* HAVE TO BE THERE FOR AYA!
AND I'LL... OOF! ...I'LL BE THERE FOR YOU!
LIFT AYA FROM THE *DEPTHS OF DESPAIR* WITH THE *POWER OF LOVE*!
Do you hear me??
YEAH, YEAH.
...SEZ THE DIMWIT WHO TRIPPED AND FELL DOWN THE STATION STAIRS!

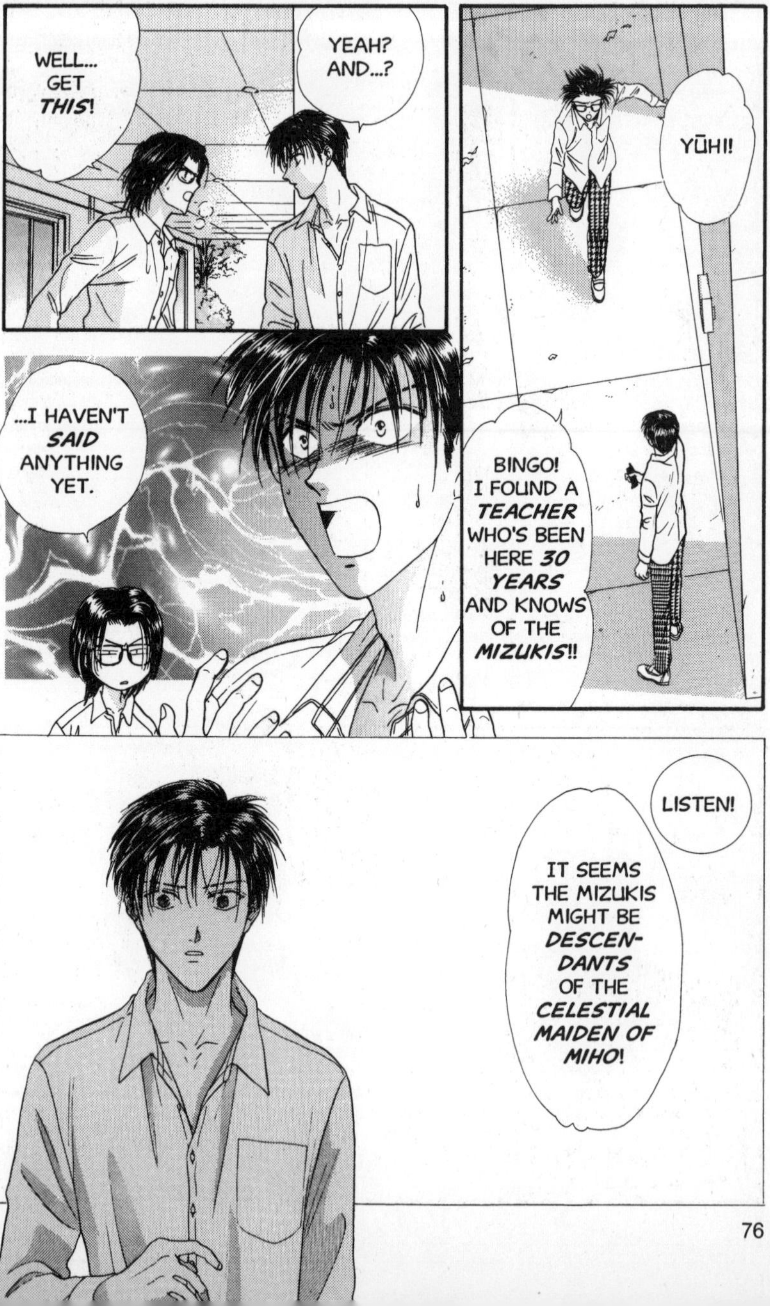
YŪHI!
BINGO! I FOUND A *TEACHER* WHO'S BEEN HERE *30 YEARS* AND KNOWS OF THE *MIZUKIS*!!
YEAH? AND...?
WELL... GET *THIS*!
...I HAVEN'T *SAID* ANYTHING YET.
LISTEN!
IT SEEMS THE MIZUKIS MIGHT BE *DESCEN-DANTS* OF THE *CELESTIAL MAIDEN OF MIHO*!

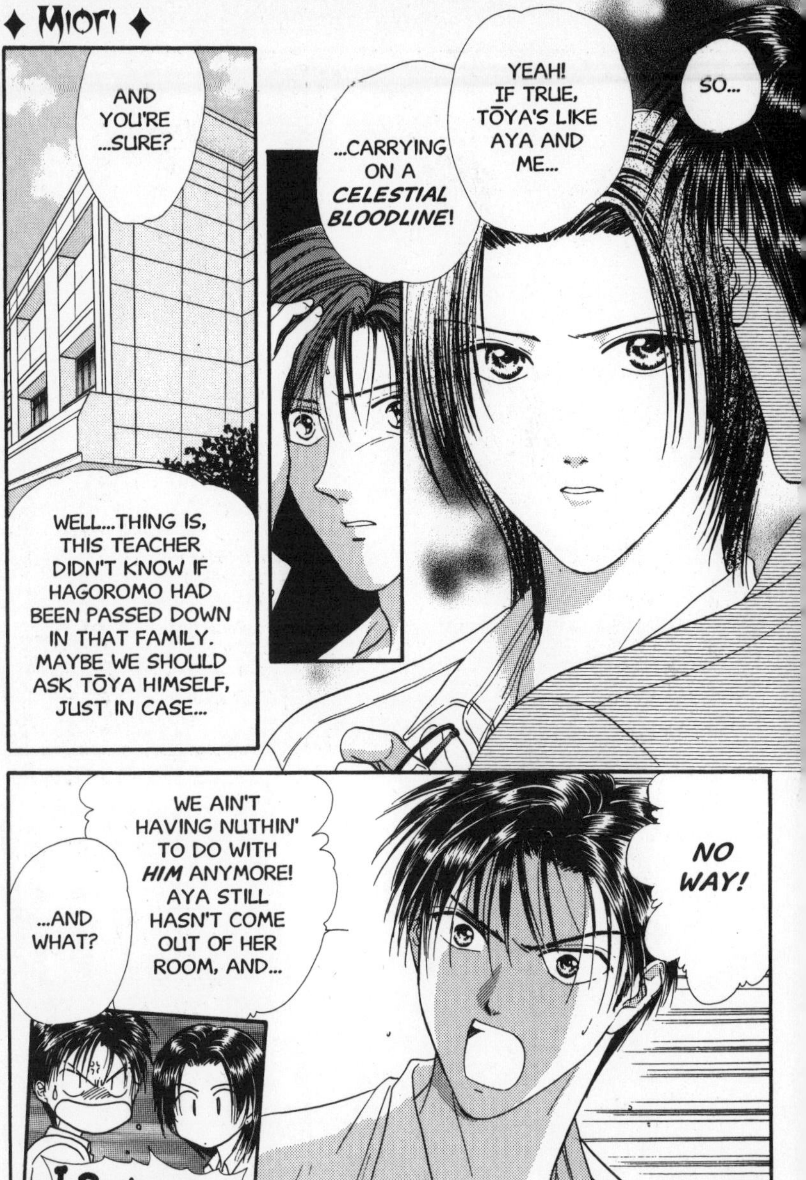
SO...
YEAH! IF TRUE, TŌYA'S LIKE AYA AND ME...
...CARRYING ON A *CELESTIAL BLOODLINE*!
AND YOU'RE ...SURE?
WELL...THING IS, THIS TEACHER DIDN'T KNOW IF HAGOROMO HAD BEEN PASSED DOWN IN THAT FAMILY. MAYBE WE SHOULD ASK TŌYA HIMSELF, JUST IN CASE...
NO WAY!
WE AIN'T HAVING NUTHIN' TO DO WITH *HIM* ANYMORE! AYA STILL HASN'T COME OUT OF HER ROOM, AND...
...AND WHAT?
I SA-A-A-ID...!

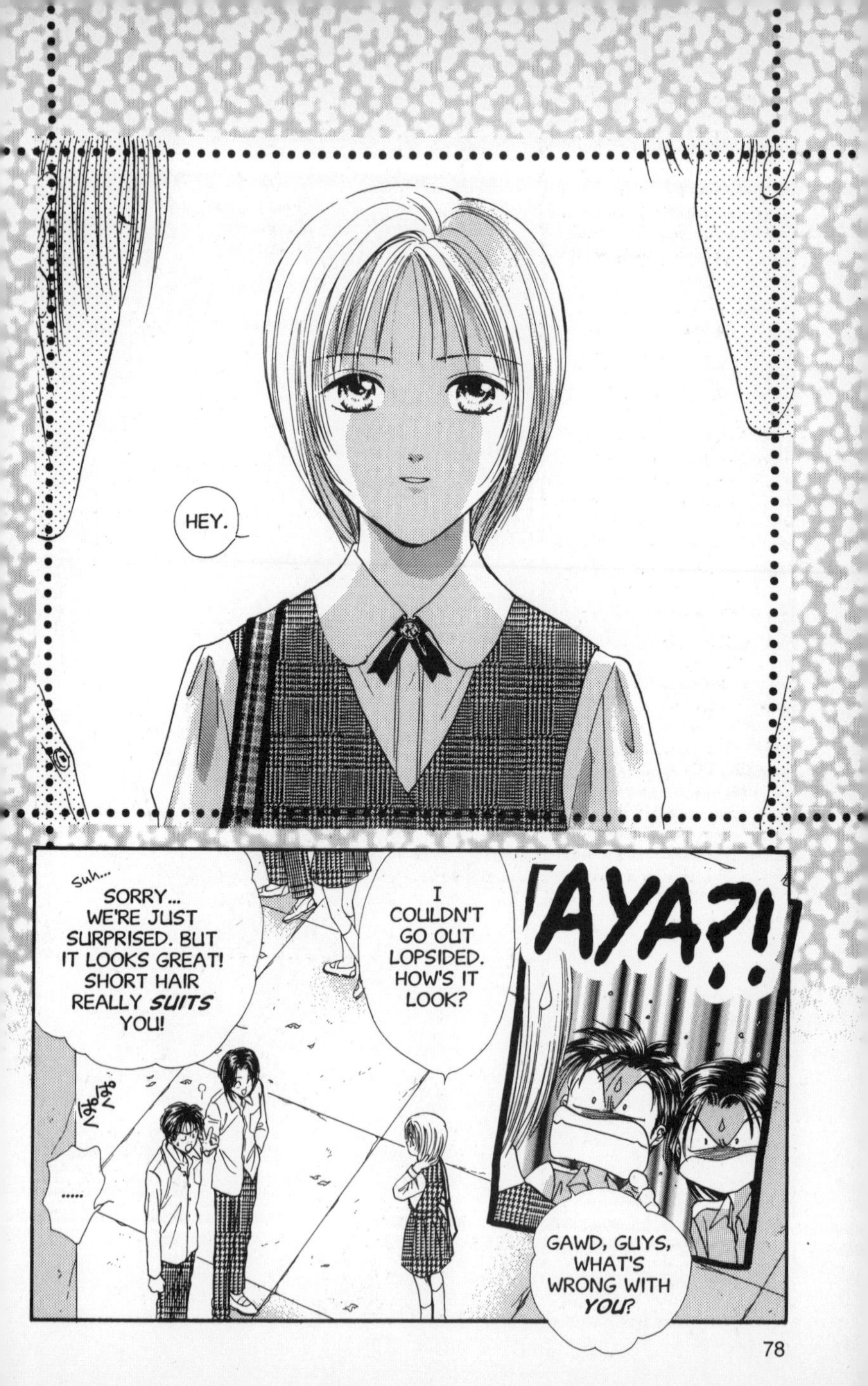
HEY.
AYA?!
GAWD, GUYS, WHAT'S WRONG WITH *YOU*?
I COULDN'T GO OUT LOPSIDED. HOW'S IT LOOK?
suh...
SORRY... WE'RE JUST SURPRISED. BUT IT LOOKS GREAT! SHORT HAIR REALLY *SUITS* YOU!
......

Ceres: 8

In the "Miyagi" arc, in Vol. 7, one of the editors checked over the lines for the dialect. But it seems like only the intonation is different, and once it's written out on paper, it's the same as standard Japanese.

Speaking of Volume 7...the sex scene. The editors and readers praised it as "innovative," which made me happy. I was relieved because they all said it wasn't obscene, but looked natural and beautiful (I was a bit worried). Among the love scenes I've written in my previous work, this was the one of which I was most pleased, and proud. ☺ It was the first time I was satisfied with such a thing, just as soon as I'd drawn it. (And, there were only a few angry Yūhi fans.)

And it wasn't just a "sex scene," it was a "making love scene" (you get the difference, right?). I've always thought that just popping sex into a story wasn't quite right; erotic manga aside, it's meaningless. People who say that characters who "make out a lot" make manga interesting are kind of missing the point. ☺ You guys are better than that! It's far more preferable when such scenes integrate with the rest of the story's events, meshing with the emotions of the characters that led up to it.

Someone wrote to talk about other manga besides mine. "I don't understand manga that goes all the way, right away. They should take more time to develop the characters' feelings..." I tend to agree. That's just my own personal opinion, though.

Actually, there was an incident which came up after my mom read that episode! ☺ I was drinking juice as she was doing the dishes and then, out of the blue, she says, "So...what was up with that?" ☺   To be continued!

WHAT? WHY, YŪHI?

I...I'M SORRY...

IT WAS *MY* FAULT! I'VE BEEN MEANING TO GET IT CUT ANYWAY.

AYA!

IT'S KILLED MY LUNCH HOUR, THOUGH! THE SALON WAS JAMMED...

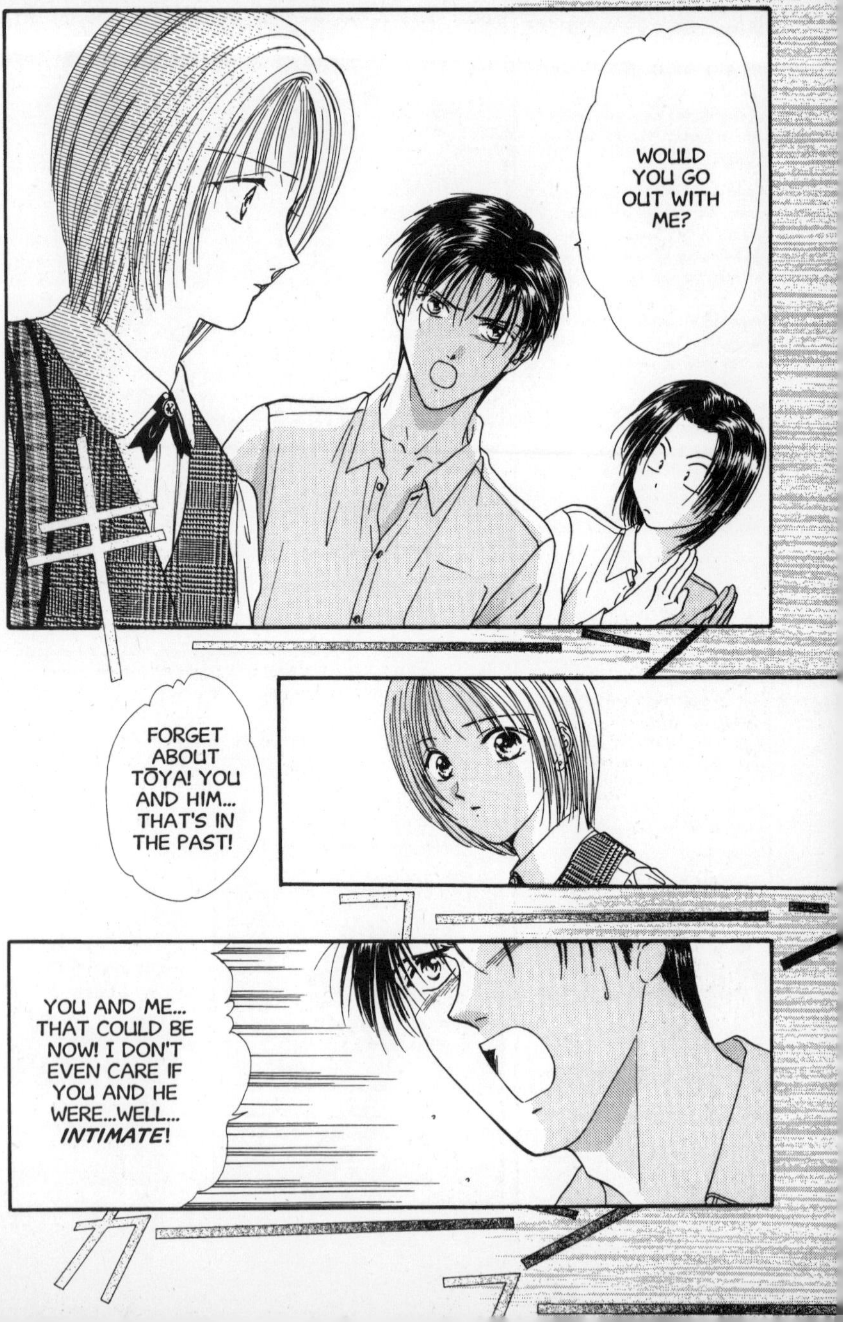
WOULD YOU GO OUT WITH ME?
FORGET ABOUT TŌYA! YOU AND HIM... THAT'S IN THE PAST!
YOU AND ME... THAT COULD BE NOW! I DON'T EVEN CARE IF YOU AND HE WERE...WELL... *INTIMATE*!

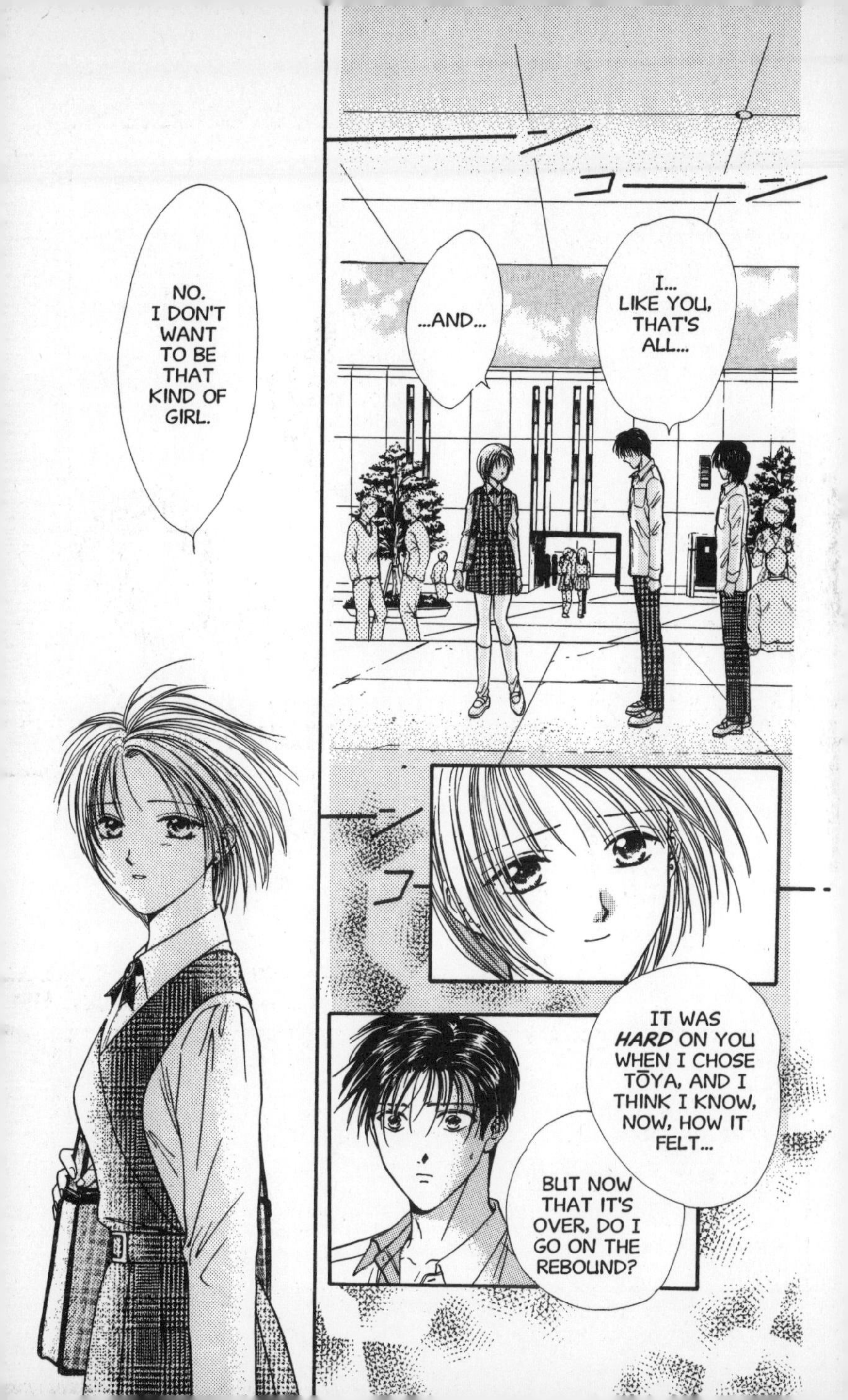
I... LIKE YOU, THAT'S ALL...
...AND...
IT WAS *HARD* ON YOU WHEN I CHOSE TŌYA, AND I THINK I KNOW, NOW, HOW IT FELT...
BUT NOW THAT IT'S OVER, DO I GO ON THE REBOUND?
NO. I DON'T WANT TO BE THAT KIND OF GIRL.

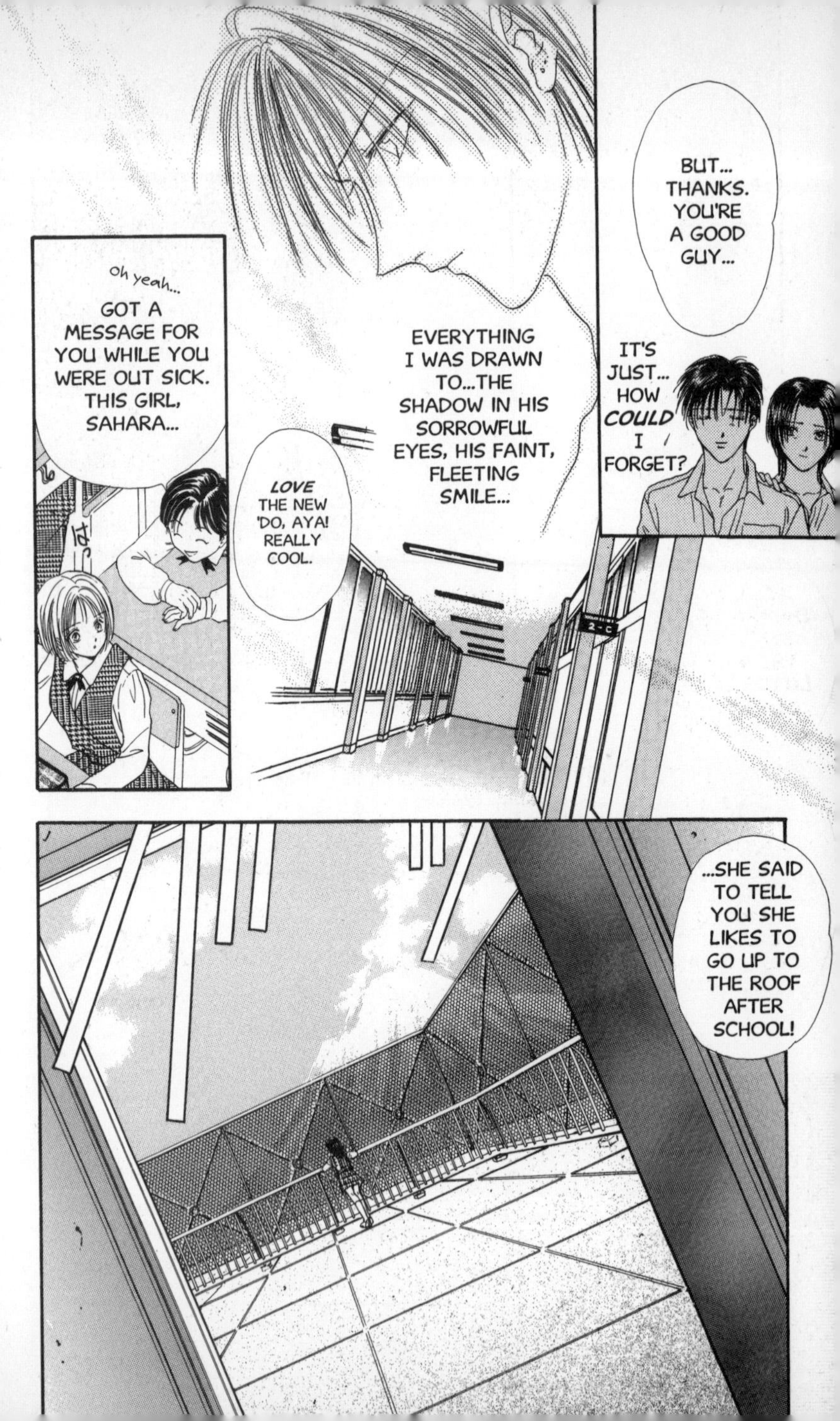

BUT... THANKS. YOU'RE A GOOD GUY...
IT'S JUST... HOW COULD I FORGET?
EVERYTHING I WAS DRAWN TO...THE SHADOW IN HIS SORROWFUL EYES, HIS FAINT, FLEETING SMILE...
LOVE THE NEW 'DO, AYA! REALLY COOL.
2-C
Oh yeah...
GOT A MESSAGE FOR YOU WHILE YOU WERE OUT SICK. THIS GIRL, SAHARA...
...SHE SAID TO TELL YOU SHE LIKES TO GO UP TO THE ROOF AFTER SCHOOL!

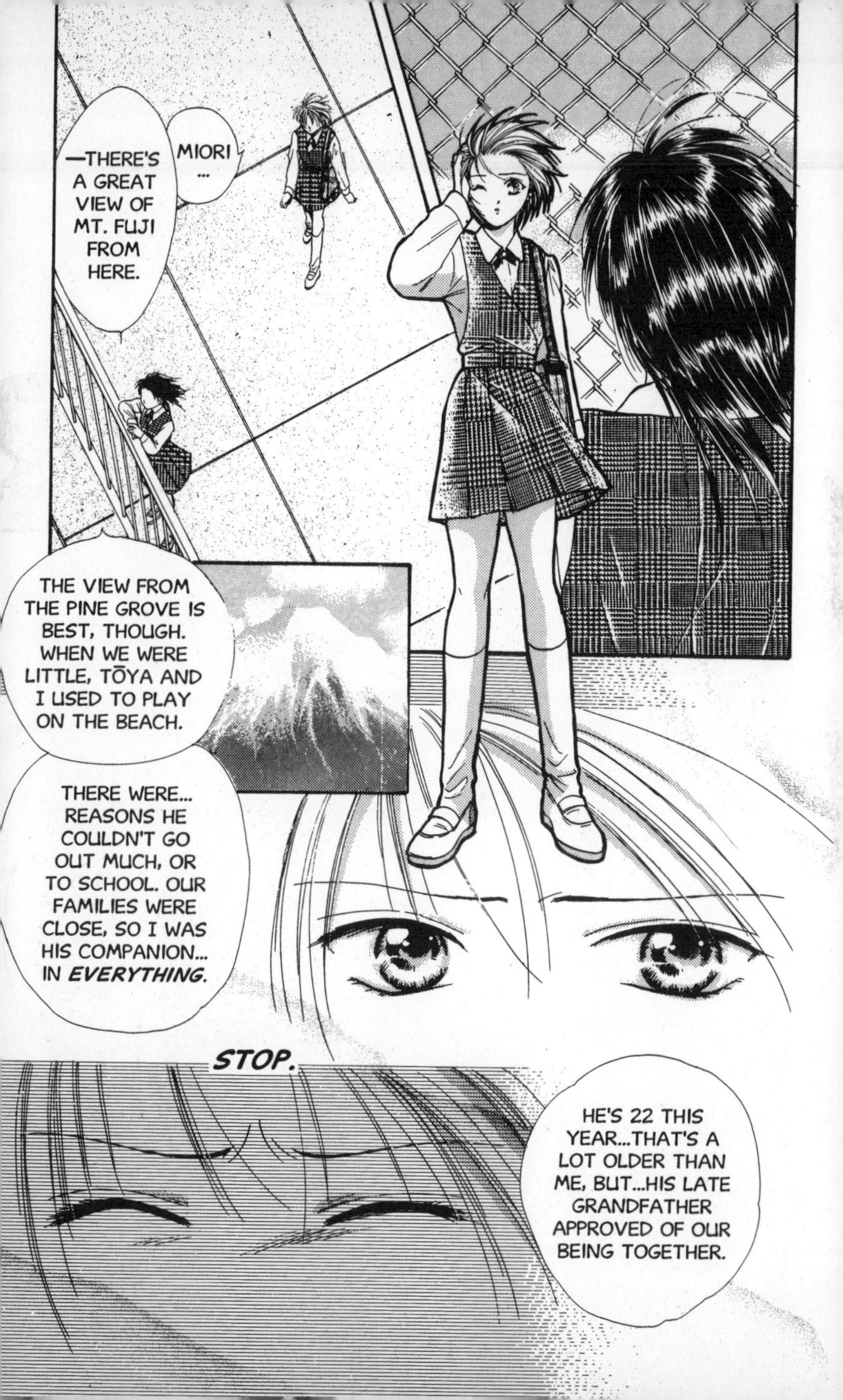
MIORI ...
—THERE'S A GREAT VIEW OF MT. FUJI FROM HERE.
THE VIEW FROM THE PINE GROVE IS BEST, THOUGH. WHEN WE WERE LITTLE, TŌYA AND I USED TO PLAY ON THE BEACH.
THERE WERE... REASONS HE COULDN'T GO OUT MUCH, OR TO SCHOOL. OUR FAMILIES WERE CLOSE, SO I WAS HIS COMPANION... IN *EVERYTHING*.
STOP.
HE'S 22 THIS YEAR...THAT'S A LOT OLDER THAN ME, BUT...HIS LATE GRANDFATHER APPROVED OF OUR BEING TOGETHER.

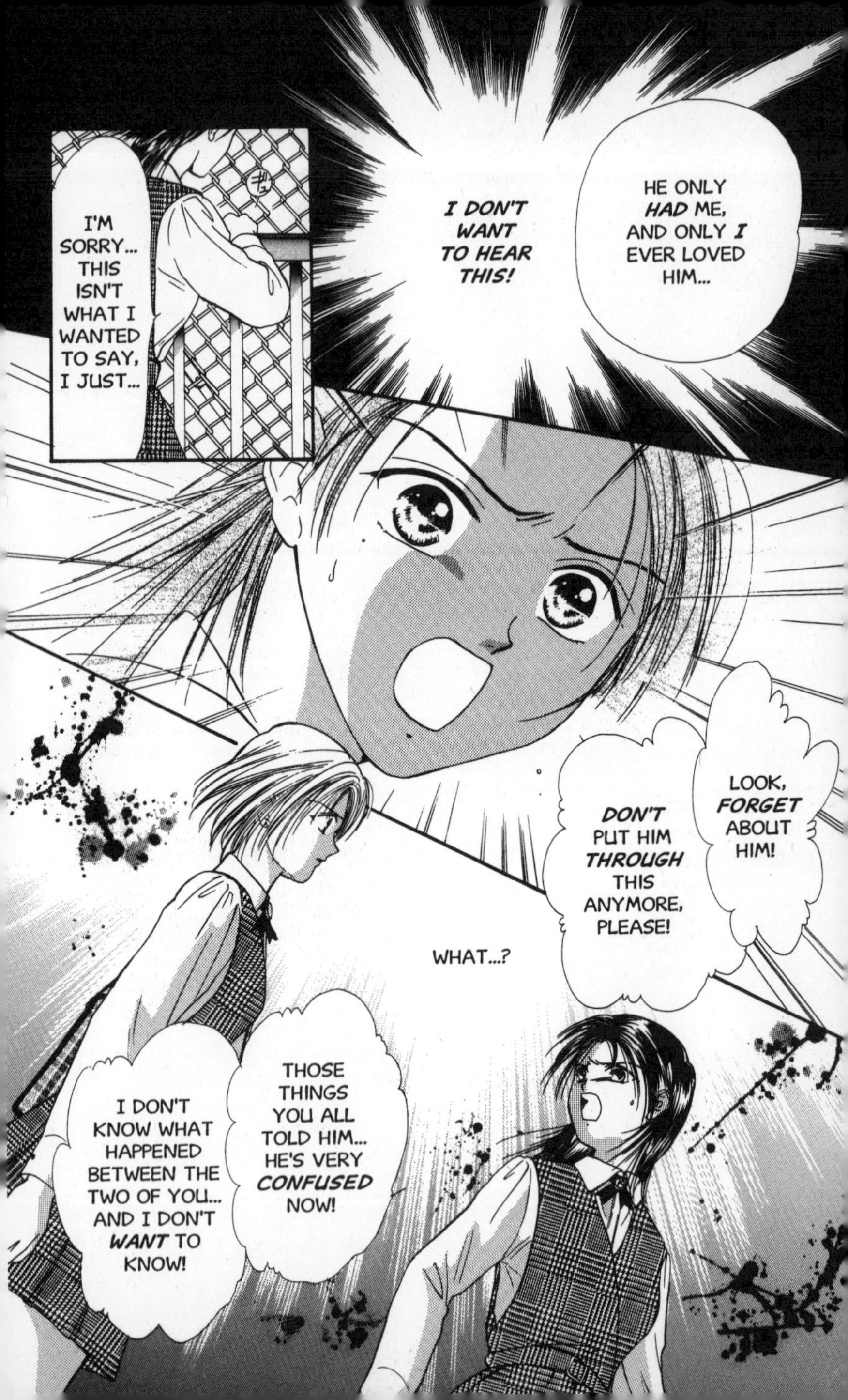
HE ONLY *HAD* ME, AND ONLY *I* EVER LOVED HIM...
I DON'T WANT TO HEAR THIS!
I'M SORRY... THIS ISN'T WHAT I WANTED TO SAY, I JUST...
LOOK, *FORGET* ABOUT HIM!
DON'T PUT HIM *THROUGH* THIS ANYMORE, PLEASE!
WHAT...?
THOSE THINGS YOU ALL TOLD HIM... HE'S VERY *CONFUSED* NOW!
I DON'T KNOW WHAT HAPPENED BETWEEN THE TWO OF YOU... AND I DON'T *WANT* TO KNOW!

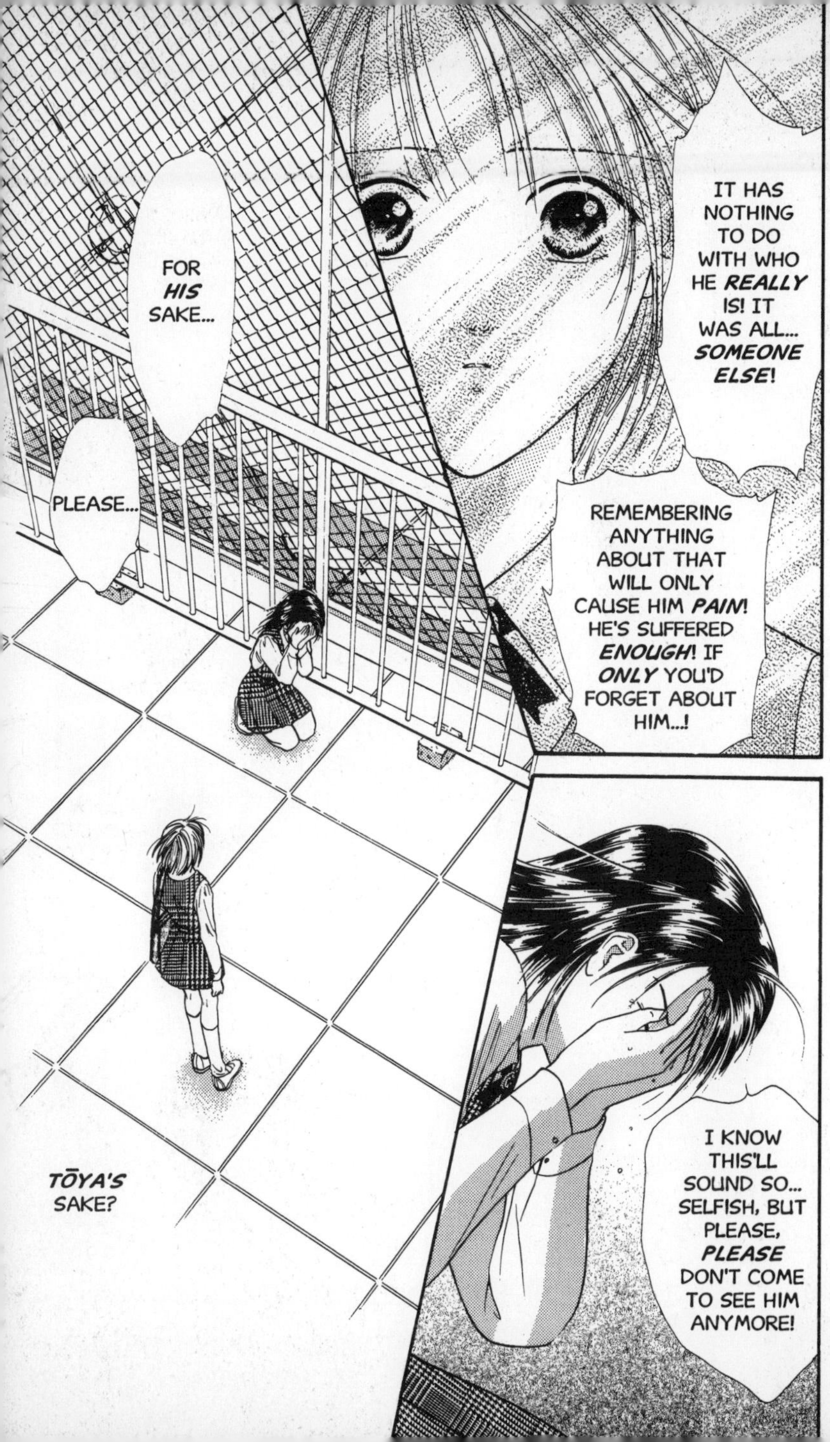
IT HAS NOTHING TO DO WITH WHO HE *REALLY* IS! IT WAS ALL... *SOMEONE ELSE*!
REMEMBERING ANYTHING ABOUT THAT WILL ONLY CAUSE HIM *PAIN*! HE'S SUFFERED *ENOUGH*! IF *ONLY* YOU'D FORGET ABOUT HIM...!
I KNOW THIS'LL SOUND SO... SELFISH, BUT PLEASE, *PLEASE* DON'T COME TO SEE HIM ANYMORE!
FOR *HIS* SAKE...
PLEASE...
TŌYA'S SAKE?

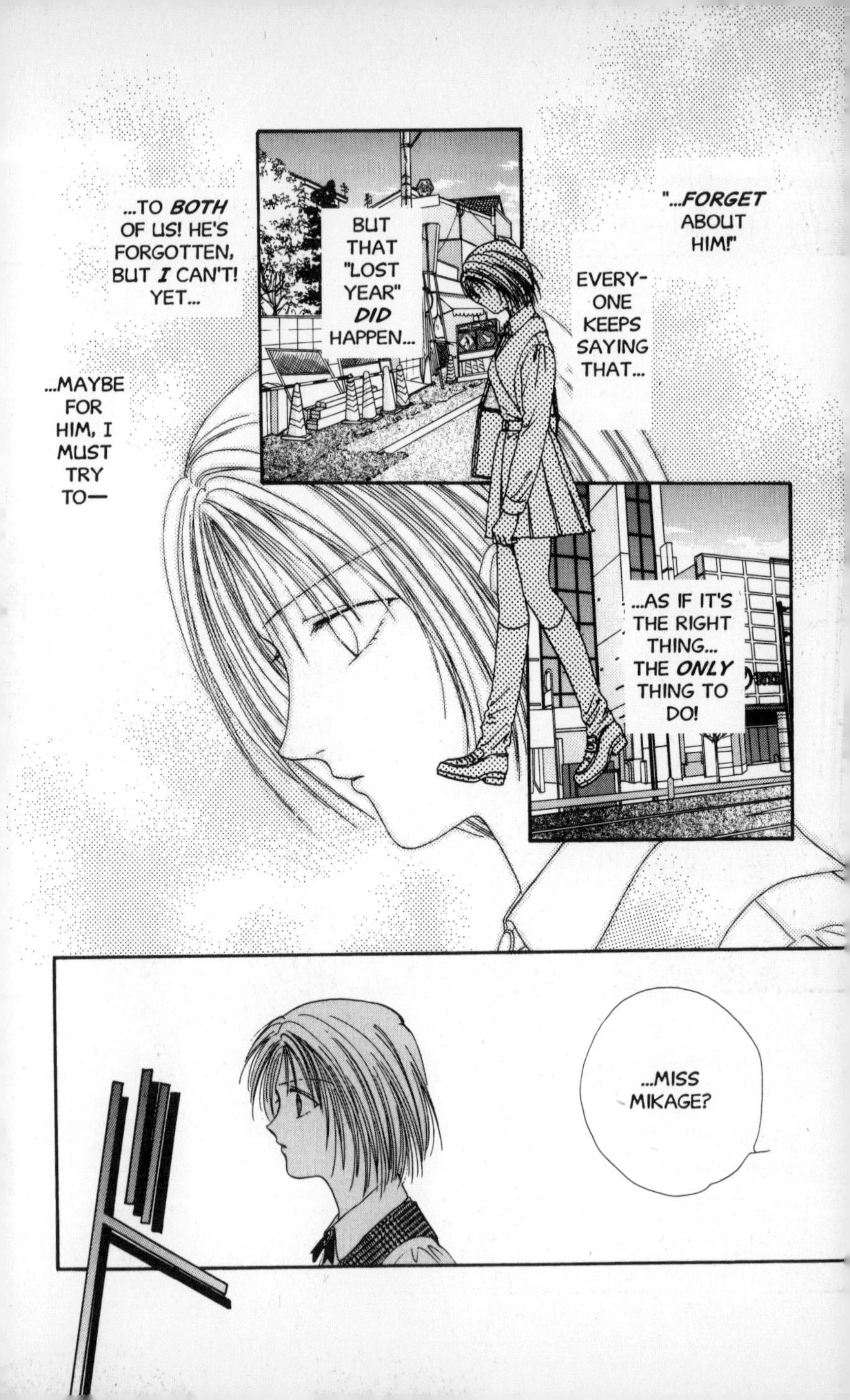
"...*FORGET* ABOUT HIM!"
EVERY-ONE KEEPS SAYING THAT...
...AS IF IT'S THE RIGHT THING... THE *ONLY* THING TO DO!
BUT THAT "LOST YEAR" *DID* HAPPEN...
...TO *BOTH* OF US! HE'S FORGOTTEN, BUT *I* CAN'T! YET...
...MAYBE FOR HIM, I MUST TRY TO—
...MISS MIKAGE?

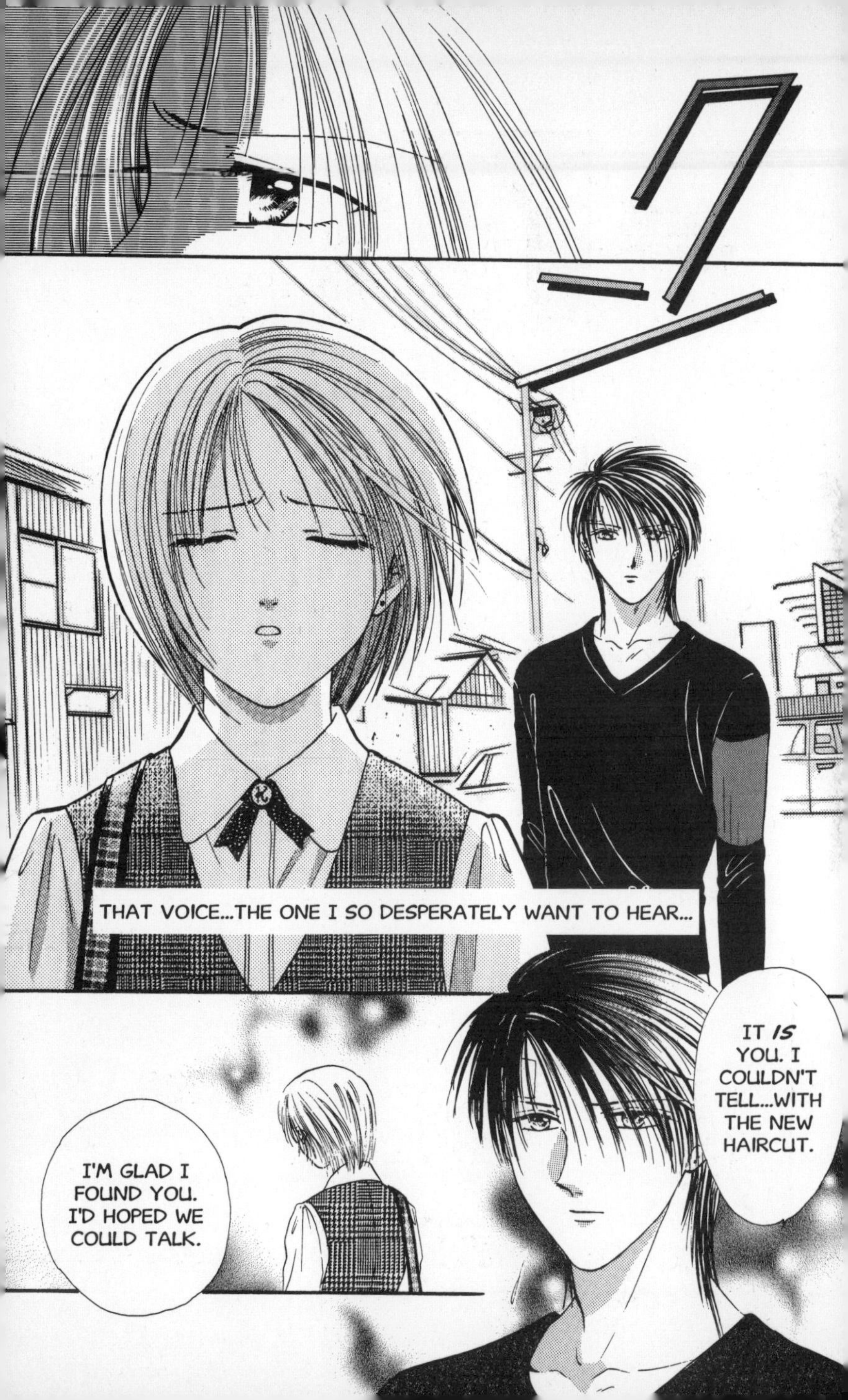
THAT VOICE...THE ONE I SO DESPERATELY WANT TO HEAR...
IT *IS* YOU. I COULDN'T TELL...WITH THE NEW HAIRCUT.
I'M GLAD I FOUND YOU. I'D HOPED WE COULD TALK.

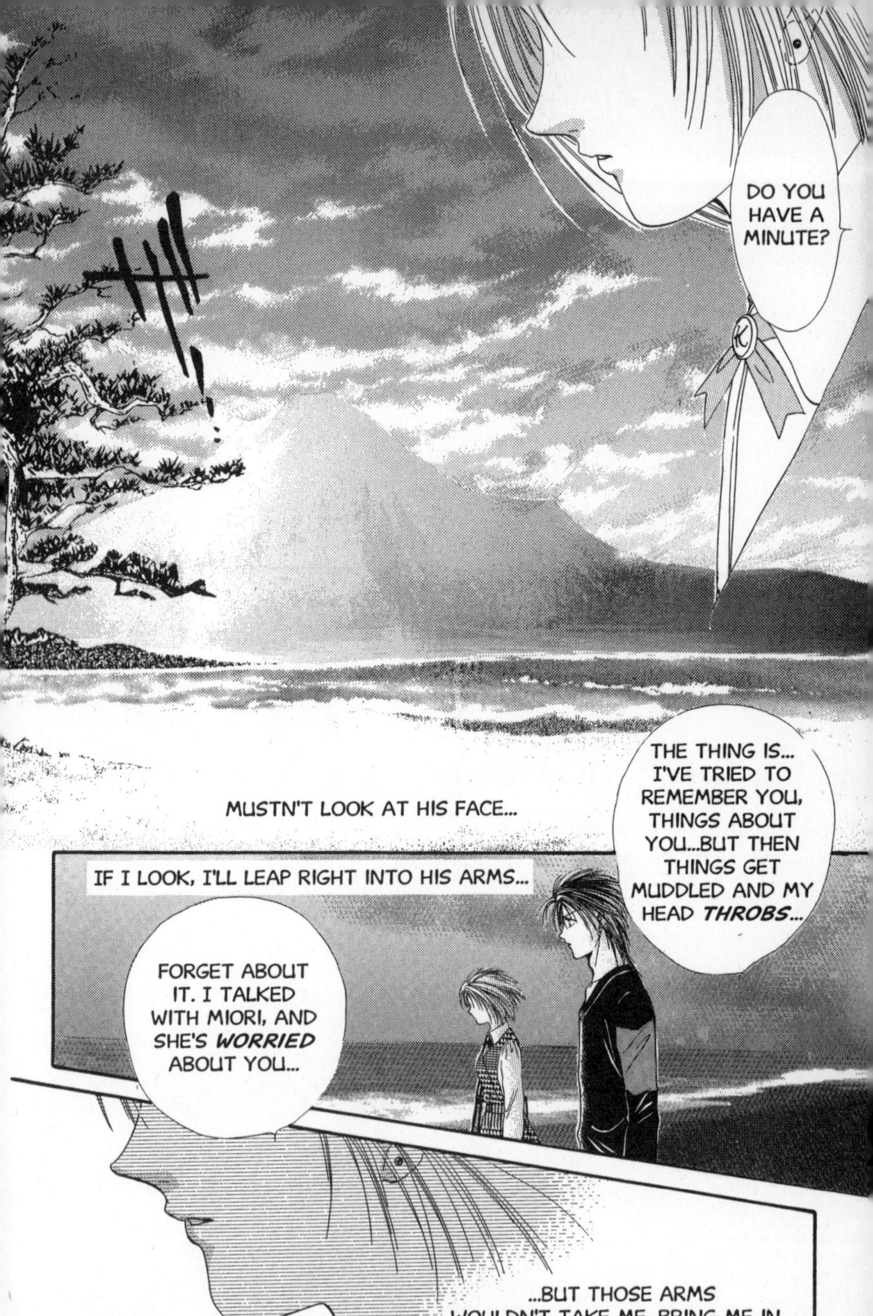
DO YOU HAVE A MINUTE?
THE THING IS... I'VE TRIED TO REMEMBER YOU, THINGS ABOUT YOU...BUT THEN THINGS GET MUDDLED AND MY HEAD *THROBS*...
MUSTN'T LOOK AT HIS FACE...
IF I LOOK, I'LL LEAP RIGHT INTO HIS ARMS...
FORGET ABOUT IT. I TALKED WITH MIORI, AND SHE'S *WORRIED* ABOUT YOU...
...BUT THOSE ARMS WOULDN'T TAKE ME, BRING ME IN...

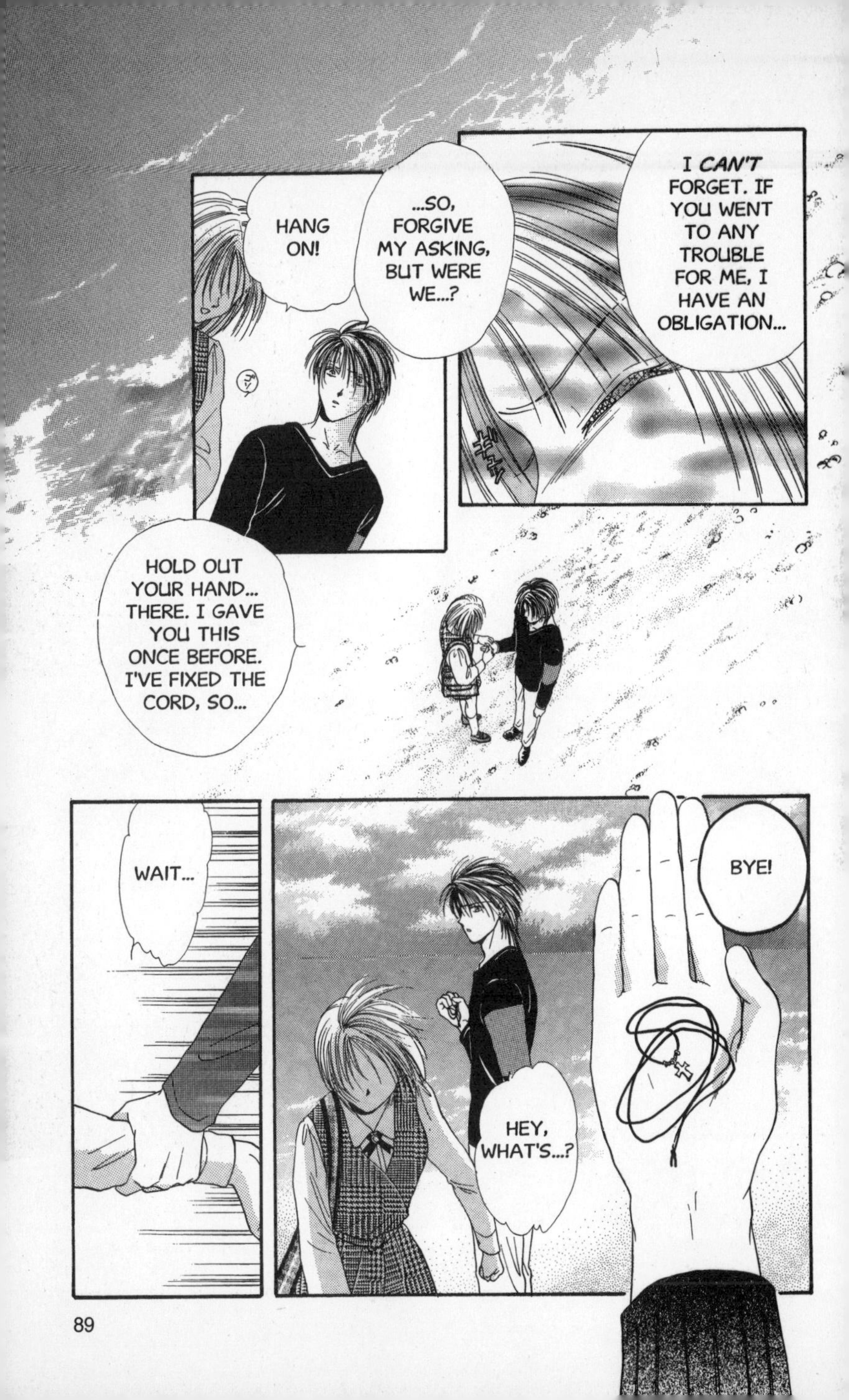
I *CAN'T* FORGET. IF YOU WENT TO ANY TROUBLE FOR ME, I HAVE AN OBLIGATION...
...SO, FORGIVE MY ASKING, BUT WERE WE...?
HANG ON!
HOLD OUT YOUR HAND... THERE. I GAVE YOU THIS ONCE BEFORE. I'VE FIXED THE CORD, SO...
BYE!
HEY, WHAT'S...?
WAIT...

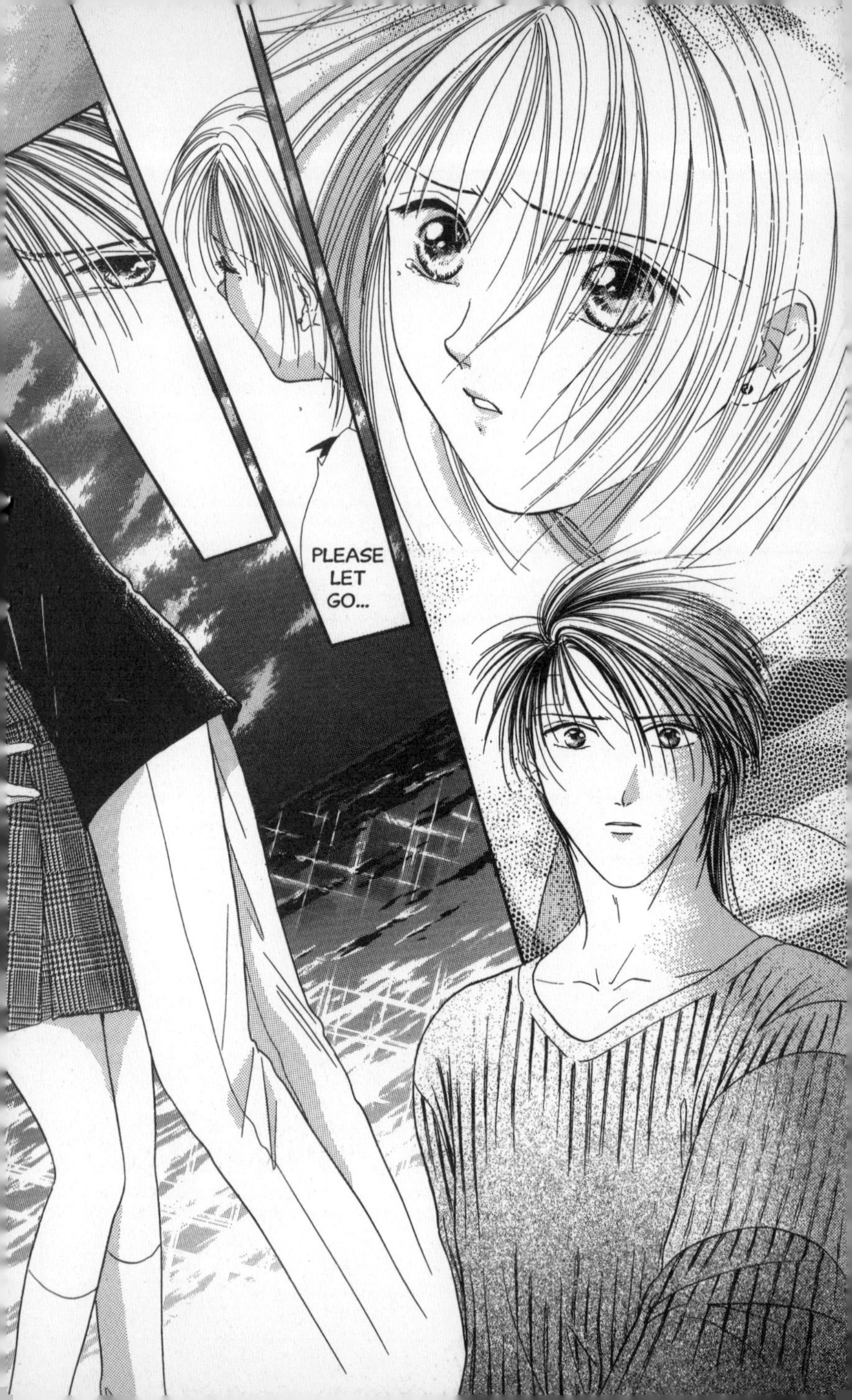
PLEASE LET GO...

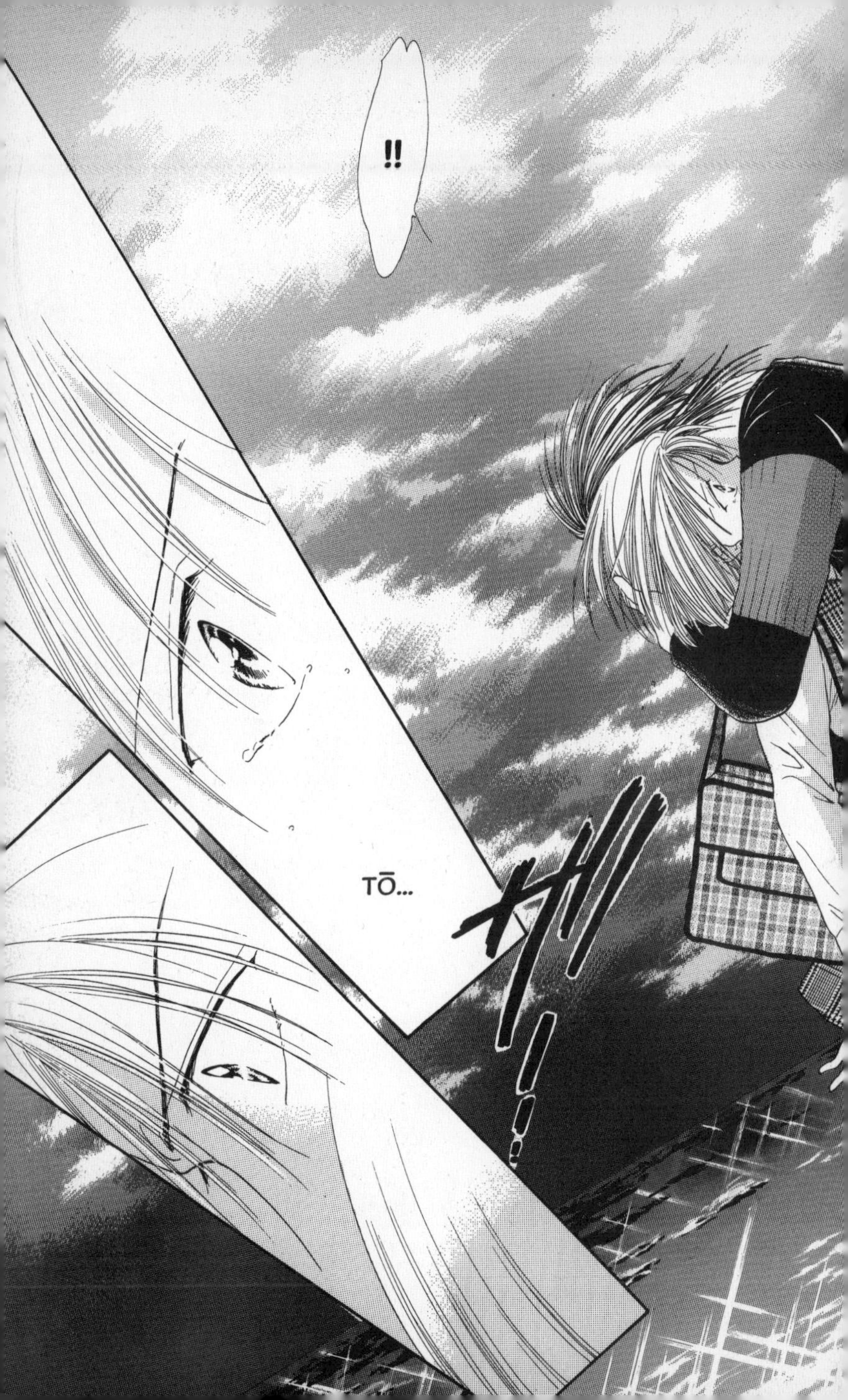
!!
TŌ...

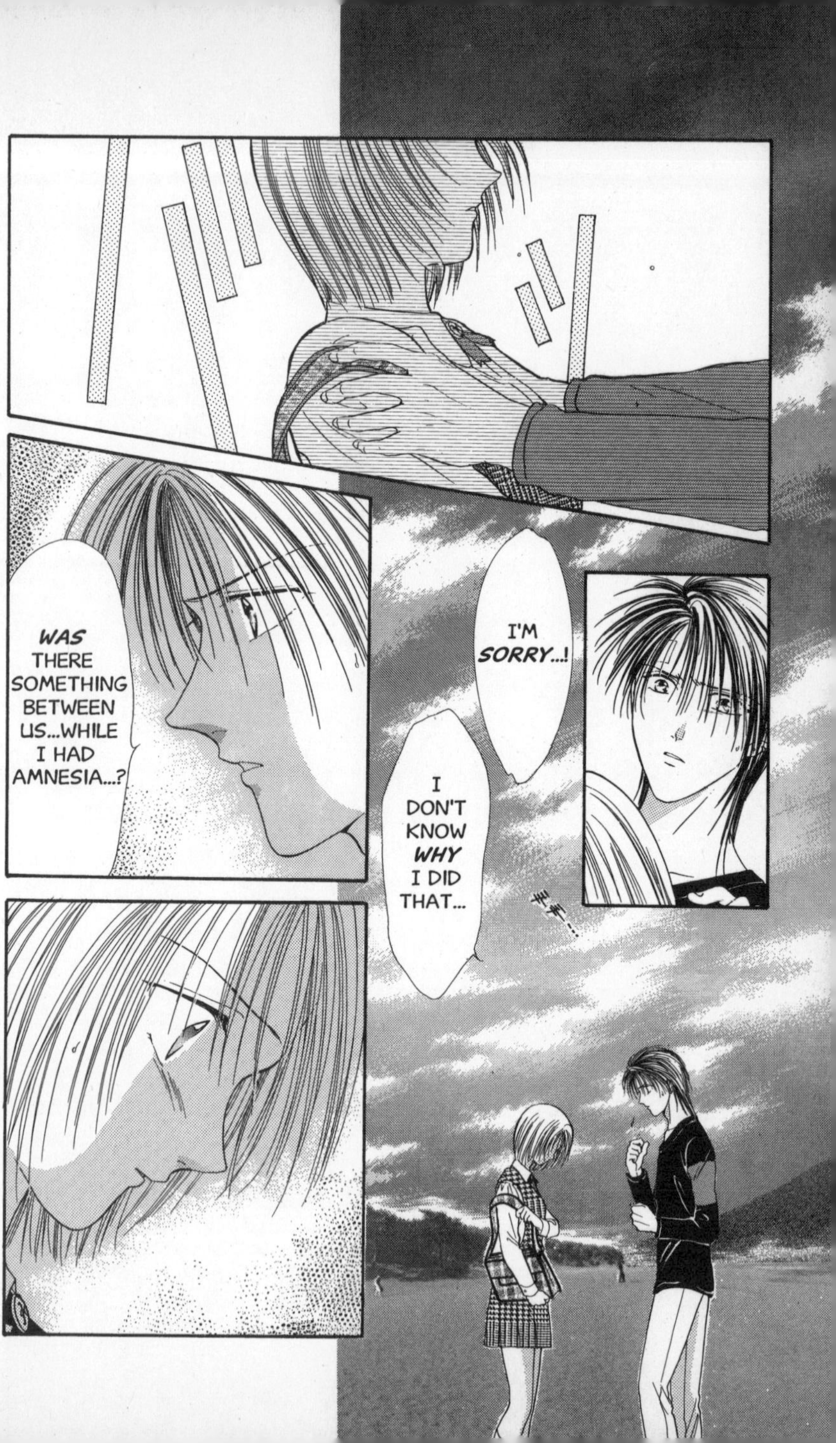
I'M *SORRY*...!
I DON'T KNOW *WHY* I DID THAT...
WAS THERE SOMETHING BETWEEN US...WHILE I HAD AMNESIA...?

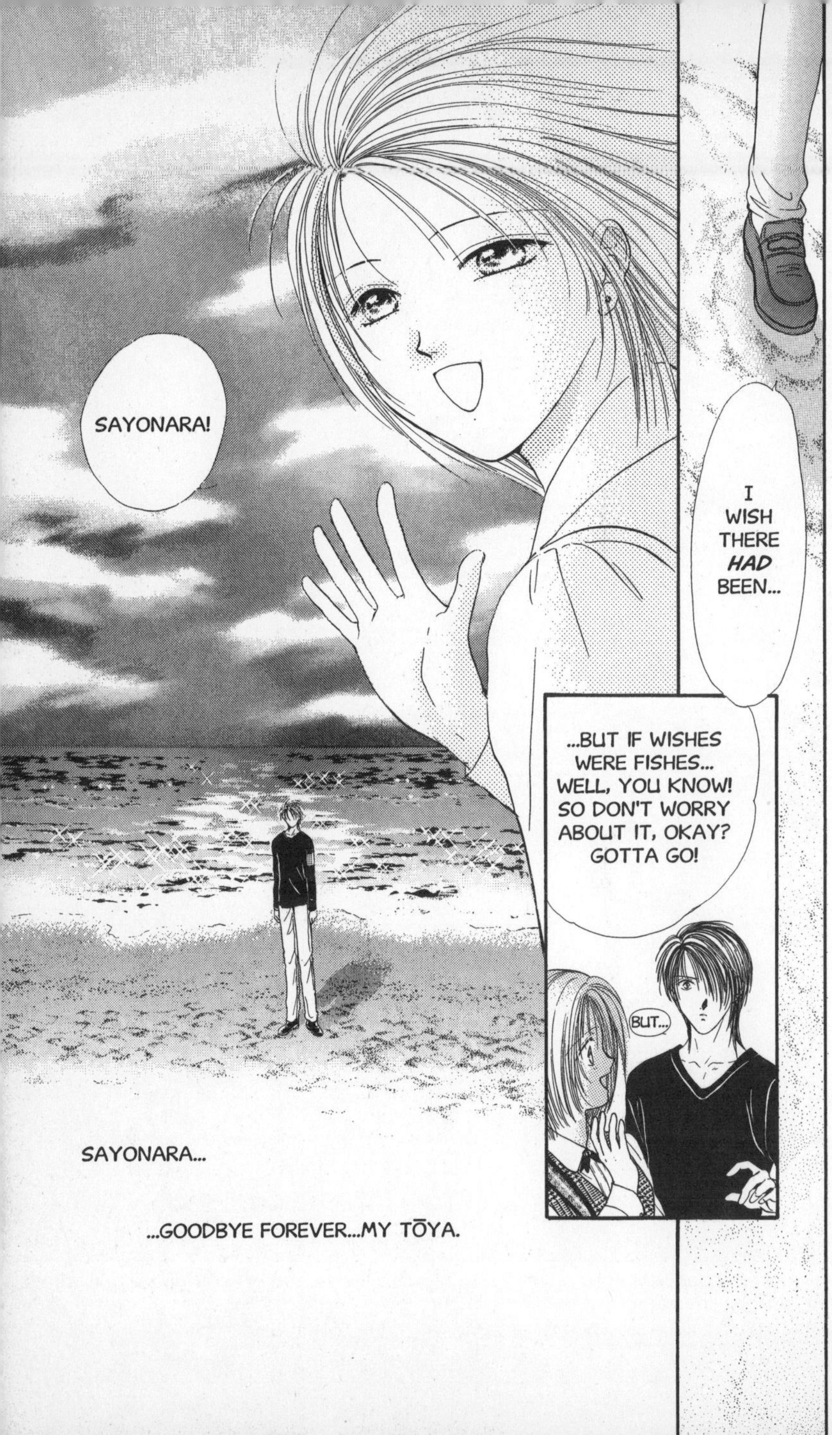
I WISH THERE *HAD* BEEN...
...BUT IF WISHES WERE FISHES... WELL, YOU KNOW! SO DON'T WORRY ABOUT IT, OKAY? GOTTA GO!
BUT...
SAYONARA!
SAYONARA...
...GOODBYE FOREVER...MY TŌYA.

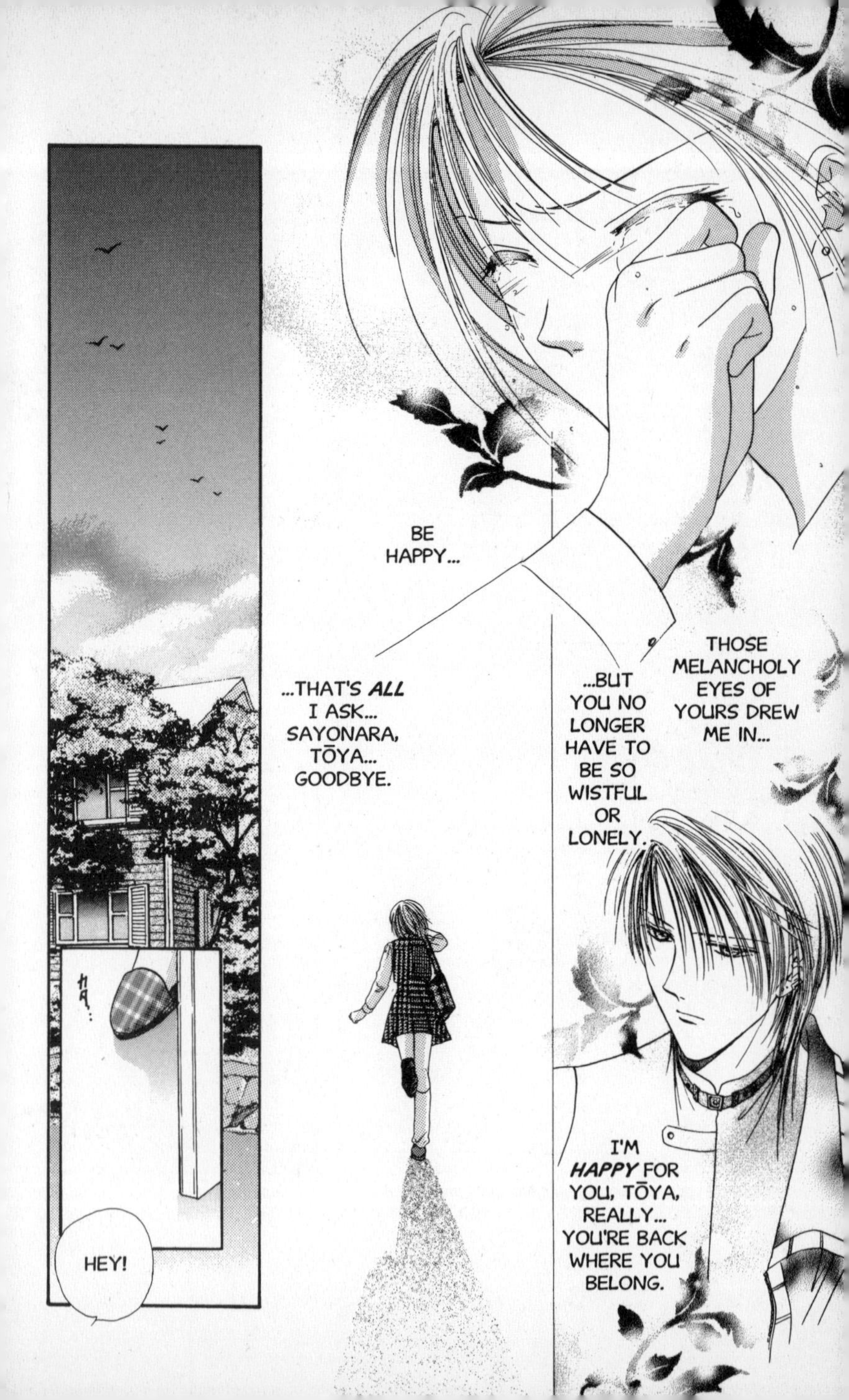
THOSE MELANCHOLY EYES OF YOURS DREW ME IN...
...BUT YOU NO LONGER HAVE TO BE SO WISTFUL OR LONELY.
I'M *HAPPY* FOR YOU, TŌYA, REALLY... YOU'RE BACK WHERE YOU BELONG.
BE HAPPY...
...THAT'S *ALL* I ASK... SAYONARA, TŌYA... GOODBYE.
HEY!

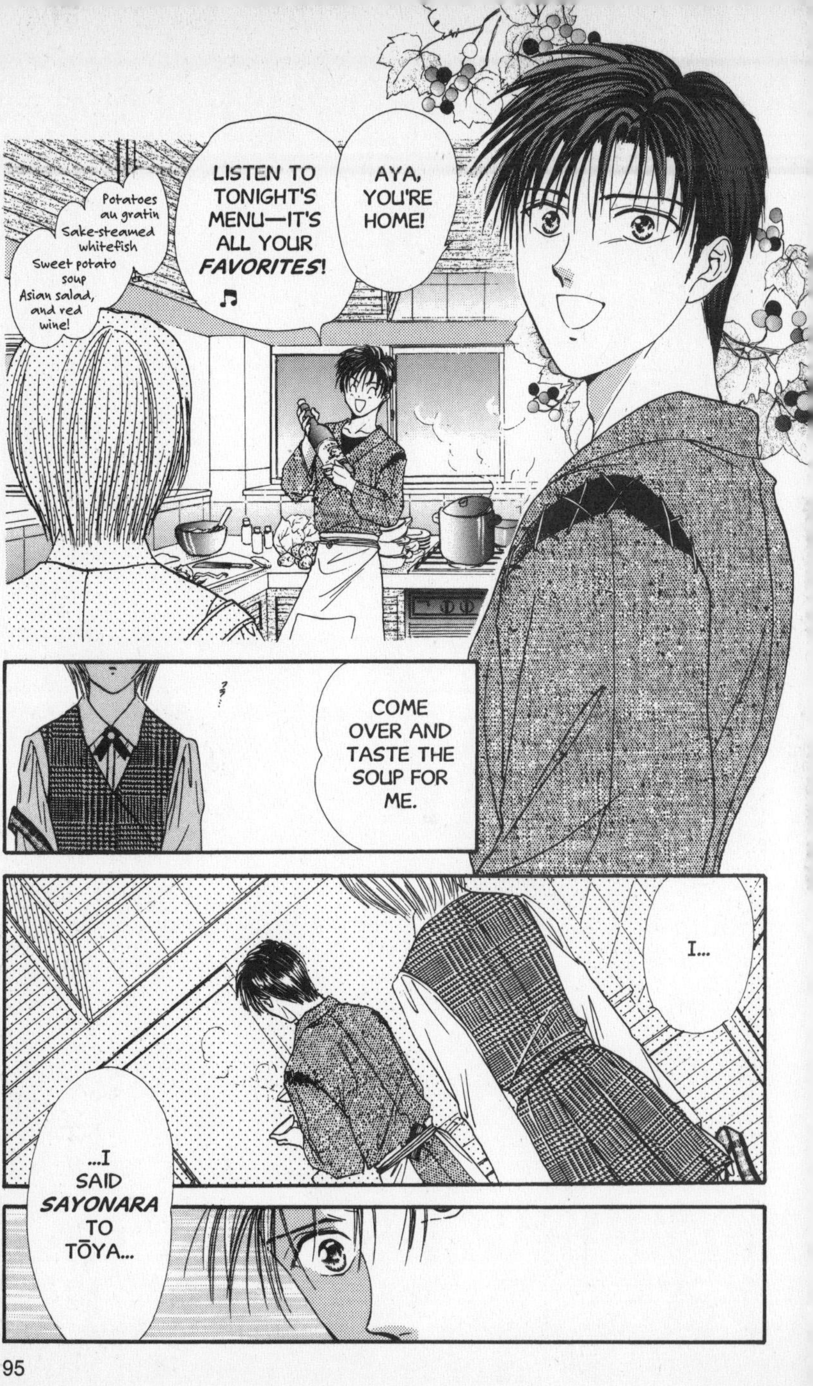
AYA, YOU'RE HOME!
LISTEN TO TONIGHT'S MENU—IT'S ALL YOUR *FAVORITES*! ♪
Potatoes au gratin
Sake-steamed whitefish
Sweet potato soup
Asian salad, and red wine!
COME OVER AND TASTE THE SOUP FOR ME.
I...
...I SAID *SAYONARA* TO TŌYA...

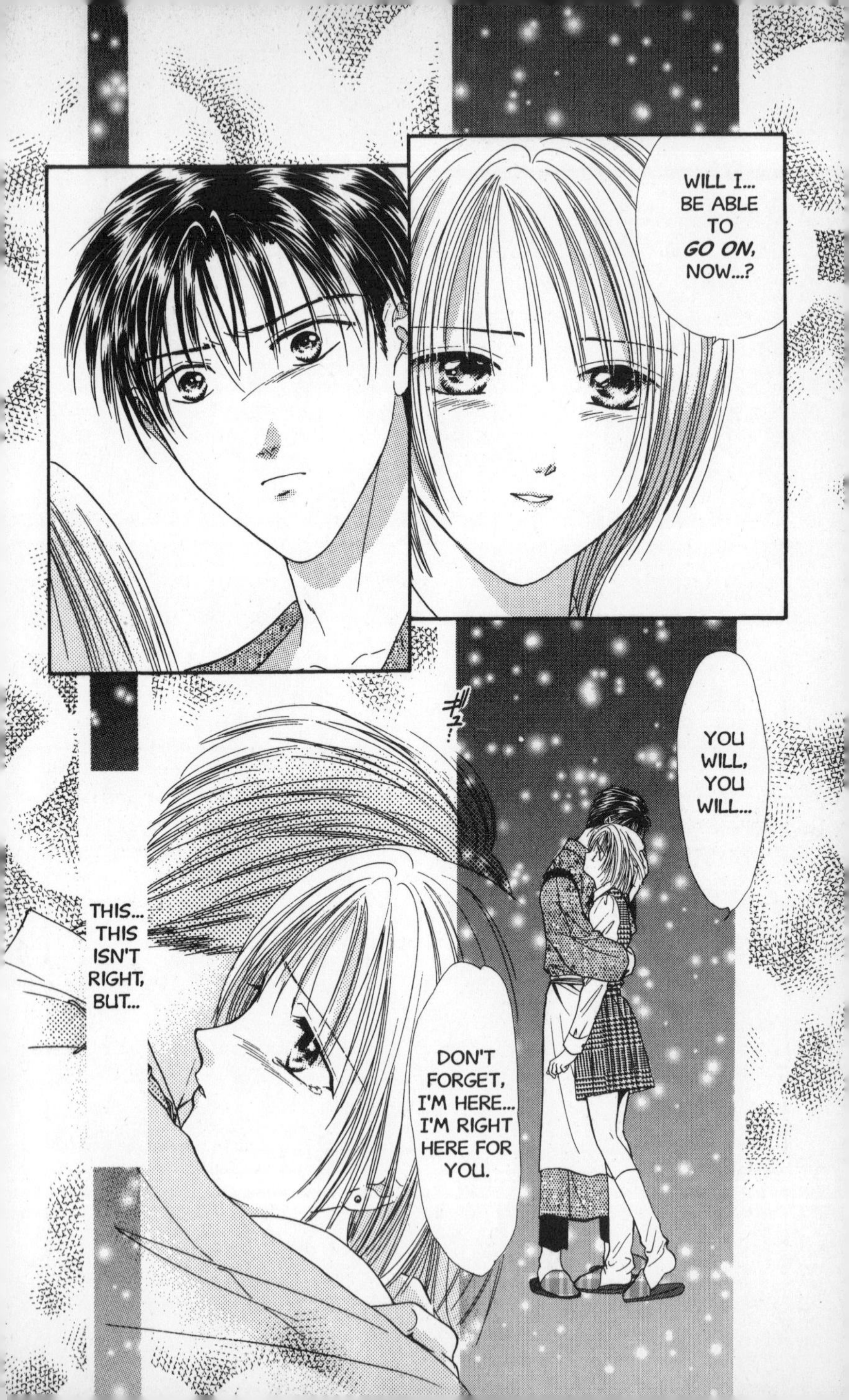
WILL I... BE ABLE TO *GO ON*, NOW...?
YOU WILL, YOU WILL...
DON'T FORGET, I'M HERE... I'M RIGHT HERE FOR YOU.
THIS... THIS ISN'T RIGHT, BUT...

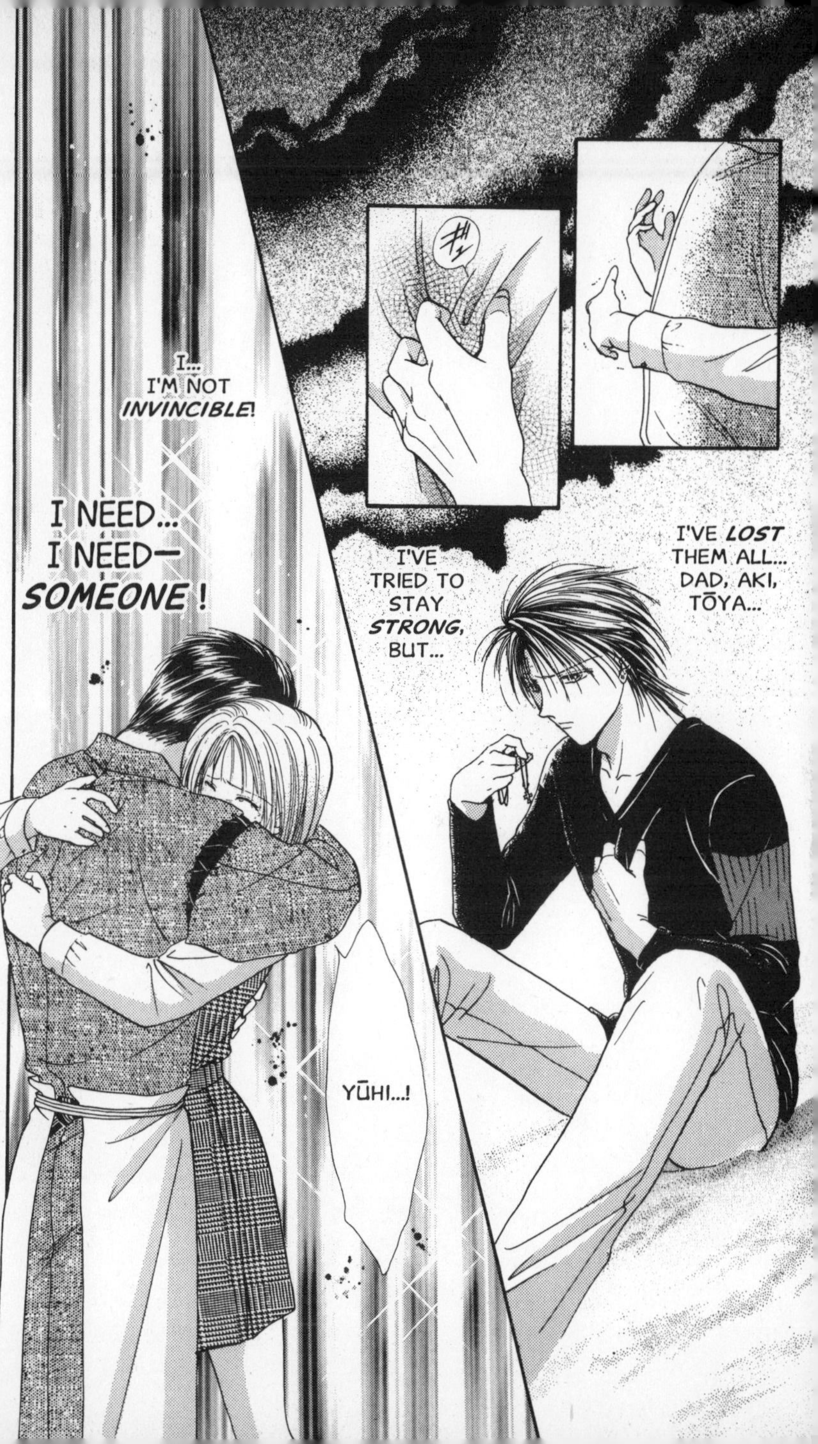

I'VE LOST THEM ALL... DAD, AKI, TŌYA...
I'VE TRIED TO STAY STRONG, BUT...
I... I'M NOT INVINCIBLE!
I NEED... I NEED— SOMEONE!
YŪHI...!

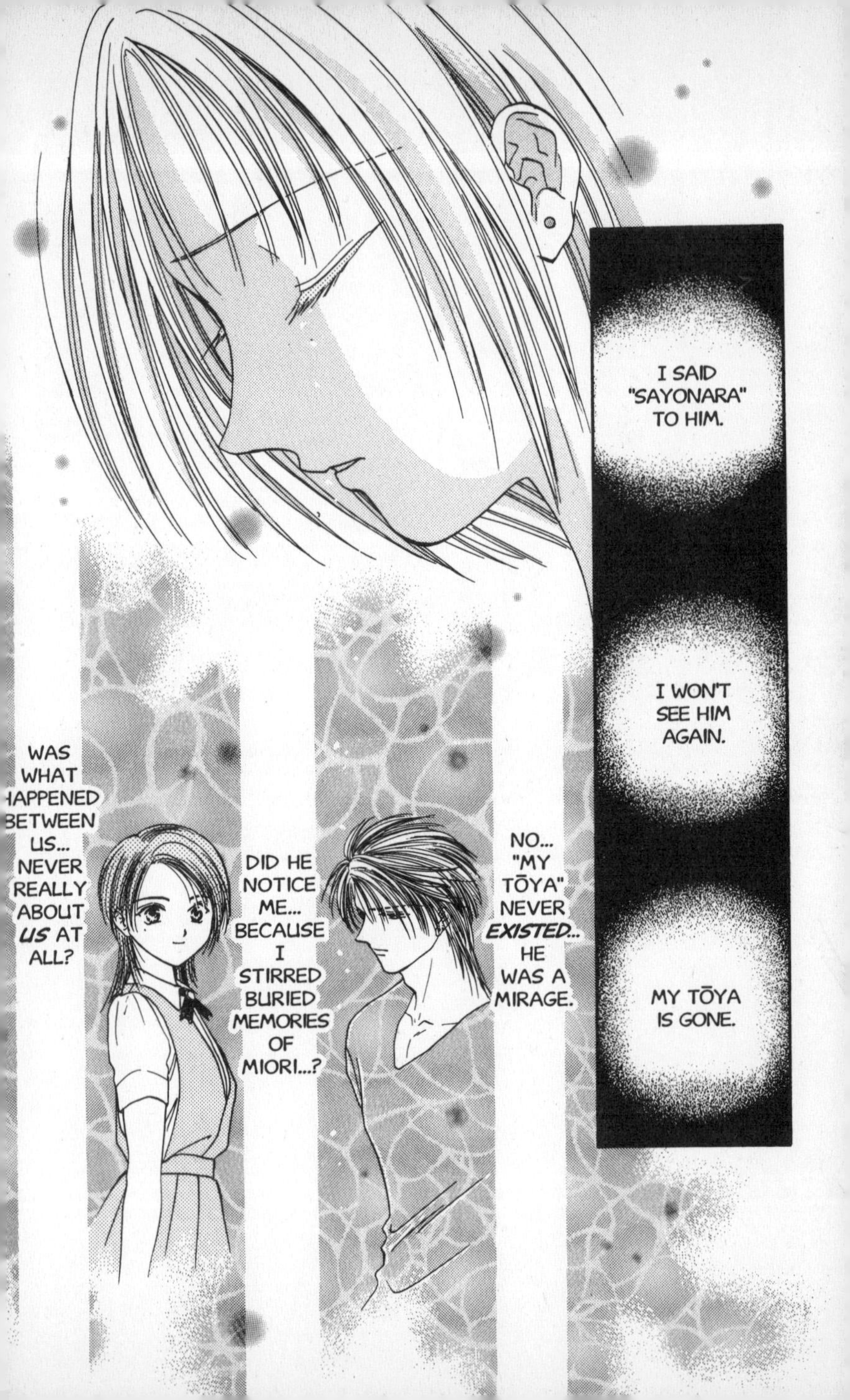
I SAID "SAYONARA" TO HIM.
I WON'T SEE HIM AGAIN.
MY TŌYA IS GONE.
NO... "MY TŌYA" NEVER *EXISTED*... HE WAS A MIRAGE.
DID HE NOTICE ME... BECAUSE I STIRRED BURIED MEMORIES OF MIORI...?
WAS WHAT HAPPENED BETWEEN US... NEVER REALLY ABOUT *US* AT ALL?

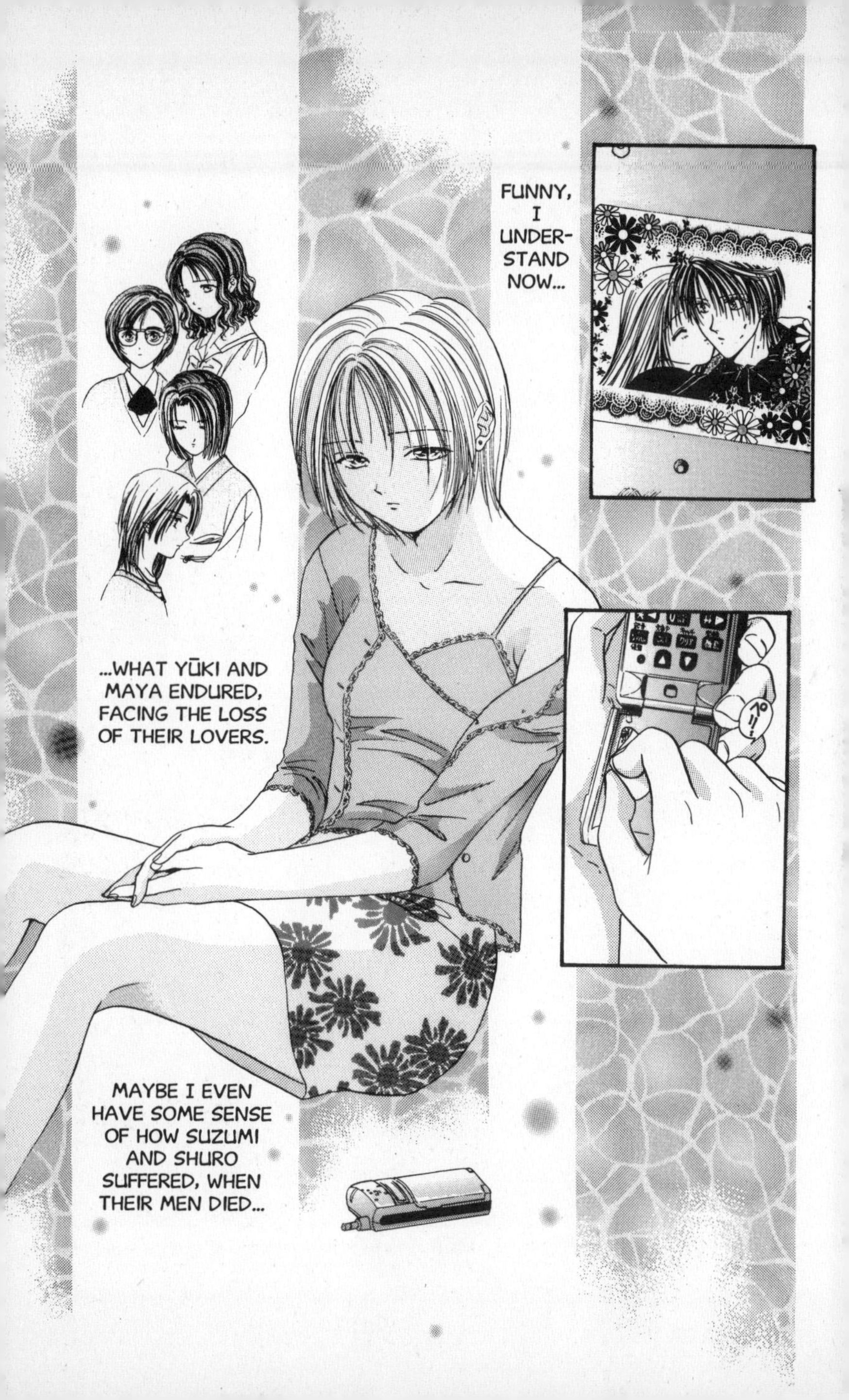
FUNNY, I UNDERSTAND NOW...
ペ!!
...WHAT YŪKI AND MAYA ENDURED, FACING THE LOSS OF THEIR LOVERS.
MAYBE I EVEN HAVE SOME SENSE OF HOW SUZUMI AND SHURO SUFFERED, WHEN THEIR MEN DIED...

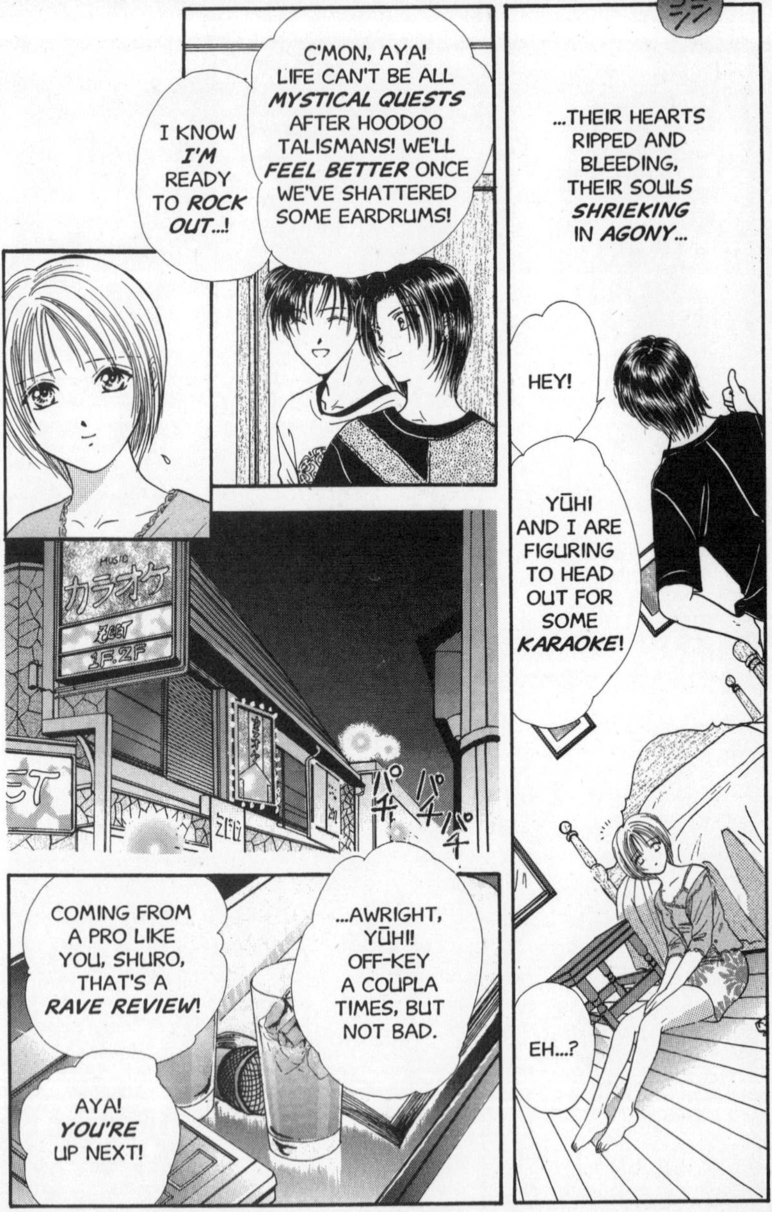
ココン
...THEIR HEARTS RIPPED AND BLEEDING, THEIR SOULS *SHRIEKING* IN *AGONY*...
HEY!
YŪHI AND I ARE FIGURING TO HEAD OUT FOR SOME *KARAOKE*!
EH...?
C'MON, AYA! LIFE CAN'T BE ALL *MYSTICAL QUESTS* AFTER HOODOO TALISMANS! WE'LL *FEEL BETTER* ONCE WE'VE SHATTERED SOME EARDRUMS!
I KNOW *I'M* READY TO *ROCK OUT*...!
カラオケ
1F.2F
パチパチパチ
...AWRIGHT, YŪHI! OFF-KEY A COUPLA TIMES, BUT NOT BAD.
COMING FROM A PRO LIKE YOU, SHURO, THAT'S A *RAVE REVIEW*!
AYA! *YOU'RE* UP NEXT!

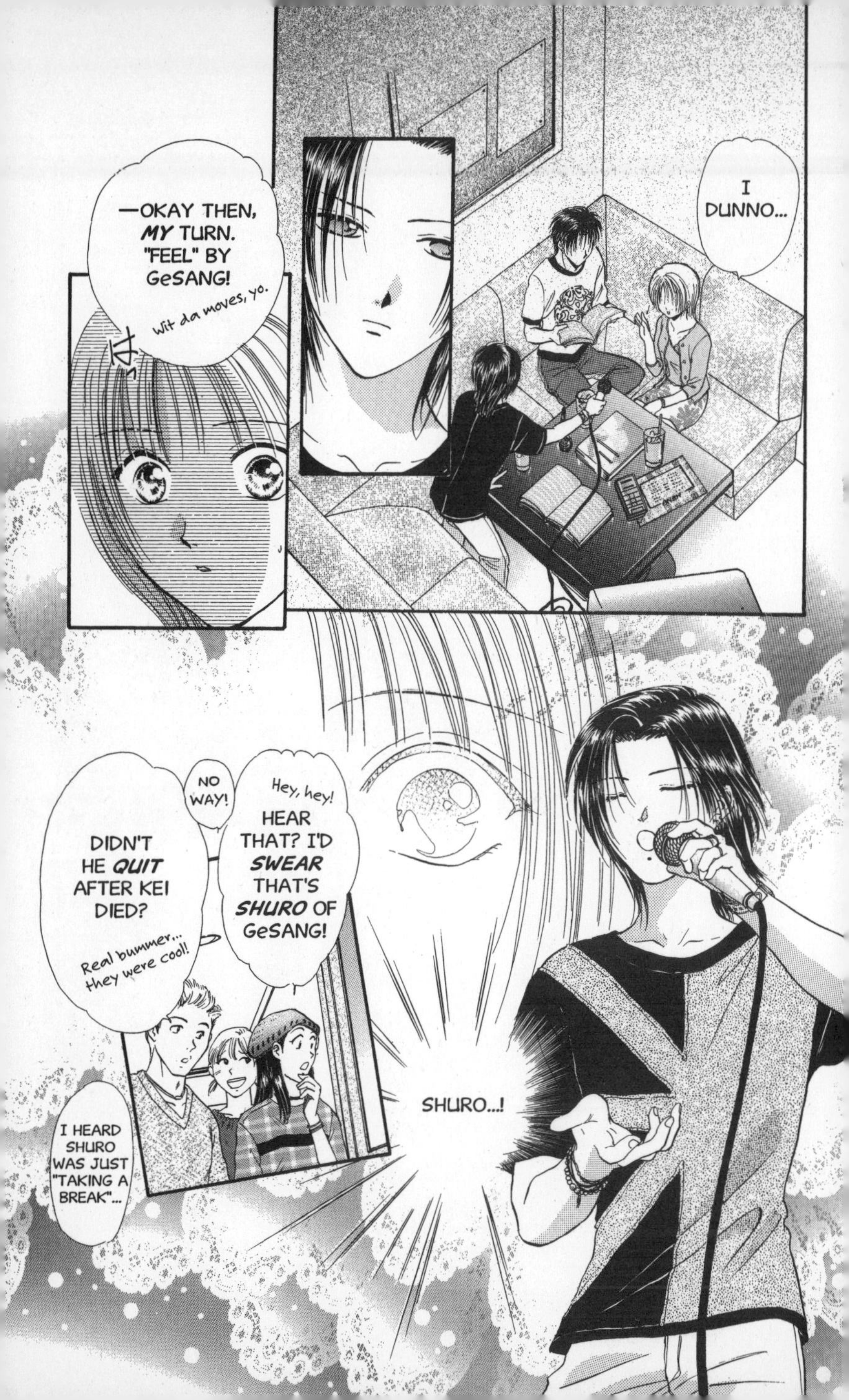
I DUNNO...
—OKAY THEN, MY TURN. "FEEL" BY GeSANG!
Wit da moves, yo.
SHURO...!
Hey, hey!
HEAR THAT? I'D SWEAR THAT'S SHURO OF GeSANG!
NO WAY!
DIDN'T HE QUIT AFTER KEI DIED?
Real bummer... they were cool!
I HEARD SHURO WAS JUST "TAKING A BREAK"...

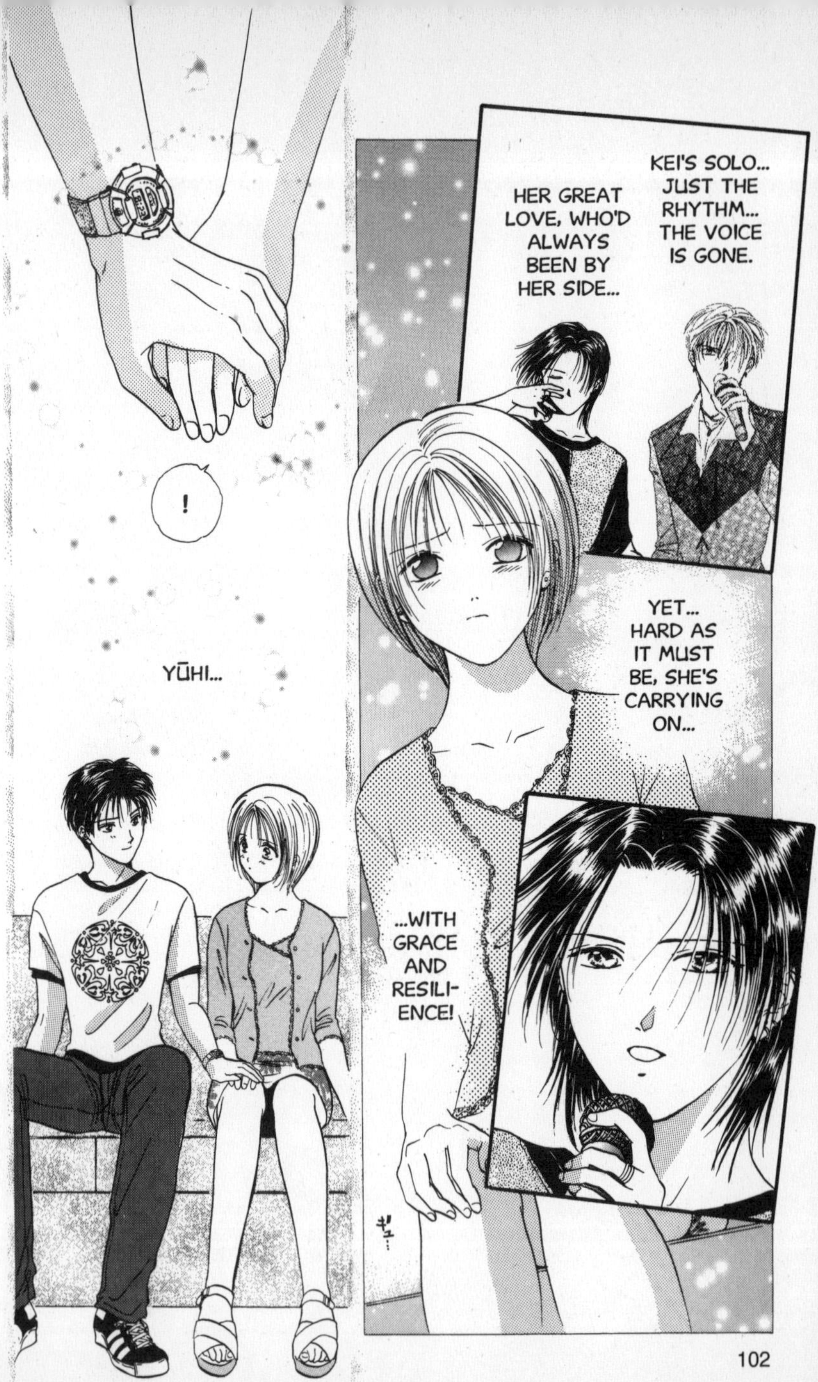
KEI'S SOLO... JUST THE RHYTHM... THE VOICE IS GONE.
HER GREAT LOVE, WHO'D ALWAYS BEEN BY HER SIDE...
YET... HARD AS IT MUST BE, SHE'S CARRYING ON...
...WITH GRACE AND RESILI-ENCE!
ギュ…
!
YŪHI...

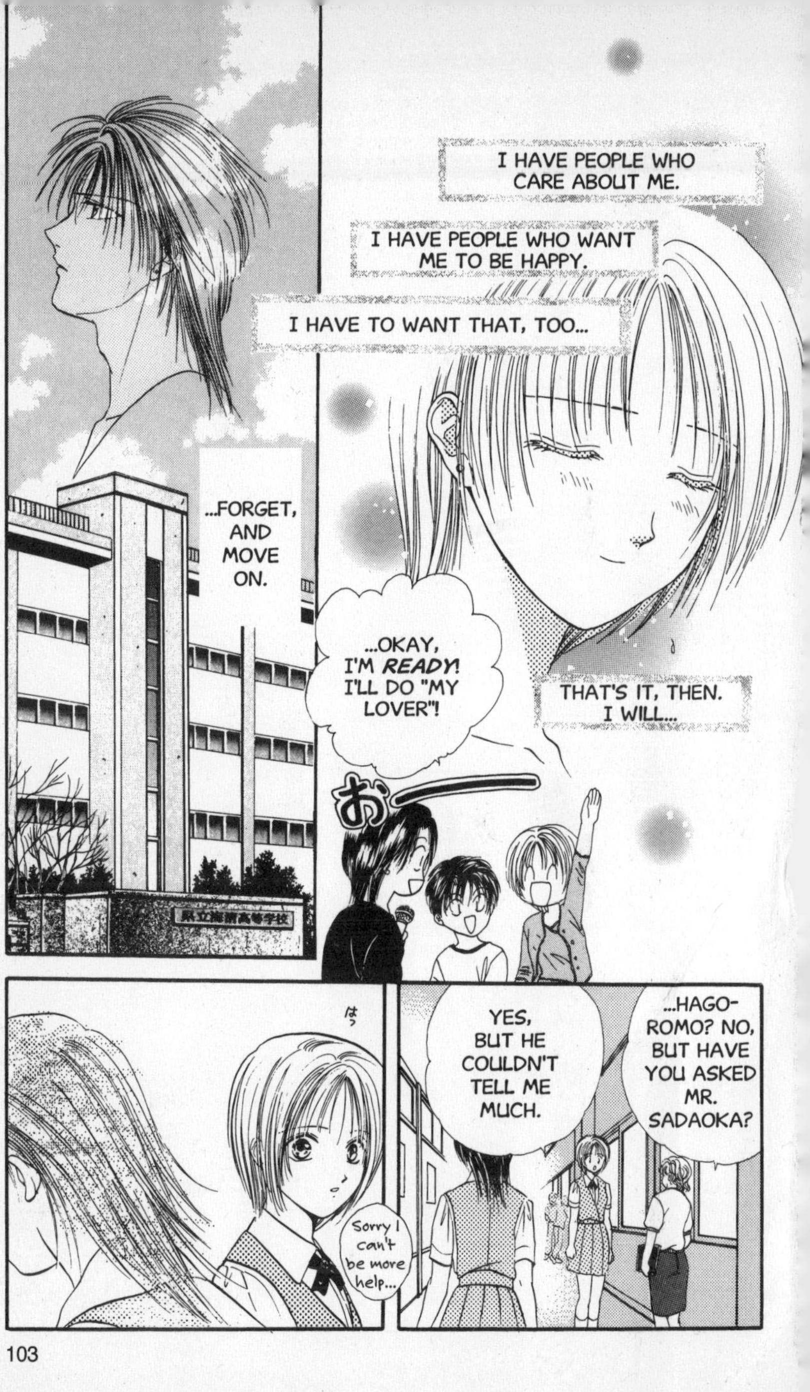
I HAVE PEOPLE WHO CARE ABOUT ME.
I HAVE PEOPLE WHO WANT ME TO BE HAPPY.
I HAVE TO WANT THAT, TOO...
THAT'S IT, THEN. I WILL...
...OKAY, I'M *READY*! I'LL DO "MY LOVER"!
お—
...FORGET, AND MOVE ON.
...HAGO-ROMO? NO, BUT HAVE YOU ASKED MR. SADAOKA?
YES, BUT HE COULDN'T TELL ME MUCH.
はっ
Sorry I can't be more help...

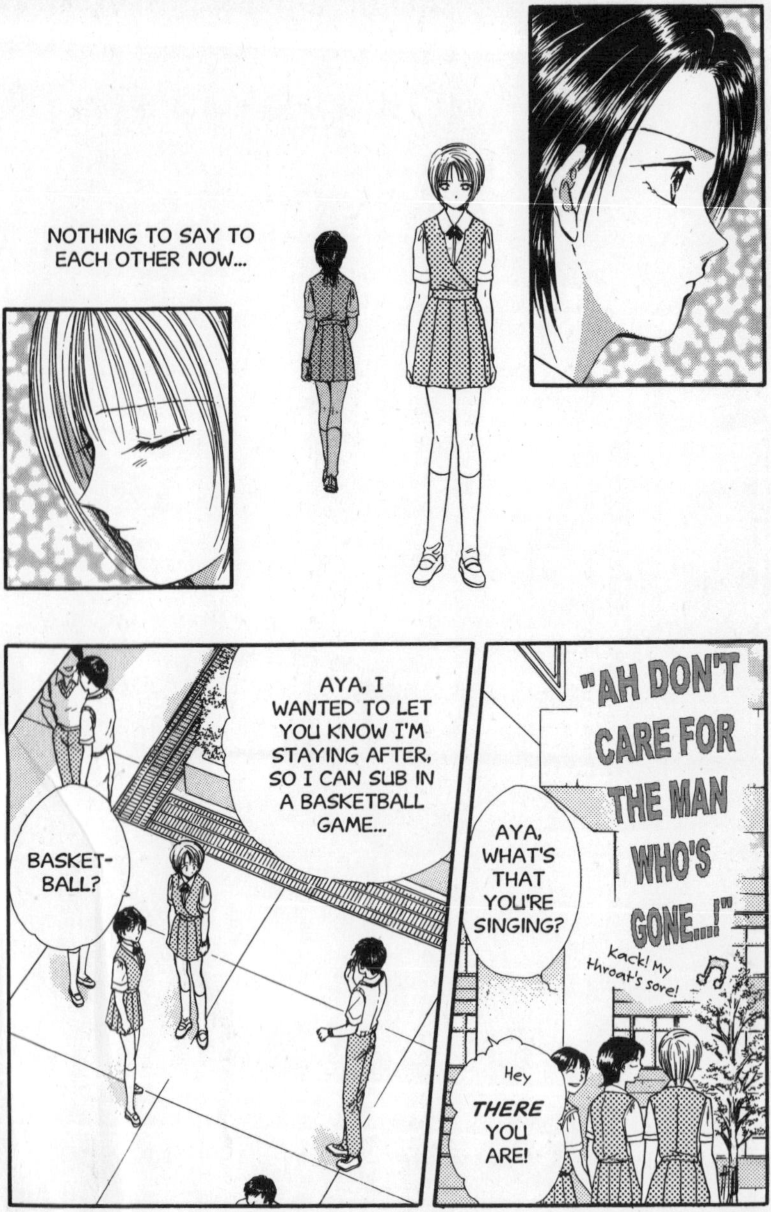
NOTHING TO SAY TO EACH OTHER NOW...
"AH DON'T CARE FOR THE MAN WHO'S GONE...!"
Kack! My throat's sore!
AYA, WHAT'S THAT YOU'RE SINGING?
Hey *THERE* YOU ARE!
AYA, I WANTED TO LET YOU KNOW I'M STAYING AFTER, SO I CAN SUB IN A BASKETBALL GAME...
BASKET-BALL?

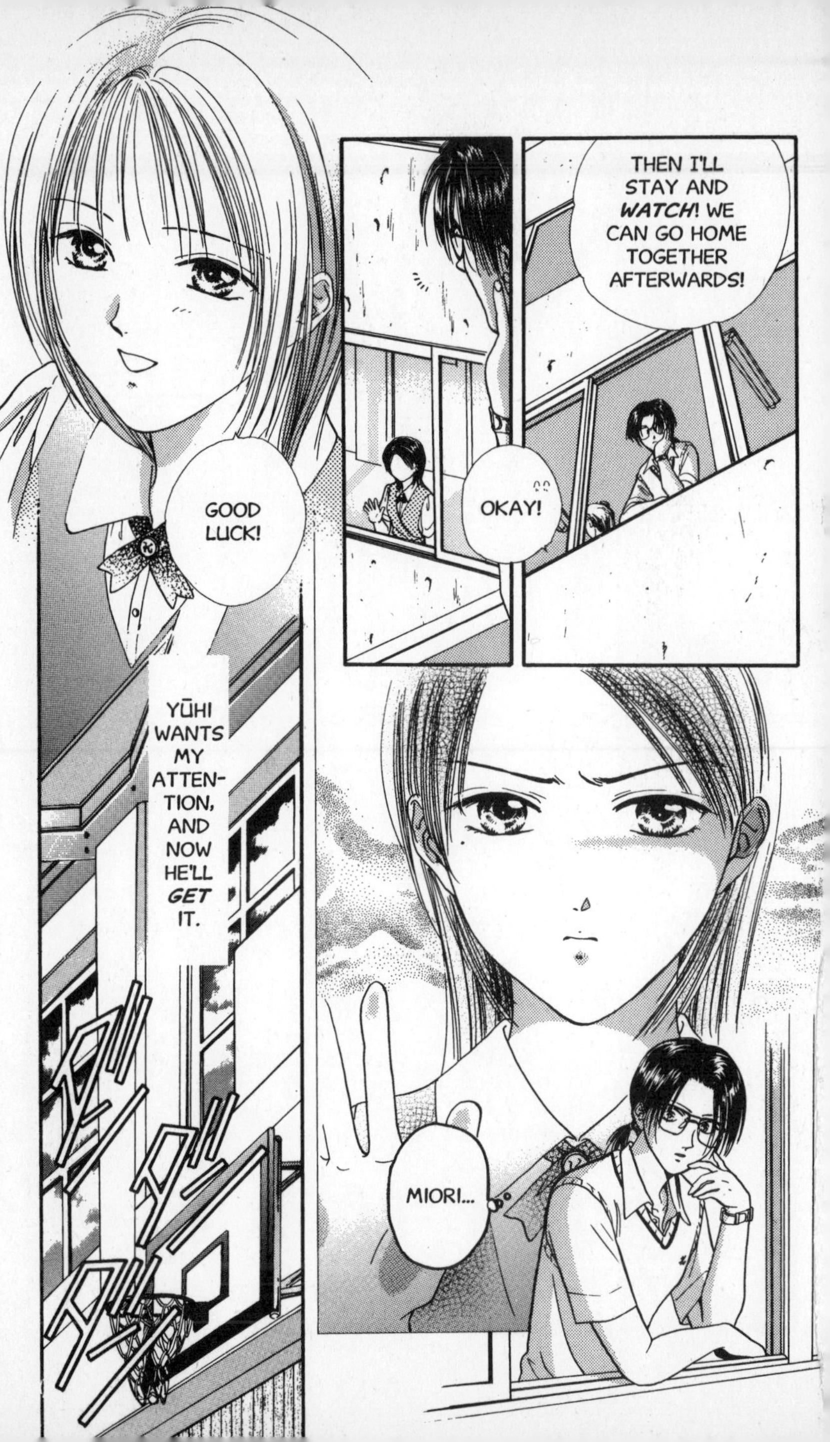
THEN I'LL STAY AND *WATCH*! WE CAN GO HOME TOGETHER AFTERWARDS!
OKAY!
MIORI...
GOOD LUCK!
YŪHI WANTS MY ATTENTION, AND NOW HE'LL *GET* IT.

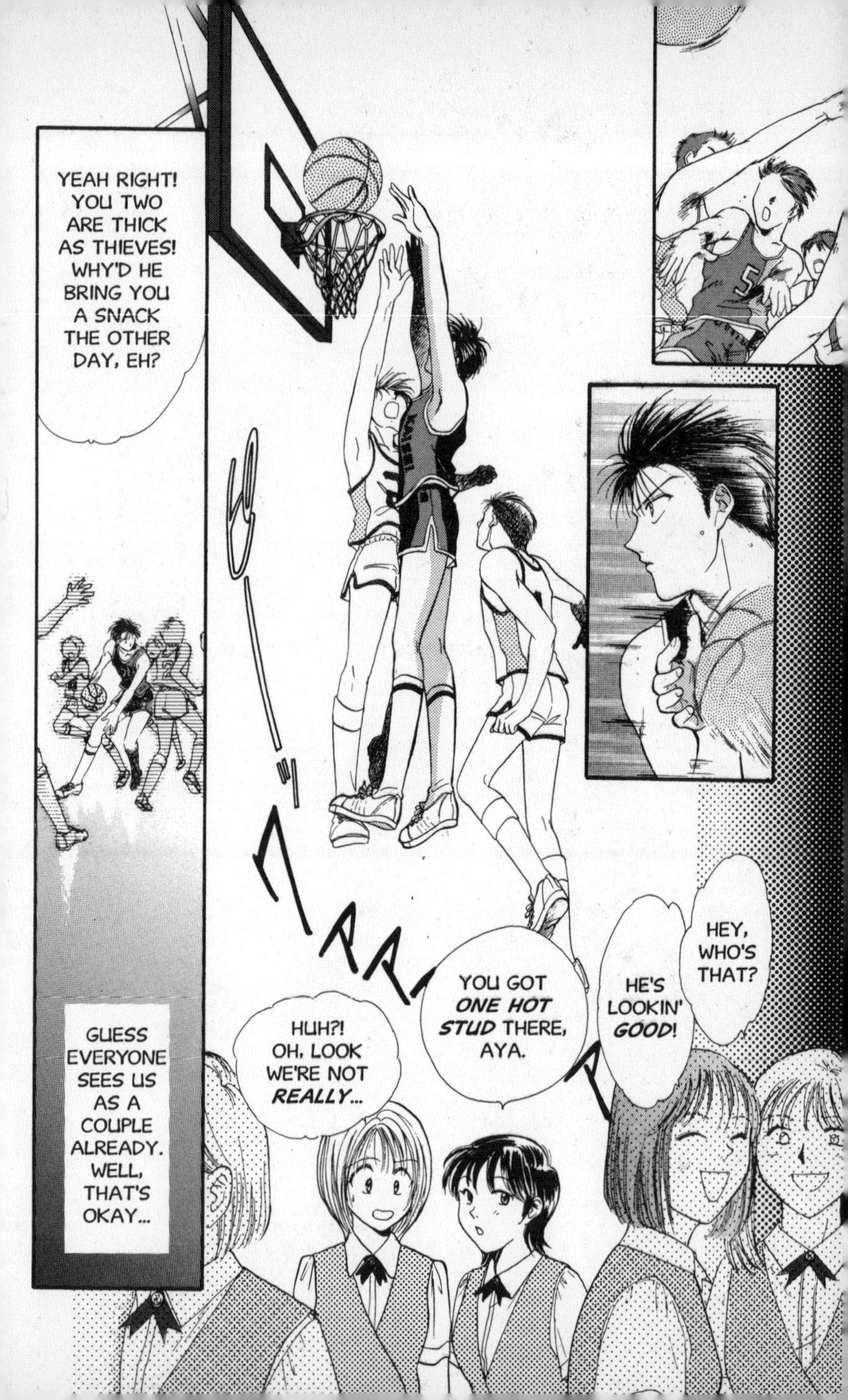
HEY, WHO'S THAT?
HE'S LOOKIN' *GOOD*!
YOU GOT *ONE HOT STUD* THERE, AYA.
HUH?! OH, LOOK WE'RE NOT *REALLY*...
YEAH RIGHT! YOU TWO ARE THICK AS THIEVES! WHY'D HE BRING YOU A SNACK THE OTHER DAY, EH?
GUESS EVERYONE SEES US AS A COUPLE ALREADY. WELL, THAT'S OKAY...

♦ Miori ♦

Continued...

...Boy, was I sweating. "Wasn't that a bit risqué, even if it **was** intended for a mature audience?" More sweat! "Parents are going to see it and complain, you know." And there's me, able only to laugh nervously. (Mom hasn't mentioned anything about it since, tho'....)

So, I'd been a bit concerned. ◡̈ Still—really—so what? There's something wrong with people who look at only **one** part of a manga and condemn the whole thing. Don't even get me started. I mean, there's nothing wrong with a couple **who loves each other** having sex. (My assistant, "M," emphatically argues that "sex isn't dirty—it's the people who claim it is who are!" She'd been touched by that sequence.) If anything, people try to pretend that sex doesn't exist. But the media treats sex (and women) as nothing more than a diversion. It's only natural that kids are going to be interested in sex. If you refuse proper sex ed, won't they only be flooded with the **wrong** kind of information? Isn't that why some teenage girls can sell sex so casually? ...Look, it's not like I'm some model citizen myself, but the sex thing is part of **Ceres**, so I'll go there when necessary. Strangely, neither Aya nor Tōya had ever discussed sex (Volume 4 was something different). Maybe that's why it seemed natural. I hope to write about all kinds of relationships, so please write me with any opinions. **Ceres** is more a love story than anything else I've ever done...maybe you can't tell. But remember, lovey-dovey "PDA"s do not a true love story make. It would be ideal if I could draw realistic and serious half the time.

And I won't forget that, the other half of the time, it's still shōjo manga.

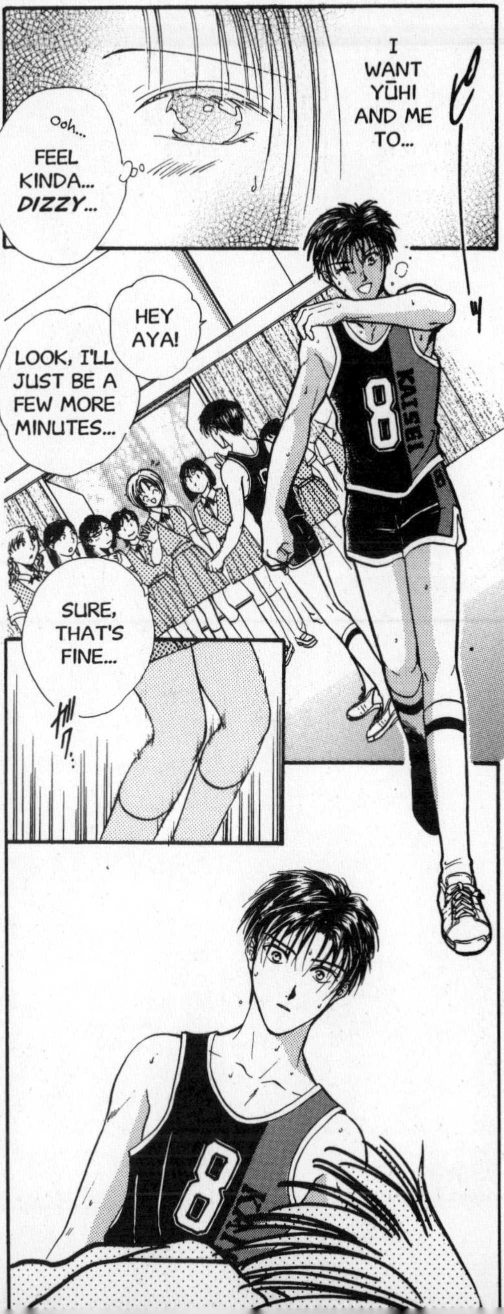

I WANT YŪHI AND ME TO...
Ooh... FEEL KINDA... DIZZY...
HEY AYA!
LOOK, I'LL JUST BE A FEW MORE MINUTES...
SURE, THAT'S FINE...

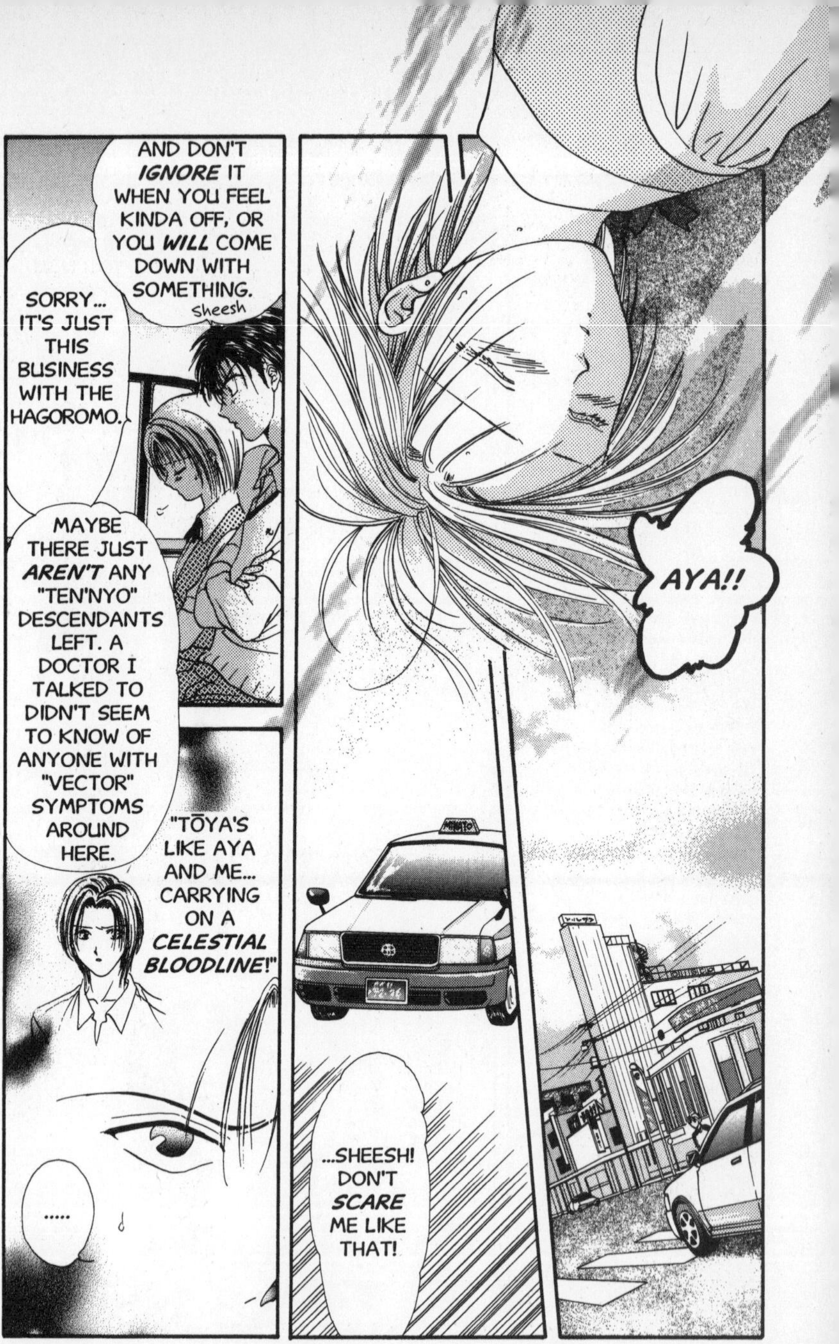
AYA!!
...SHEESH! DON'T SCARE ME LIKE THAT!
AND DON'T IGNORE IT WHEN YOU FEEL KINDA OFF, OR YOU WILL COME DOWN WITH SOMETHING.
Sheesh
SORRY... IT'S JUST THIS BUSINESS WITH THE HAGOROMO.
MAYBE THERE JUST AREN'T ANY "TEN'NYO" DESCENDANTS LEFT. A DOCTOR I TALKED TO DIDN'T SEEM TO KNOW OF ANYONE WITH "VECTOR" SYMPTOMS AROUND HERE.
"TŌYA'S LIKE AYA AND ME... CARRYING ON A CELESTIAL BLOODLINE!"
.....

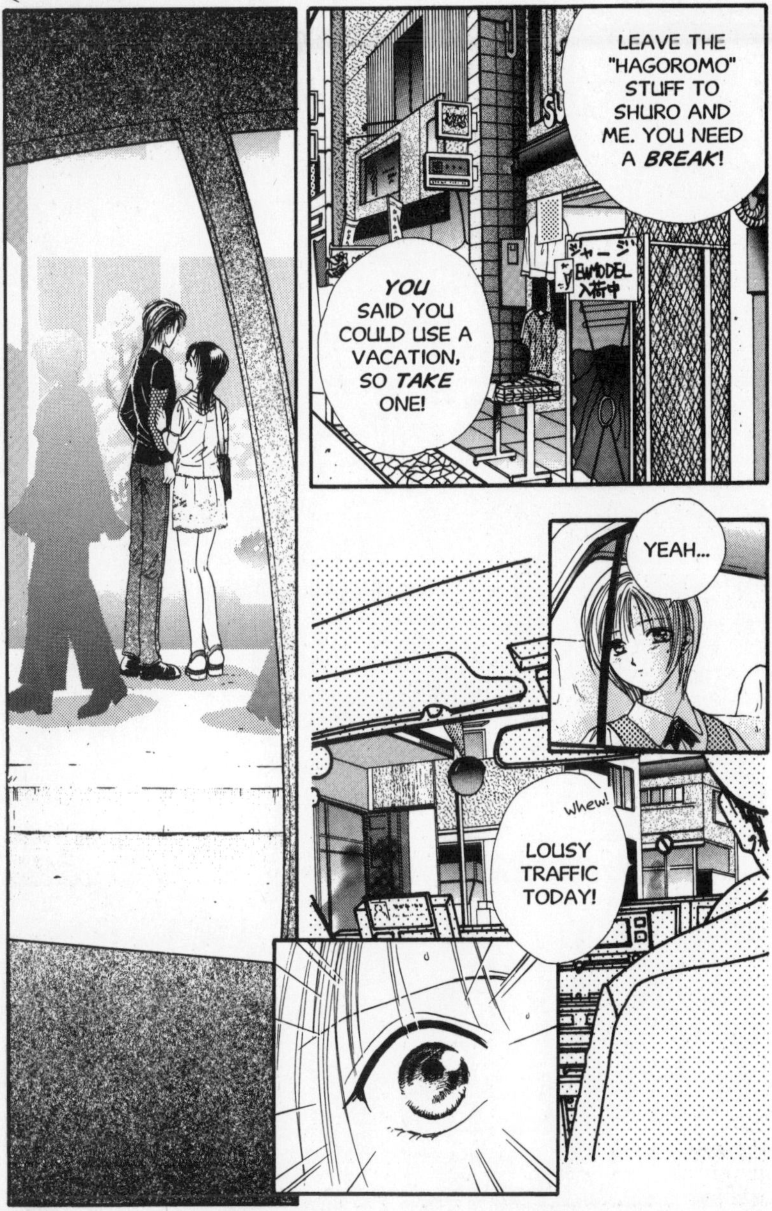
LEAVE THE "HAGOROMO" STUFF TO SHURO AND ME. YOU NEED A ***BREAK***!
ジャージ
EWMODEL
入荷中
YOU SAID YOU COULD USE A VACATION, SO ***TAKE*** ONE!
YEAH...
Whew!
LOUSY TRAFFIC TODAY!

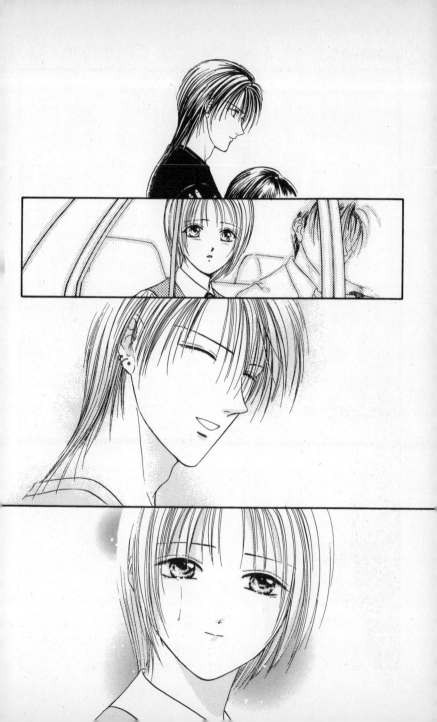

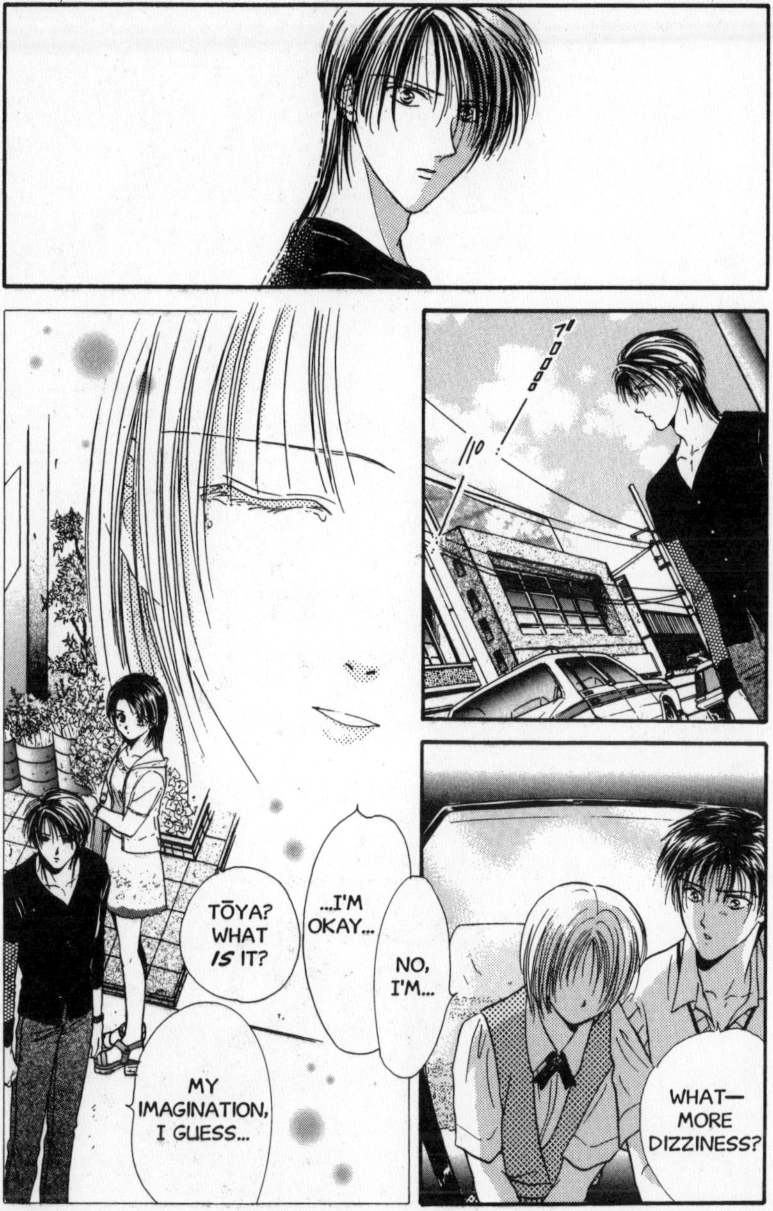
WHAT— MORE DIZZINESS?
...I'M OKAY...
NO, I'M...
TŌYA? WHAT *IS* IT?
MY IMAGINATION, I GUESS...

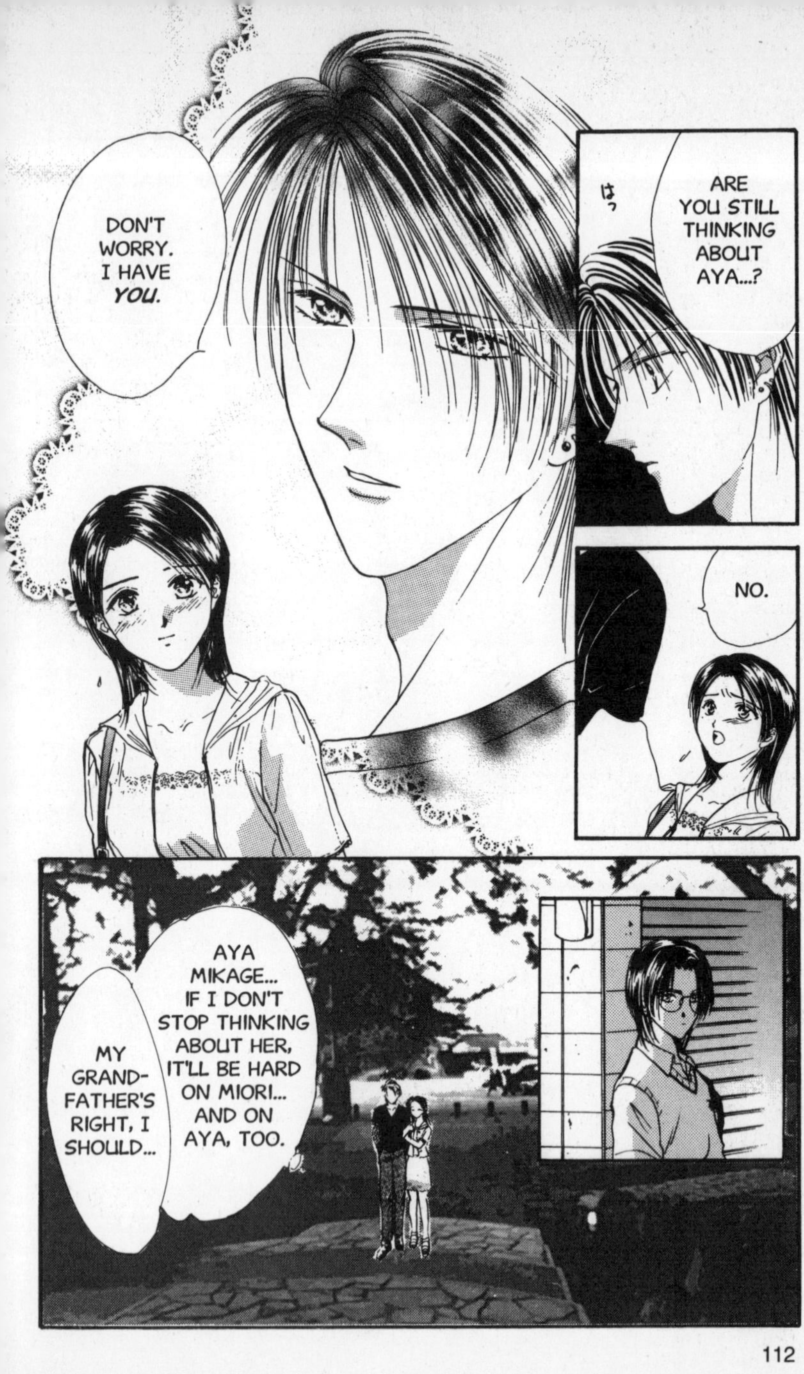
ARE YOU STILL THINKING ABOUT AYA...?
はっ
NO.
DON'T WORRY. I HAVE *YOU*.
AYA MIKAGE... IF I DON'T STOP THINKING ABOUT HER, IT'LL BE HARD ON MIORI... AND ON AYA, TOO.
MY GRANDFATHER'S RIGHT, I SHOULD...

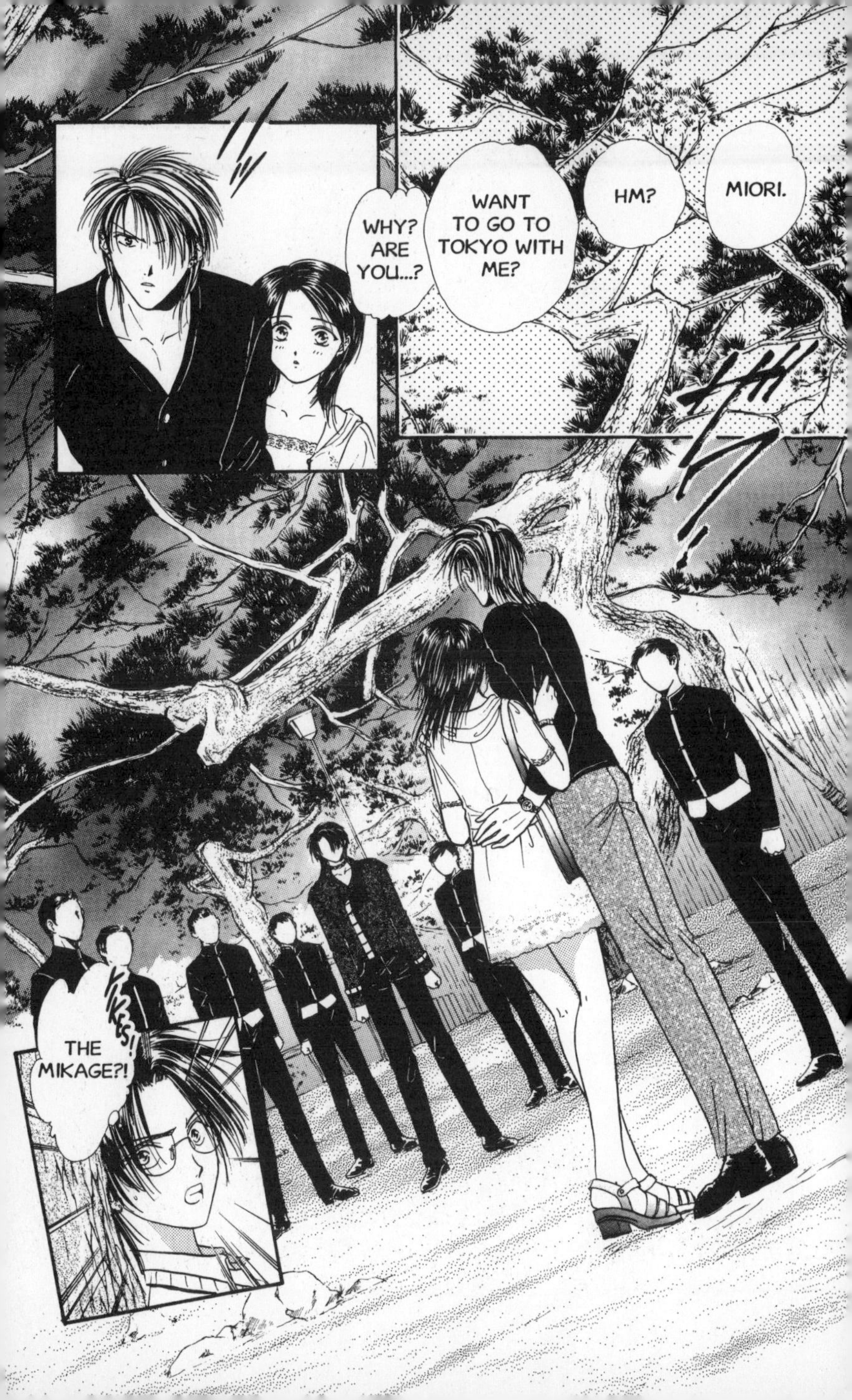
MIORI.
HM?
WANT TO GO TO TOKYO WITH ME?
WHY? ARE YOU...?
YIKES!
THE MIKAGE?!

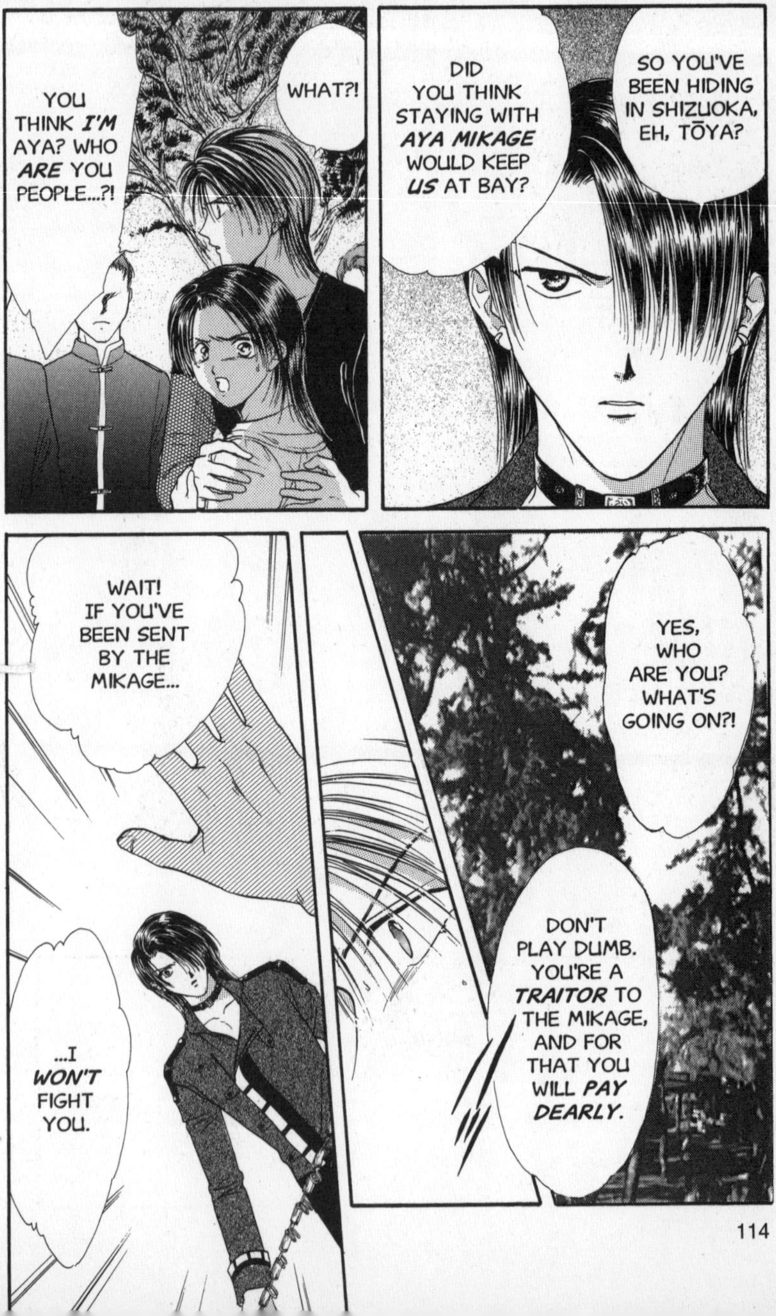
SO YOU'VE BEEN HIDING IN SHIZUOKA, EH, TŌYA?
DID YOU THINK STAYING WITH *AYA MIKAGE* WOULD KEEP *US* AT BAY?
WHAT?!
YOU THINK *I'M* AYA? WHO *ARE* YOU PEOPLE...?!
YES, WHO ARE YOU? WHAT'S GOING ON?!
DON'T PLAY DUMB. YOU'RE A *TRAITOR* TO THE MIKAGE, AND FOR THAT YOU WILL *PAY DEARLY*.
WAIT! IF YOU'VE BEEN SENT BY THE MIKAGE...
...I *WON'T* FIGHT YOU.

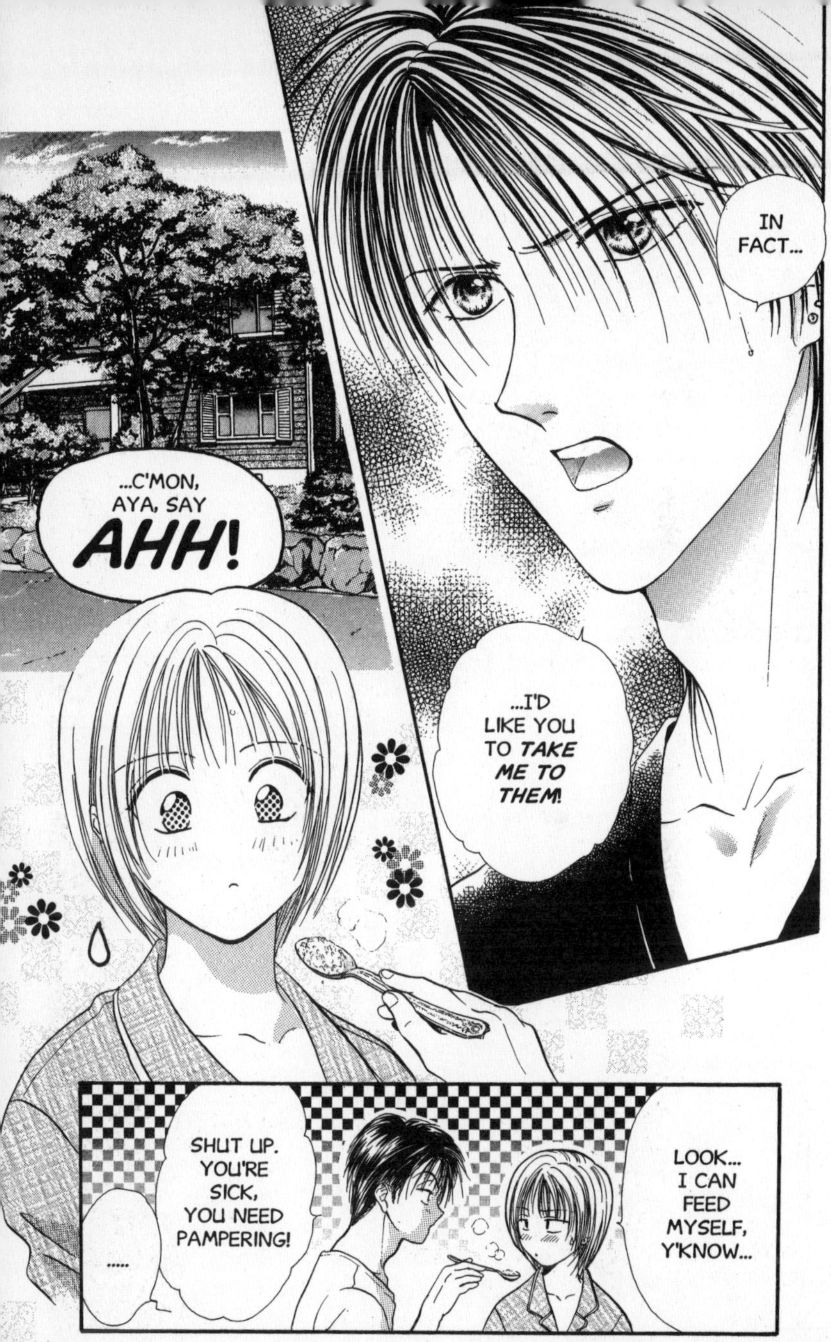
IN FACT...
...I'D LIKE YOU TO *TAKE ME TO THEM*!
...C'MON, AYA, SAY **AHH**!
LOOK... I CAN FEED MYSELF, Y'KNOW...
SHUT UP. YOU'RE SICK, YOU NEED PAMPERING!
......

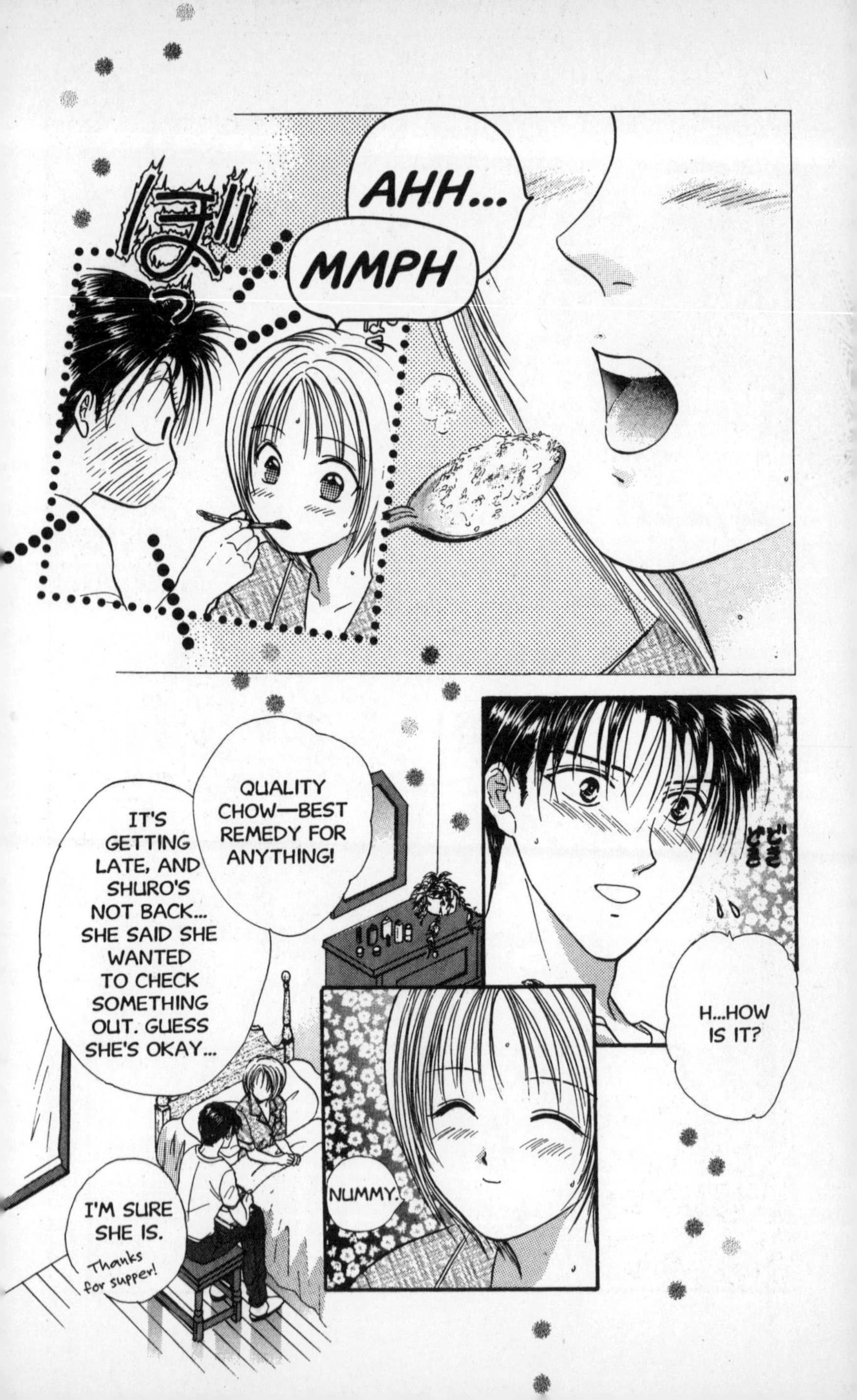
AHH...
MMPH
H...HOW IS IT?
NUMMY.
QUALITY CHOW—BEST REMEDY FOR ANYTHING!
IT'S GETTING LATE, AND SHURO'S NOT BACK... SHE SAID SHE WANTED TO CHECK SOMETHING OUT. GUESS SHE'S OKAY...
I'M SURE SHE IS.
Thanks for supper!

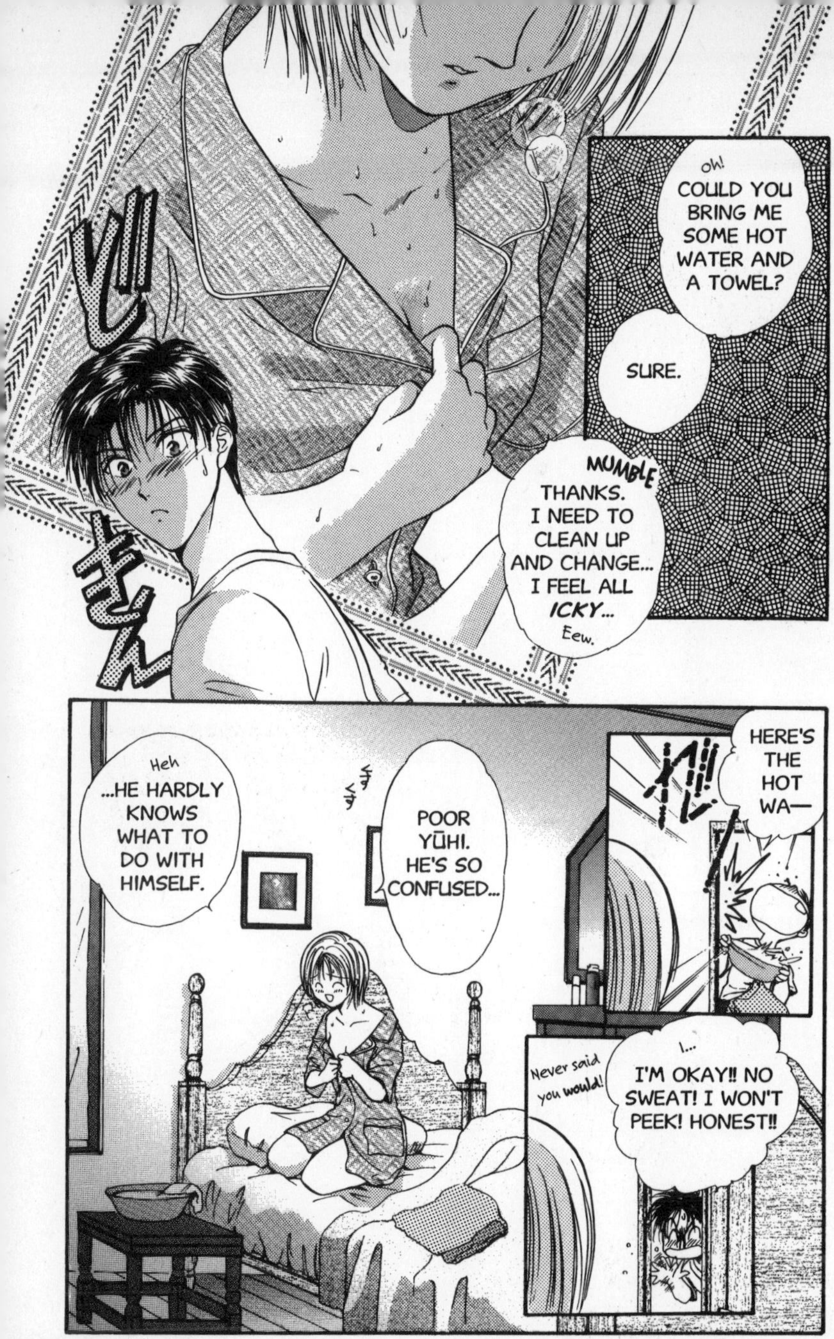
oh!
COULD YOU BRING ME SOME HOT WATER AND A TOWEL?
SURE.
MUMBLE
THANKS. I NEED TO CLEAN UP AND CHANGE... I FEEL ALL *ICKY*...
Eew.
HERE'S THE HOT WA—
I...
I'M OKAY!! NO SWEAT! I WON'T PEEK! HONEST!!
Never said you would!
POOR YŪHI. HE'S SO CONFUSED...
Heh
...HE HARDLY KNOWS WHAT TO DO WITH HIMSELF.

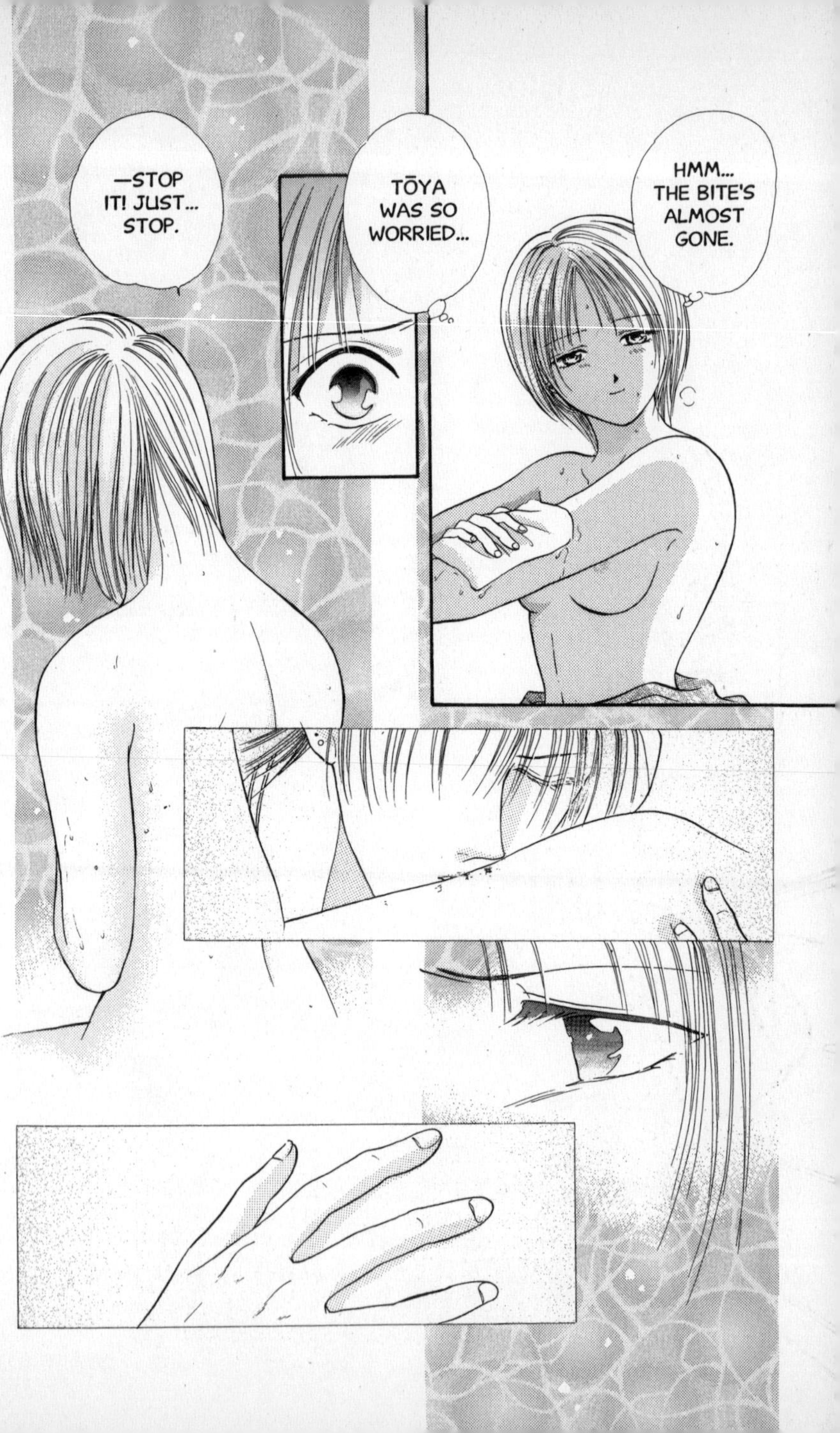
HMM... THE BITE'S ALMOST GONE.
TŌYA WAS SO WORRIED...
—STOP IT! JUST... STOP.

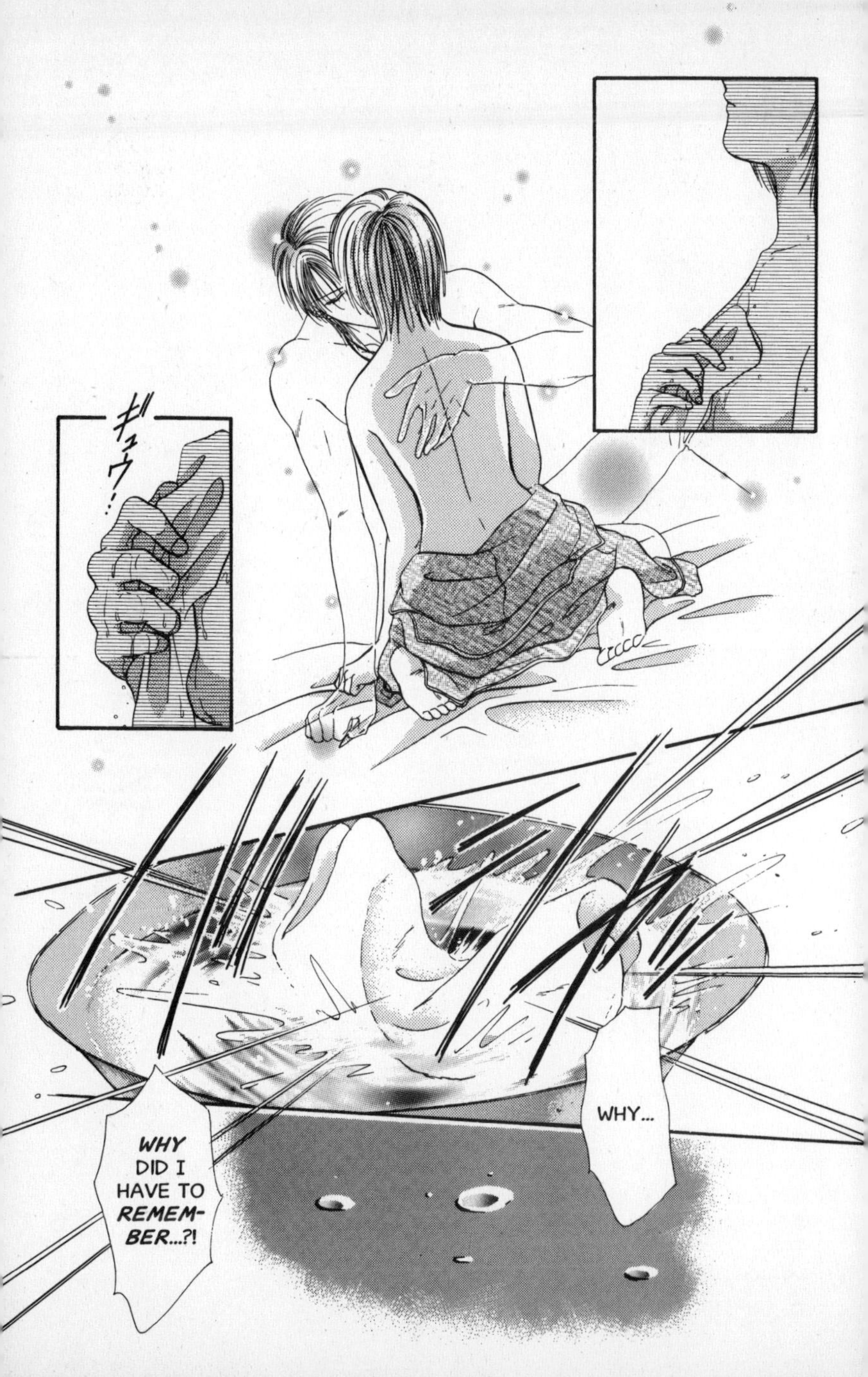
ギュウ!!
WHY...
WHY DID I HAVE TO *REMEMBER*...?!

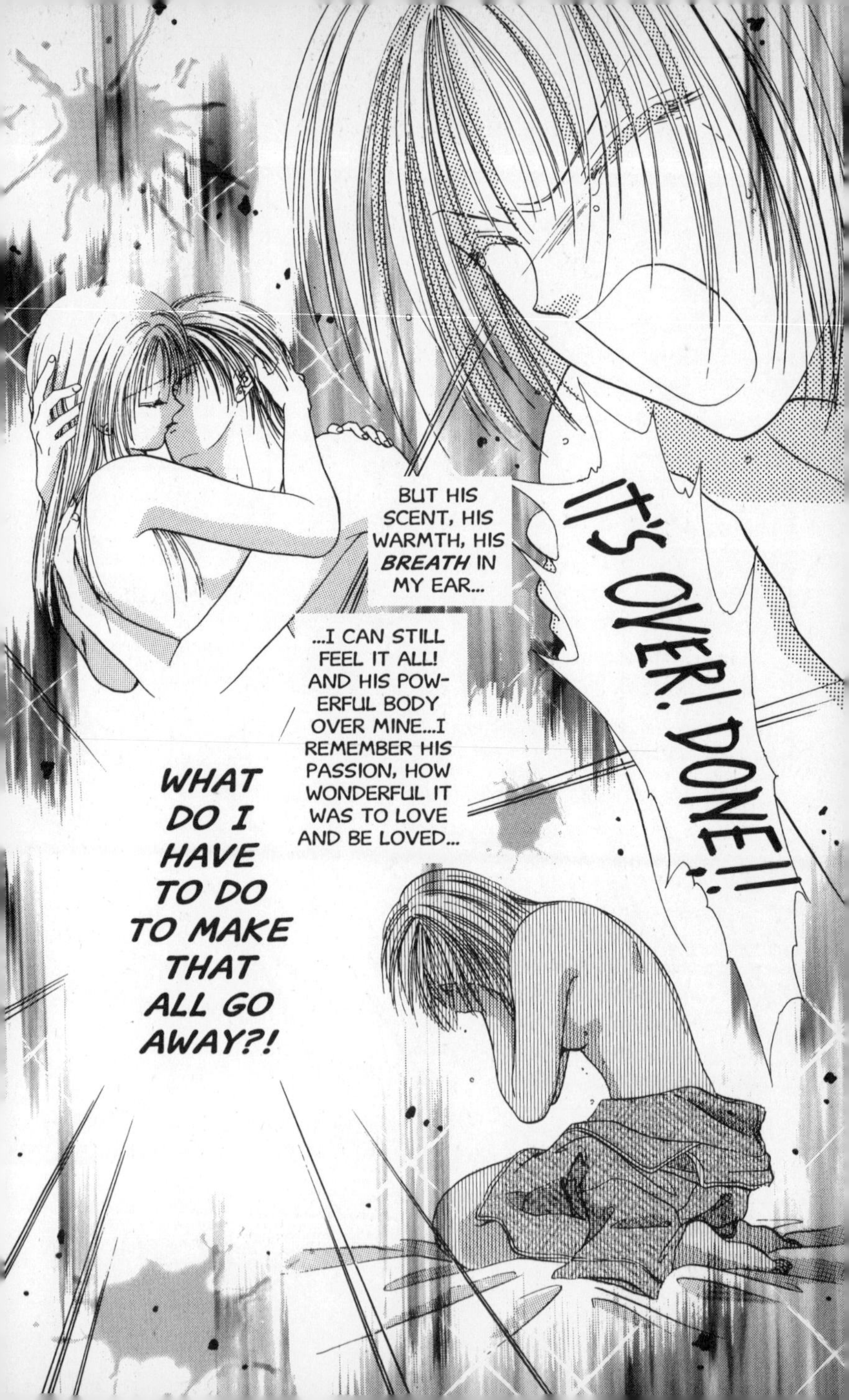
IT'S OVER! DONE!!
BUT HIS SCENT, HIS WARMTH, HIS *BREATH* IN MY EAR...
...I CAN STILL FEEL IT ALL! AND HIS POW-ERFUL BODY OVER MINE...I REMEMBER HIS PASSION, HOW WONDERFUL IT WAS TO LOVE AND BE LOVED...
WHAT DO I HAVE TO DO TO MAKE THAT ALL GO AWAY?!

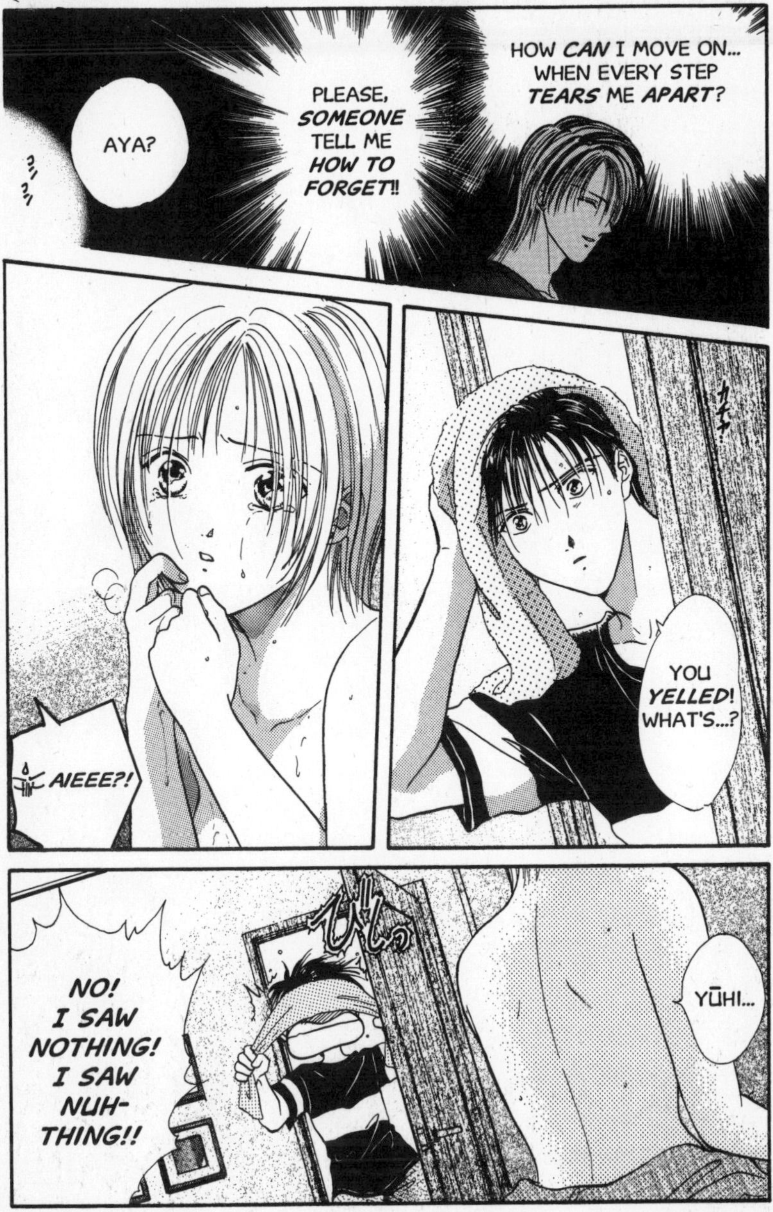
HOW CAN I MOVE ON... WHEN EVERY STEP TEARS ME APART?
PLEASE, SOMEONE TELL ME HOW TO FORGET!!
AYA?
YOU YELLED! WHAT'S...?
AIEEE?!
YŪHI...
NO! I SAW NOTHING! I SAW NUH-THING!!

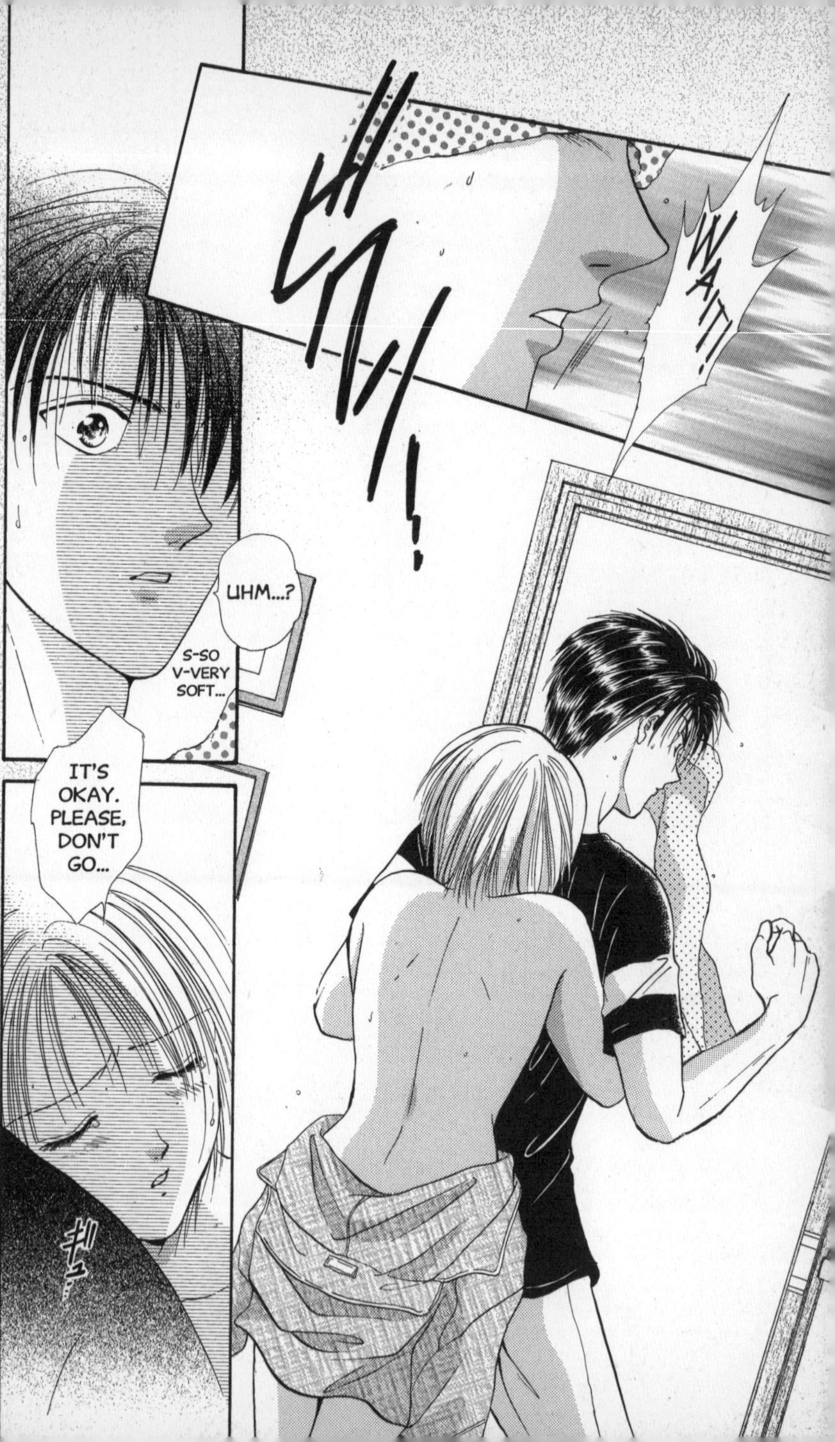
WAIT!!
UHM...?
S-SO V-VERY SOFT...
IT'S OKAY. PLEASE, DON'T GO...

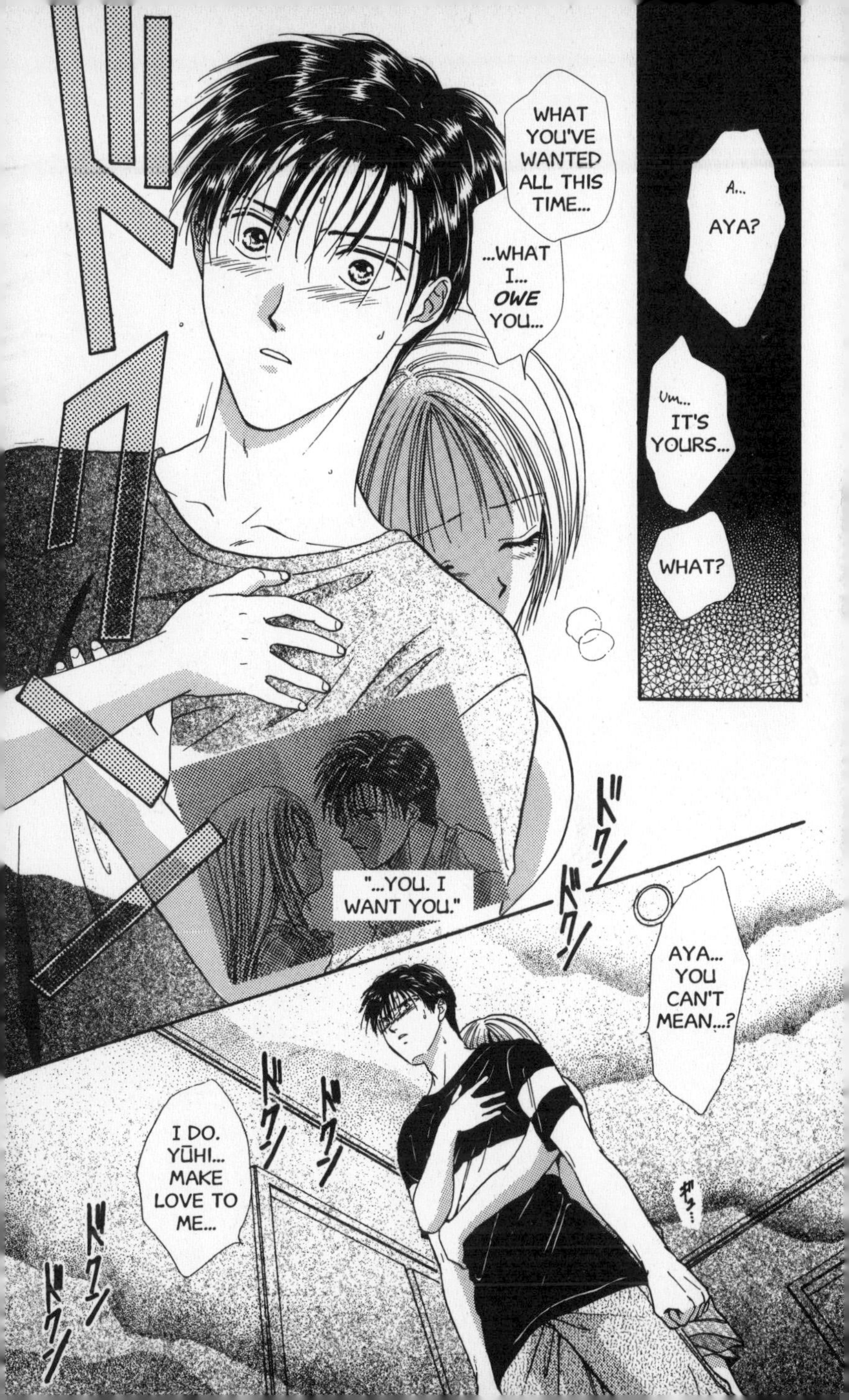
A... AYA?
Um... IT'S YOURS...
WHAT?
WHAT YOU'VE WANTED ALL THIS TIME...
...WHAT I... OWE YOU...
"...YOU. I WANT YOU."
AYA... YOU CAN'T MEAN...?
I DO. YŪHI... MAKE LOVE TO ME...

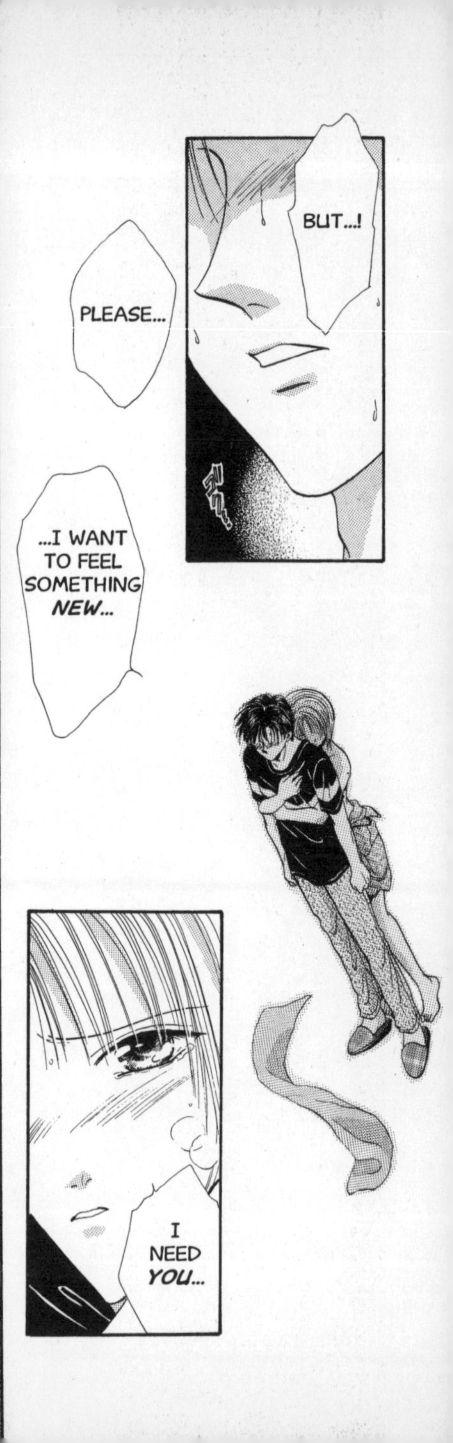
BUT...!
PLEASE...
...I WANT TO FEEL SOMETHING *NEW*...
I NEED *YOU*...
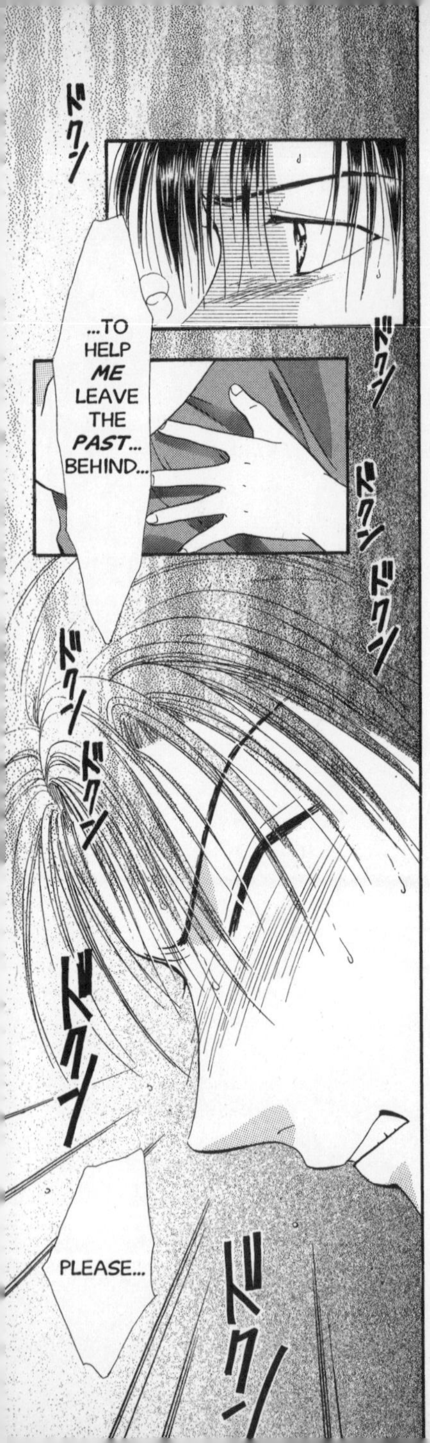
...TO HELP *ME* LEAVE THE *PAST*... BEHIND...
PLEASE...

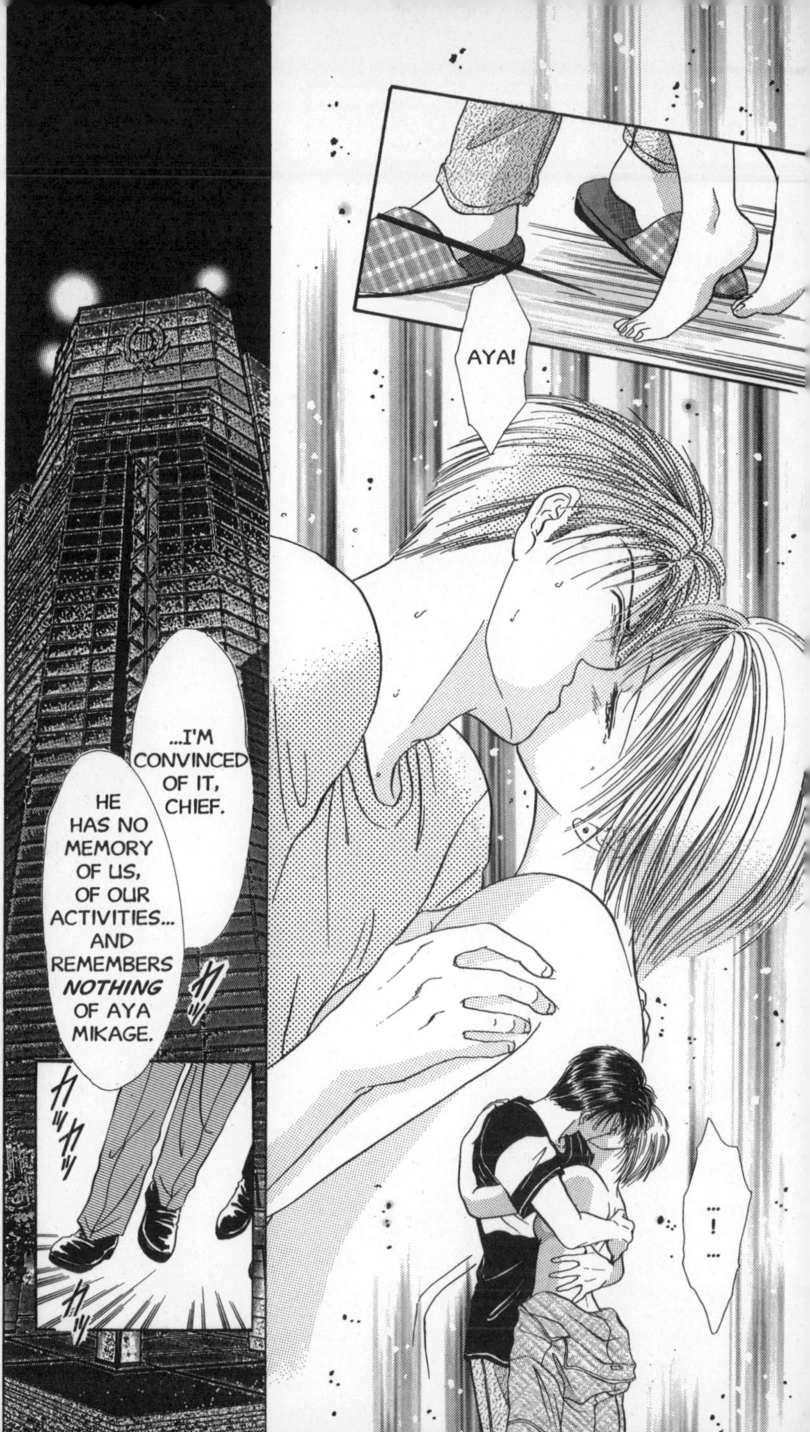
AYA!
...!...
...I'M CONVINCED OF IT, CHIEF.
HE HAS NO MEMORY OF US, OF OUR ACTIVITIES... AND REMEMBERS *NOTHING* OF AYA MIKAGE.

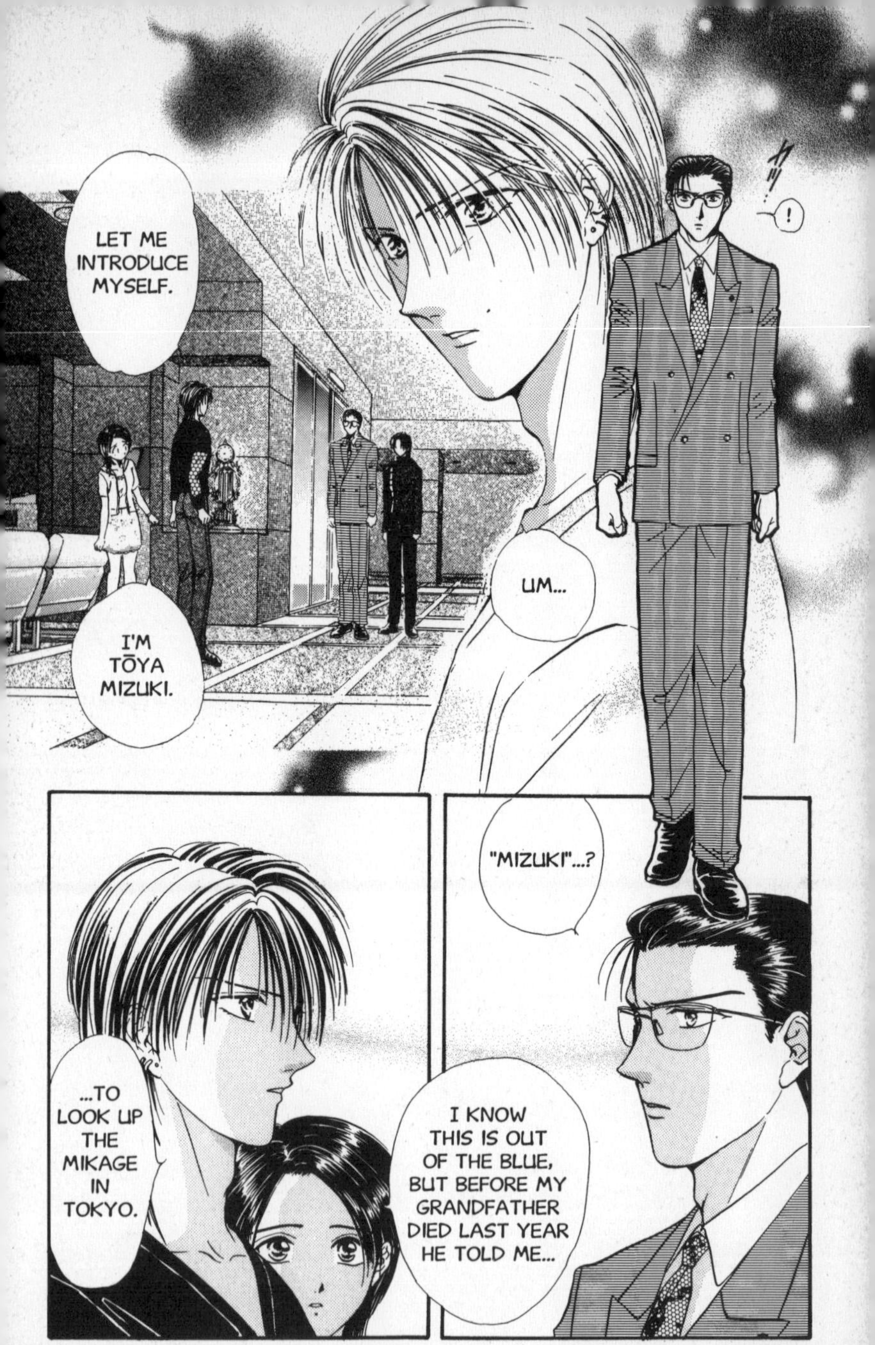
!
LET ME INTRODUCE MYSELF.
UM...
I'M TŌYA MIZUKI.
"MIZUKI"...?
I KNOW THIS IS OUT OF THE BLUE, BUT BEFORE MY GRANDFATHER DIED LAST YEAR HE TOLD ME...
...TO LOOK UP THE MIKAGE IN TOKYO.

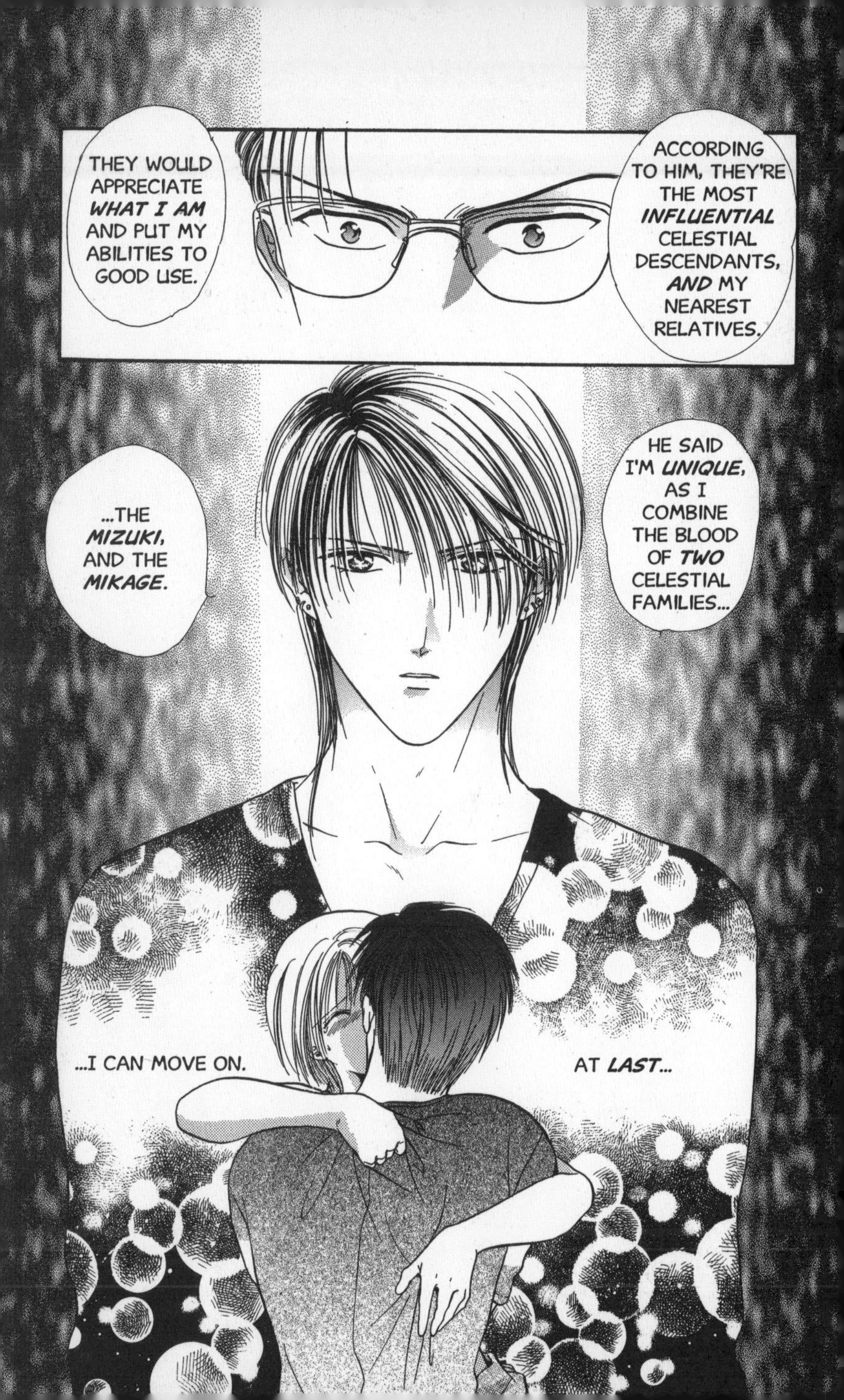
ACCORDING TO HIM, THEY'RE THE MOST *INFLUENTIAL* CELESTIAL DESCENDANTS, *AND* MY NEAREST RELATIVES.
THEY WOULD APPRECIATE *WHAT I AM* AND PUT MY ABILITIES TO GOOD USE.
HE SAID I'M *UNIQUE*, AS I COMBINE THE BLOOD OF *TWO* CELESTIAL FAMILIES...
...THE *MIZUKI*, AND THE *MIKAGE*.
AT *LAST*...
...I CAN MOVE ON.

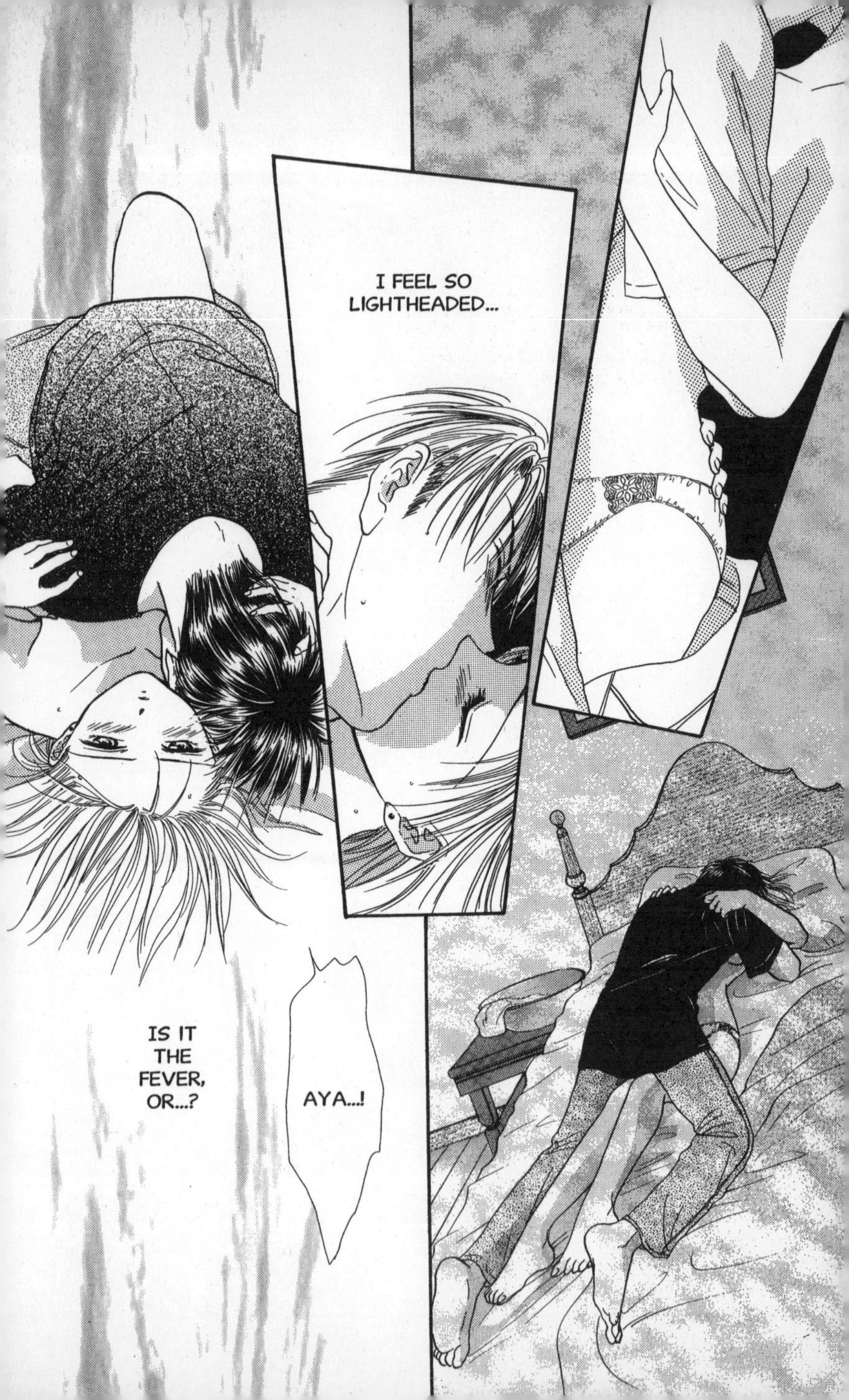
I FEEL SO LIGHTHEADED...
AYA...!
IS IT THE FEVER, OR...?

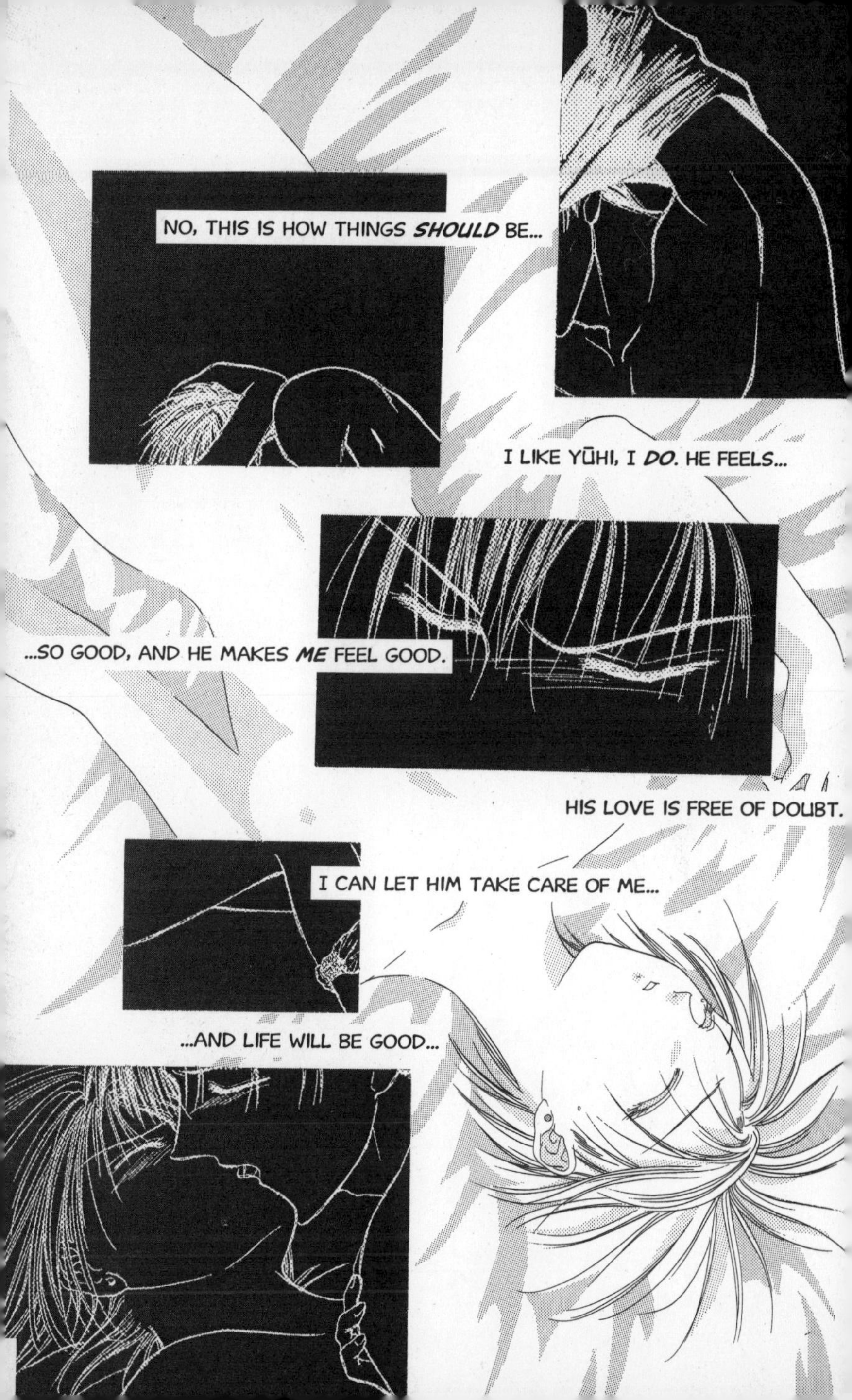
NO, THIS IS HOW THINGS *SHOULD* BE...
I LIKE YŪHI, I *DO*. HE FEELS...
...SO GOOD, AND HE MAKES *ME* FEEL GOOD.
HIS LOVE IS FREE OF DOUBT.
I CAN LET HIM TAKE CARE OF ME...
...AND LIFE WILL BE GOOD...

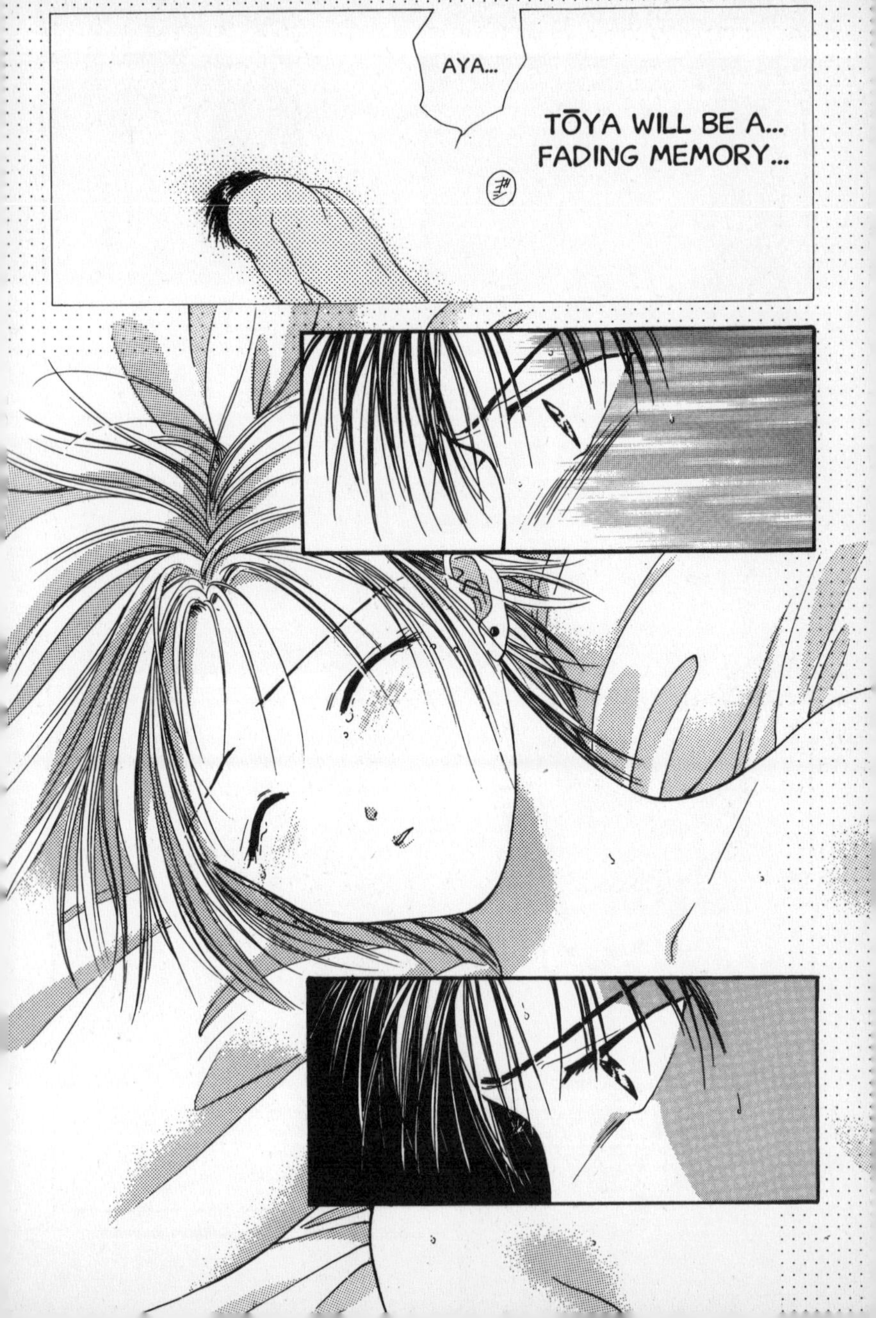
TŌYA WILL BE A...
FADING MEMORY...
AYA...

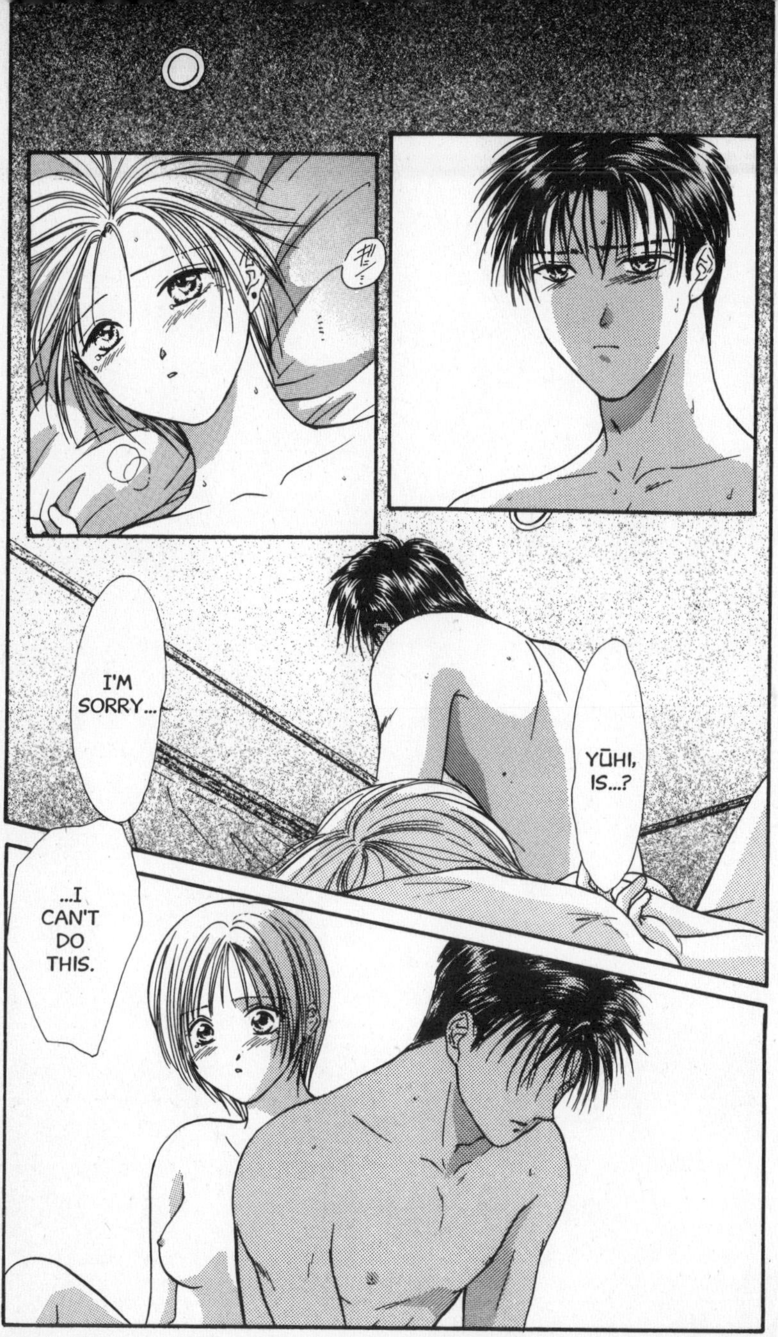
YŪHI, IS...?
I'M SORRY...
...I CAN'T DO THIS.

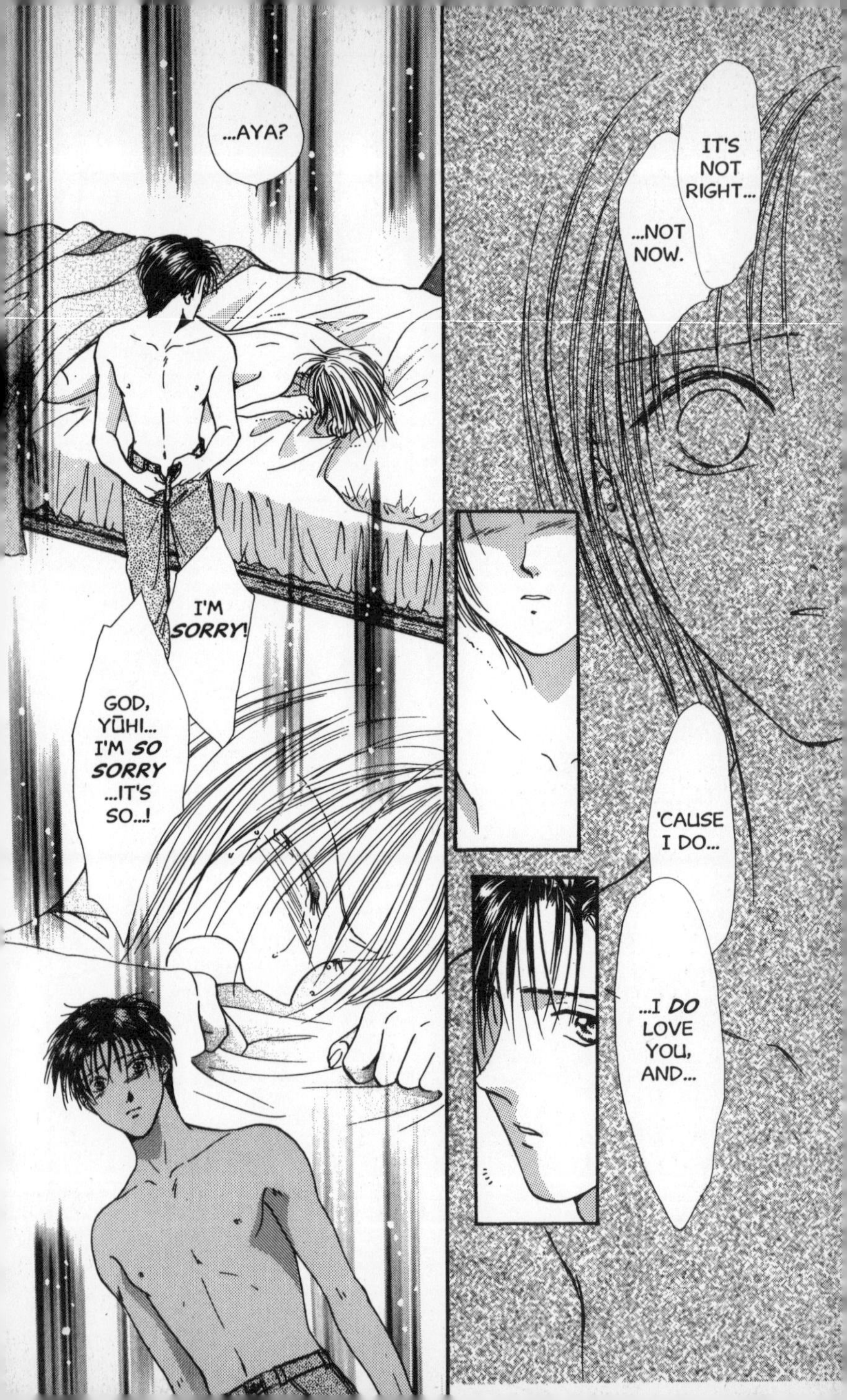
IT'S NOT RIGHT...
...NOT NOW.
'CAUSE I DO...
...I *DO* LOVE YOU, AND...
...AYA?
I'M *SORRY*!
GOD, YŪHI... I'M *SO SORRY* ...IT'S SO...!

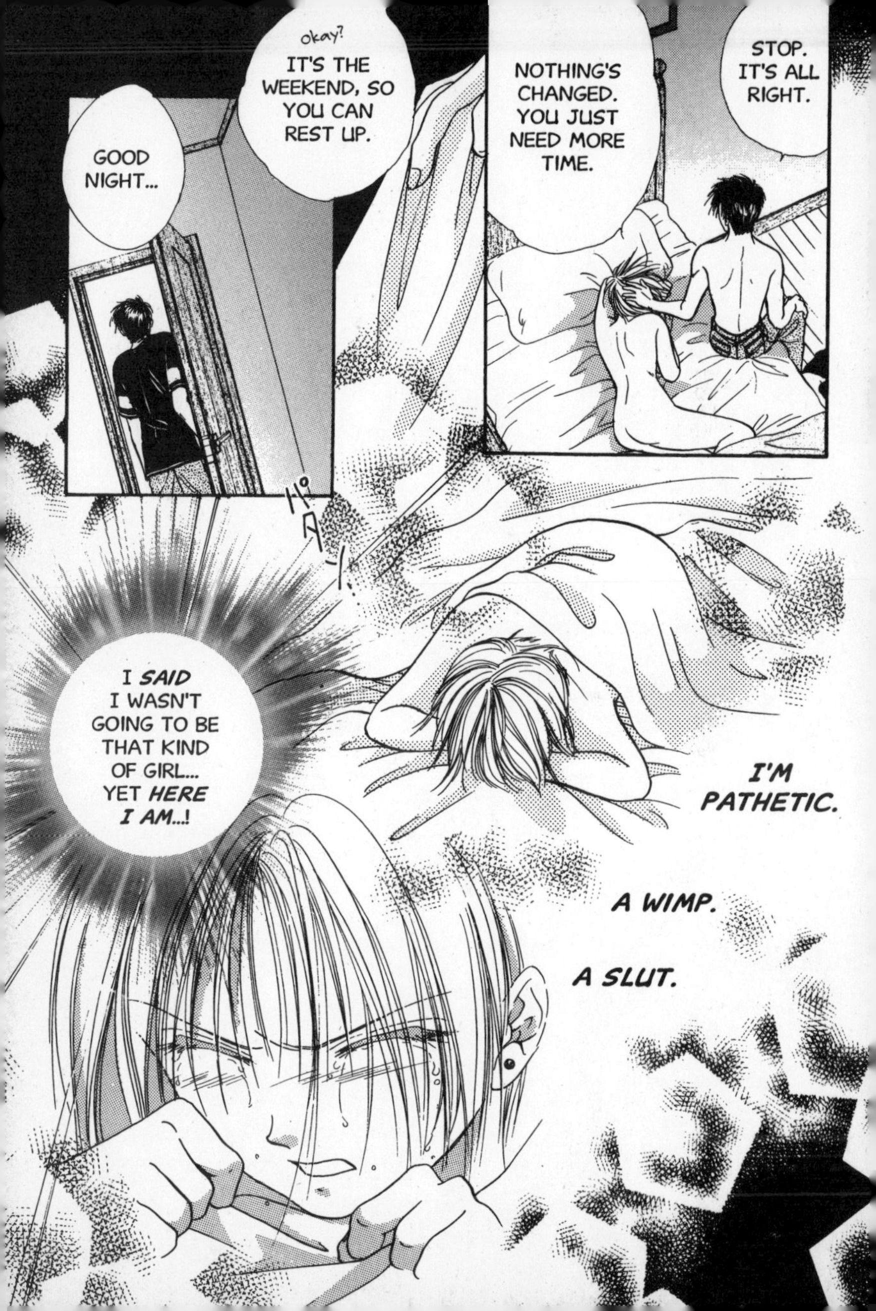
STOP. IT'S ALL RIGHT.
NOTHING'S CHANGED. YOU JUST NEED MORE TIME.
okay?
IT'S THE WEEKEND, SO YOU CAN REST UP.
GOOD NIGHT...
I'M PATHETIC.
A WIMP.
A SLUT.
I *SAID* I WASN'T GOING TO BE THAT KIND OF GIRL... YET *HERE I AM*...!

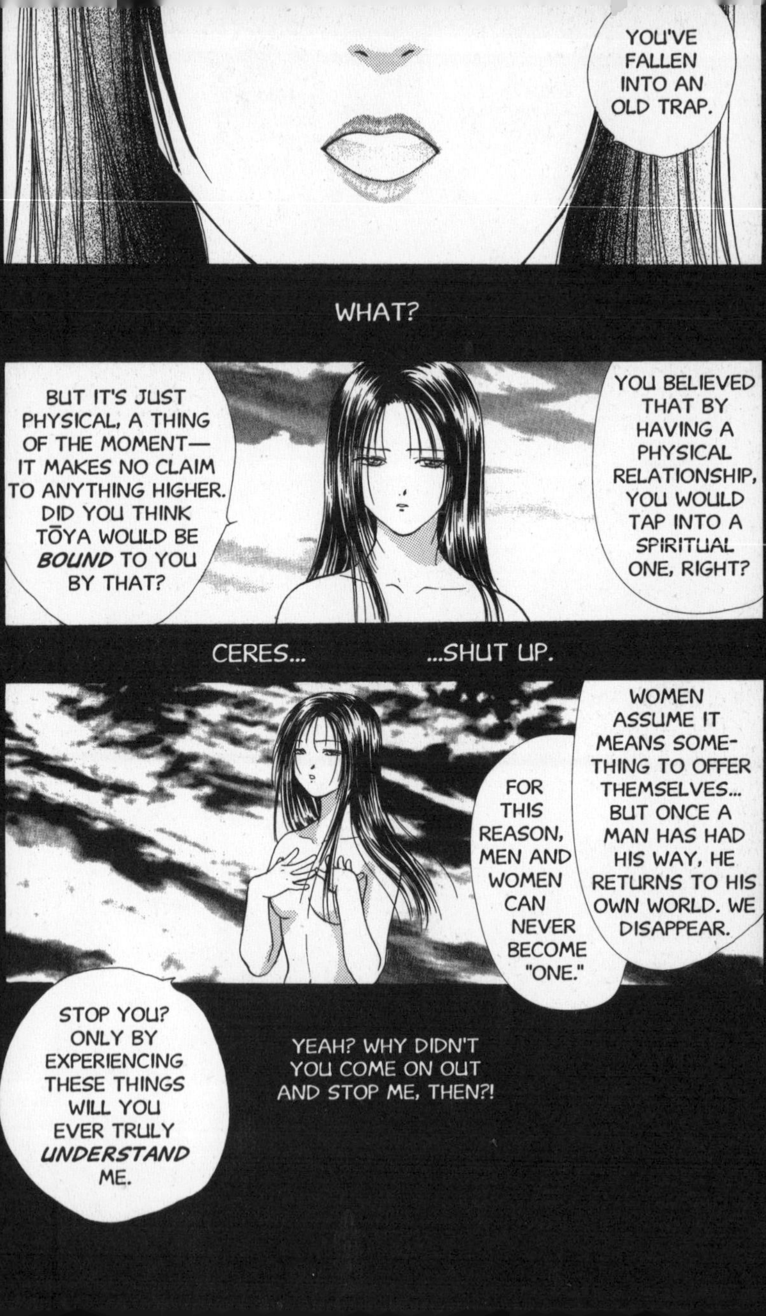
YOU'VE FALLEN INTO AN OLD TRAP.
WHAT?
YOU BELIEVED THAT BY HAVING A PHYSICAL RELATIONSHIP, YOU WOULD TAP INTO A SPIRITUAL ONE, RIGHT?
BUT IT'S JUST PHYSICAL, A THING OF THE MOMENT— IT MAKES NO CLAIM TO ANYTHING HIGHER. DID YOU THINK TŌYA WOULD BE *BOUND* TO YOU BY THAT?
CERES...
...SHUT UP.
WOMEN ASSUME IT MEANS SOME-THING TO OFFER THEMSELVES... BUT ONCE A MAN HAS HAD HIS WAY, HE RETURNS TO HIS OWN WORLD. WE DISAPPEAR.
FOR THIS REASON, MEN AND WOMEN CAN NEVER BECOME "ONE."
YEAH? WHY DIDN'T YOU COME ON OUT AND STOP ME, THEN?!
STOP YOU? ONLY BY EXPERIENCING THESE THINGS WILL YOU EVER TRULY *UNDERSTAND* ME.

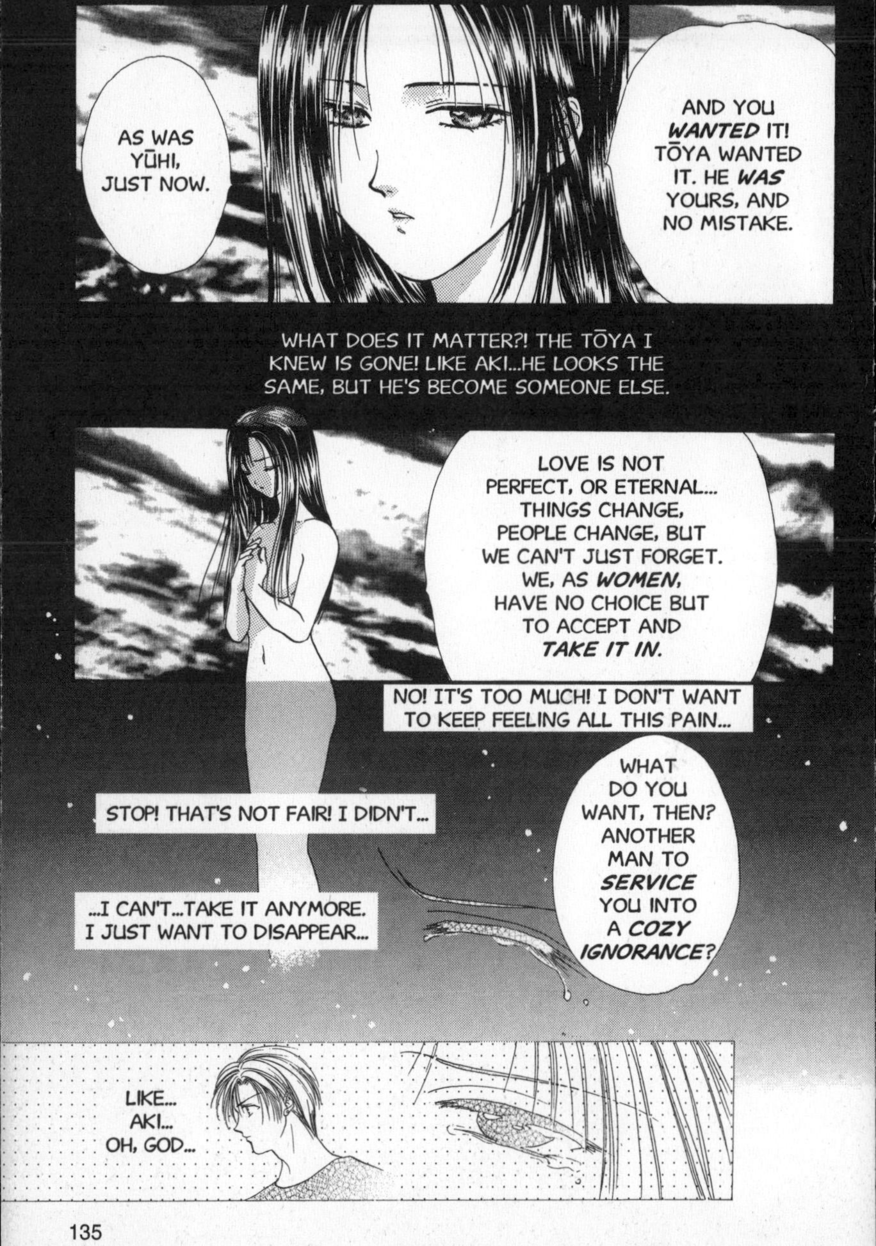
AND YOU WANTED IT! TŌYA WANTED IT. HE WAS YOURS, AND NO MISTAKE.
AS WAS YŪHI, JUST NOW.
WHAT DOES IT MATTER?! THE TŌYA I KNEW IS GONE! LIKE AKI...HE LOOKS THE SAME, BUT HE'S BECOME SOMEONE ELSE.
LOVE IS NOT PERFECT, OR ETERNAL... THINGS CHANGE, PEOPLE CHANGE, BUT WE CAN'T JUST FORGET. WE, AS WOMEN, HAVE NO CHOICE BUT TO ACCEPT AND TAKE IT IN.
NO! IT'S TOO MUCH! I DON'T WANT TO KEEP FEELING ALL THIS PAIN...
WHAT DO YOU WANT, THEN? ANOTHER MAN TO SERVICE YOU INTO A COZY IGNORANCE?
STOP! THAT'S NOT FAIR! I DIDN'T...
...I CAN'T...TAKE IT ANYMORE. I JUST WANT TO DISAPPEAR...
LIKE... AKI... OH, GOD...

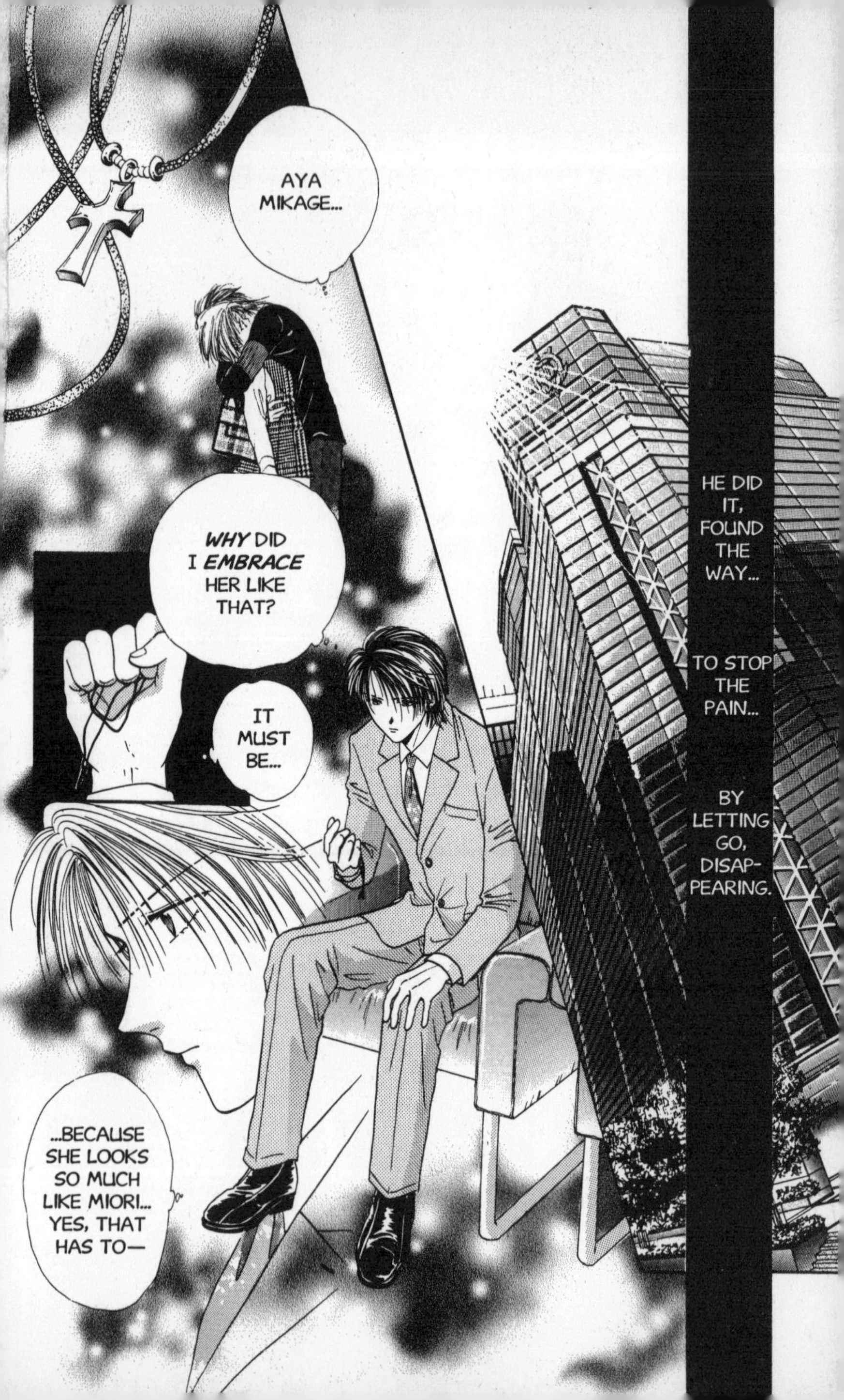
HE DID IT, FOUND THE WAY...
TO STOP THE PAIN...
BY LETTING GO, DISAPPEARING.
AYA MIKAGE...
WHY DID I EMBRACE HER LIKE THAT?
IT MUST BE...
...BECAUSE SHE LOOKS SO MUCH LIKE MIORI... YES, THAT HAS TO—

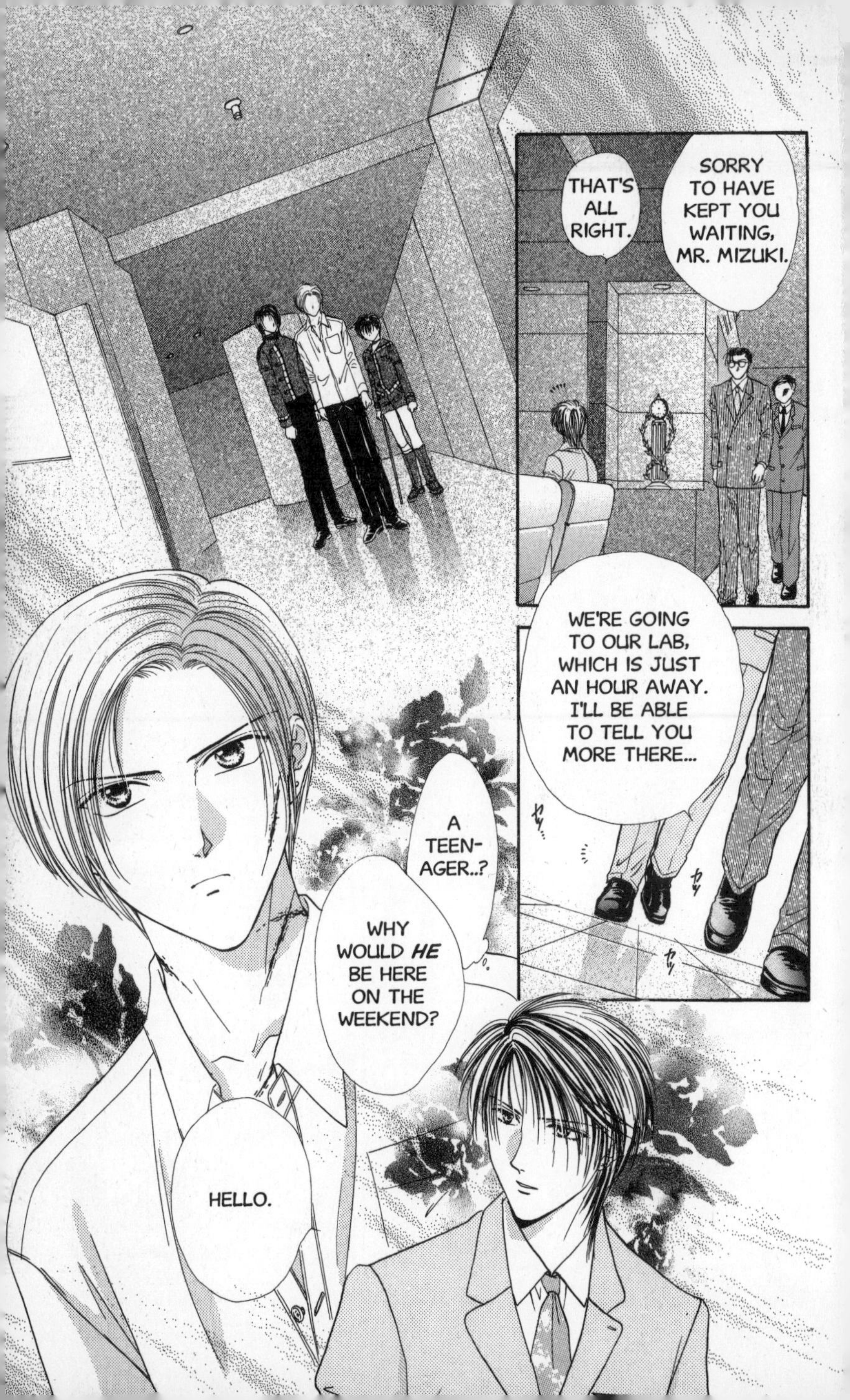
SORRY TO HAVE KEPT YOU WAITING, MR. MIZUKI.
THAT'S ALL RIGHT.
WE'RE GOING TO OUR LAB, WHICH IS JUST AN HOUR AWAY. I'LL BE ABLE TO TELL YOU MORE THERE...
A TEEN-AGER..?
WHY WOULD *HE* BE HERE ON THE WEEKEND?
HELLO.

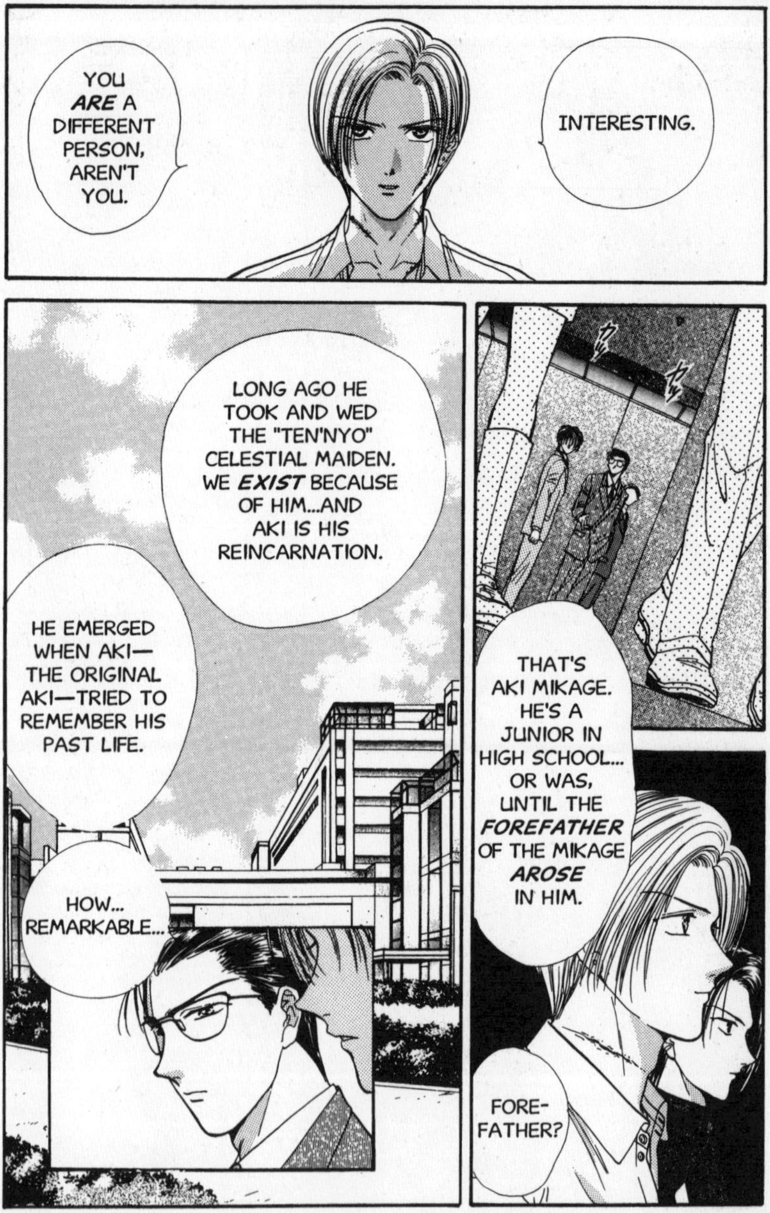
INTERESTING.
YOU *ARE* A DIFFERENT PERSON, AREN'T YOU.
THAT'S AKI MIKAGE. HE'S A JUNIOR IN HIGH SCHOOL... OR WAS, UNTIL THE *FOREFATHER* OF THE MIKAGE *AROSE* IN HIM.
FORE-FATHER?
LONG AGO HE TOOK AND WED THE "TEN'NYO" CELESTIAL MAIDEN. WE *EXIST* BECAUSE OF HIM...AND AKI IS HIS REINCARNATION.
HE EMERGED WHEN AKI—THE ORIGINAL AKI—TRIED TO REMEMBER HIS PAST LIFE.
HOW... REMARKABLE...

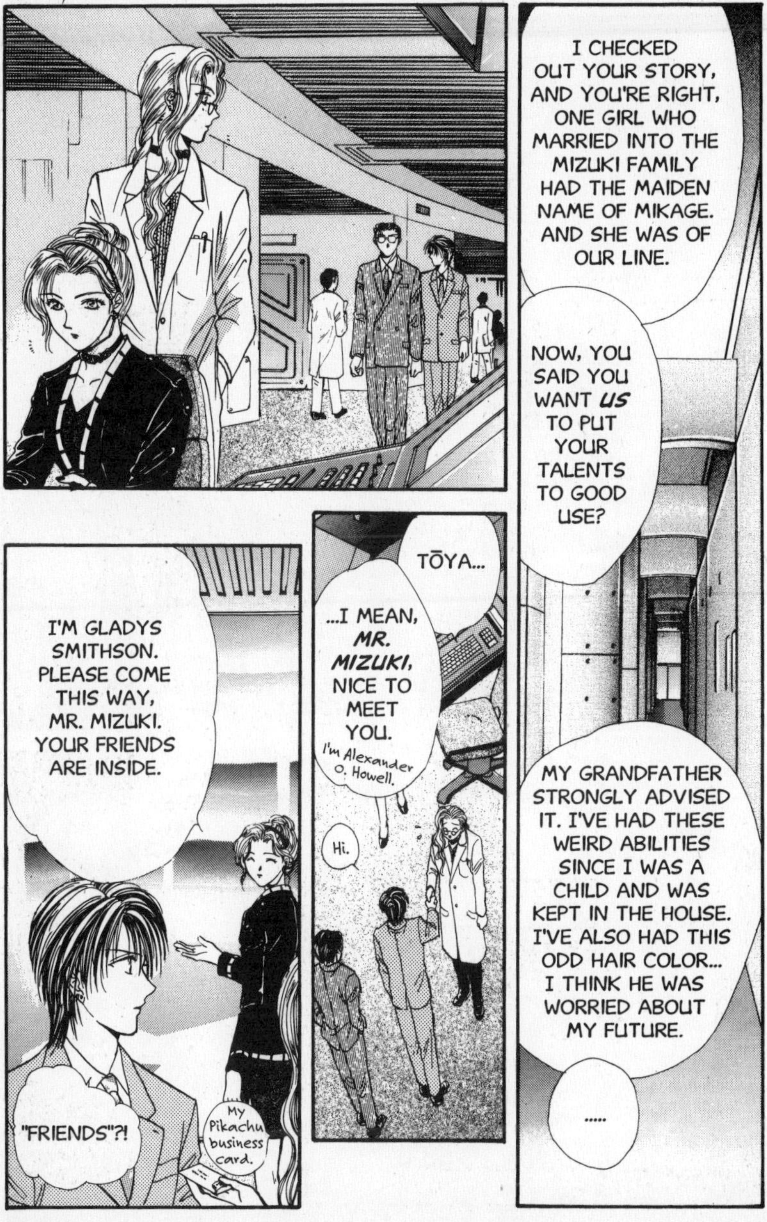
I CHECKED OUT YOUR STORY, AND YOU'RE RIGHT, ONE GIRL WHO MARRIED INTO THE MIZUKI FAMILY HAD THE MAIDEN NAME OF MIKAGE. AND SHE WAS OF OUR LINE.
NOW, YOU SAID YOU WANT *US* TO PUT YOUR TALENTS TO GOOD USE?
MY GRANDFATHER STRONGLY ADVISED IT. I'VE HAD THESE WEIRD ABILITIES SINCE I WAS A CHILD AND WAS KEPT IN THE HOUSE. I'VE ALSO HAD THIS ODD HAIR COLOR... I THINK HE WAS WORRIED ABOUT MY FUTURE.
.....
TŌYA...
...I MEAN, ***MR. MIZUKI***, NICE TO MEET YOU.
I'm Alexander O. Howell.
Hi.
I'M GLADYS SMITHSON. PLEASE COME THIS WAY, MR. MIZUKI. YOUR FRIENDS ARE INSIDE.
"FRIENDS"?!
My Pikachu business card.

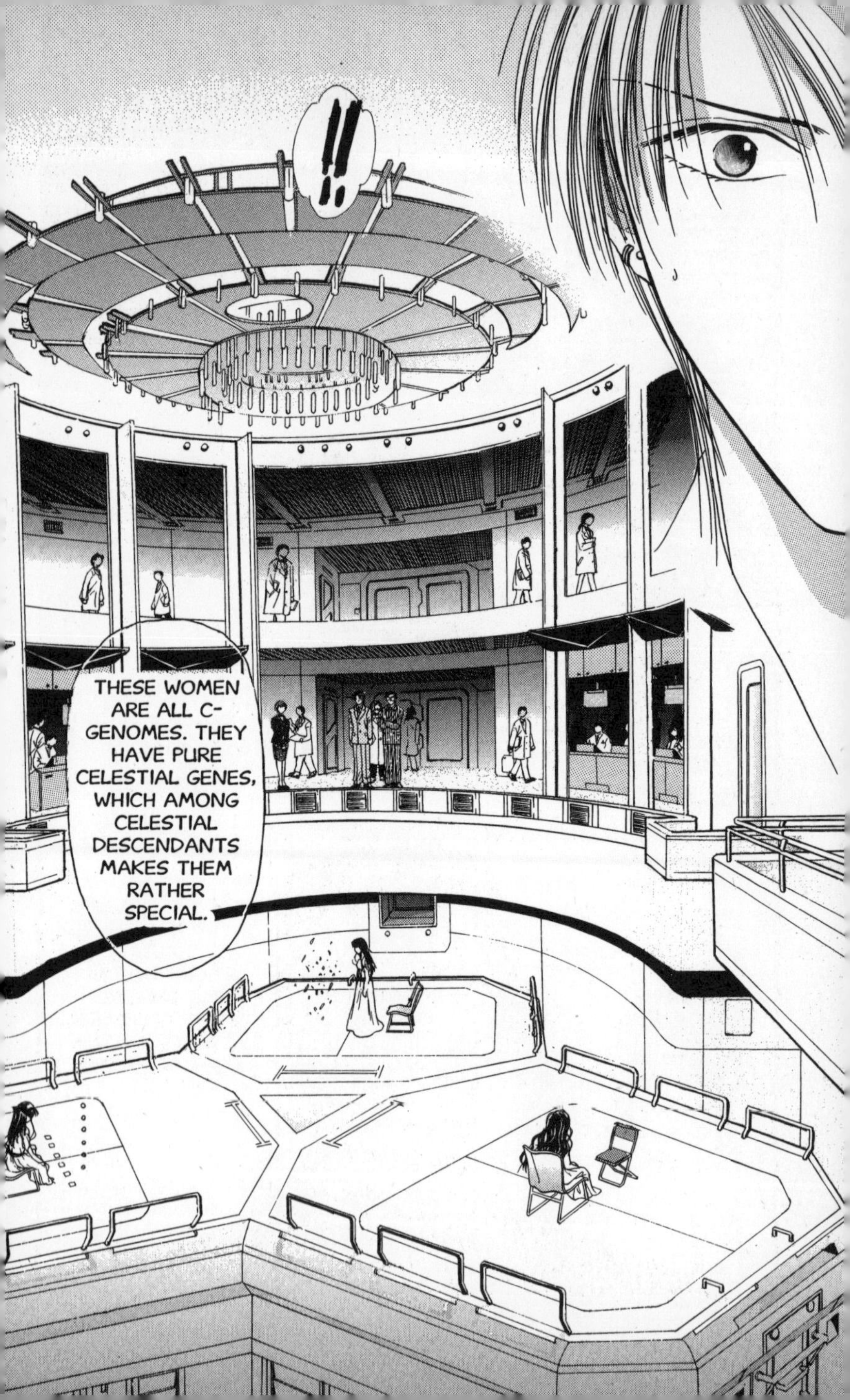
!!
THESE WOMEN ARE ALL C-GENOMES. THEY HAVE PURE CELESTIAL GENES, WHICH AMONG CELESTIAL DESCENDANTS MAKES THEM RATHER SPECIAL.

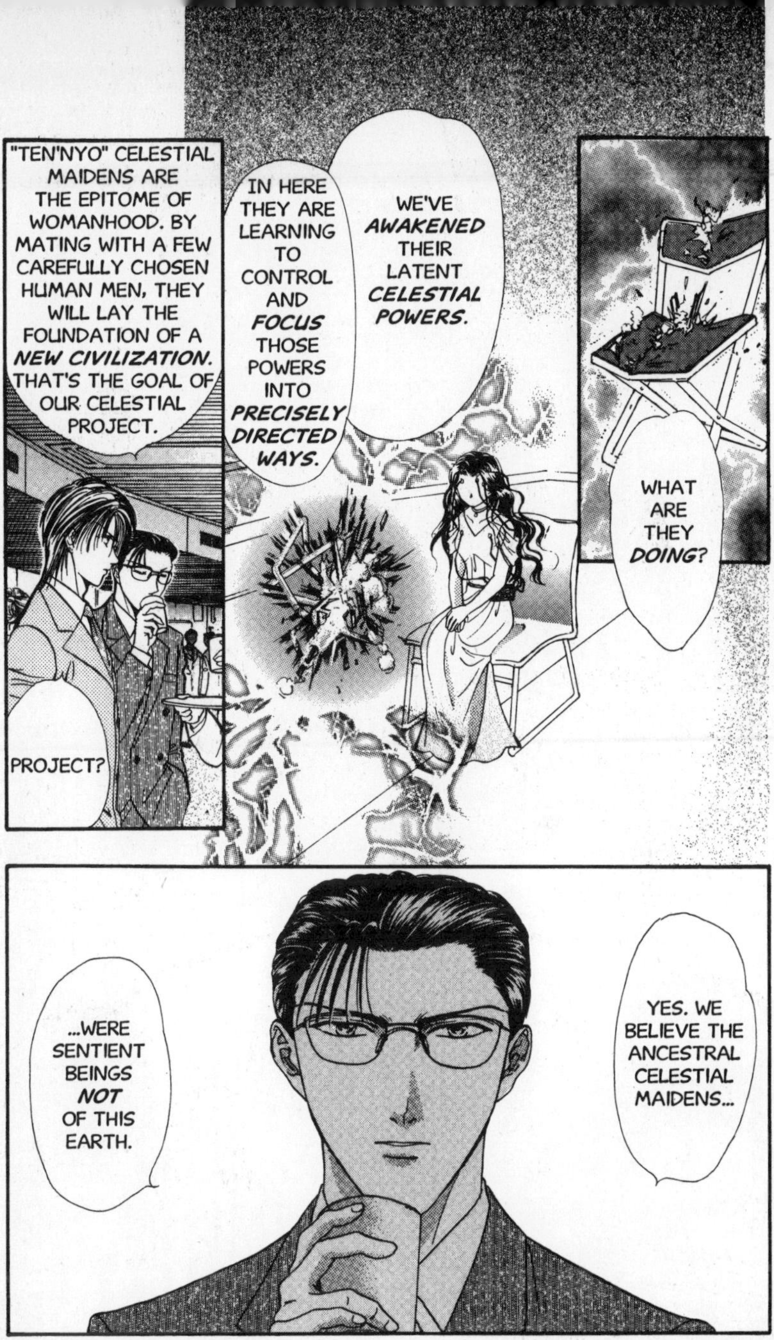
WHAT ARE THEY *DOING?*
WE'VE *AWAKENED* THEIR LATENT *CELESTIAL POWERS.*
IN HERE THEY ARE LEARNING TO CONTROL AND *FOCUS* THOSE POWERS INTO *PRECISELY DIRECTED WAYS.*
"TEN'NYO" CELESTIAL MAIDENS ARE THE EPITOME OF WOMANHOOD. BY MATING WITH A FEW CAREFULLY CHOSEN HUMAN MEN, THEY WILL LAY THE FOUNDATION OF A *NEW CIVILIZATION.* THAT'S THE GOAL OF OUR CELESTIAL PROJECT.
PROJECT?
YES. WE BELIEVE THE ANCESTRAL CELESTIAL MAIDENS...
...WERE SENTIENT BEINGS *NOT* OF THIS EARTH.

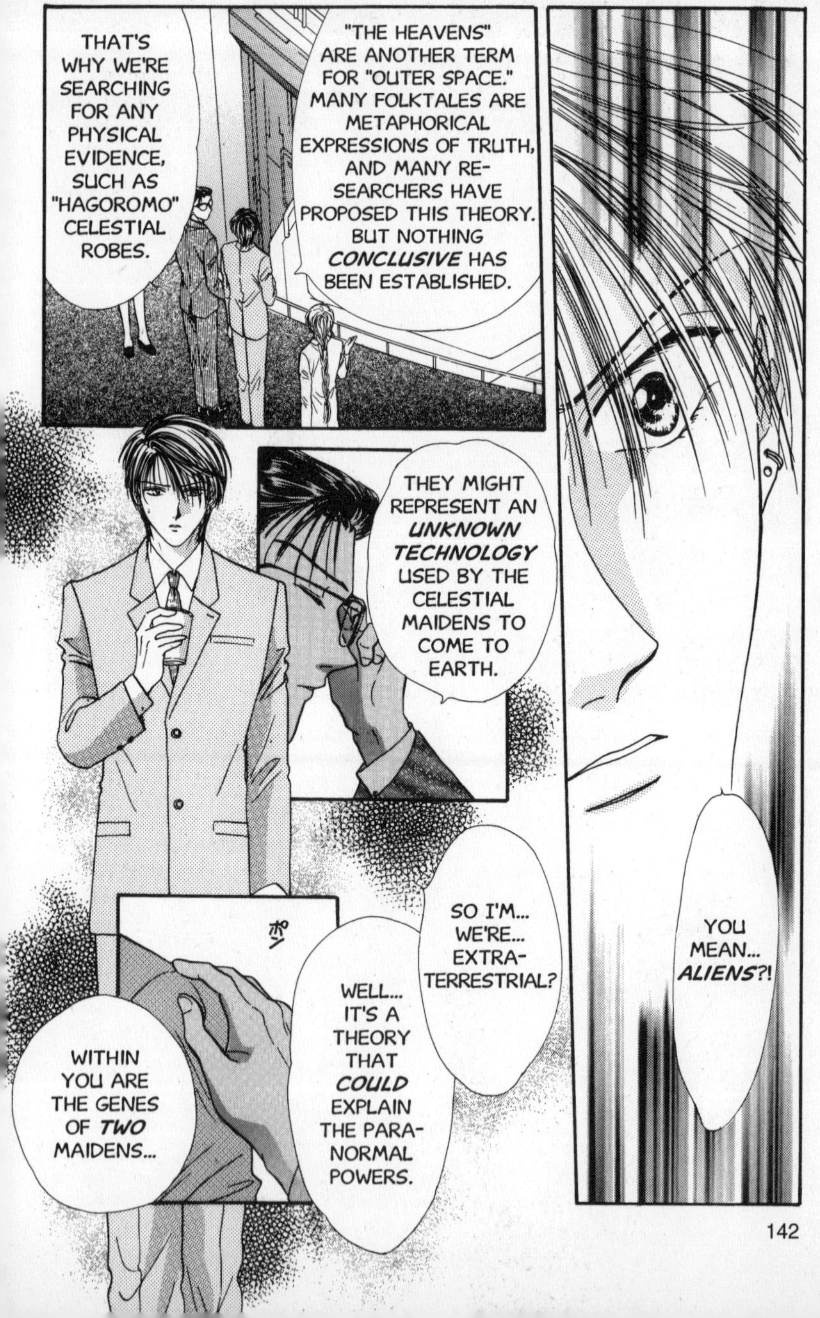
YOU MEAN... ALIENS?!
"THE HEAVENS" ARE ANOTHER TERM FOR "OUTER SPACE." MANY FOLKTALES ARE METAPHORICAL EXPRESSIONS OF TRUTH, AND MANY RE-SEARCHERS HAVE PROPOSED THIS THEORY. BUT NOTHING CONCLUSIVE HAS BEEN ESTABLISHED.
THAT'S WHY WE'RE SEARCHING FOR ANY PHYSICAL EVIDENCE, SUCH AS "HAGOROMO" CELESTIAL ROBES.
THEY MIGHT REPRESENT AN UNKNOWN TECHNOLOGY USED BY THE CELESTIAL MAIDENS TO COME TO EARTH.
SO I'M... WE'RE... EXTRA-TERRESTRIAL?
WELL... IT'S A THEORY THAT COULD EXPLAIN THE PARA-NORMAL POWERS.
ポン
WITHIN YOU ARE THE GENES OF TWO MAIDENS...

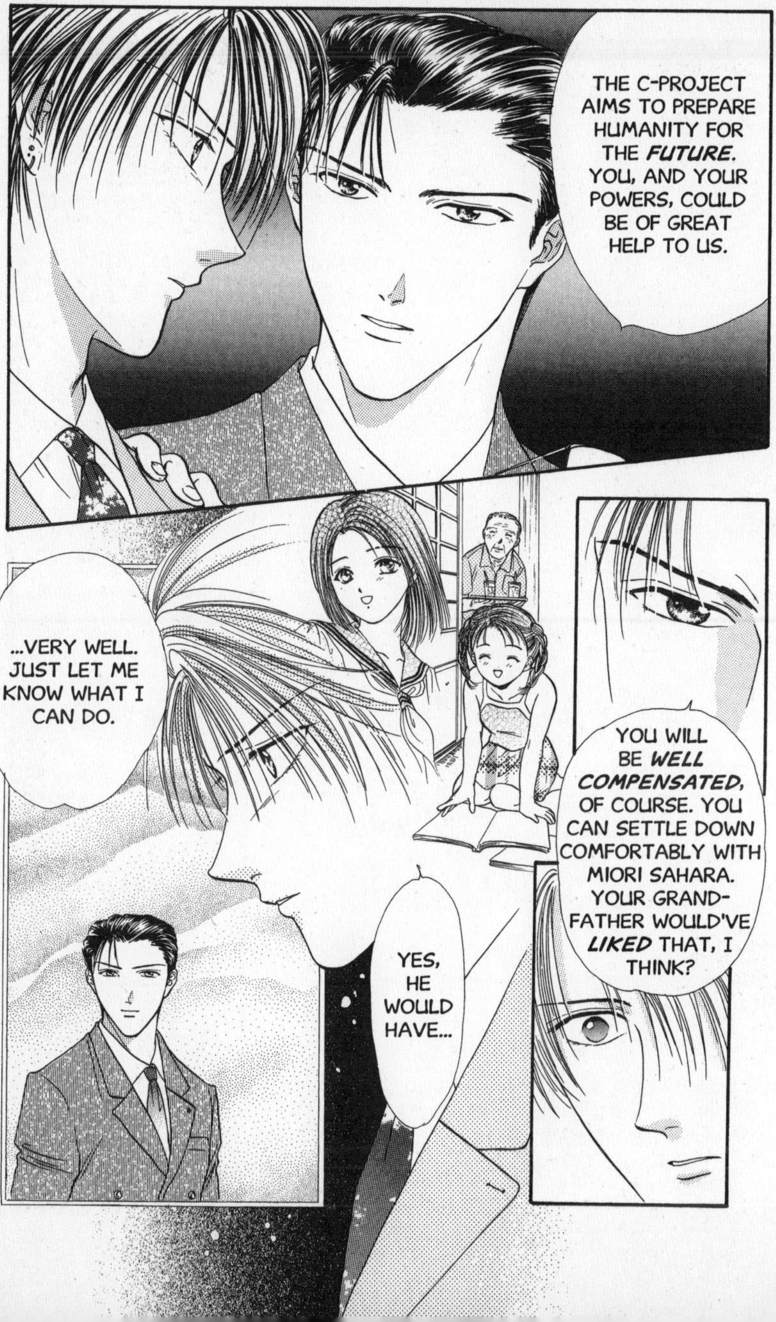
THE C-PROJECT AIMS TO PREPARE HUMANITY FOR THE *FUTURE*. YOU, AND YOUR POWERS, COULD BE OF GREAT HELP TO US.
YOU WILL BE ***WELL COMPENSATED***, OF COURSE. YOU CAN SETTLE DOWN COMFORTABLY WITH MIORI SAHARA. YOUR GRANDFATHER WOULD'VE ***LIKED*** THAT, I THINK?
YES, HE WOULD HAVE...
...VERY WELL. JUST LET ME KNOW WHAT I CAN DO.

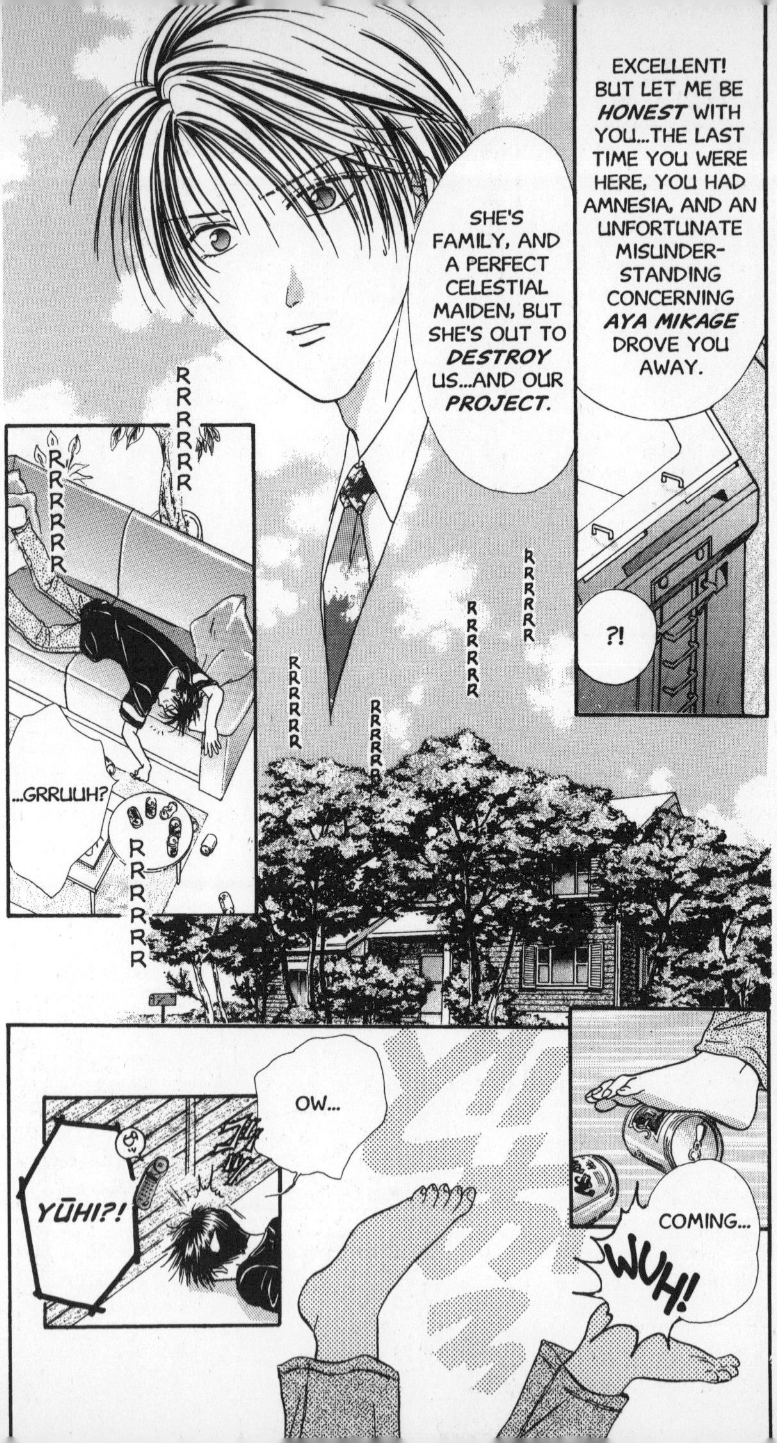
EXCELLENT! BUT LET ME BE HONEST WITH YOU...THE LAST TIME YOU WERE HERE, YOU HAD AMNESIA, AND AN UNFORTUNATE MISUNDER-STANDING CONCERNING AYA MIKAGE DROVE YOU AWAY.
SHE'S FAMILY, AND A PERFECT CELESTIAL MAIDEN, BUT SHE'S OUT TO DESTROY US...AND OUR PROJECT.
?!
RRRRRR
RRRRRR
RRRRRR
RRRRRR
RRRRRR
RRRRRR
...GRRUUH?
RRRRRR
COMING...
WUH!
OW...
YŪHI?!

◆ Miori ◆

...Hey, it's tough to explain. And if I myself have no idea, why am I writing about it?!

I do want each and every one of you to know you're special—especially you girls. Please, take better care of yourselves! Whenever someone young is in the news (whether violence- or sex-related), there's a storm of commentary by adults, but I get the feeling that they don't really "get" where the kids are coming from. I'm an adult too, of course, so maybe I'm just as bad, but I also think that it's not age that determines maturity. Among readers, there are junior-high kids who are remarkably mature...and then there are adults who make me question their age. Uhh...where was I going with this, again?

My previous editor once made the observation that many of the letters I receive are from people who want to tell me their problems. Why?? I do get quite a few "I luv so-and-so! ♡" letters, but others write about relationships, illness, school, friends and family, etc....and sometimes nothing else! ...So, what do you think of the manga? I welcome feedback, read every last letter I get—and pretty closely, too! I get mad, sympathize (?), and make a big fuss; my parents yell at me to "read more quietly," which is why I tend to get so passionate here, for those of you who look forward to these little columns, 'cause I can't directly write you back... ...sorry 'bout that. Sometimes I worry about how so-and-so is doing with her problem, but I shouldn't really be playing favorites. Thanks to everyone who's sent music tapes!

"Rain" by LUNA SEA is perfect for Tōya!! L'ARC-EN-CIEL, too.

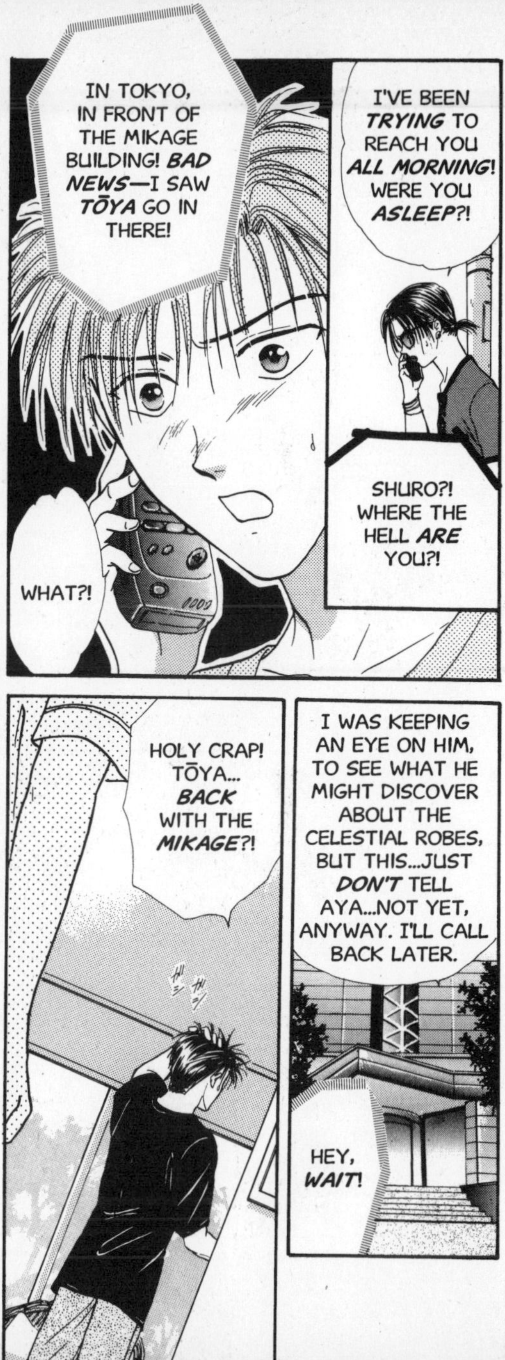
I'VE BEEN *TRYING* TO REACH YOU *ALL MORNING*! WERE YOU *ASLEEP*?!
SHURO?! WHERE THE HELL *ARE* YOU?!
IN TOKYO, IN FRONT OF THE MIKAGE BUILDING! *BAD NEWS*—I SAW *TŌYA* GO IN THERE!
WHAT?!
I WAS KEEPING AN EYE ON HIM, TO SEE WHAT HE MIGHT DISCOVER ABOUT THE CELESTIAL ROBES, BUT THIS...JUST *DON'T* TELL AYA...NOT YET, ANYWAY. I'LL CALL BACK LATER.
HEY, *WAIT*!
HOLY CRAP! TŌYA... *BACK* WITH THE *MIKAGE*?!

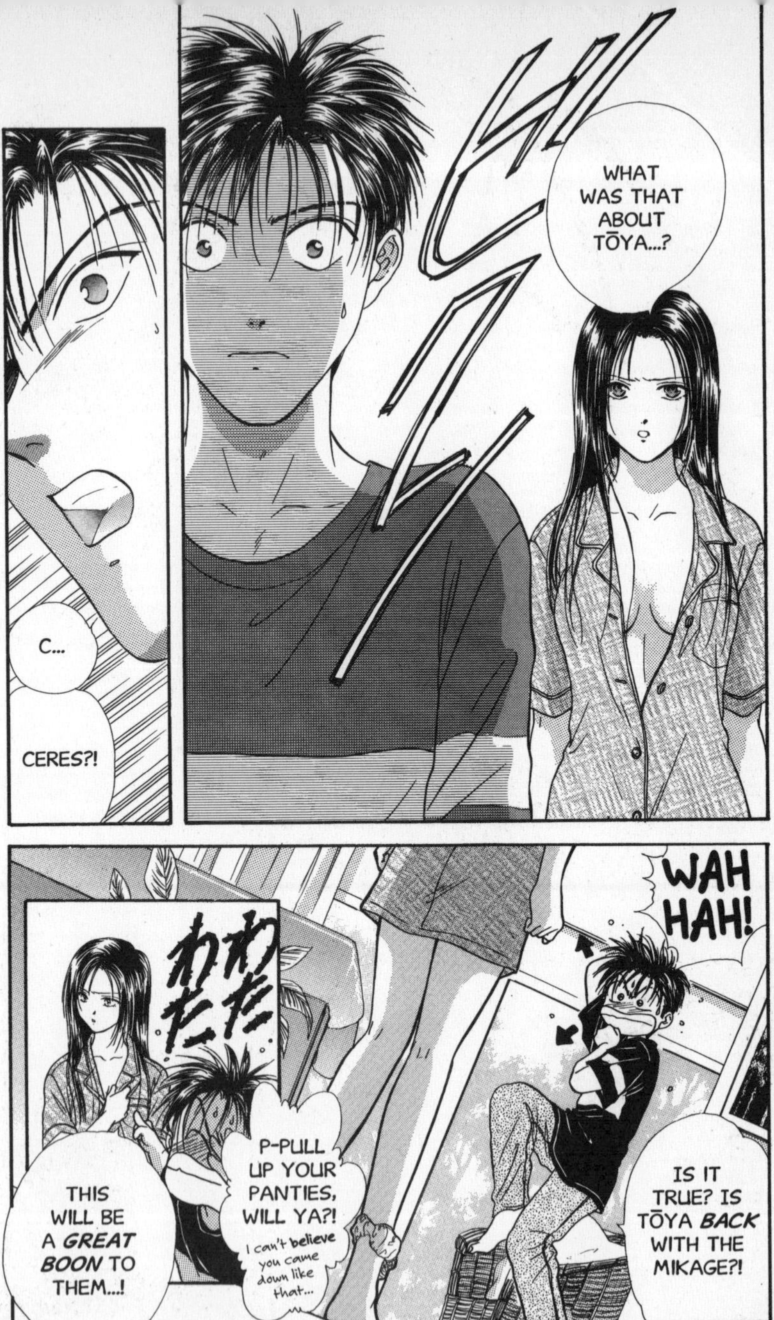
WHAT WAS THAT ABOUT TŌYA...?
C...
CERES?!
WAH HAH!
IS IT TRUE? IS TŌYA *BACK* WITH THE MIKAGE?!
P-PULL UP YOUR PANTIES, WILL YA?!
I can't believe you came down like that...
わたわた
THIS WILL BE A *GREAT BOON* TO THEM...!

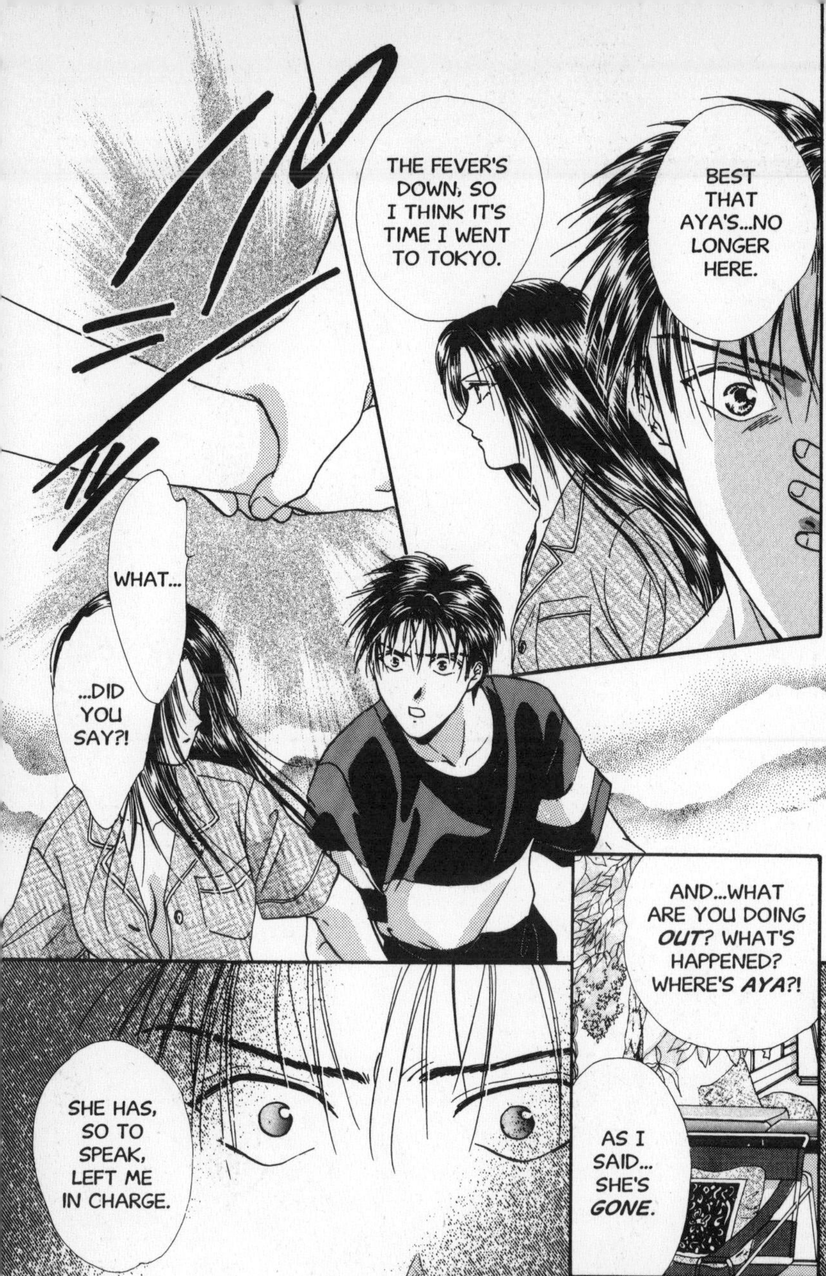
BEST THAT AYA'S...NO LONGER HERE.
THE FEVER'S DOWN, SO I THINK IT'S TIME I WENT TO TOKYO.
WHAT...
...DID YOU SAY?!
AND...WHAT ARE YOU DOING *OUT*? WHAT'S HAPPENED? WHERE'S *AYA*?!
AS I SAID... SHE'S *GONE*.
SHE HAS, SO TO SPEAK, LEFT ME IN CHARGE.

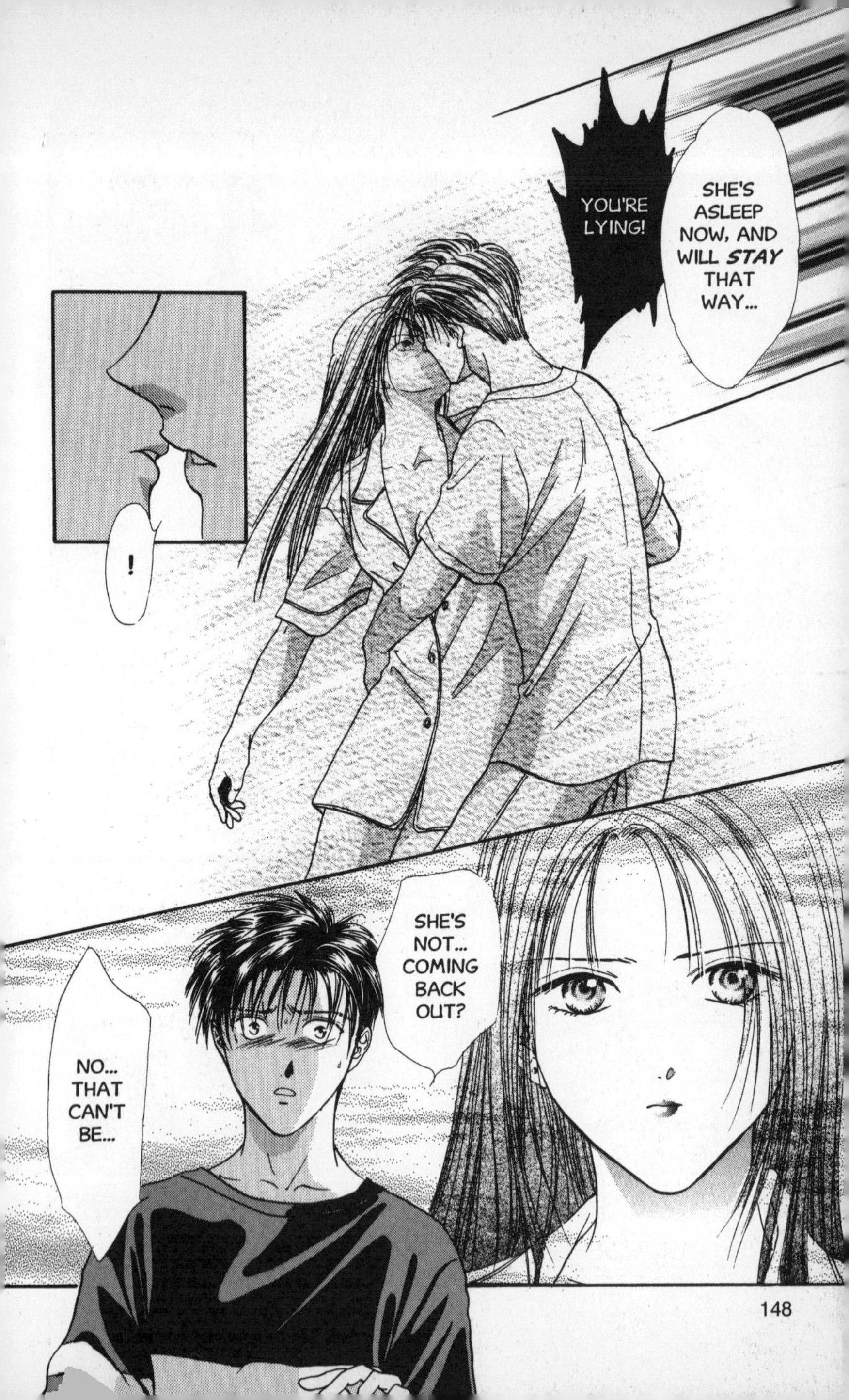
SHE'S ASLEEP NOW, AND WILL *STAY* THAT WAY...
YOU'RE LYING!
!
SHE'S NOT... COMING BACK OUT?
NO... THAT CAN'T BE...

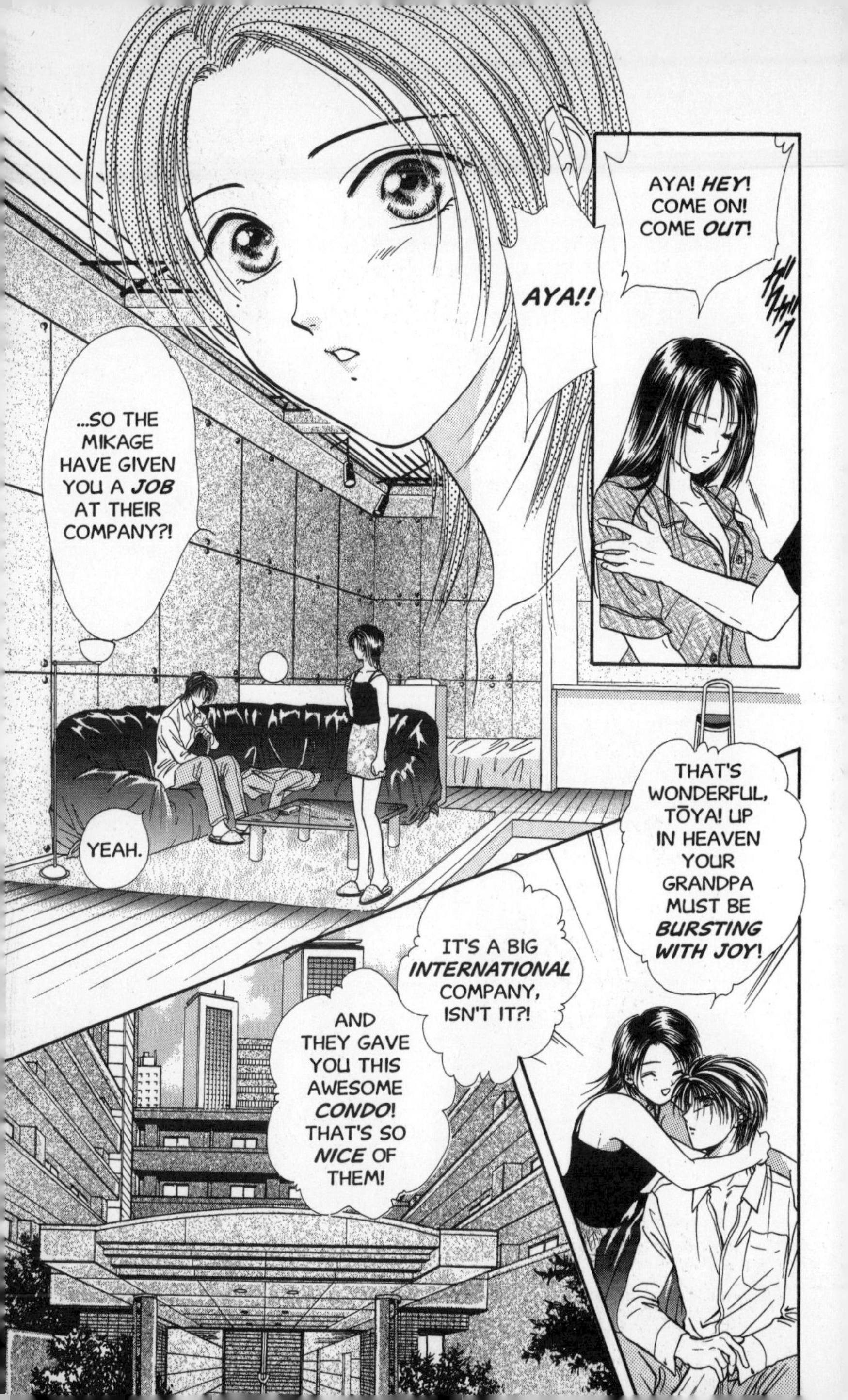
AYA! HEY! COME ON! COME OUT!
AYA!!
...SO THE MIKAGE HAVE GIVEN YOU A JOB AT THEIR COMPANY?!
YEAH.
THAT'S WONDERFUL, TŌYA! UP IN HEAVEN YOUR GRANDPA MUST BE BURSTING WITH JOY!
IT'S A BIG INTERNATIONAL COMPANY, ISN'T IT?!
AND THEY GAVE YOU THIS AWESOME CONDO! THAT'S SO NICE OF THEM!

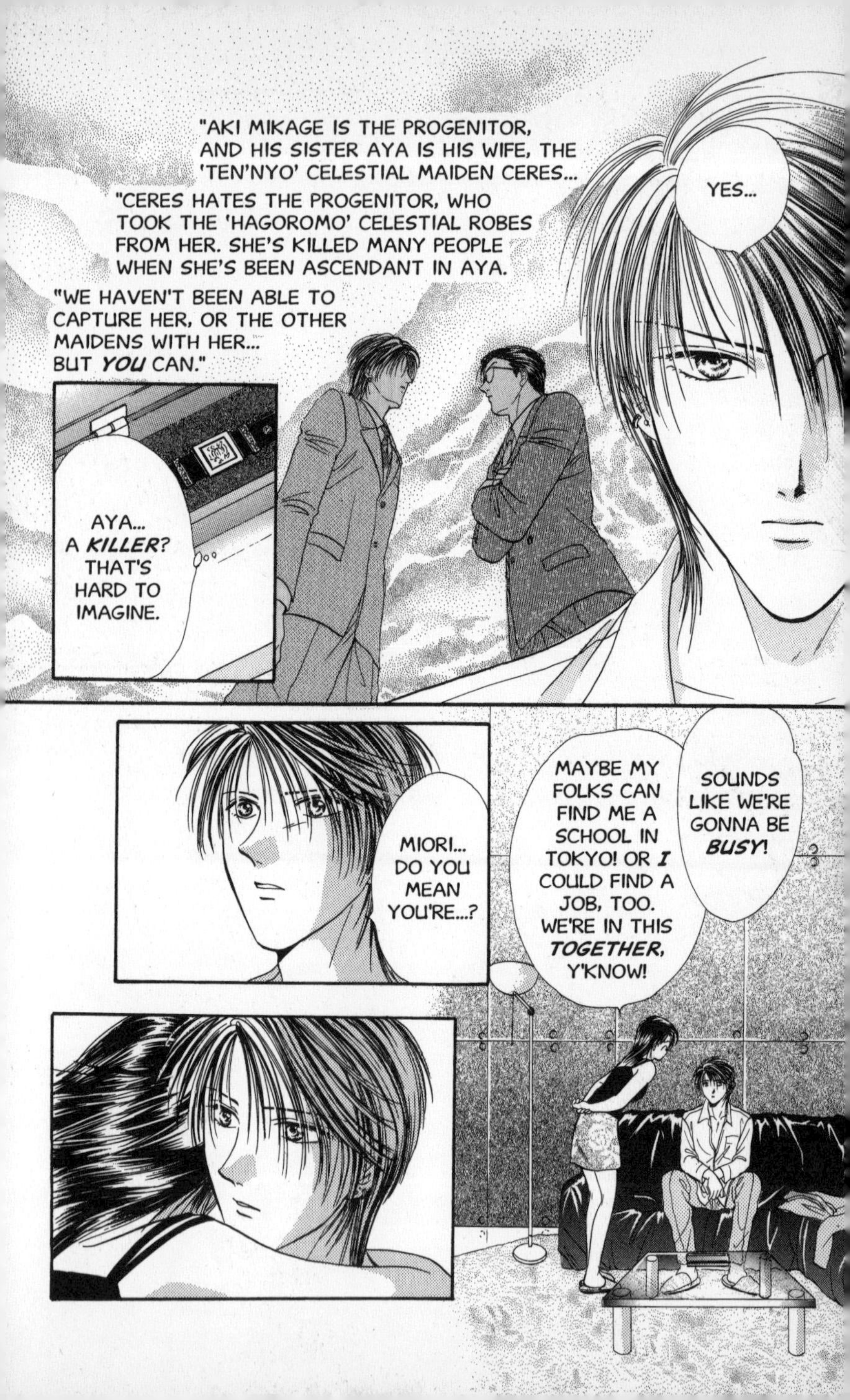
"AKI MIKAGE IS THE PROGENITOR, AND HIS SISTER AYA IS HIS WIFE, THE 'TEN'NYO' CELESTIAL MAIDEN CERES...
"CERES HATES THE PROGENITOR, WHO TOOK THE 'HAGOROMO' CELESTIAL ROBES FROM HER. SHE'S KILLED MANY PEOPLE WHEN SHE'S BEEN ASCENDANT IN AYA.
"WE HAVEN'T BEEN ABLE TO CAPTURE HER, OR THE OTHER MAIDENS WITH HER... BUT *YOU* CAN."
YES...
AYA... A *KILLER*? THAT'S HARD TO IMAGINE.
SOUNDS LIKE WE'RE GONNA BE *BUSY*!
MAYBE MY FOLKS CAN FIND ME A SCHOOL IN TOKYO! OR *I* COULD FIND A JOB, TOO. WE'RE IN THIS *TOGETHER*, Y'KNOW!
MIORI... DO YOU MEAN YOU'RE...?

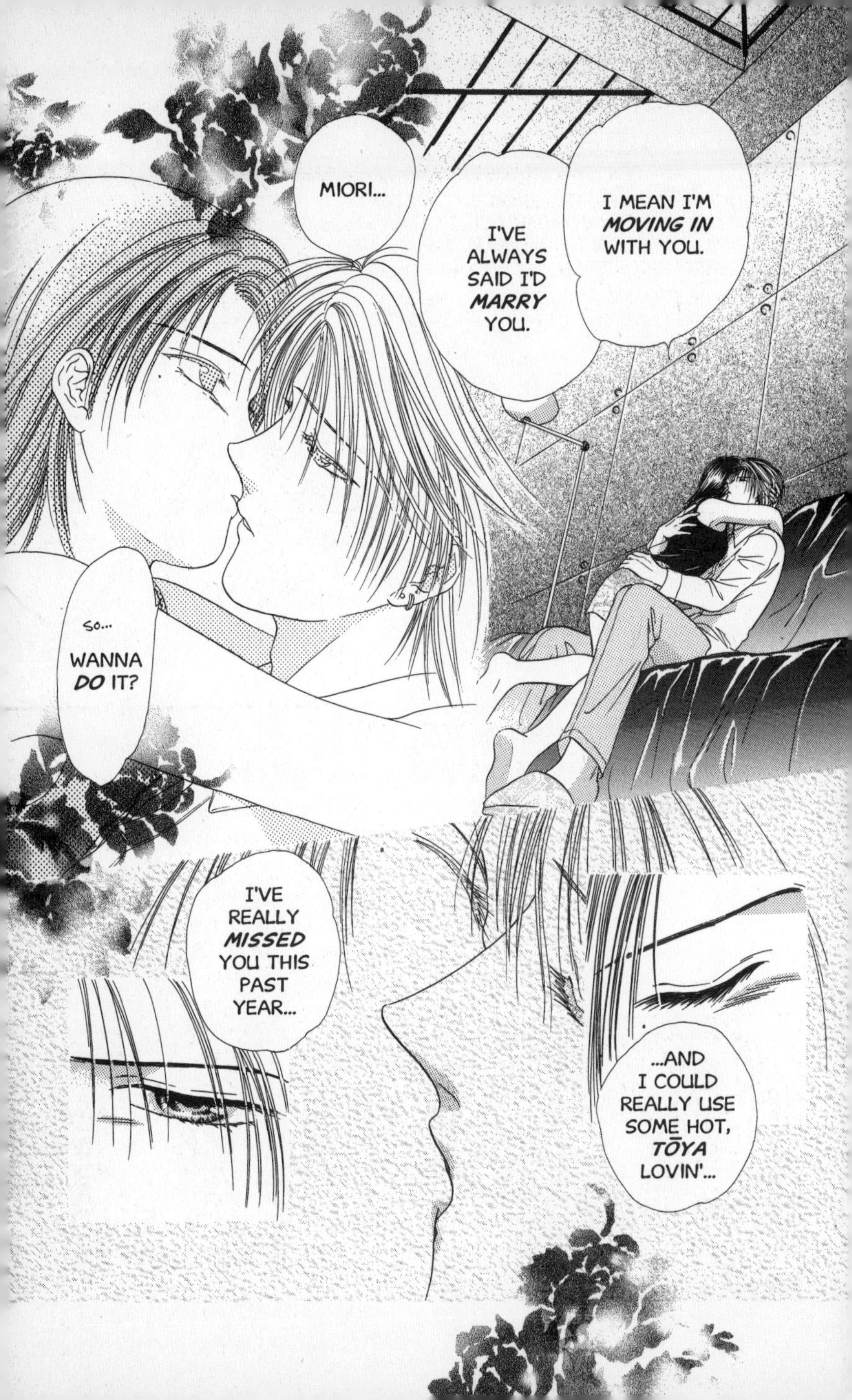
I MEAN I'M *MOVING IN* WITH YOU.
I'VE ALWAYS SAID I'D *MARRY* YOU.
MIORI...
SO... WANNA *DO* IT?
I'VE REALLY *MISSED* YOU THIS PAST YEAR...
...AND I COULD REALLY USE SOME HOT, *TŌYA* LOVIN'...

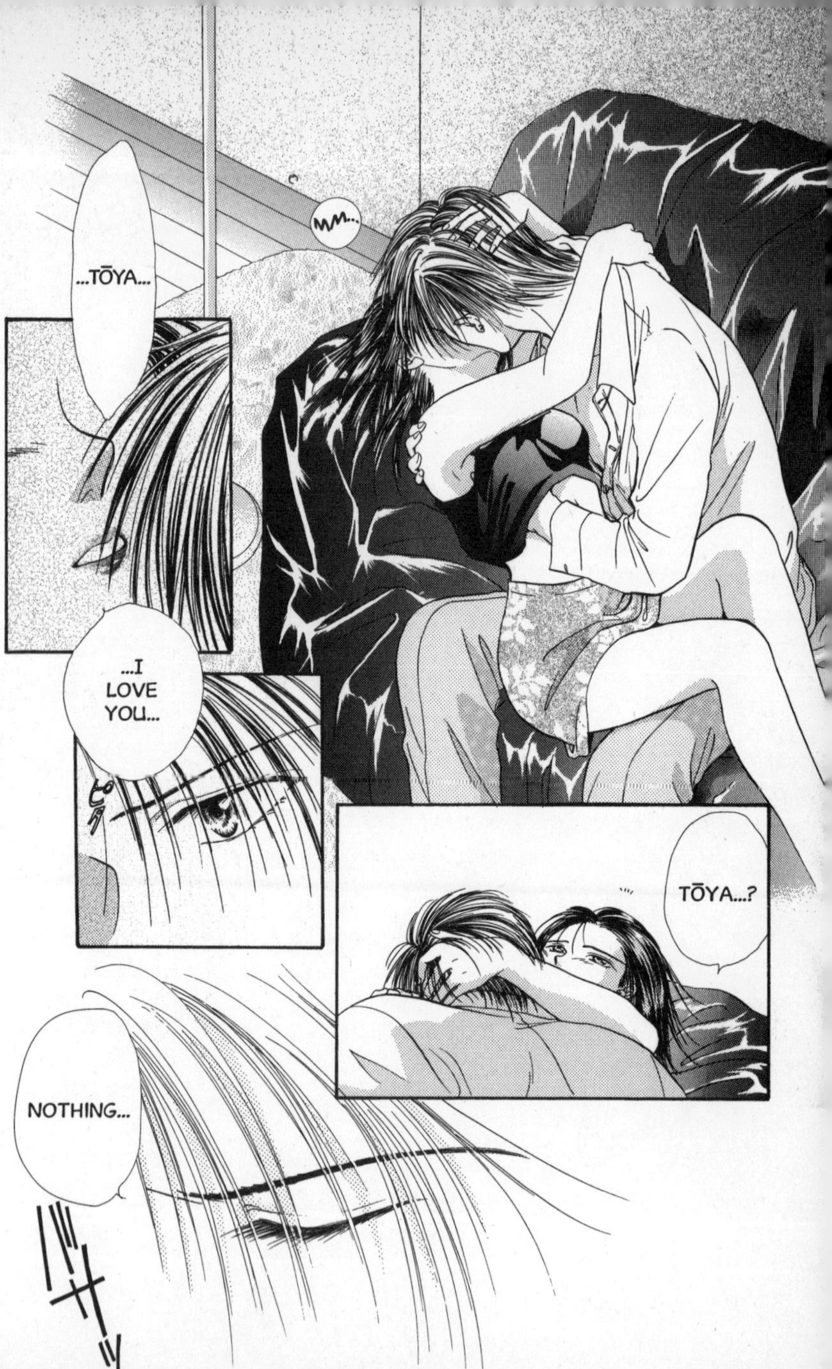
MM...
...TŌYA...
...I LOVE YOU...
TŌYA...?
NOTHING...

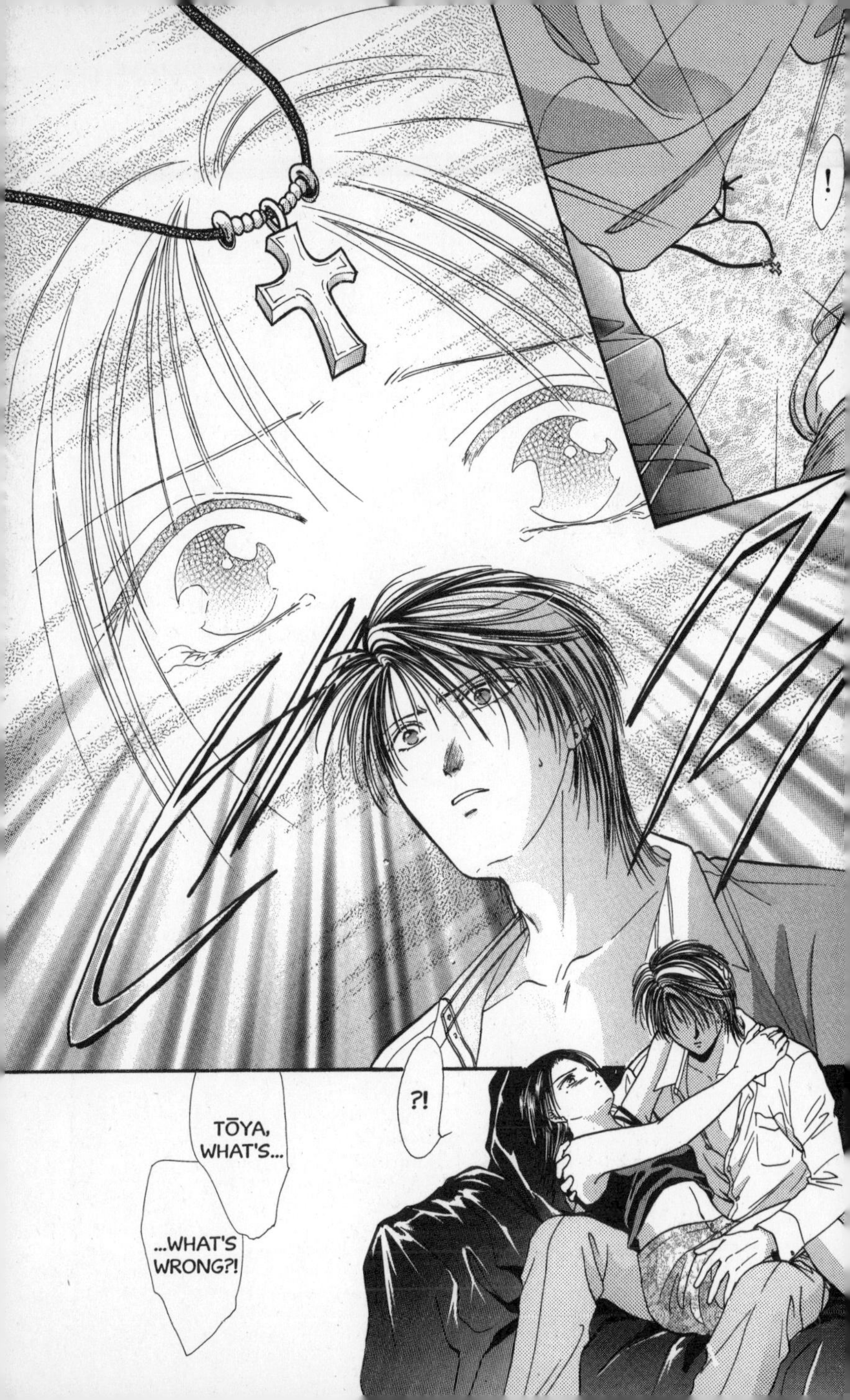
!
?!
TŌYA, WHAT'S...
...WHAT'S WRONG?!

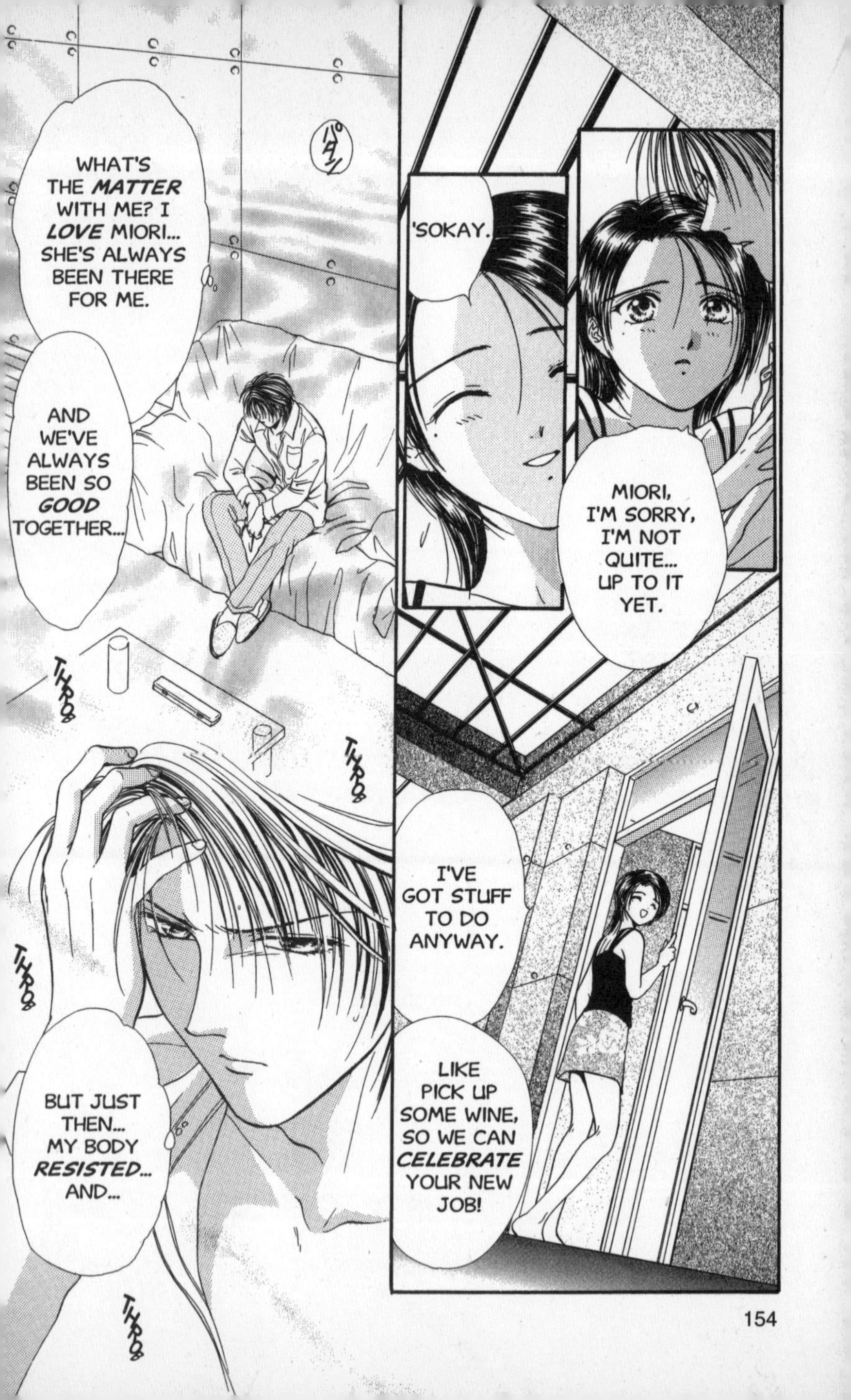
MIORI, I'M SORRY, I'M NOT QUITE... UP TO IT YET.
'SOKAY.
I'VE GOT STUFF TO DO ANYWAY.
LIKE PICK UP SOME WINE, SO WE CAN *CELEBRATE* YOUR NEW JOB!
パタン
WHAT'S THE *MATTER* WITH ME? I *LOVE* MIORI... SHE'S ALWAYS BEEN THERE FOR ME.
AND WE'VE ALWAYS BEEN SO *GOOD* TOGETHER...
THROB
THROB
THROB
BUT JUST THEN... MY BODY *RESISTED*... AND...
THROB

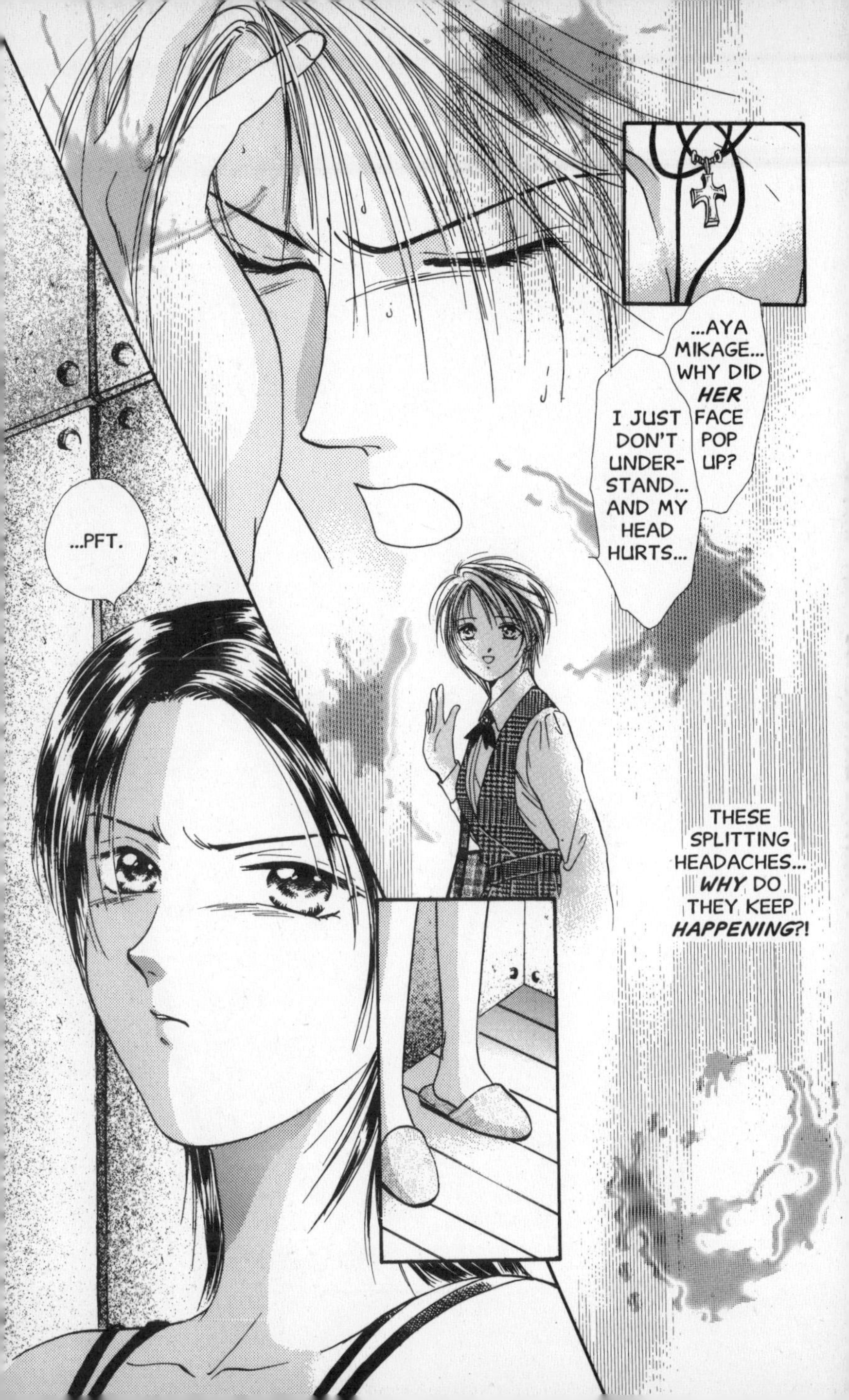
...AYA MIKAGE... WHY DID HER FACE POP UP?
I JUST DON'T UNDER-STAND... AND MY HEAD HURTS...
THESE SPLITTING HEADACHES... WHY DO THEY KEEP HAPPENING?!
...PFT.

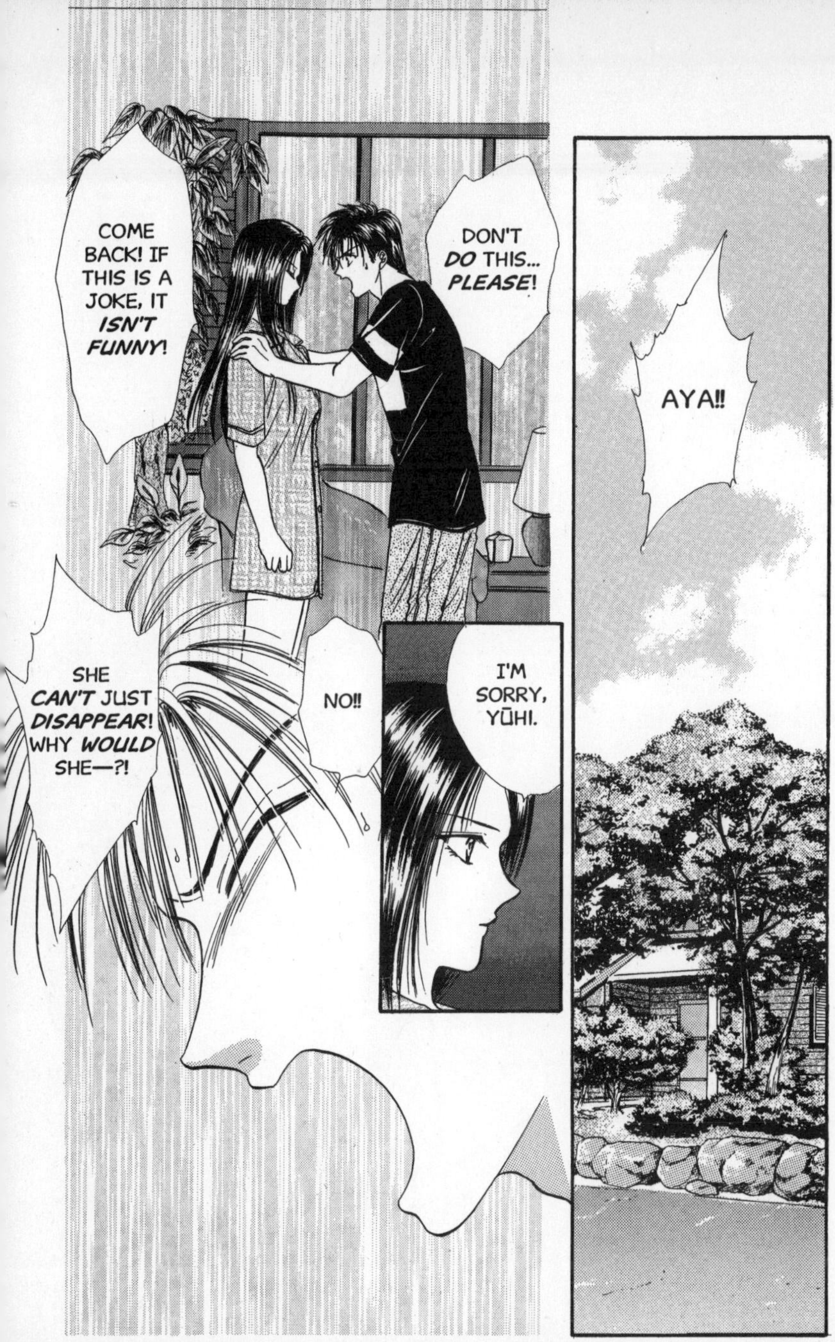

AYA!!
DON'T *DO* THIS... ***PLEASE***!
COME BACK! IF THIS IS A JOKE, IT ***ISN'T FUNNY***!
I'M SORRY, YŪHI.
NO!!
SHE ***CAN'T*** JUST ***DISAPPEAR***! WHY ***WOULD*** SHE—?!

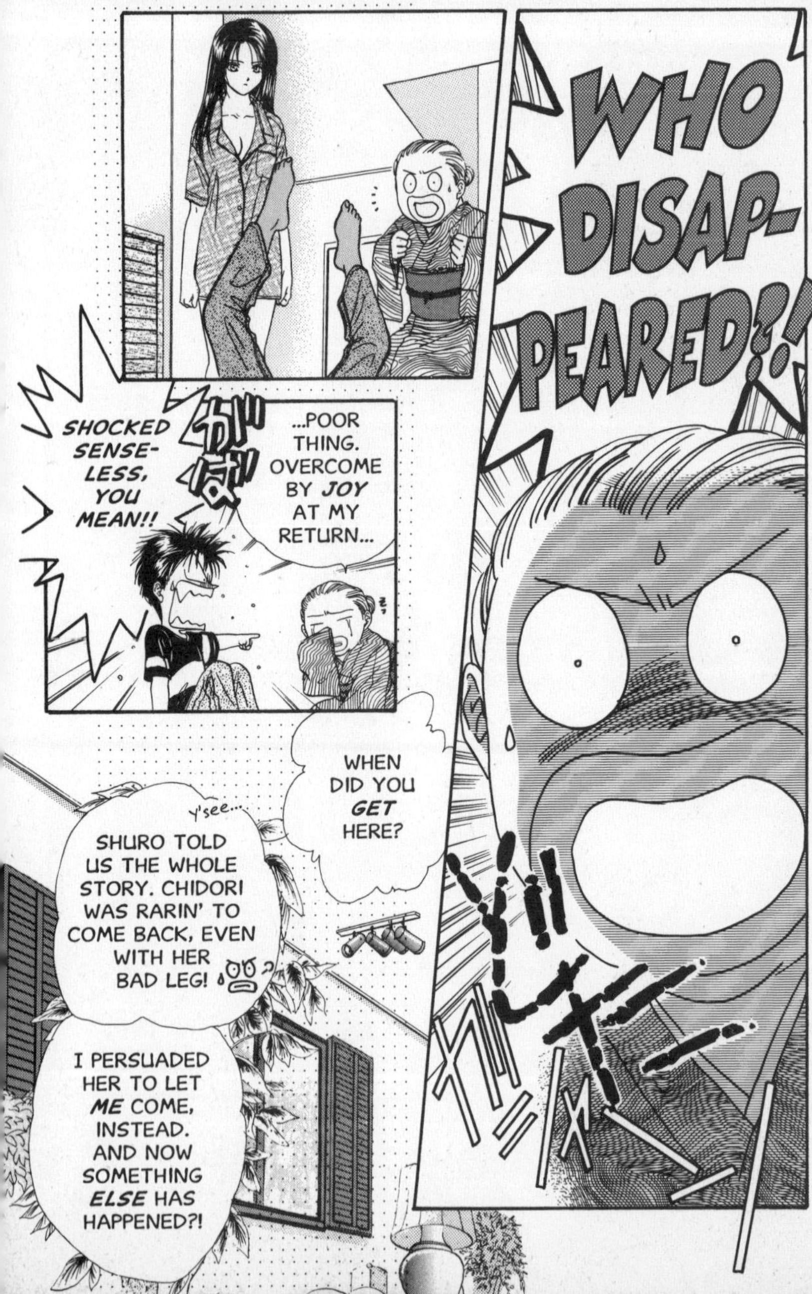
WHO DISAPPEARED?!
...POOR THING. OVERCOME BY *JOY* AT MY RETURN...
がば
SHOCKED SENSELESS, YOU MEAN!!
WHEN DID YOU *GET* HERE?
Y'see...
SHURO TOLD US THE WHOLE STORY. CHIDORI WAS RARIN' TO COME BACK, EVEN WITH HER BAD LEG!
I PERSUADED HER TO LET *ME* COME, INSTEAD. AND NOW SOMETHING *ELSE* HAS HAPPENED?!

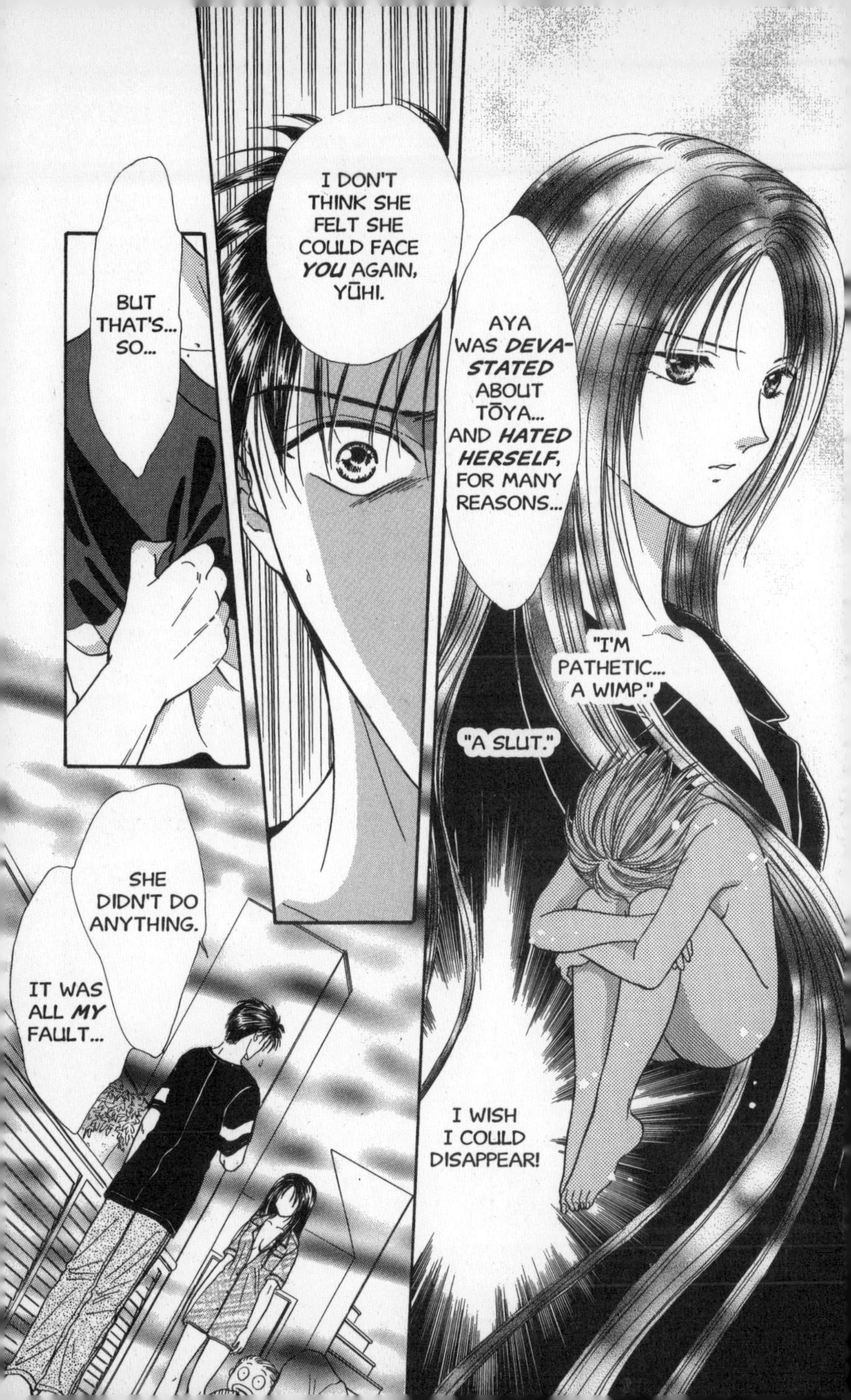
I DON'T THINK SHE FELT SHE COULD FACE *YOU* AGAIN, YŪHI.
AYA WAS ***DEVASTATED*** ABOUT TŌYA... AND ***HATED HERSELF***, FOR MANY REASONS...
"I'M PATHETIC... A WIMP."
"A SLUT."
I WISH I COULD DISAPPEAR!
BUT THAT'S... SO...
SHE DIDN'T DO ANYTHING.
IT WAS ALL *MY* FAULT...

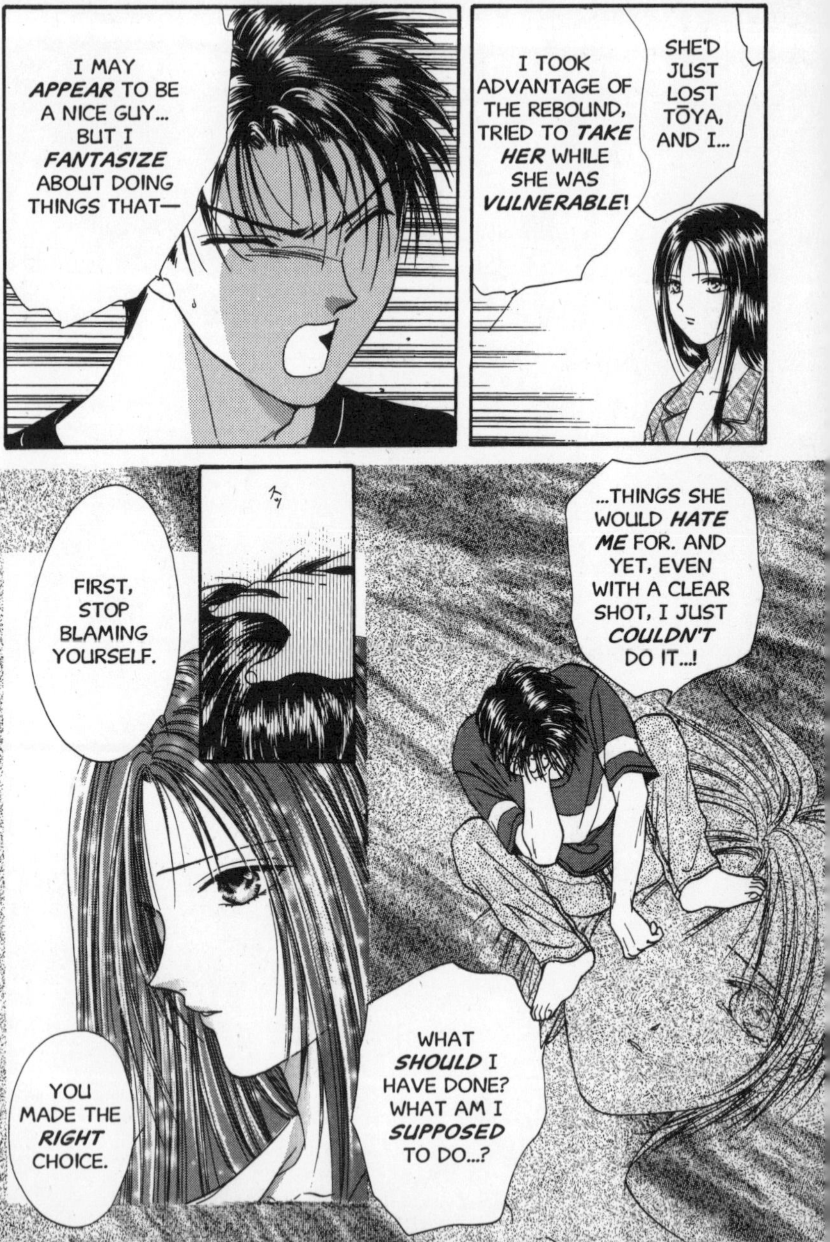
SHE'D JUST LOST TŌYA, AND I...
I TOOK ADVANTAGE OF THE REBOUND, TRIED TO TAKE HER WHILE SHE WAS VULNERABLE!
I MAY APPEAR TO BE A NICE GUY... BUT I FANTASIZE ABOUT DOING THINGS THAT—
...THINGS SHE WOULD HATE ME FOR. AND YET, EVEN WITH A CLEAR SHOT, I JUST COULDN'T DO IT...!
WHAT SHOULD I HAVE DONE? WHAT AM I SUPPOSED TO DO...?
FIRST, STOP BLAMING YOURSELF.
YOU MADE THE RIGHT CHOICE.

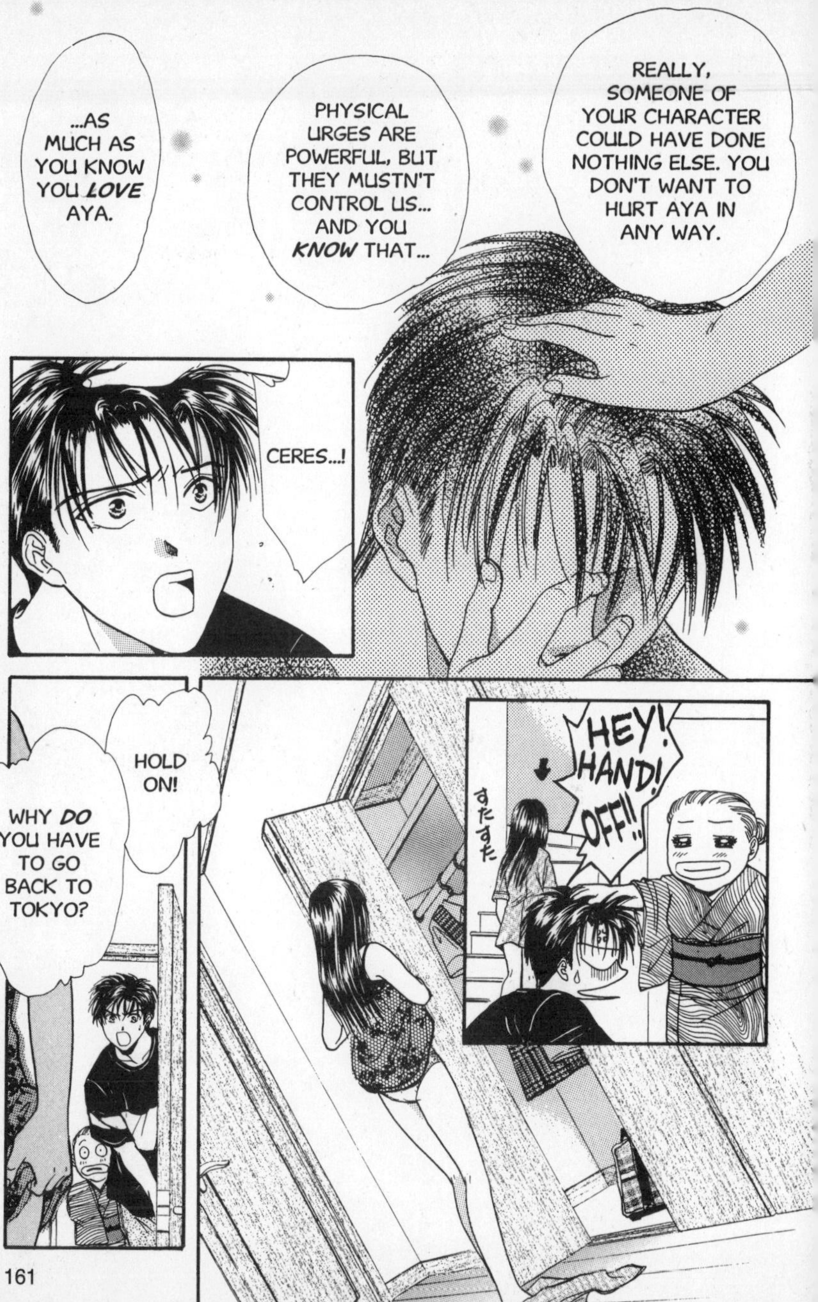
REALLY, SOMEONE OF YOUR CHARACTER COULD HAVE DONE NOTHING ELSE. YOU DON'T WANT TO HURT AYA IN ANY WAY.
PHYSICAL URGES ARE POWERFUL, BUT THEY MUSTN'T CONTROL US... AND YOU *KNOW* THAT...
...AS MUCH AS YOU KNOW YOU *LOVE* AYA.
CERES...!
HEY! HAND! OFF!!
すたすた
HOLD ON!
WHY *DO* YOU HAVE TO GO BACK TO TOKYO?

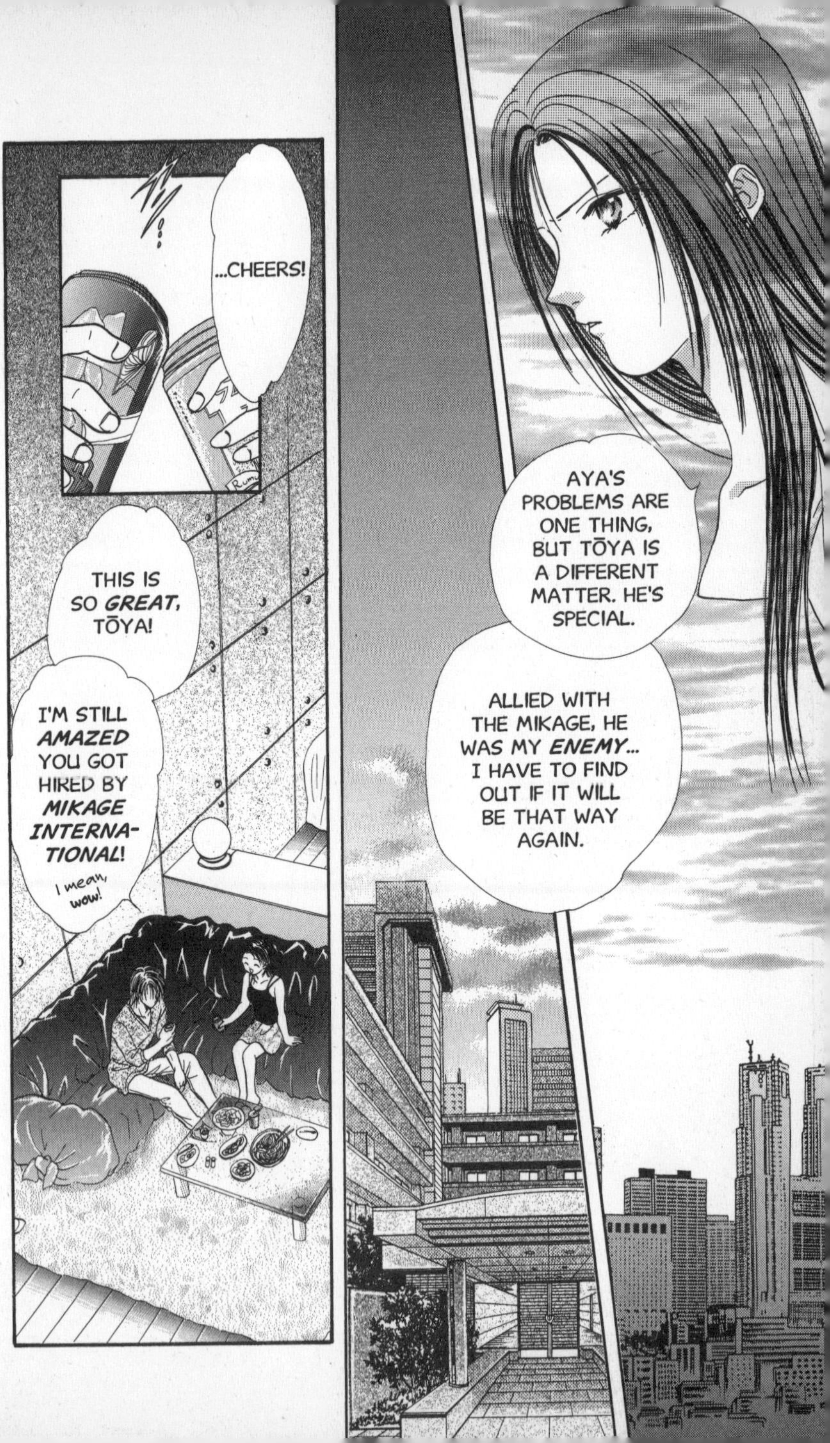
AYA'S PROBLEMS ARE ONE THING, BUT TŌYA IS A DIFFERENT MATTER. HE'S SPECIAL.
ALLIED WITH THE MIKAGE, HE WAS MY *ENEMY*... I HAVE TO FIND OUT IF IT WILL BE THAT WAY AGAIN.
...CHEERS!
THIS IS SO *GREAT*, TŌYA!
I'M STILL *AMAZED* YOU GOT HIRED BY *MIKAGE INTERNATIONAL*!
I mean, wow!

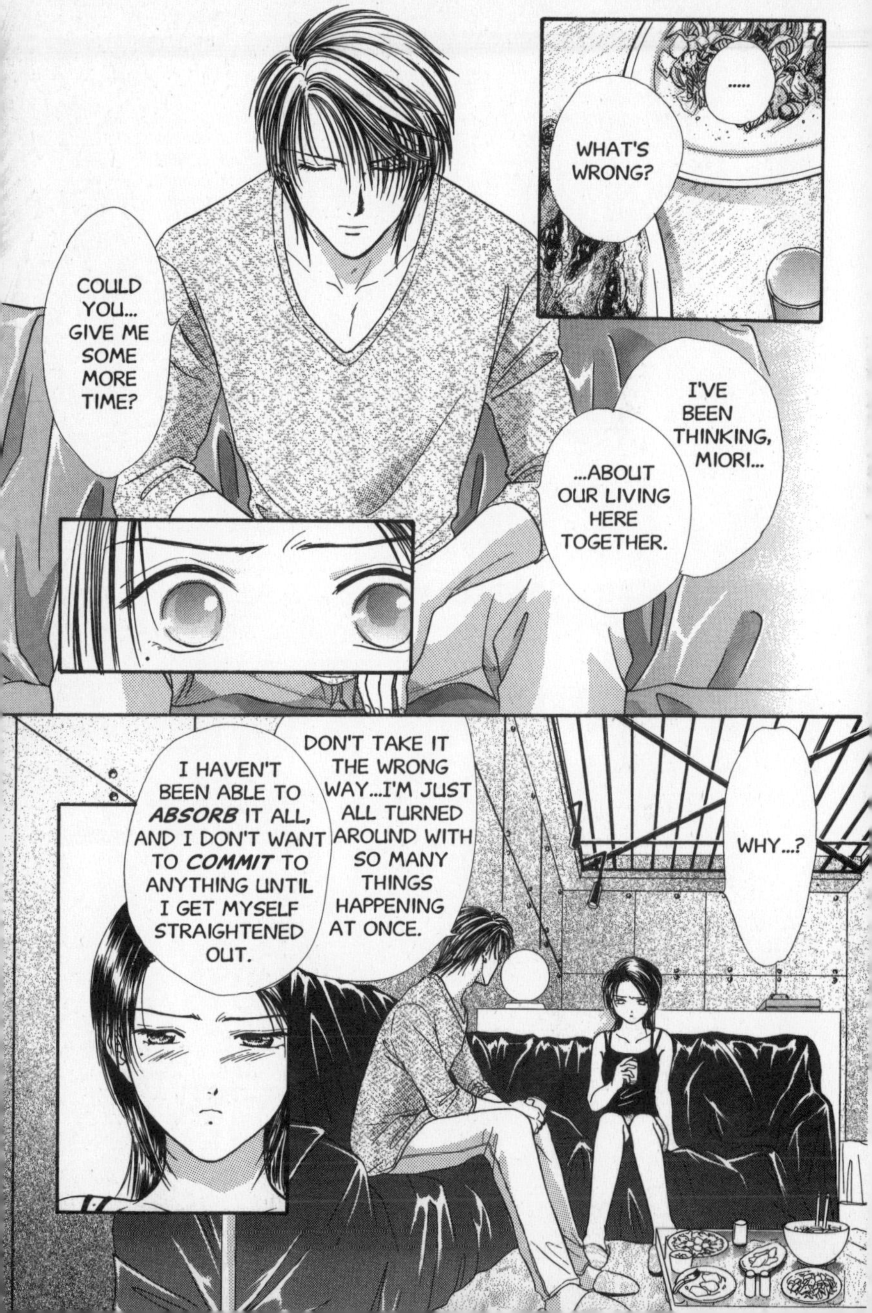
.....
WHAT'S WRONG?
I'VE BEEN THINKING, MIORI...
...ABOUT OUR LIVING HERE TOGETHER.
COULD YOU... GIVE ME SOME MORE TIME?
WHY...?
DON'T TAKE IT THE WRONG WAY...I'M JUST ALL TURNED AROUND WITH SO MANY THINGS HAPPENING AT ONCE.
I HAVEN'T BEEN ABLE TO ABSORB IT ALL, AND I DON'T WANT TO COMMIT TO ANYTHING UNTIL I GET MYSELF STRAIGHTENED OUT.

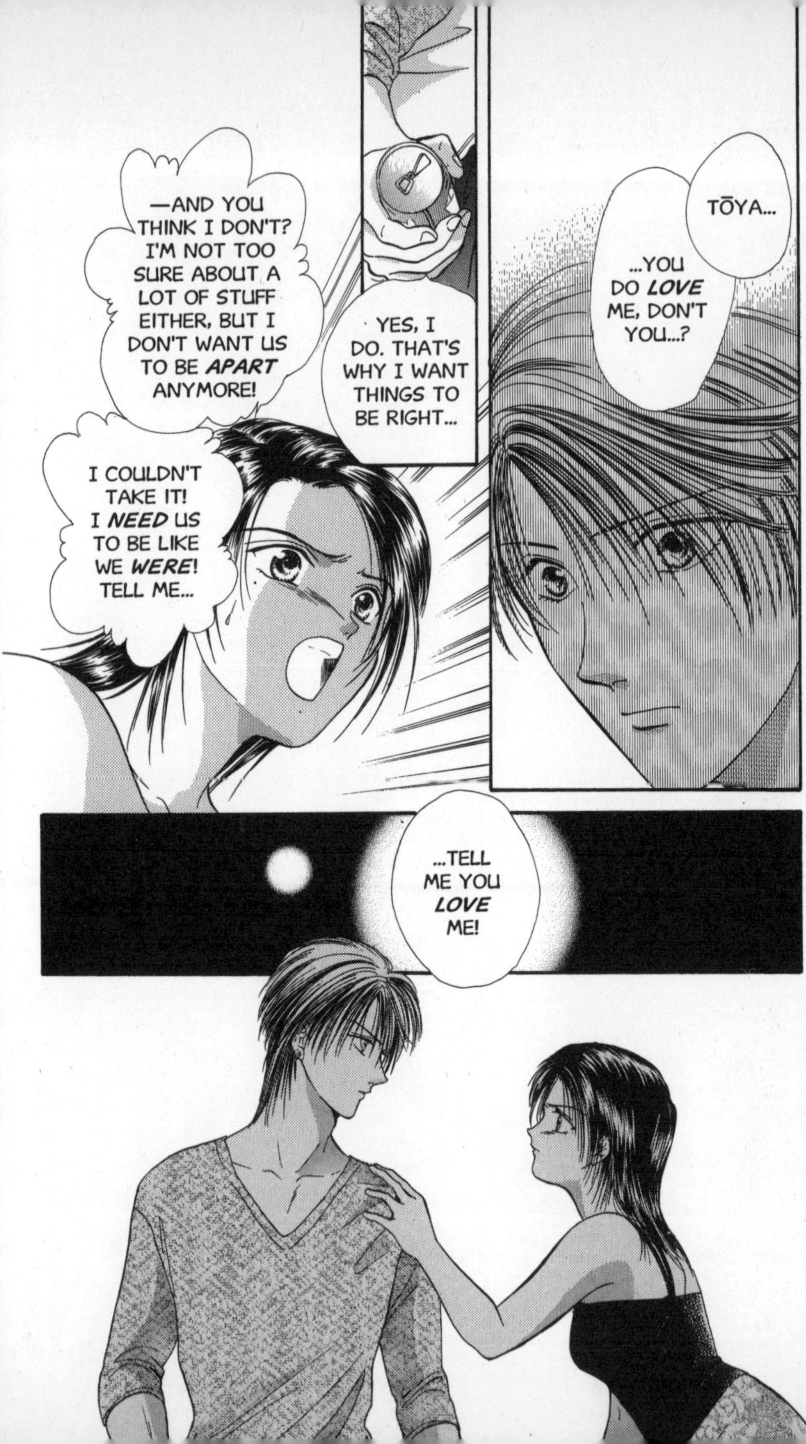
TŌYA...
...YOU DO LOVE ME, DON'T YOU...?
YES, I DO. THAT'S WHY I WANT THINGS TO BE RIGHT...
—AND YOU THINK I DON'T? I'M NOT TOO SURE ABOUT A LOT OF STUFF EITHER, BUT I DON'T WANT US TO BE APART ANYMORE!
I COULDN'T TAKE IT! I NEED US TO BE LIKE WE WERE! TELL ME...
...TELL ME YOU LOVE ME!

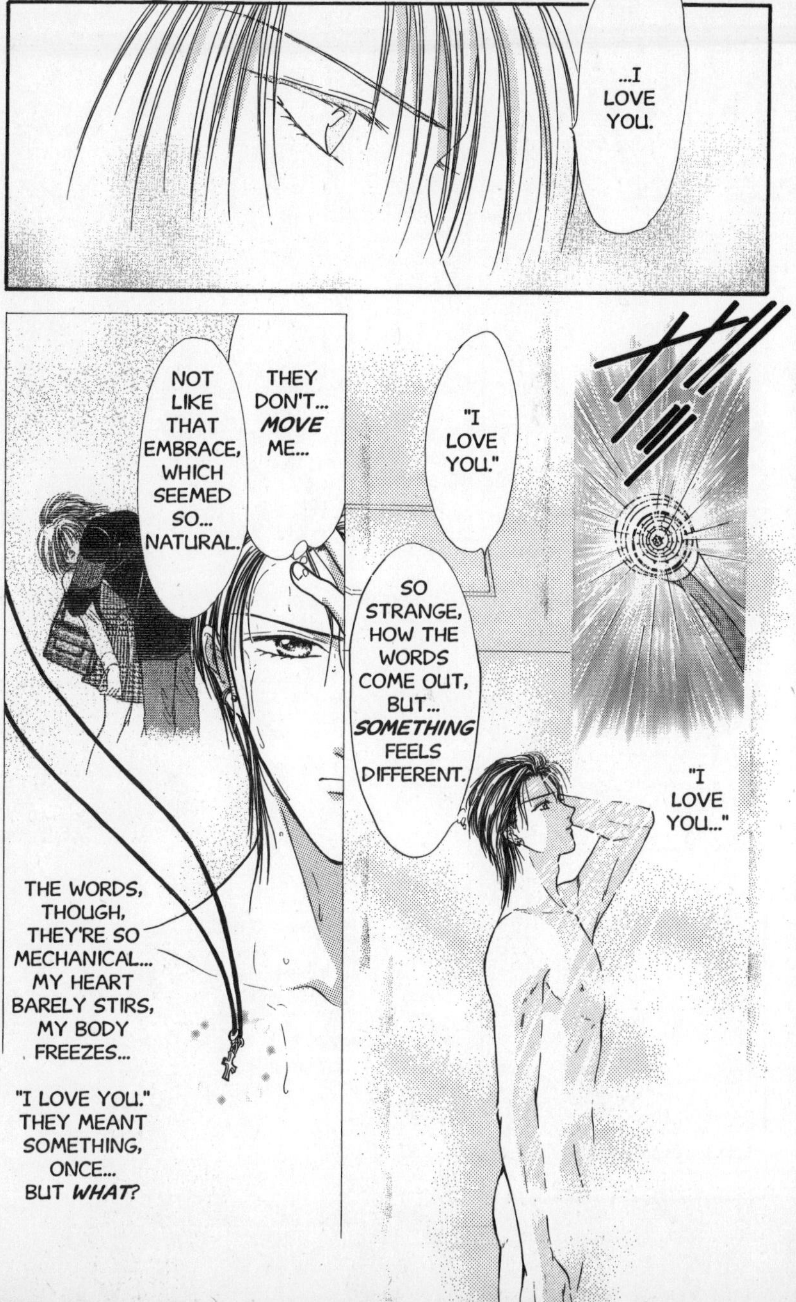
...I LOVE YOU.
"I LOVE YOU."
SO STRANGE, HOW THE WORDS COME OUT, BUT... *SOMETHING* FEELS DIFFERENT.
"I LOVE YOU..."
THEY DON'T... *MOVE* ME...
NOT LIKE THAT EMBRACE, WHICH SEEMED SO... NATURAL.
THE WORDS, THOUGH, THEY'RE SO MECHANICAL... MY HEART BARELY STIRS, MY BODY FREEZES...
"I LOVE YOU." THEY MEANT SOMETHING, ONCE... BUT *WHAT*?

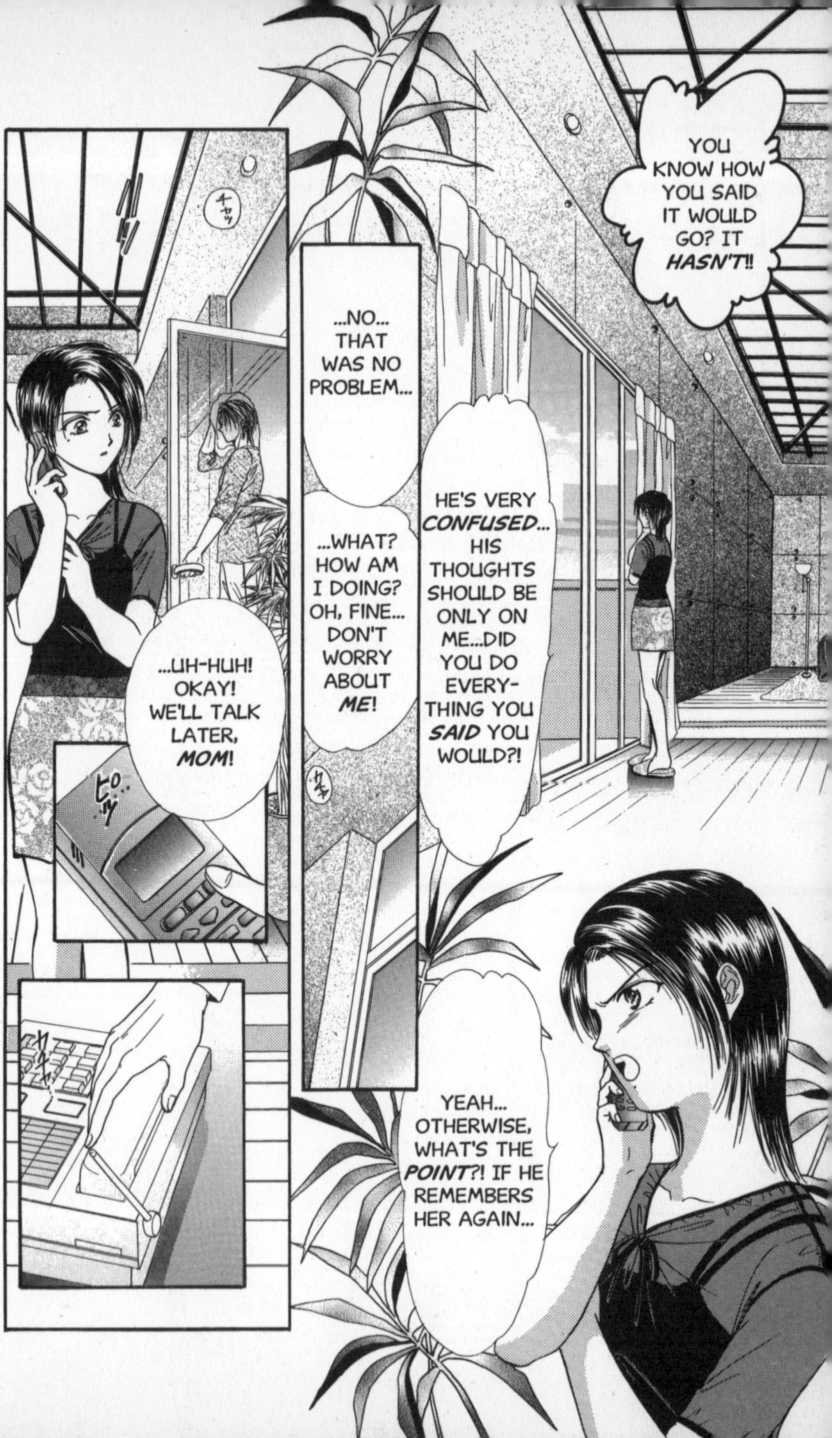
YOU KNOW HOW YOU SAID IT WOULD GO? IT *HASN'T*!!
HE'S VERY *CONFUSED*... HIS THOUGHTS SHOULD BE ONLY ON ME...DID YOU DO EVERY-THING YOU *SAID* YOU WOULD?!
YEAH... OTHERWISE, WHAT'S THE *POINT*?! IF HE REMEMBERS HER AGAIN...
...NO... THAT WAS NO PROBLEM...
...WHAT? HOW AM I DOING? OH, FINE... DON'T WORRY ABOUT *ME*!
...UH-HUH! OKAY! WE'LL TALK LATER, *MOM*!

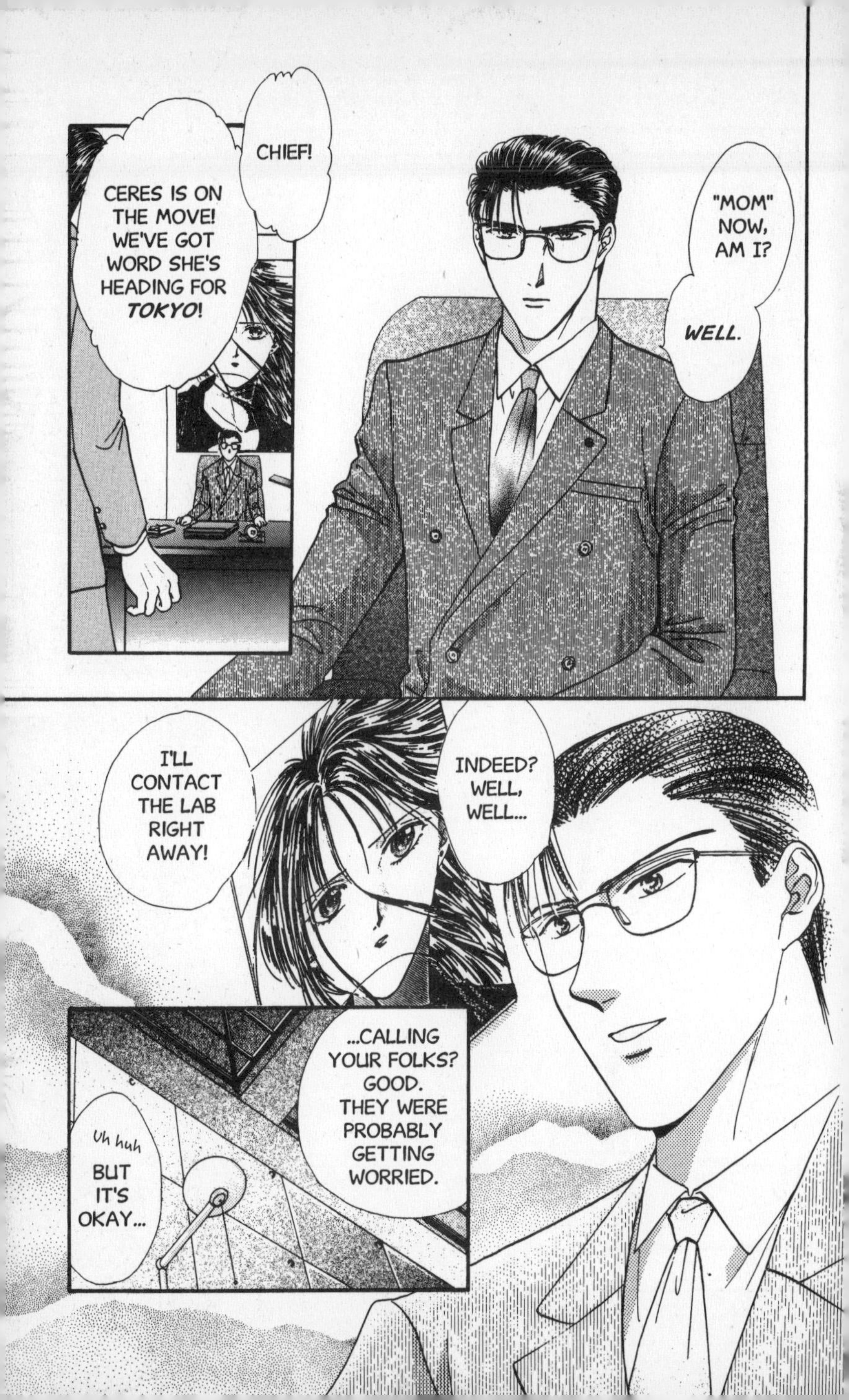
"MOM" NOW, AM I?
WELL.
CHIEF!
CERES IS ON THE MOVE! WE'VE GOT WORD SHE'S HEADING FOR *TOKYO*!
INDEED? WELL, WELL...
I'LL CONTACT THE LAB RIGHT AWAY!
...CALLING YOUR FOLKS? GOOD. THEY WERE PROBABLY GETTING WORRIED.
Uh huh
BUT IT'S OKAY...

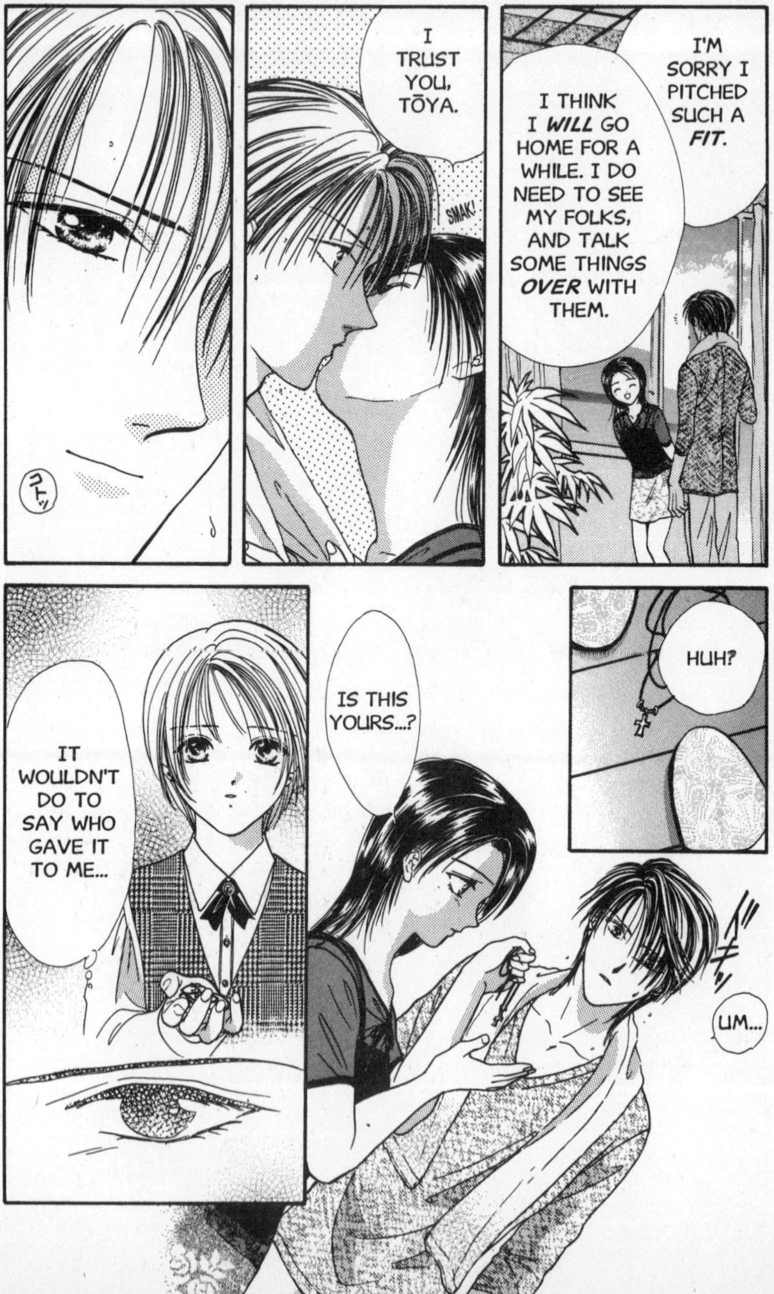
I'M SORRY I PITCHED SUCH A *FIT*.
I THINK I ***WILL*** GO HOME FOR A WHILE. I DO NEED TO SEE MY FOLKS, AND TALK SOME THINGS ***OVER*** WITH THEM.
SMAK!
I TRUST YOU, TŌYA.
コトッ
HUH?
IS THIS YOURS...?
UM...
IT WOULDN'T DO TO SAY WHO GAVE IT TO ME...

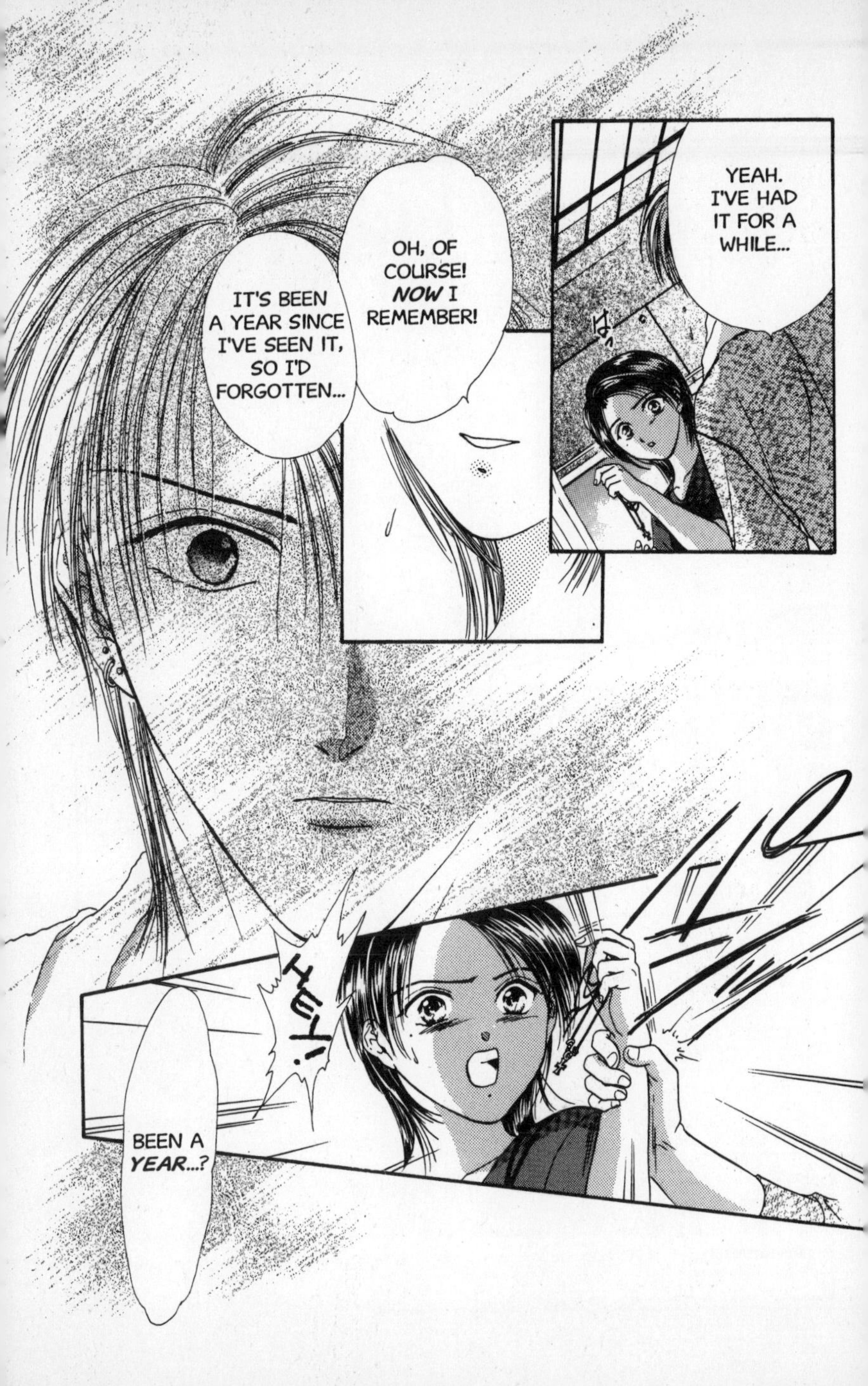
YEAH. I'VE HAD IT FOR A WHILE...
OH, OF COURSE! *NOW* I REMEMBER!
IT'S BEEN A YEAR SINCE I'VE SEEN IT, SO I'D FORGOTTEN...
HEY!
BEEN A *YEAR*...?

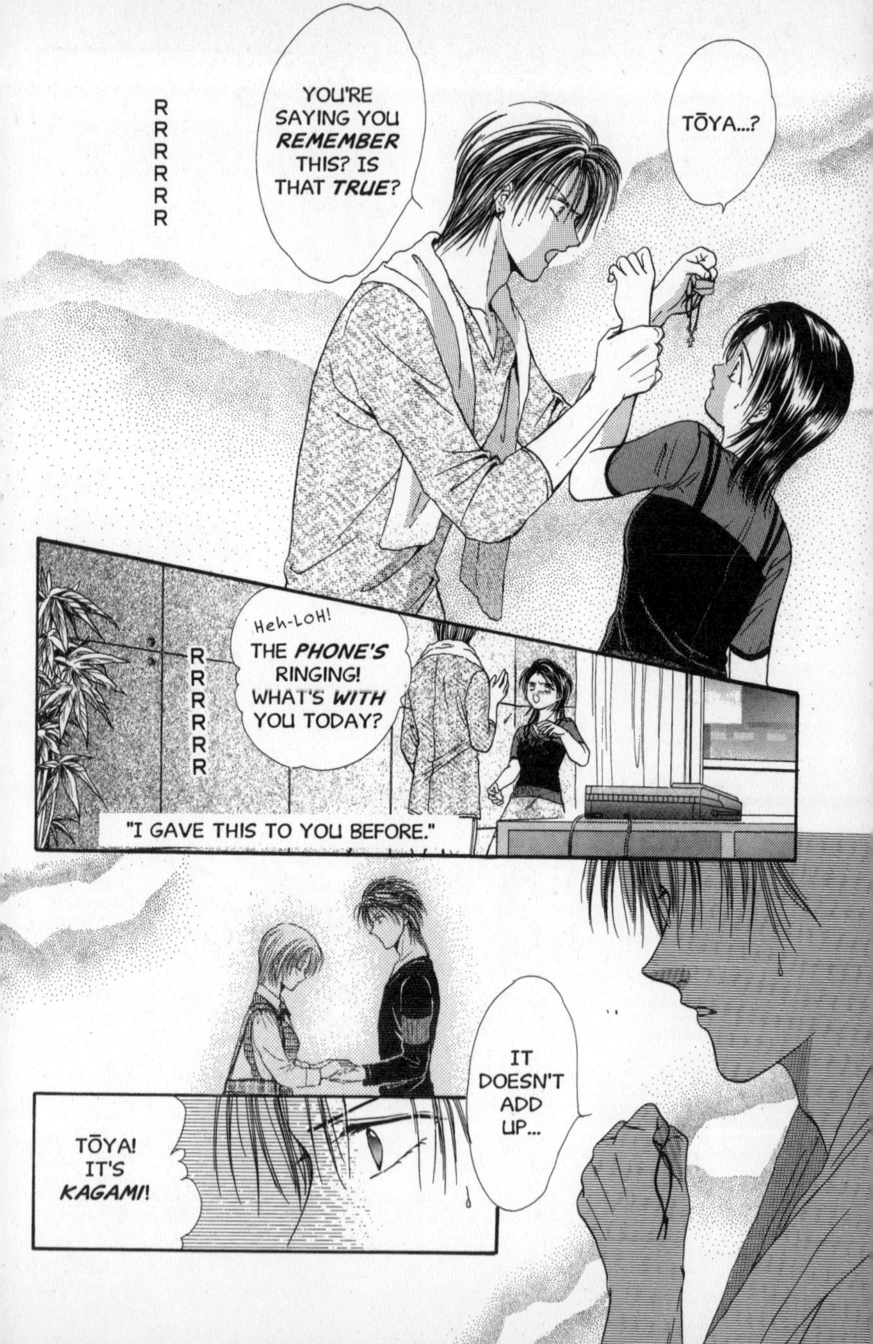
TŌYA...?
YOU'RE SAYING YOU *REMEMBER* THIS? IS THAT *TRUE*?
RRRRRR
Heh-LOH! THE *PHONE'S* RINGING! WHAT'S *WITH* YOU TODAY?
RRRRRR
"I GAVE THIS TO YOU BEFORE."
IT DOESN'T ADD UP...
TŌYA! IT'S *KAGAMI*!

✦ Miori ✦

Gack! The last note for this volume already?!

The "Shizuoka" arc sure has had some interesting feedback. ◡̈ Most of it has been about how sorry people feel for Aya, and how more are mad at Miori than at Tōya. Wonder what people will say after the next volume...? 💧 An assistant points out that the person who most deserves sympathy is Tōya. It's true...I like Tōya...more than Yūhi. 💧 Tōya's a type of guy I've never drawn before, and I've put so much into how he looks. 💧 He can pull off a more dramatic relationship, too. Yūhi does have a juicy role. Plus, he's cute. I've gotten a letter saying, "Since Aya and Tōya are apart all the time, I love how it gets so emotionally charged when they do get together!" Real relationships are like that, too—you keep a healthy distance. If you're constantly clinging to the guy, the relationship is doomed. There are exceptions, tho'. Assistant "H" says people don't recognize the effort Tōya makes. "He's trying just as hard as Yūhi, but it doesn't show in his face..." Yeah. I mean, he's risking his life...! ◡̈ But that's okay, my love compensates for all. ◡̈

Guess what?! They're making a **Ceres** calendar for 1999! And it's all-new art! I think it'll go on sale [in Japan] in November.... Also, the last volume of the **Fushigi Yūgi** OAV, Part 2, comes out in October! It's 50 mins. long, so it's a bit expensive, but it'll be the last **FY** anime... probably. Watch for it! The second **FY** novelization, "The Chichiri Story: Legend of Shoryu," is on sale from Shogakukan Palette Books now! The next? "The Nuriko Story"...

The first—"The Tasuki Story: Legend of Genrō"—has also been reprinted, so go find one!

Have a nice day, everyone. Next time might be epic (?), too...see you in December!

8/98

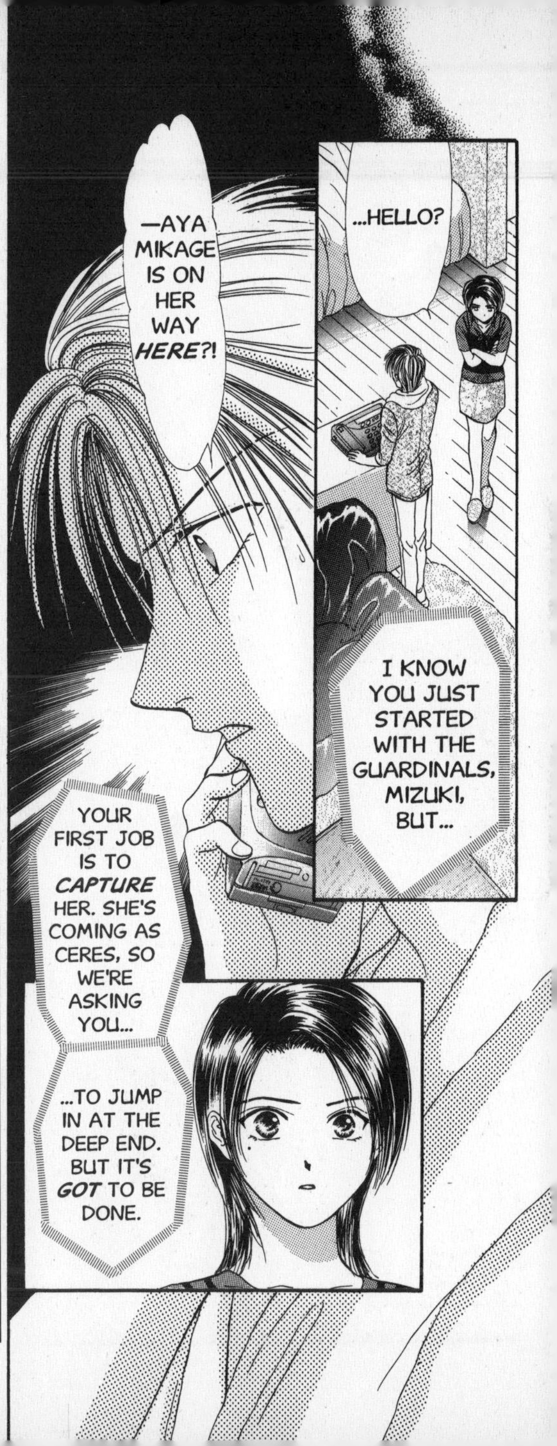
...HELLO?
—AYA MIKAGE IS ON HER WAY *HERE*?!
I KNOW YOU JUST STARTED WITH THE GUARDINALS, MIZUKI, BUT...
YOUR FIRST JOB IS TO *CAPTURE* HER. SHE'S COMING AS CERES, SO WE'RE ASKING YOU...
...TO JUMP IN AT THE DEEP END. BUT IT'S *GOT* TO BE DONE.

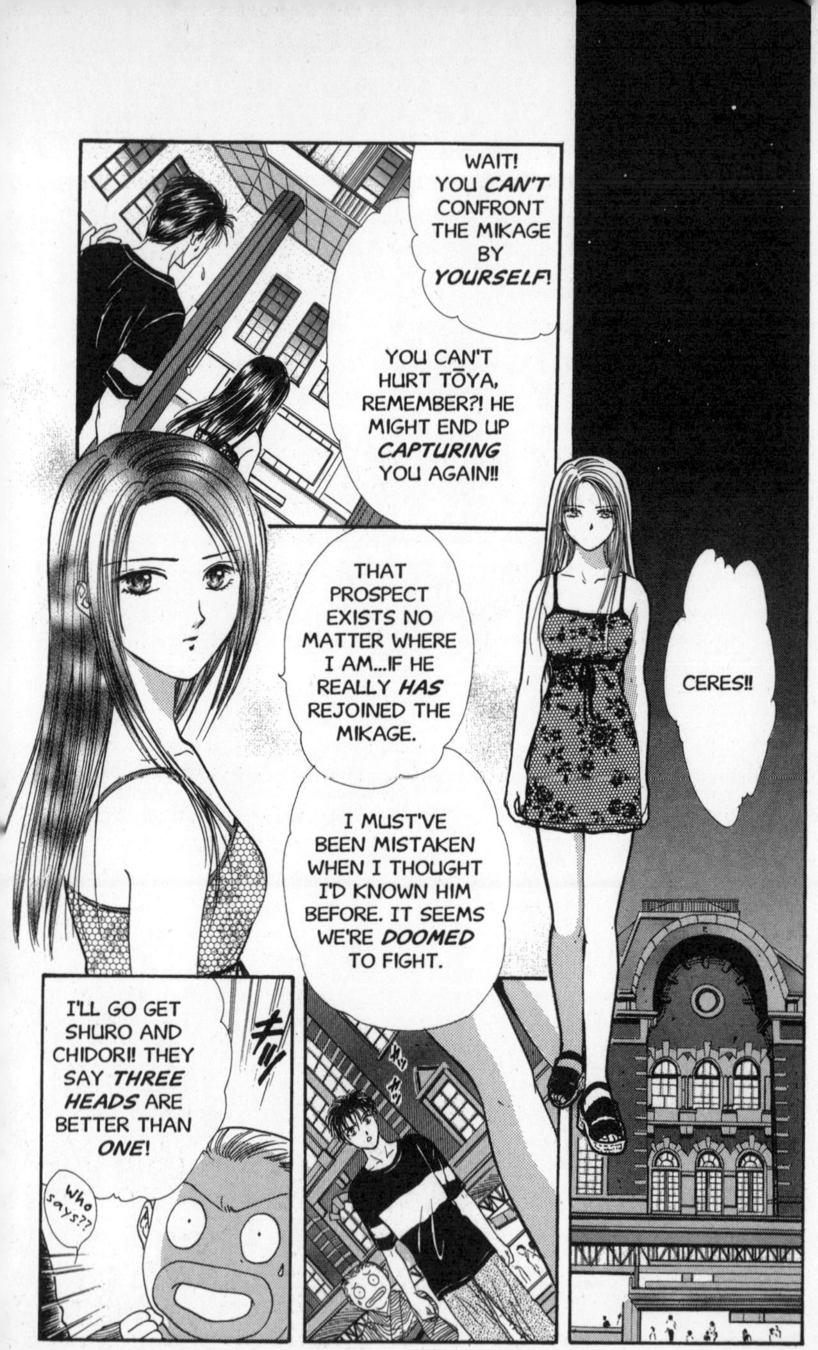
CERES!!
WAIT! YOU *CAN'T* CONFRONT THE MIKAGE BY ***YOURSELF***!
YOU CAN'T HURT TŌYA, REMEMBER?! HE MIGHT END UP ***CAPTURING*** YOU AGAIN!!
THAT PROSPECT EXISTS NO MATTER WHERE I AM...IF HE REALLY ***HAS*** REJOINED THE MIKAGE.
I MUST'VE BEEN MISTAKEN WHEN I THOUGHT I'D KNOWN HIM BEFORE. IT SEEMS WE'RE ***DOOMED*** TO FIGHT.
I'LL GO GET SHURO AND CHIDORI!! THEY SAY ***THREE HEADS*** ARE BETTER THAN ***ONE***!
Who says??

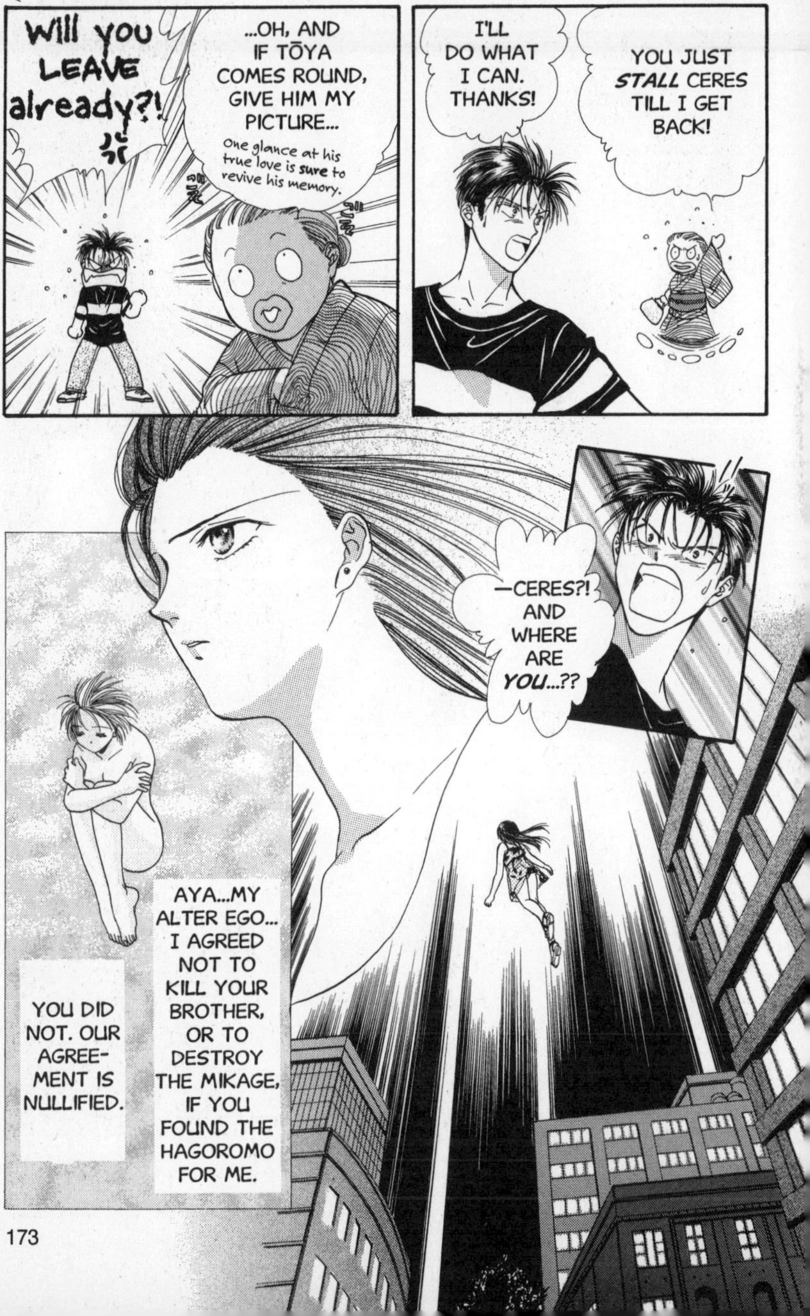
YOU JUST STALL CERES TILL I GET BACK!
I'LL DO WHAT I CAN. THANKS!
...OH, AND IF TŌYA COMES ROUND, GIVE HIM MY PICTURE...
One glance at his true love is sure to revive his memory.
Will you LEAVE already?!
—CERES?! AND WHERE ARE YOU...??
AYA...MY ALTER EGO... I AGREED NOT TO KILL YOUR BROTHER, OR TO DESTROY THE MIKAGE, IF YOU FOUND THE HAGOROMO FOR ME.
YOU DID NOT. OUR AGREEMENT IS NULLIFIED.

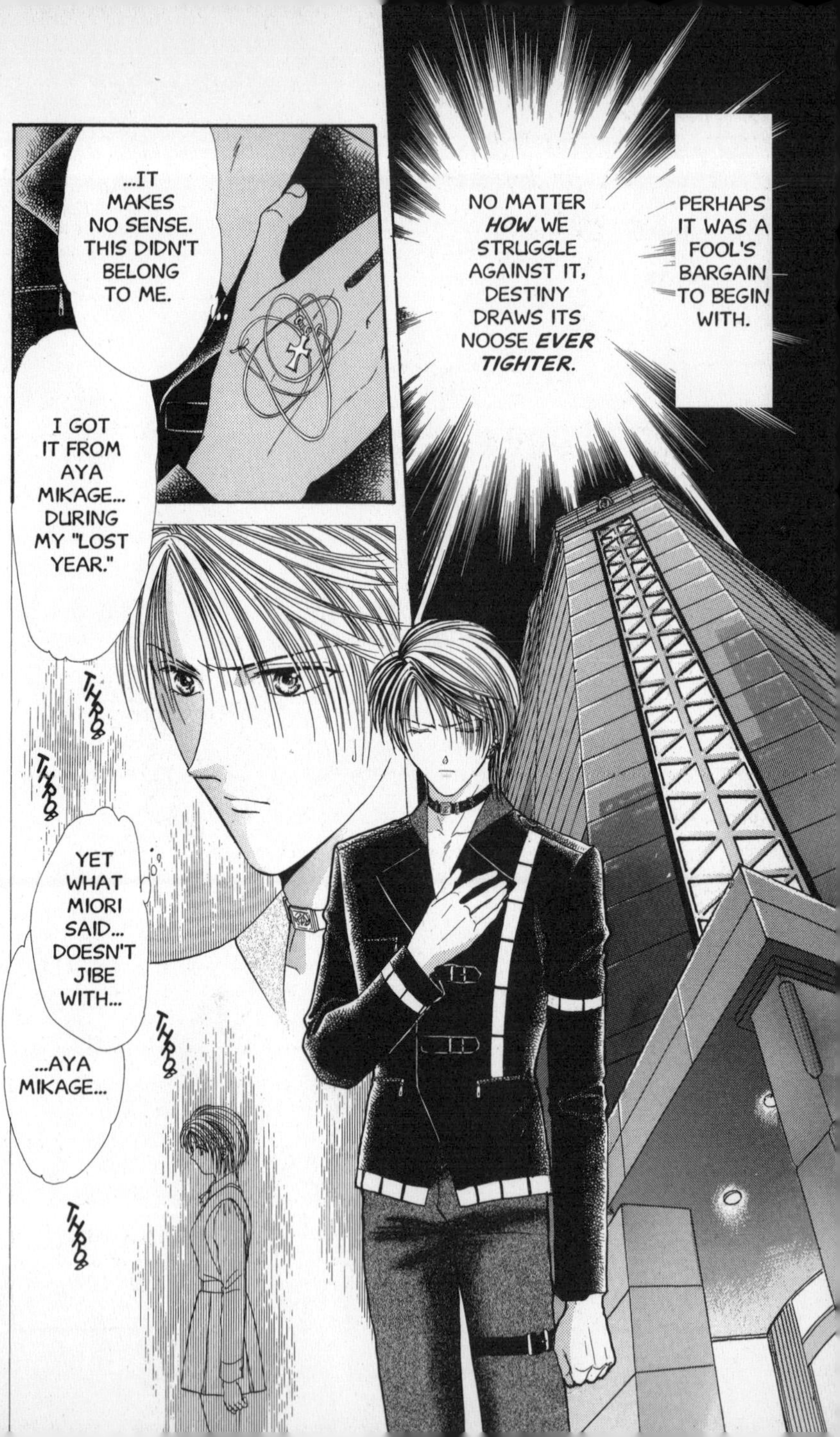
PERHAPS IT WAS A FOOL'S BARGAIN TO BEGIN WITH.
NO MATTER *HOW* WE STRUGGLE AGAINST IT, DESTINY DRAWS ITS NOOSE *EVER TIGHTER.*
...IT MAKES NO SENSE. THIS DIDN'T BELONG TO ME.
I GOT IT FROM AYA MIKAGE... DURING MY "LOST YEAR."
THROB
THROB
YET WHAT MIORI SAID... DOESN'T JIBE WITH...
THROB
...AYA MIKAGE...
THROB

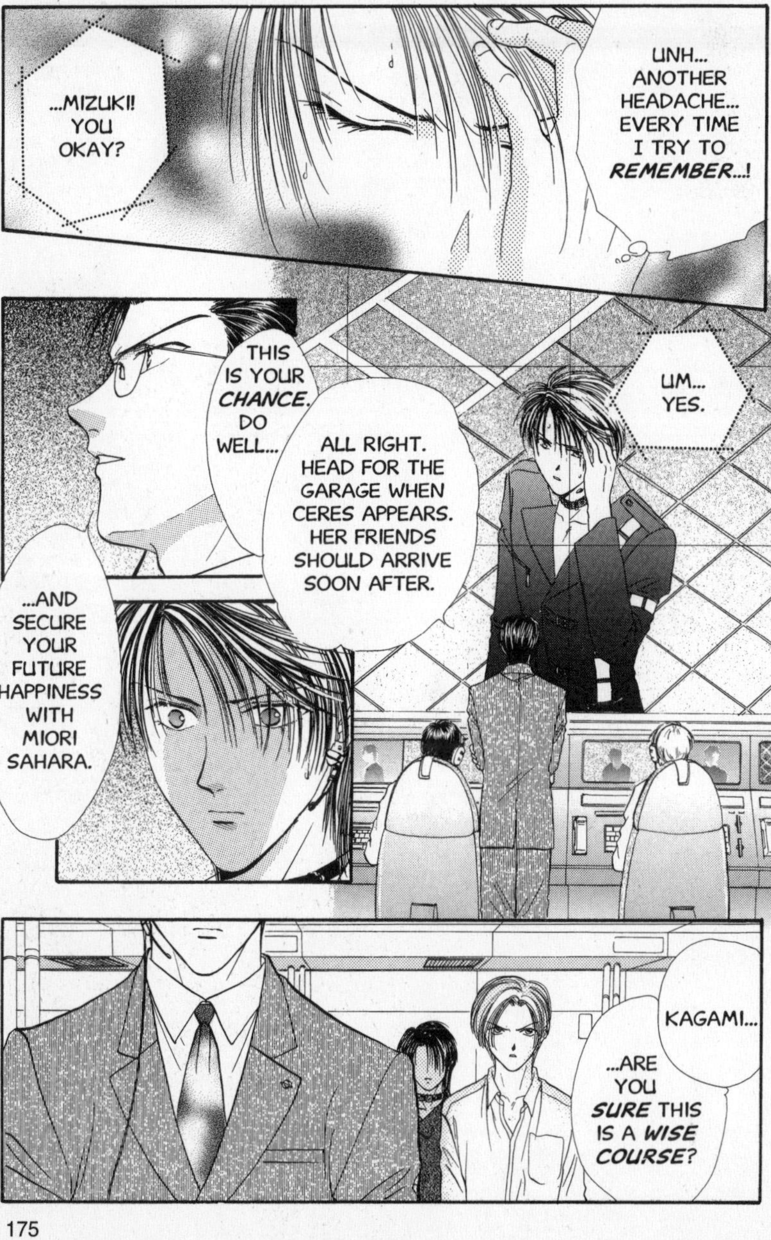
UNH... ANOTHER HEADACHE... EVERY TIME I TRY TO *REMEMBER*...!
...MIZUKI! YOU OKAY?
UM... YES.
ALL RIGHT. HEAD FOR THE GARAGE WHEN CERES APPEARS. HER FRIENDS SHOULD ARRIVE SOON AFTER.
THIS IS YOUR *CHANCE*. DO WELL...
...AND SECURE YOUR FUTURE HAPPINESS WITH MIORI SAHARA.
KAGAMI...
...ARE YOU *SURE* THIS IS A *WISE COURSE*?

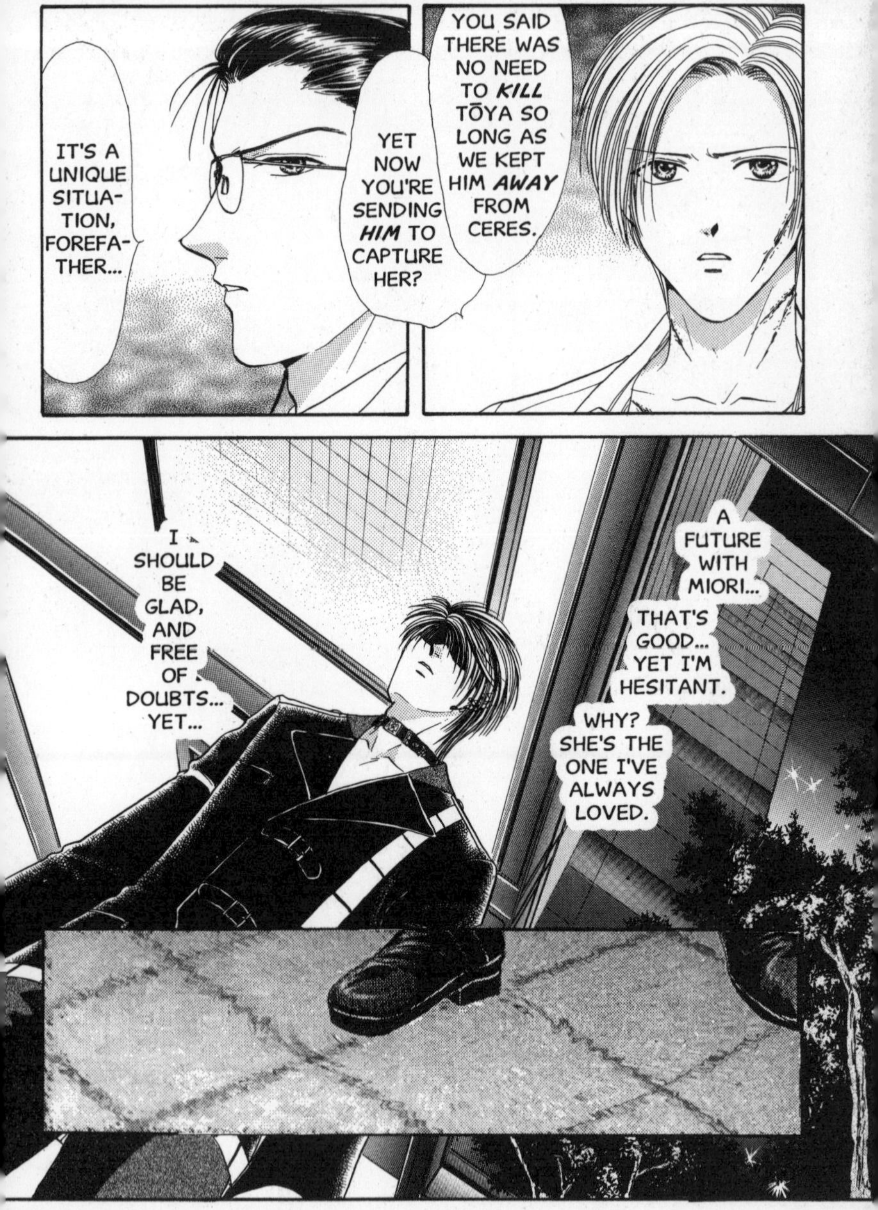
YOU SAID THERE WAS NO NEED TO *KILL* TŌYA SO LONG AS WE KEPT HIM *AWAY* FROM CERES.
YET NOW YOU'RE SENDING *HIM* TO CAPTURE HER?
IT'S A UNIQUE SITUATION, FOREFATHER...
A FUTURE WITH MIORI...
THAT'S GOOD... YET I'M HESITANT.
WHY? SHE'S THE ONE I'VE ALWAYS LOVED.
I SHOULD BE GLAD, AND FREE OF DOUBTS... YET...

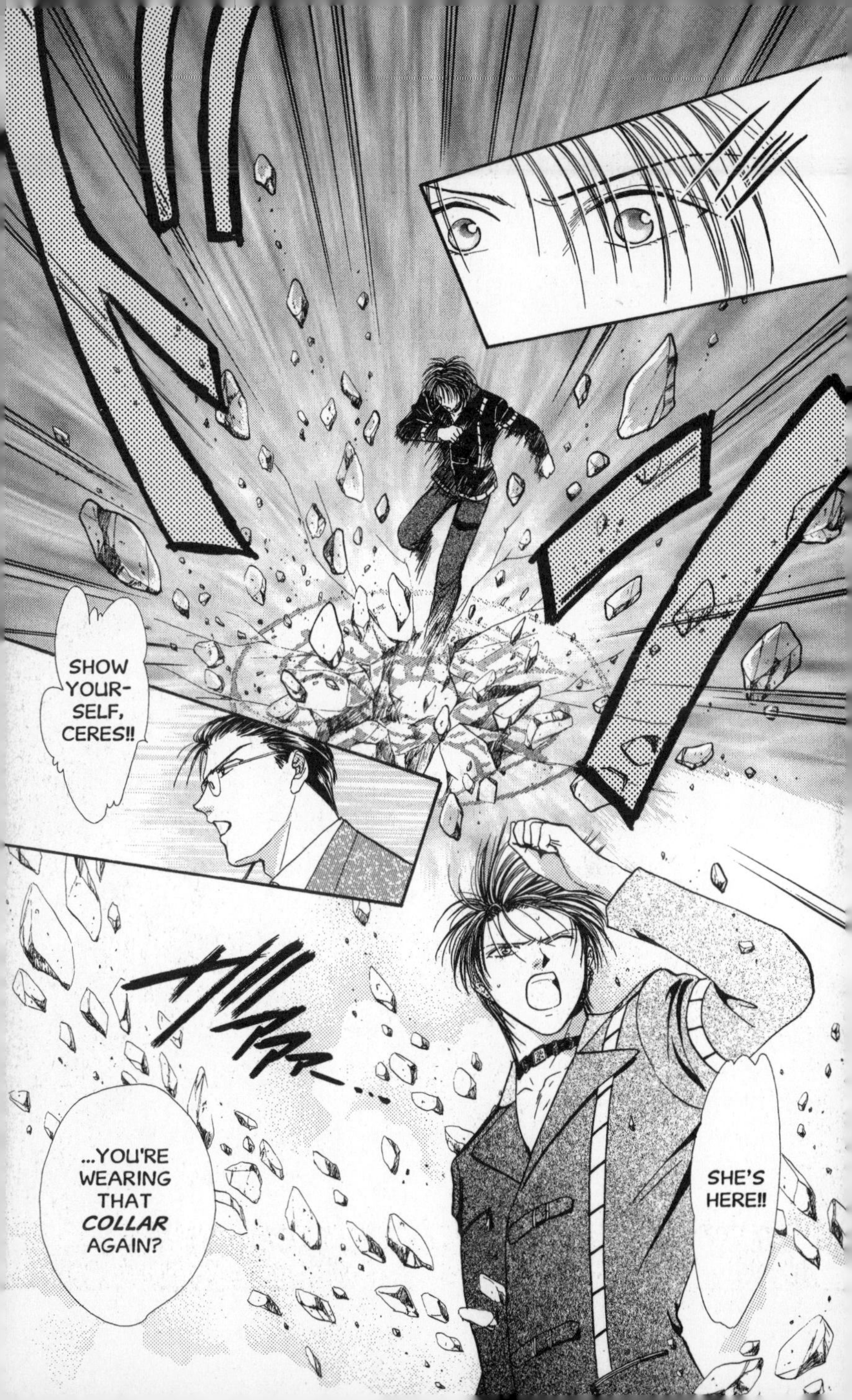
SHOW YOUR-SELF, CERES!!
SHE'S HERE!!
...YOU'RE WEARING THAT *COLLAR* AGAIN?

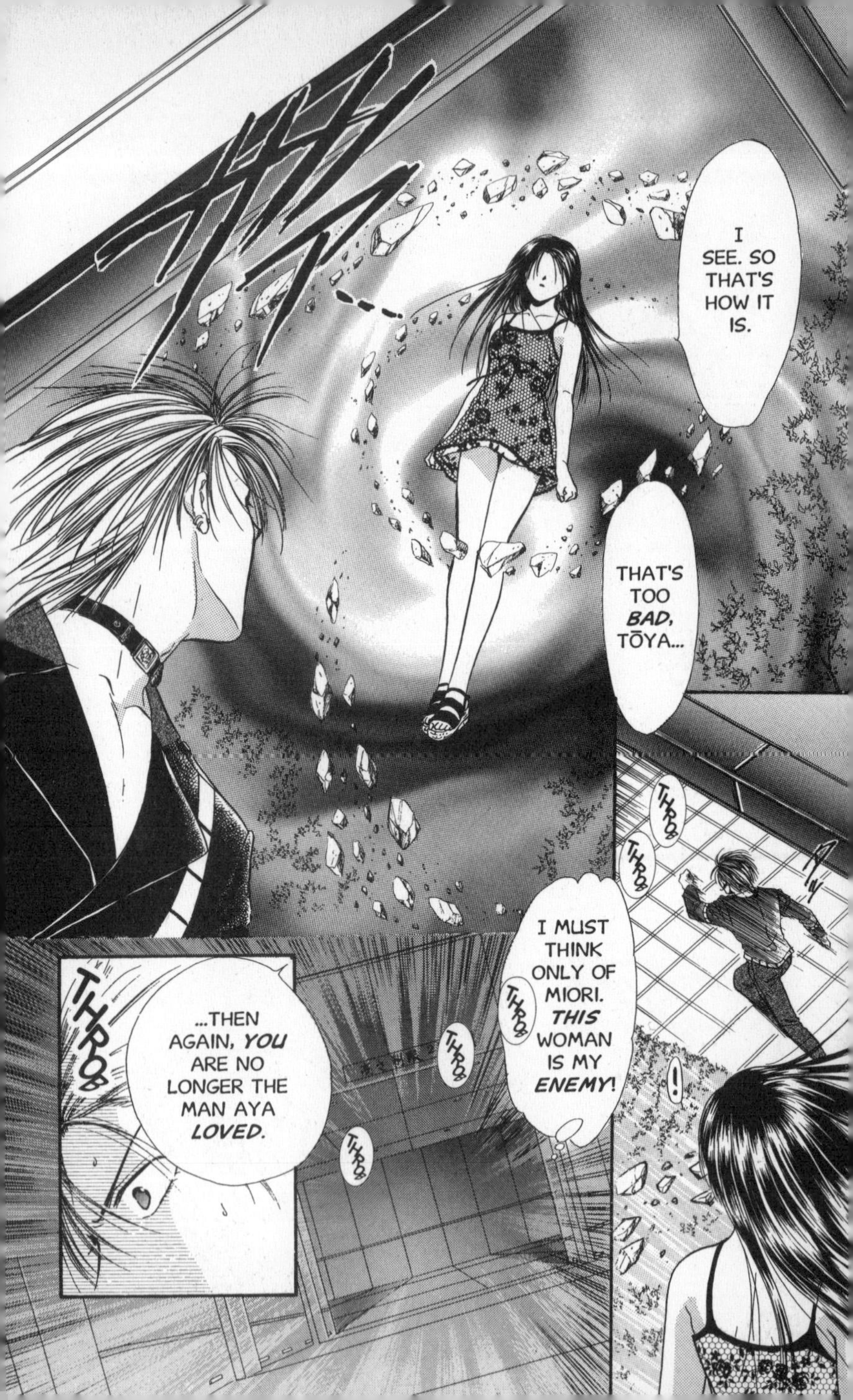
I SEE. SO THAT'S HOW IT IS.
THAT'S TOO BAD, TŌYA...
THROB
THROB
I MUST THINK ONLY OF MIORI. THIS WOMAN IS MY ENEMY!
THROB
!
THROB
THROB
...THEN AGAIN, YOU ARE NO LONGER THE MAN AYA LOVED.
THROB

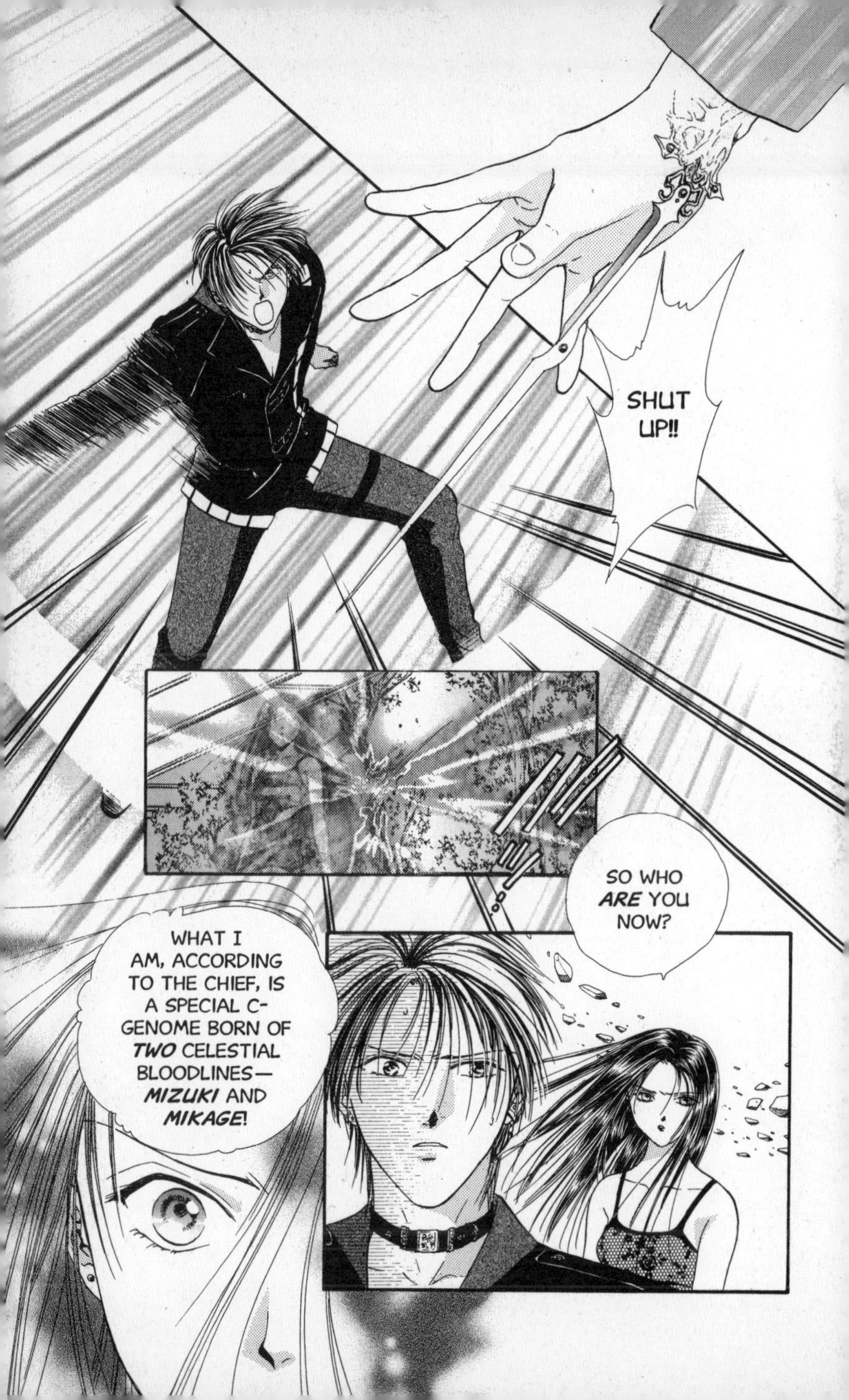
SHUT UP!!
SO WHO *ARE* YOU NOW?
WHAT I AM, ACCORDING TO THE CHIEF, IS A SPECIAL C-GENOME BORN OF *TWO* CELESTIAL BLOODLINES—*MIZUKI* AND *MIKAGE*!

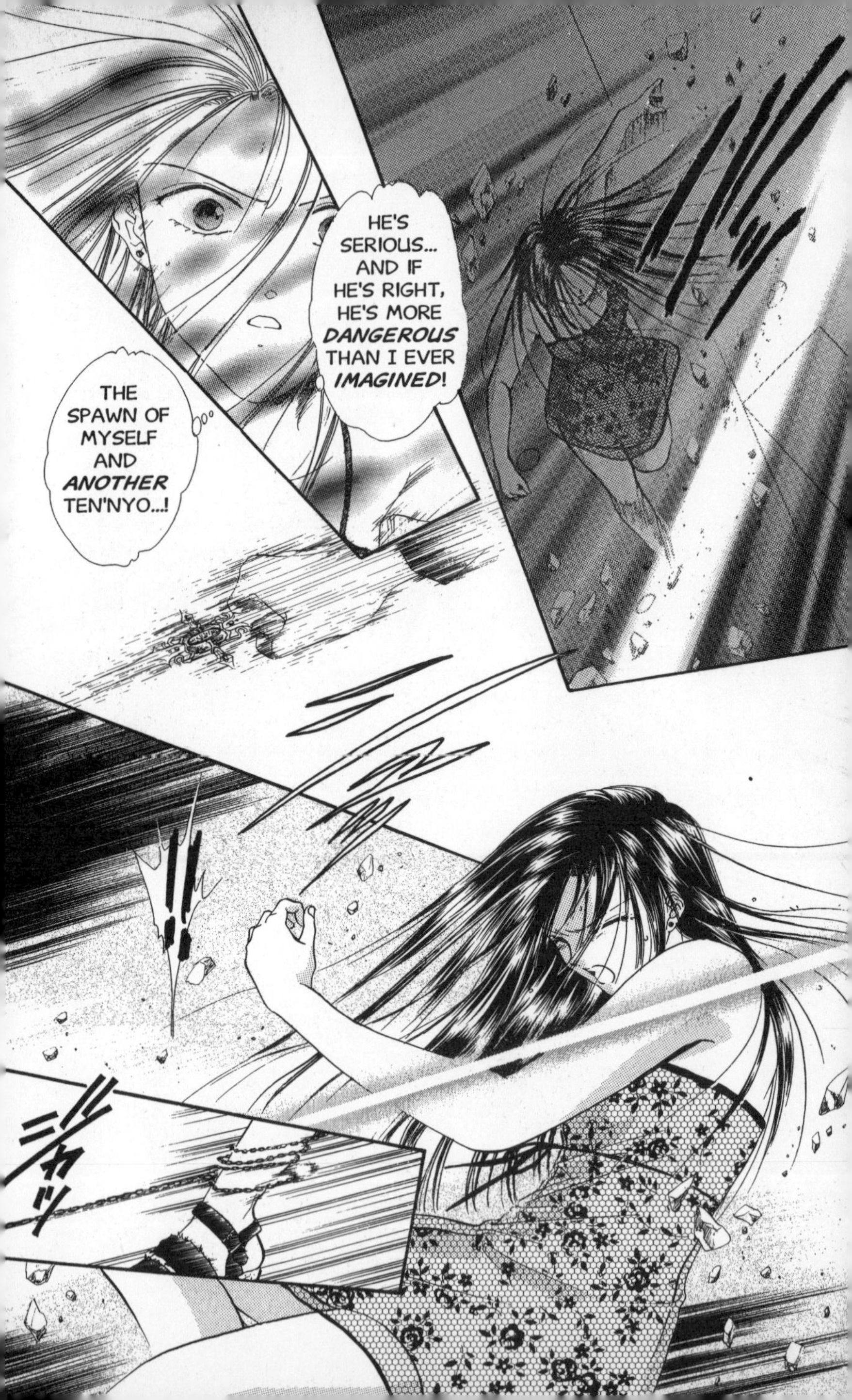
HE'S SERIOUS... AND IF HE'S RIGHT, HE'S MORE *DANGEROUS* THAN I EVER *IMAGINED*!
THE SPAWN OF MYSELF AND *ANOTHER* TEN'NYO...!
ジャッ

Ceres: 8

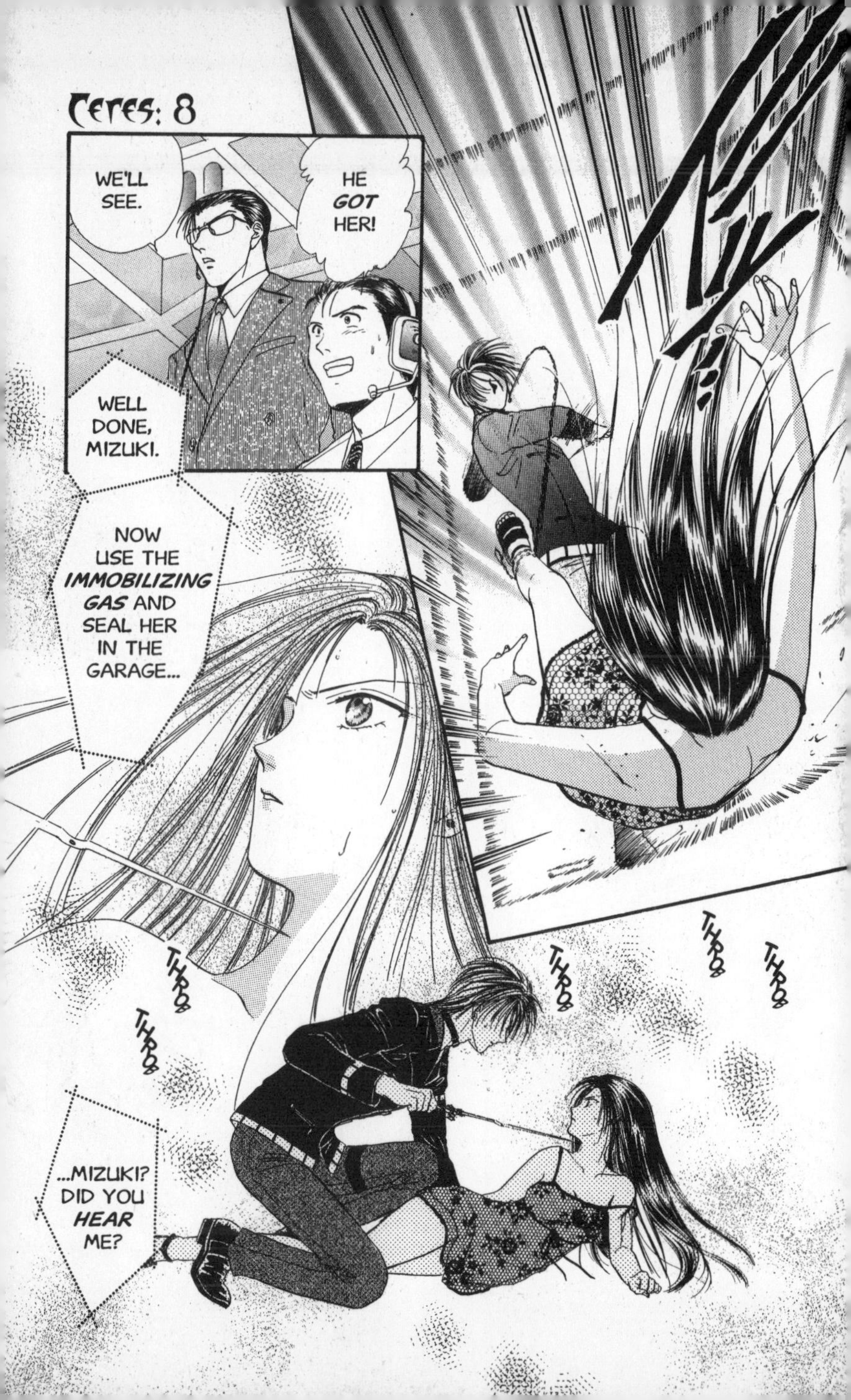
HE *GOT* HER!
WE'LL SEE.
WELL DONE, MIZUKI.
NOW USE THE *IMMOBILIZING GAS* AND SEAL HER IN THE GARAGE...
THROB THROB
THROB THROB
...MIZUKI? DID YOU *HEAR* ME?

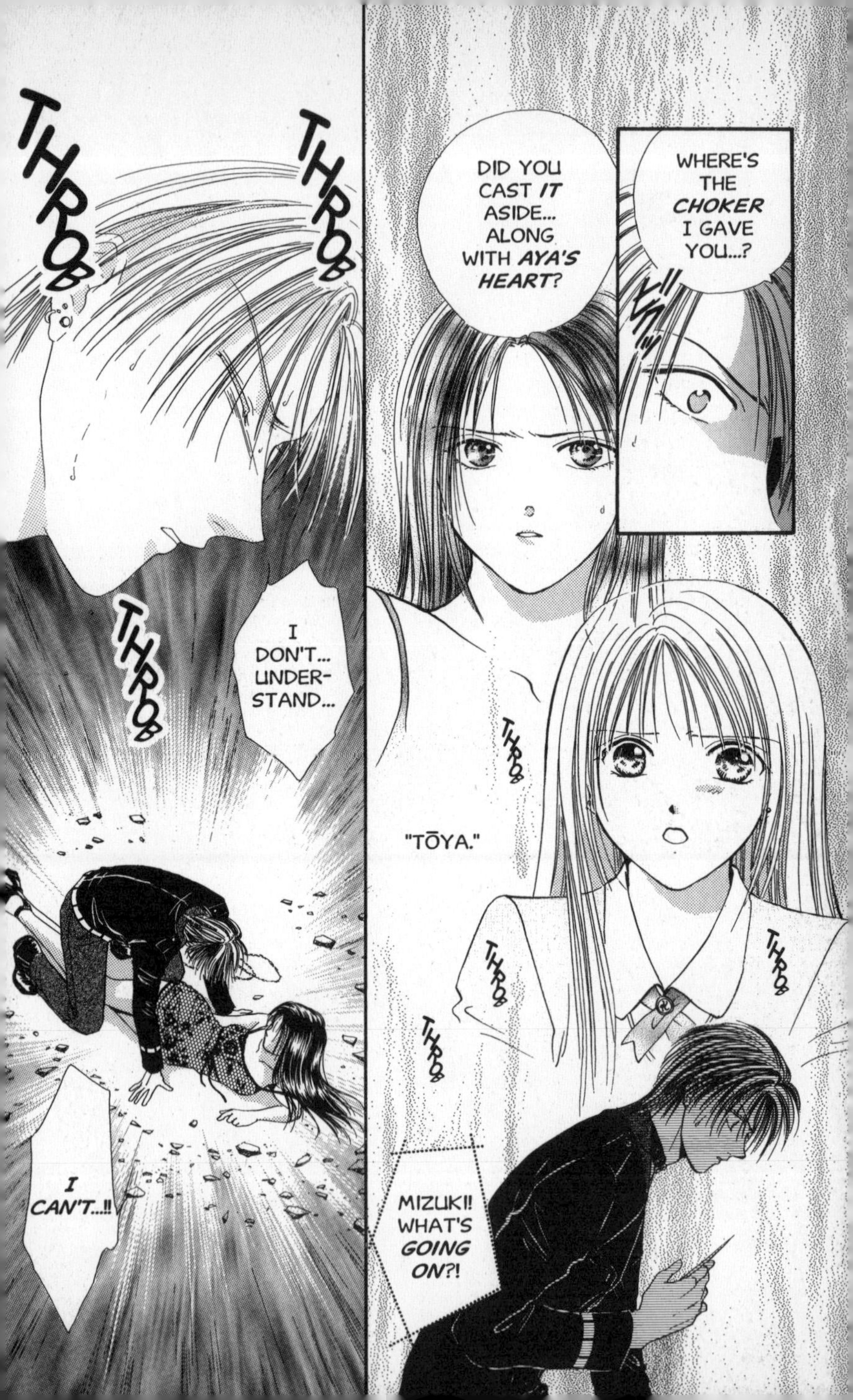
WHERE'S THE *CHOKER* I GAVE YOU...?
DID YOU CAST *IT* ASIDE... ALONG WITH *AYA'S HEART*?
THROB
THROB
THROB
"TŌYA."
THROB
MIZUKI! WHAT'S *GOING ON*?!
THROB
THROB
THROB
I DON'T... UNDER-STAND...
I CAN'T...!!

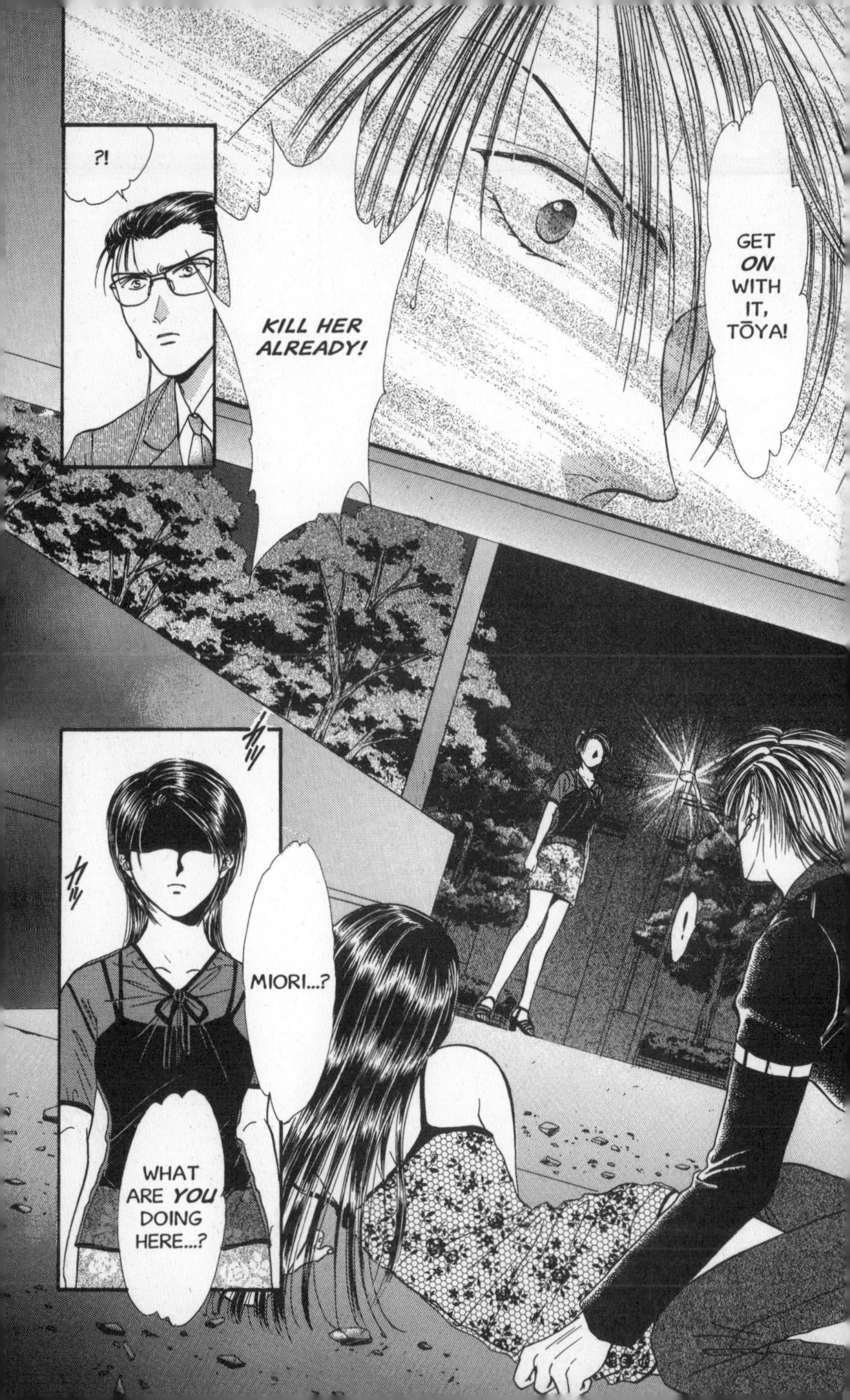
GET *ON* WITH IT, TŌYA!
KILL HER ALREADY!
?!
!
MIORI...?
WHAT ARE *YOU* DOING HERE...?

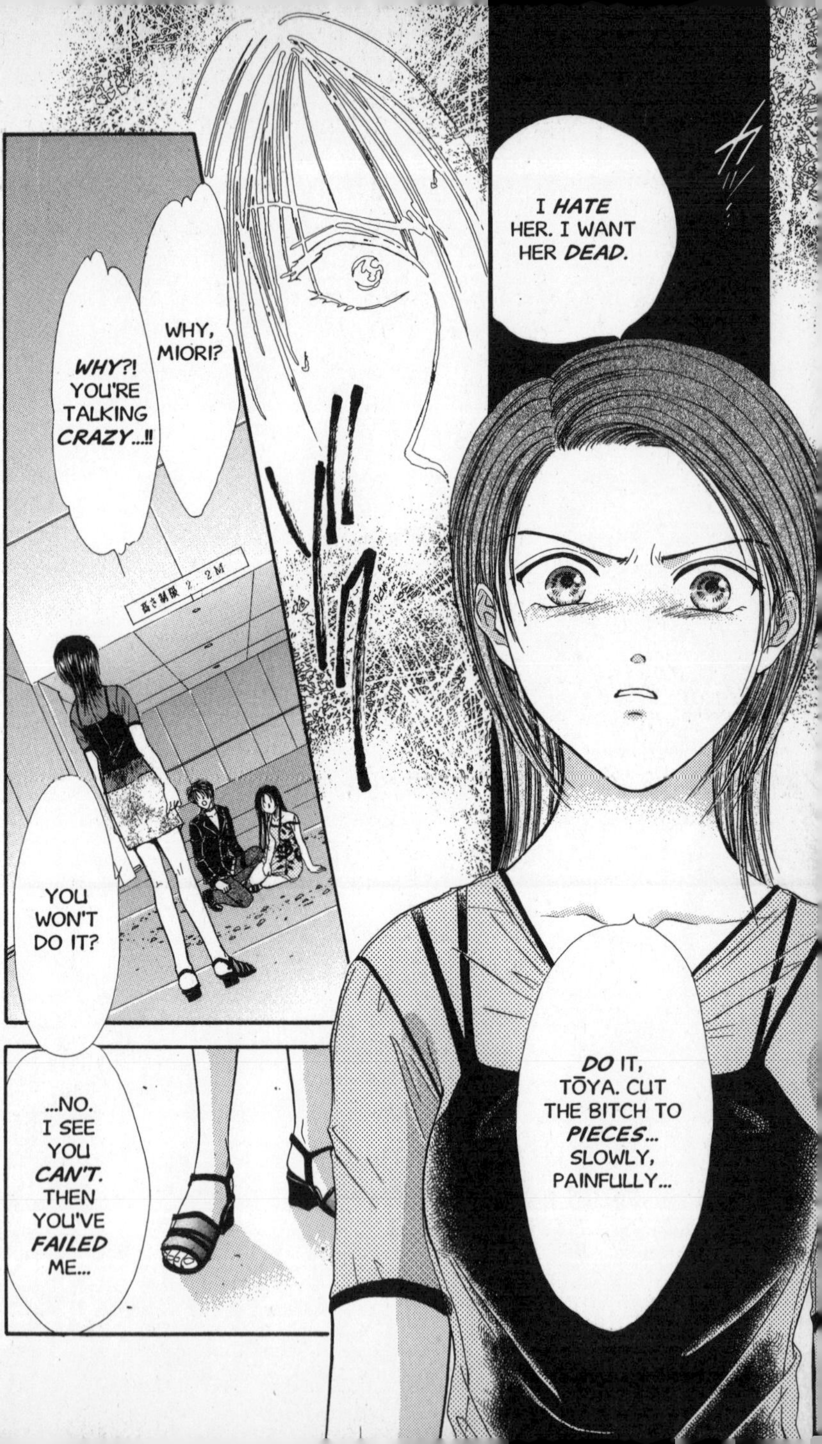
I *HATE* HER. I WANT HER *DEAD*.
DO IT, TŌYA. CUT THE BITCH TO *PIECES*... SLOWLY, PAINFULLY...
WHY, MIORI?
WHY?! YOU'RE TALKING *CRAZY*...!!
YOU WON'T DO IT?
...NO. I SEE YOU *CAN'T*. THEN YOU'VE *FAILED* ME...

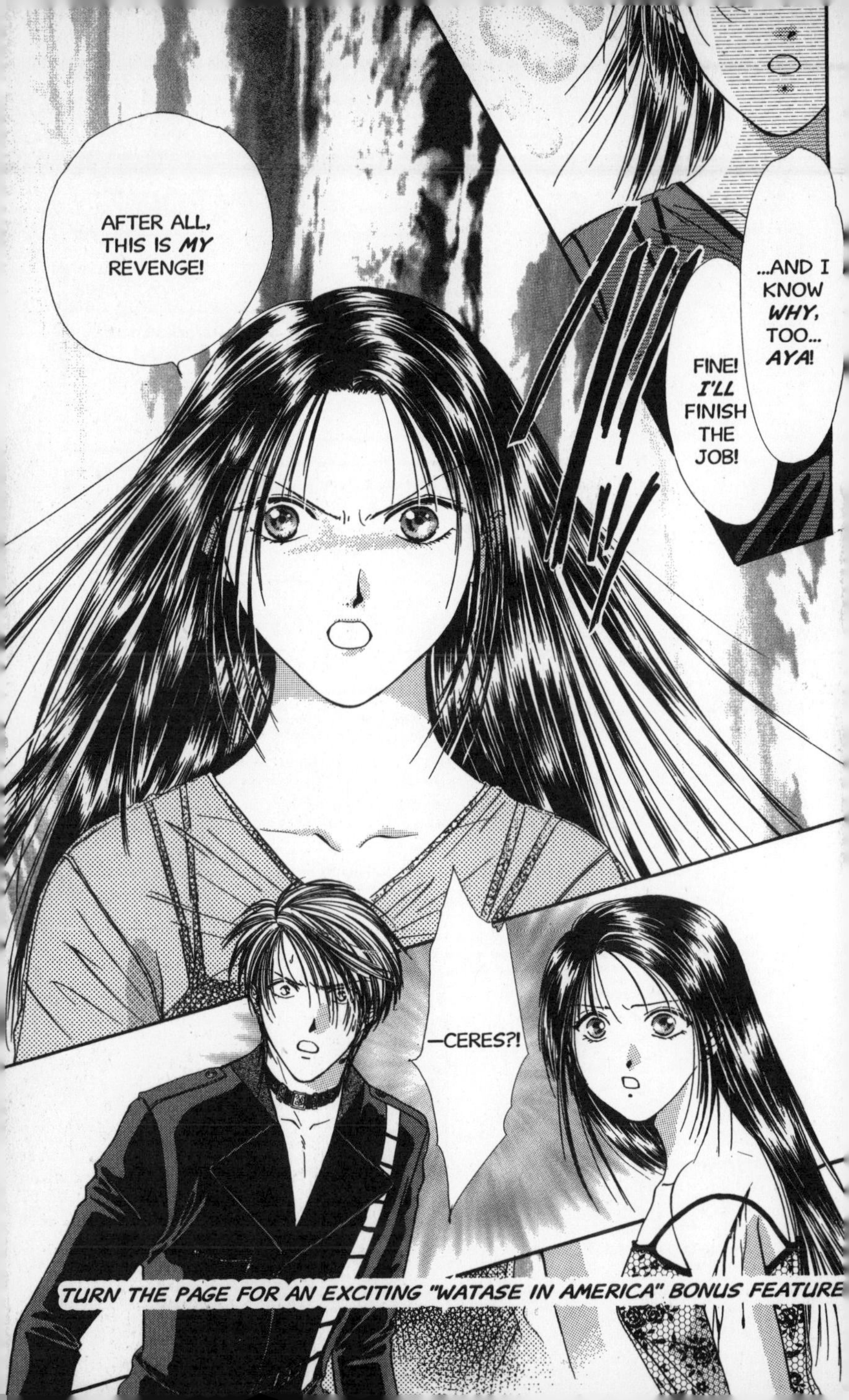
...AND I KNOW WHY, TOO... AYA!
FINE! I'LL FINISH THE JOB!
AFTER ALL, THIS IS MY REVENGE!
—CERES?!
TURN THE PAGE FOR AN EXCITING "WATASE IN AMERICA" BONUS FEATURE

I had pages left over, so...

'98 ANIME EXPO in L.A. REPORT

"In which the Author discovers how big a deal anime is overseas"

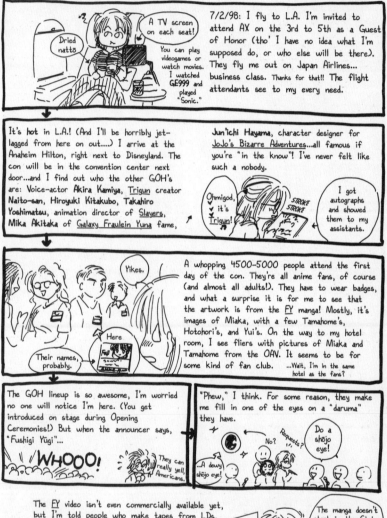

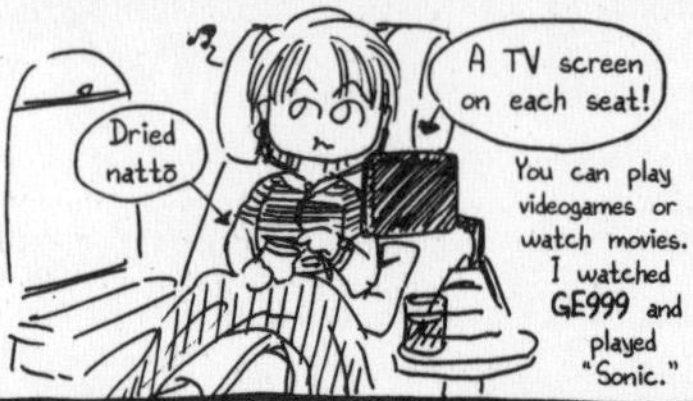
A TV screen on each seat!
Dried nattō
You can play videogames or watch movies. I watched GE999 and played "Sonic."

7/2/98: I fly to L.A. I'm invited to attend AX on the 3rd to 5th as a Guest of Honor (tho' I have no idea what I'm supposed do, or who else will be there). They fly me out on Japan Airlines... business class. Thanks for that!! The flight attendants see to my every need.

It's **hot** in L.A.! (And I'll be horribly jet-lagged from here on out....) I arrive at the Anaheim Hilton, right next to Disneyland. The con will be in the convention center next door...and I find out who the other GOH's are: Voice-actor **Akira Kamiya**, Trigun creator **Naito-san**, **Hiroyuki Kitakubo**, **Takahiro Yoshimatsu**, animation director of Slayers, **Mika Akitaka** of Galaxy Fraulein Yuna fame, **Jun'ichi Hayama**, character designer for JoJo's Bizarre Adventures...all famous if you're "in the know"! I've never felt like such a nobody.

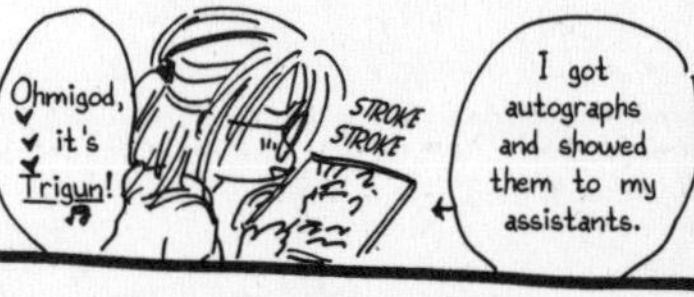
I got autographs and showed them to my assistants.
STROKE STROKE
Ohmigod, it's Trigun!

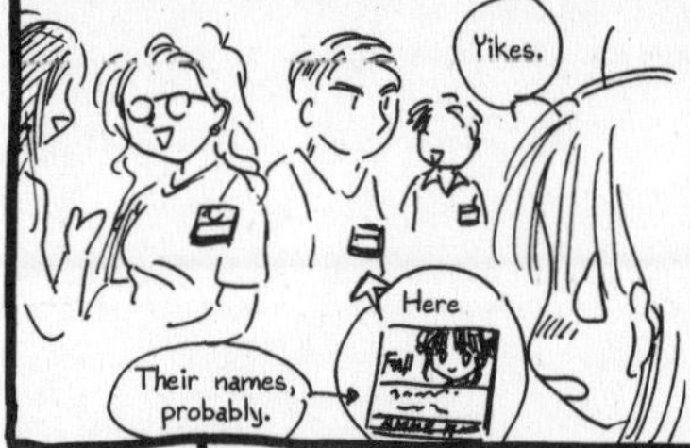
Yikes.
Here
Their names, probably.

A whopping 4500-5000 people attend the first day of the con. They're all anime fans, of course (and almost all adults!). They have to wear badges, and what a surprise it is for me to see that the artwork is from the FY manga! Mostly, it's images of Miaka, with a few Tamahome's, Hotohori's, and Yui's. On the way to my hotel room, I see fliers with pictures of Miaka and Tamahome from the OAV. It seems to be for some kind of fan club. ...Wait, I'm in the same hotel as the fans?

The GOH lineup is so awesome, I'm worried no one will notice I'm here. (You get introduced on stage during Opening Ceremonies!) But when the announcer says, "Fushigi Yūgi"...

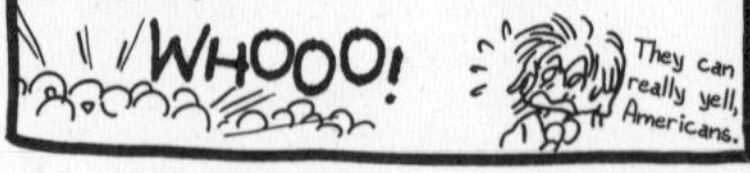
WHOOO!
They can really yell, Americans.

"Phew," I think. For some reason, they make me fill in one of the eyes on a "daruma" they have.

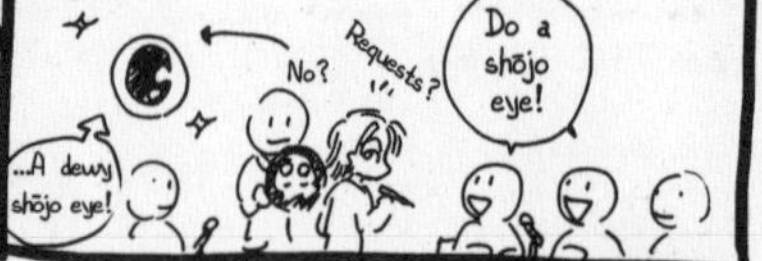
Do a shōjo eye!
Requests?
No?
...A dewy shōjo eye!

The FY video isn't even commercially available yet, but I'm told people who make tapes from LDs, etc., that they get from Japan, do it out of a sense of duty (?). I think some of anime's popularity comes from this sense of scarcity.

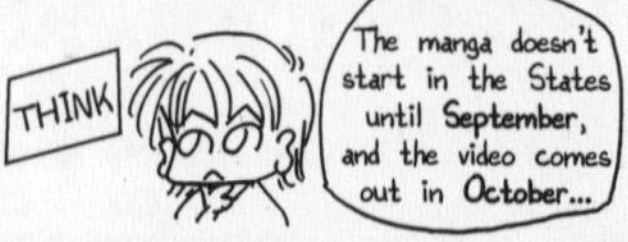
THINK
The manga doesn't start in the States until September, and the video comes out in October...

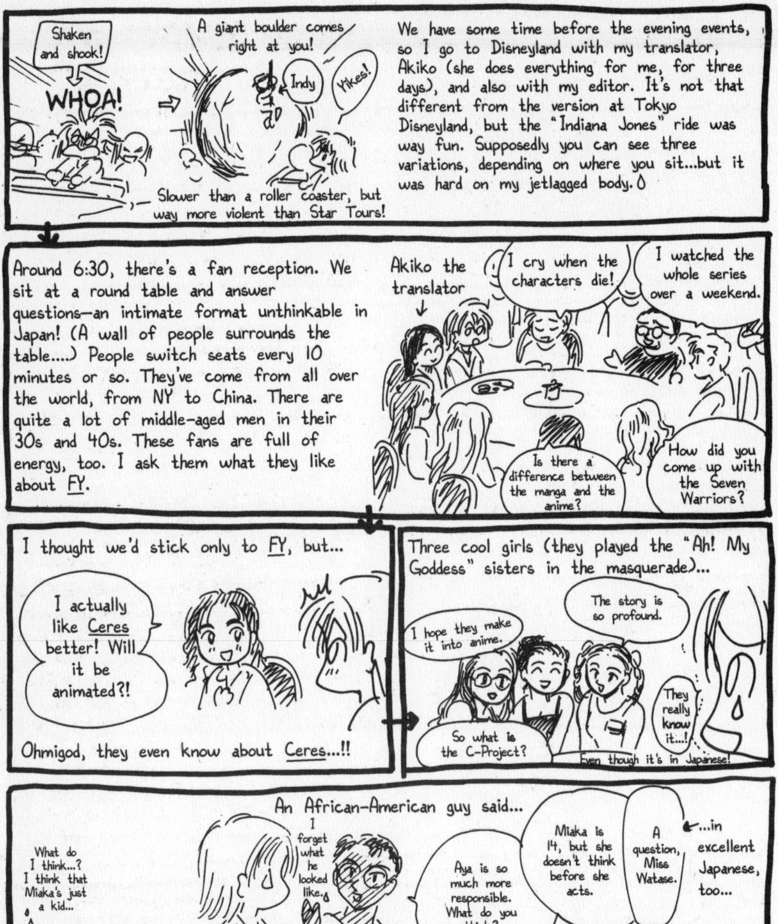
We have some time before the evening events, so I go to Disneyland with my translator, Akiko (she does everything for me, for three days), and also with my editor. It's not that different from the version at Tokyo Disneyland, but the "Indiana Jones" ride was way fun. Supposedly you can see three variations, depending on where you sit...but it was hard on my jetlagged body.
A giant boulder comes right at you!
Yikes!
Indy
Shaken and shook!
WHOA!
Slower than a roller coaster, but way more violent than Star Tours!
Around 6:30, there's a fan reception. We sit at a round table and answer questions—an intimate format unthinkable in Japan! (A wall of people surrounds the table....) People switch seats every 10 minutes or so. They've come from all over the world, from NY to China. There are quite a lot of middle-aged men in their 30s and 40s. These fans are full of energy, too. I ask them what they like about FY.
I watched the whole series over a weekend.
I cry when the characters die!
Akiko the translator
How did you come up with the Seven Warriors?
Is there a difference between the manga and the anime?
I thought we'd stick only to FY, but...
I actually like Ceres better! Will it be animated?!
Ohmigod, they even know about Ceres...!!
Three cool girls (they played the "Ah! My Goddess" sisters in the masquerade)...
The story is so profound.
I hope they make it into anime.
They really know it...!
So what is the C-Project?
Even though it's in Japanese!
An African-American guy said...
...in excellent Japanese, too...
A question, Miss Watase.
Miaka is 14, but she doesn't think before she acts.
Aya is so much more responsible. What do you think?
I forget what he looked like.
What do I think...? I think that Miaka's just a kid...

People in Japan tend to identify more with main characters who are kind of ditzy (it makes them more approachable), but, in comparison, girls in other countries seem much more studious. (I guess that's why she seems extra stupid, to them....) I've heard that, in some circles, Japanese people—even those over 20—are considered no better than kids themselves, mentally. Maybe young people in Japan should study more, so they won't come under this kind of criticism from other countries....

I include myself, of course

(Though the "manga" Miaka and the "anime" Miaka have their differences, too.)

And then! The next day! Panel discussions start!!

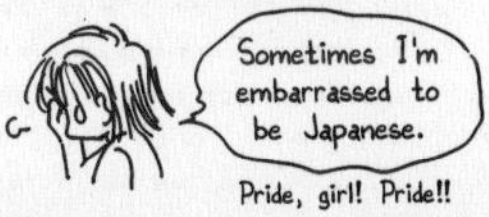
Sometimes I'm embarrassed to be Japanese.
Pride, girl! Pride!!

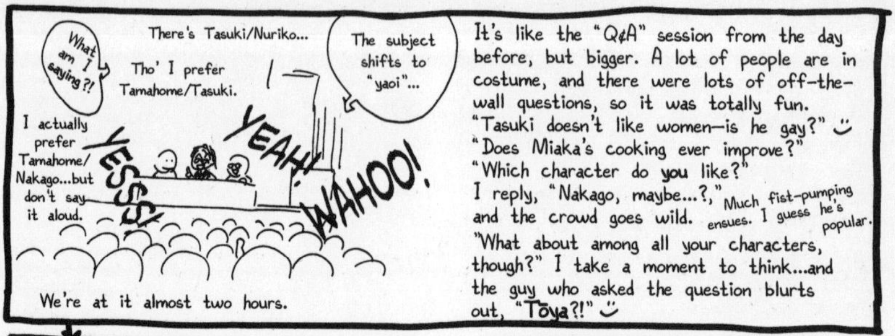
It's like the "Q&A" session from the day before, but bigger. A lot of people are in costume, and there were lots of off-the-wall questions, so it was totally fun.
"Tasuki doesn't like women—is he gay?"
"Does Miaka's cooking ever improve?"
"Which character do you like?"
I reply, "Nakago, maybe...?," and the crowd goes wild.
Much fist-pumping ensues. I guess he's popular.
"What about among all your characters, though?" I take a moment to think...and the guy who asked the question blurts out, "Tōya?!"
The subject shifts to "yaoi"...
There's Tasuki/Nuriko...
Tho' I prefer Tamahome/Tasuki.
What am I saying?!
YEAH!
WAHOO!
YESS!
I actually prefer Tamahome/Nakago...but don't say it aloud.
We're at it almost two hours.

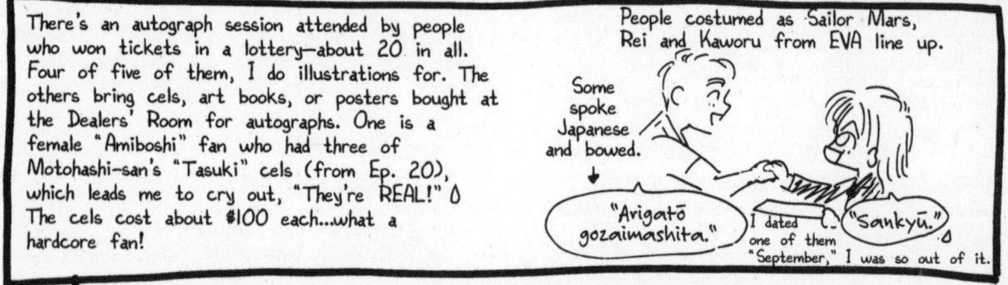
People costumed as Sailor Mars, Rei and Kaworu from EVA line up.
"Sankyū."
I dated one of them "September," I was so out of it.
Some spoke Japanese and bowed.
"Arigatō gozaimashita."
There's an autograph session attended by people who won tickets in a lottery—about 20 in all. Four of five of them, I do illustrations for. The others bring cels, art books, or posters bought at the Dealers' Room for autographs. One is a female "Amiboshi" fan who had three of Motohashi-san's "Tasuki" cels (from Ep. 20), which leads me to cry out, "They're REAL!" The cels cost about $100 each...what a hardcore fan!

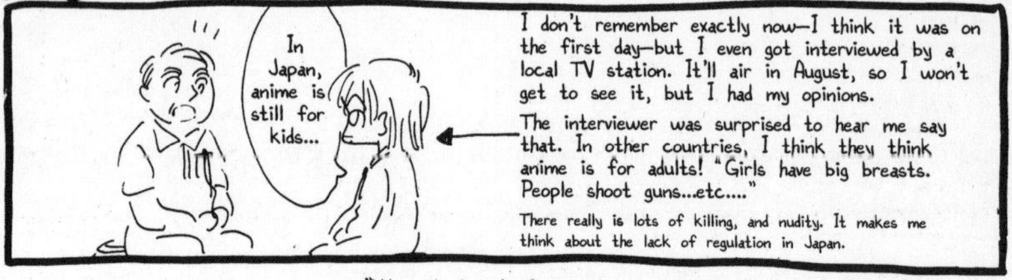
I don't remember exactly now—I think it was on the first day—but I even got interviewed by a local TV station. It'll air in August, so I won't get to see it, but I had my opinions.
The interviewer was surprised to hear me say that. In other countries, I think they think anime is for adults! "Girls have big breasts. People shoot guns...etc...."
There really is lots of killing, and nudity. It makes me think about the lack of regulation in Japan.
In Japan, anime is still for kids...

"Was it tough for you, as a woman, to break into the field?" I'm surprised to hear that, even in the States, where things are more progressive, "even actresses lose the best roles to men." I reply, "In this line of work, there's no gender. I'm no less passionate than any man about it." He tells me it's a good answer.

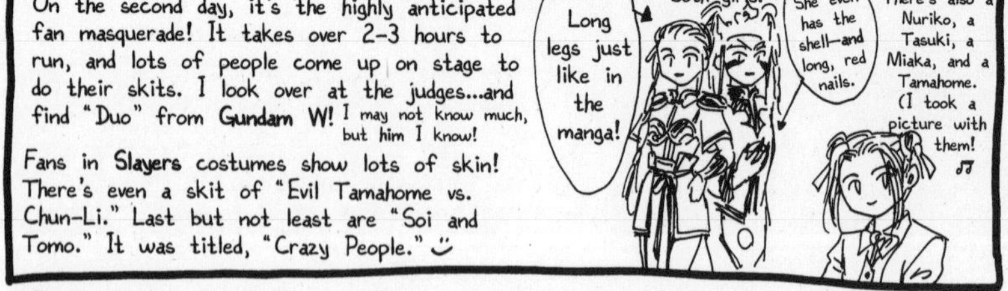
There's also a Nuriko, a Tasuki, a Miaka, and a Tamahome. (I took a picture with them!
She even has the shell—and long, red nails.
Both girls.
Long legs just like in the manga!
On the second day, it's the highly anticipated fan masquerade! It takes over 2-3 hours to run, and lots of people come up on stage to do their skits. I look over at the judges...and find "Duo" from Gundam W!
I may not know much, but him I know!
Fans in Slayers costumes show lots of skin! There's even a skit of "Evil Tamahome vs. Chun-Li." Last but not least are "Soi and Tomo." It was titled, "Crazy People."

I'm messing up the order of events, but after the autograph session there was a magazine interview—with reporters from magazines of several countries! They tell me there's lots of FY fans in Europe, too. The female reporter from Germany is dressed in a kung-fu outfit.

On the third day, at 10:00 a.m., I have a panel with an American author and Naito-san. I'm sick from jetlag, though (and my stomach isn't handling the food...). Naito-san, Kamiya-san and the other GOH's were all super nice, BTW.

Japanese food, puriizu...!

My Japanese stomach is so picky.

AND THEN, ANOTHER AUTOGRAPH SESSION.

This time, there's a Miaka, a Nuriko, and a Kenshin lined up.

All money is donated to a cancer-research charity.

Sign-board

After a break, I get asked to donate an autograph for the auction (plus a few individual requests). I borrow some Copic markers from Naito-san, and draw the popular Nakago, Miaka, and Tamahome combo in color. I also sign a cel of Chichiri, and the first art book. I stay behind until the last minute and listen to Kamiya-san. When I get there, lots of anime stuff is being auctioned off.

My autograph is the last item auctioned. I keep nodding off, but this one I wake up for and tape with my camcorder. I assume it'll go quickly...but the price keeps going up, and the crowd keeps going wild! Amazingly, the winning bid comes in at $3200. The winner is a woman, and I go up on stage to hand it to her personally and shake her hand. I'm not worthy...

In Japan, they give this kind of stuff away as reader prizes...!!

A new record is set! 🜚 You could live in this country for THREE MONTHS with that kind of money!! 🜚

AT LAST, CLOSING CEREMONIES. I FILL IN THE OTHER "DARUMA" EYE.

I'm given some kind of trophy. The FY OAV seems to have received First Place in the "Best OAV" category...and it's not even released yet...!!

It should be Studio Pierrot's award, not mine.

Fatigue, lack of sleep, and inability to eat **anything** almost does me in. But, boy, I looked good for the camera...! There must have been at least 100 pictures taken of me, with various people. (This adds to the eyestrain.)

Recovery comes with the beauty of San Francisco—where I visit after the con—plus, I finally get JAPANESE FOOD!! ↘ It really is a beautiful city.

My thanks to everyone at Anime Expo and Viz Communications.

Man, this took long to write.

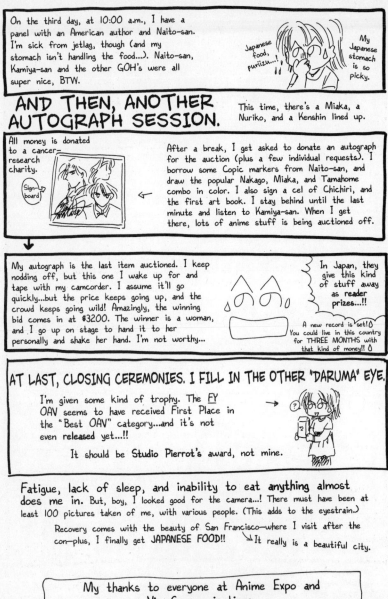

BY THE WAY...

There were members from the FY mailing list at the "Meet the GOH's" reception at the con, and they gave me a scrapbook.

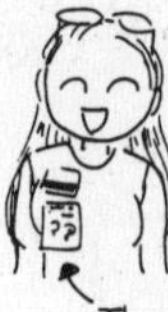
??

There were 7-8 of them, I think...?

They had homemade badges of their favorite characters.

The URLs of each character's fan club were written inside, so let me introduce some...

心宿 • NAKAGO'S RULING CLASS
www.geocities.com/Tokyo/Garden/8332/nakago_fanclub.html

氐宿 • THE CACKLING TOMO FAN CLUB
www.geocities.com/Tokyo/Bay/6286/

井宿 • CHICHIRI'S DA (DELIRIOUS ADDICTS) CLUB
www.geocities.com/Tokyo/Bay/6409/

THE NO DA! MISSION
www.geocities.com/Tokyo/Flats/6643/nodaindex.html

翼宿 THE DROOLING TASUKI FAN CLUB www.geocities.com/Tokyo/Temple/8545/

星宿 THE SWOONING HOTOHORI FANCLUB www.geocities.com/Tokyo/Pagoda/4705

柳宿 THE NURIKO FAN CLUB www.ryuuen.com/nuriko/

亢宿 角宿 THE SEIRYŪ TWINS FAN CLUB www.angelfire.com/anime/seiryuutwins/index.html

鬼宿 TAMAHOME'S FANCLUB http://Pages.nyu.edu/~gss200/FY/fanclub/fanclub.html

And last but not least...!!

十夜 TŌYA FAN CLUB (AYASHI NO CERES) www.geocities.com/Tokyo/6827/tooya.html

A big hit abroad?

If you've got a computer, why not look 'em up?

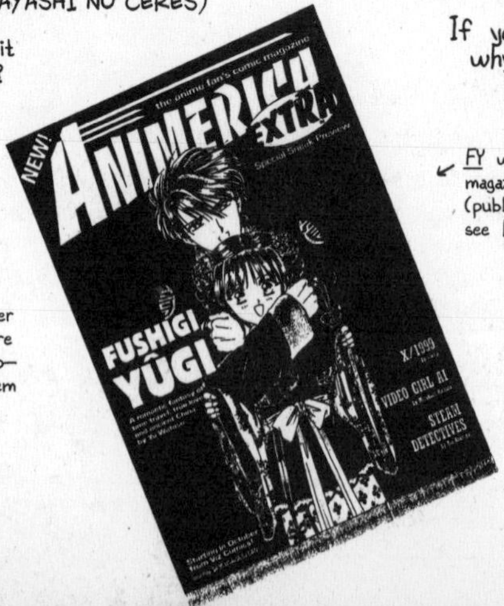
NEW!
ANIMERICA EXTRA
the anime fan's comic magazine
Special Sneak Preview
FUSHIGI YÛGI
X/1999
VIDEO GIRL AI
STEAM DETECTIVES

American version

FY will be running in this magazine, starting Autumn '98 (published by Viz). The issue you see here is a promo copy.

The other titles are good, too—check 'em out!

Maybe those of us in Japan can get a copy by visiting the States...?

This'll be the sixth language it's translated into. I keep hearing rumors of an Italian version. Italian...?!

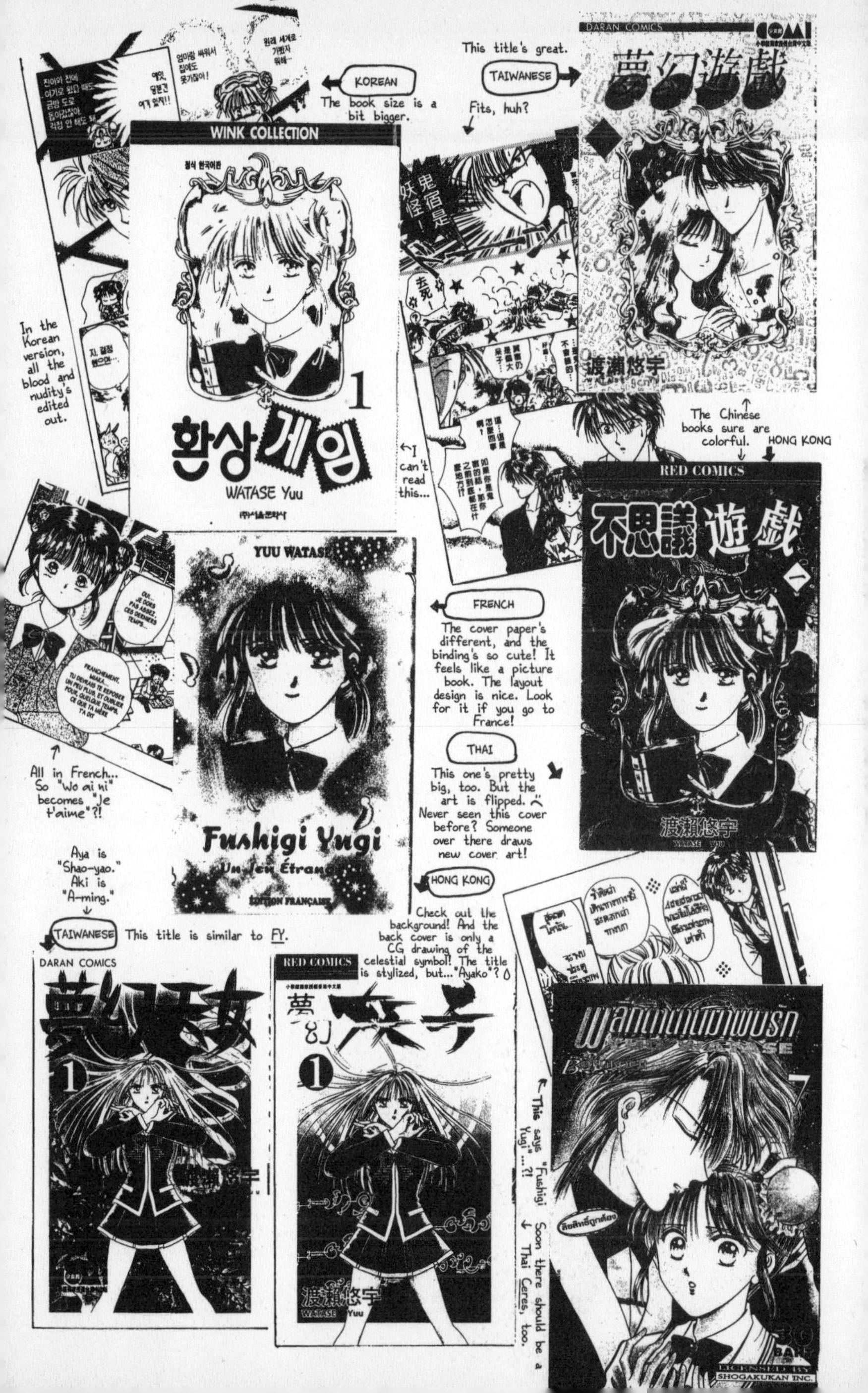
DARAN COMICS
夢幻遊戲
渡瀨悠宇
This title's great.
TAIWANESE
Fits, huh?
KOREAN
The book size is a bit bigger.
WINK COLLECTION
1
환상게임
WATASE Yuu
In the Korean version, all the blood and nudity's edited out.
I can't read this...
The Chinese books sure are colorful.
HONG KONG
RED COMICS
不思議遊戲
渡瀨悠宇
WATASE YUU
YUU WATASE
Fushigi Yugi
Un Jeu Étrange
ÉDITION FRANÇAISE
FRENCH
The cover paper's different, and the binding's so cute! It feels like a picture book. The layout design is nice. Look for it if you go to France!
All in French... So "Wo ai ni" becomes "Je t'aime"?!
THAI
This one's pretty big, too. But the art is flipped. Never seen this cover before? Someone over there draws new cover art!
Aya is "Shao-yao." Aki is "A-ming."
HONG KONG
Check out the background! And the back cover is only a CG drawing of the celestial symbol! The title is stylized, but..."Ayako"?
TAIWANESE
This title is similar to FY.
DARAN COMICS
1
RED COMICS
1
渡瀨悠宇
WATASE Yuu
This says "Fushigi Yugi"...?!
Soon there should be a Thai Ceres, too.
LICENSED BY SHOGAKUKAN INC.

The CERES Guide to Sound Effects

We've left most of the sound effects in CERES as Yû Watase originally created them–in Japanese. VIZ has created this glossary to help you decipher, page-by-page and panel-by-panel, what all those foreign words and background noises mean. Use this guide to impress your friends with your new Japanese vocabulary. The glossary lists the page number then panel. For example, 3.1 indicates page 3, panel 1.

007.1 FX: Chi Chi Chi Chi ("Tic-Toc, Tic-Toc")
008.1 FX: Bururururu (vibration of phone)
008.2 FX: Ha ("Gasp!," exclamation)
013.4 FX: Za (waves)
013.5 FX: Musu ("Hmph!")
015.1 FX: Zân (more prolonged wave-sounds)
015.3 FX: Za (waves)
015.4 FX: Basha Basha (flailing splash)
016.1 FX: Ha ("Gasp!," exclamation)
017.3 FX: Dopûn (big splash)
017.4 FX: Gobo Gobo (burble, burble [typically, drowning])
018.4 FX: Pon ("pat," controlled "touch" sound)
020.3 FX: Ha ("Gasp!," exclamation)
021.5 FX: Bururuku (vibration of phone)
025.2 FX: Ta ("dash")
025.3 FX: Dôn (heavy dramatic turn ["da-dah-DAH!"])
025.5 FX: Gan Gan Gan Gan (smacking head against wall)
026.3 FX: Gashân-Doka ("crash! smash!")
026.5 FX: Pa ("blink")
026.6 FX: Su ("fwish," light "brushing against" sound)
027.2 FX: Gyu ("squeeze" sound)
029.2 FX: Chi Chi Chi ("tweeting" birds)
029.3 FX: Su ("fwish," light "brushing against" sound)
029.4 FX: Chi Chi Chi ("tweeting" birds)
030.2 FX: Su ("fwish," light "brushing against" sound)
032.1 FX: Hyuuuuu (sound of whistling wind; can suggest loneliness)
032.2 FX: Pa ("blink")
034.1 FX: Za (waves)
035.1 FX: Zan (heavy-ish sound of waves)
036.1 FX: Biku ("twitch"; can indicate fear, alarm)
036.2 FX: Yoro ("stagger")
039.4 FX: Ha ("Gasp!," exclamation)
040.1 FX: Ki Ki Ki Ki Ki (screech of car brakes)
044.3 FX: Burororoo ("Vroom!")
045.1 FX: Zawa ("rustle," as in leaves)
045.4 FX: Sa (sound of light rain)
046.1 FX: Za (sound of heavy rain)
047.1 FX: Wân (comedic wailing)

047.2 FX: Ki ("glare")
048.2 FX: Piku (lighter "twitch" sound)
048.4 FX: Noro Noro (slow, deliberate movement)
049.3 FX: Za (sound of heavy rain)
049.5 FX: Putsu ("clik")
050.3 FX: Pi (light "tearing" sound)
052.2 FX: Peshi ("whap")
053.2 FX: Gatan ("clunk")
053.3 FX: Za (sound of heavy rain)
054.2 FX: Karari ("rattle," as in sliding door)
054.2 FX: Ha ("Gasp!," exclamation)
058.2 FX: Zukin ("throb")
059.2 FX: Su ("fwish," light "brushing against" sound [in this case, rising to stand])
060.1 FX: Ha Ha Ha Ha Ha (laughter)
060.1 FX: Pushu (escaping carbonation; opening a can)
060.1 FX: Kampai ("Cheers!")
060.2 FX: Puha ("Ahhh" [as in after a long sip of beer])
060.3 FX: Yoro ("stagger"—usually drunken)
061.2 FX: Ha ("Gasp!," exclamation)
061.4 FX: A—! ("Hey-y-y!," "Watch it!")
061.5 FX: Ba ("yank," "shove," "whoosh")
062.1 FX: Gashân ("Craash!")
062.3 FX: Su ("fwish," light "brushing against"—in this case, the sound of displaced air)
063.2 FX: Pasa ("fwish" of Aya's severed lock)
063.4 FX: Sa (sound of light rain)
067.2 FX: Gyu ("squeeze" sound, or "clench")
067.3 FX: Za (sound of heavy rain)
068.2 FX: Pinpôn ("Ding-dong!")
068.3 FX: Kara ("rattle," as of sliding door)
069.1 FX: Basha Basha Basha ("splish"-ing splash)
070.4 FX: Ha ("Gasp!," exclamation)
071.2 FX: Basha Basha ("spish-spash")
071.4 FX: Ha ("Gasp!," exclamation)
072.5 FX: Sa (sound of light rain)
075.1 FX: Ki—! (frustrated wail)
075.2 FX: Doka ("bonk")
075.3 FX: Piki (sound of chagrin)
078.3 FX: Paku Paku (empty flapping of Yûhi's soundless mouth)
080.1 FX: Ki'in (chime of school bell)
080.2 FX: Kôn (chime of school bell)
080.3 FX: Kân Kôn (chime of school bell)
081.1 FX: [Ki'i]n Kôn (chime of school bell)
081.2 FX: [Ki'i]n Kôn (chime of school bell)
082.3 FX: Ha ("Gasp!," exclamation)
082.4 FX: Ba ("yank," "shove," "whoosh"—in this case, "zoom"-ing in of "camera")
084.2 FX: Gyu ("squeeze," "clench")

086.5 FX: Do[kun] (heavy heartbeat)
087.1 FX: [Do]kun (heavy heartbeat)
088.1 FX: Za (waves)
089.1 FX: Gyu ("squeeze," "clench"—in this case, her eyes)
089.2 FX: Goso ("rummaging" sound)
091.1 FX: Za (waves)
092.1 FX: Ba (rough "grab," or shake)
092.3 FX: Zaza (sound of "short" waves)
094.4 FX: Kata ("chk")
095.2 FX: Fura ("wavering" where she stands)
096.3 FX: Gyu ("squeeze," "clench")
097.2 FX: Gyu ("squeeze," "clench")
099.2 FX: Peri (small "tearing," "peeling" sound)
100.1 FX: Kon Kon ("knock knock")
100.4 FX: Pachi Pachi Pachi ("clap clap clap")
101.3 FX: Ha ("Gasp!," exclamation)
102.2 FX: Gyu ("squeeze," "clench")
103.1 FX: O—! ("Whoa!," "Awright!," "Way t' go!")
103.4 FX: Ha ("Gasp!," exclamation)
105.4 FX: Dan Dan Dan (rhythmic dribbling of basketball)
106.3 FX: Pi— ("fweet"—sound of whistle)
106.3 FX: Wa— (cheering crowd)
107.1 FX: Pi— ("fweet"—whistle)
107.3 FX: Gaku (buckling of Aya's knees)
111.2 FX: Burororoo pa— (traffic noises)
112.1 FX: Ha ("Gasp!," exclamation)
113.2 FX: Ha ("Gasp!," exclamation)
113.3 FX: Zawa ("rustle")
114.4 FX: Ha ("Gasp!," exclamation)
116.2 FX: Paku ("chomp")
116.2 FX: Bo (sound of a "blush")
116.3 FX: Doki Doki (quickening heartbeat)
117.2 FX: Dokin ("gulp")
117.3 FX: Gan ("bonk")
117.5 FX: Kusu Kusu ("tee-hee")
119.3 FX: Gyu— ("squeeze," "clench")
119.4 FX: Basha ("splash")
121.1 FX: Kon Kon ("knock knock")
121.2 FX: Kacha ("chk")
121.4 FX: Bishi ("whap")
122.1 FX: Bikun (a "startled," "taken-aback" sound)
122.4 FX: Gyu ("squeeze," "clench")
123.2 FX: Dokun (heavy heartbeat)
123.4 FX: Dokun Dokun... (heavy heartbeat)
123.4 FX: Gyu ("squeeze," "clench")
124.1 FX: Goku ("Gulp!")
124.5 FX: Dokun Dokun... (heavy heartbeat)
125.4 FX: Ka Ka Ka... (sound of footsteps)
126.1 FX: Ka (footsteps)
130.1 FX: Gishi ("creak," as in bedsprings)
131.2 FX: Gishi ("creak")

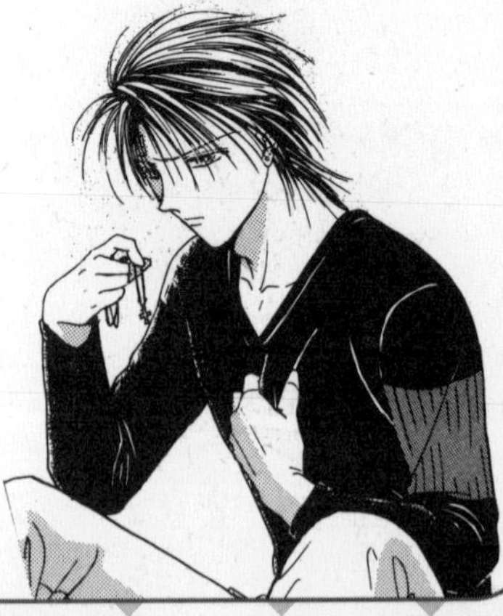

133.3 FX: Patan (sound of a door... closing with finality)
137.2 FX: Ka Ka Ka (footsteps)
138.2 FX: Ka Ka (footsteps)
142.5 FX: Pon ("pat," controlled "touch" sound)
144.6 FX: Go ("bonk")
144.6 FX: Pi ("beep")
145.4 FX: Gashi Gashi ("skritch, skritch")
146.1 FX: Bikun (a "startled," "taken-aback" sound)
146.4 FX: Wata Wata (sound of flailing panic)
147.2 FX: Pashi ("whap")
149.1 FX: Gaku Gaku ("shake, shake")
152.3 FX: Piku ("twitch")
152.5 FX: Basa ("fwap")
153.2 FX: Bikun (a "startled," "taken-aback" sound)
154.4 FX: Patan (closing door)
158.1 FX: Dota Gashân ("Thunk!" "Crash!")
158.3 FX: Gaba ("pop"; sound of sudden rising)
160.4 FX: Su ("fwish," light "brushing against" sound)
161.3 FX: Suta Suta (sound of purposefully walking away)
162.3 FX: Kan ("clink")
165.2 FX: Za ("fshh"—the sound of a shower)
166.3 FX: Cha ("chk")
166.3 FX: Ha ("Gasp!," exclamation)
166.4 FX: Pi ("beep")
166.5 FX: Kacha ("chk")
168.3 FX: Koto ("clunk")
168.5 FX: Doki (quickening heartbeat)
169.1 FX: Ha ("Gasp!," exclamation)
169.4 FX: Pashi ("whap," sudden grab)
172.4 FX: Ka Ka (footsteps)
172.5 FX: Ki (fixed, intense stare)
173.2 FX: Goso Goso ("rummaging" sound)
173.3 FX: Ha ("Gasp!," exclamation)
177.1 FX: Ha ("Gasp!," exclamation)
177.2 FX: Don ("Boom!")
177.4 FX: Za— (sound of "buoyancy")
178.1 FX: Za— (sound of "buoyancy")
178.2 FX: Ta ("dash")
179.3 FX: Ba ("yank," "shove," "whoosh")
180.1 FX: Ba ("yank," "shove," "whoosh")
180.3 FX: Shu ("slash")
180.5 FX: Ja ("jangle")
181.1 FX: Do ("thud")
182.1 FX: Biku ("twitch"; can indicate fear, alarm)
183.4 FX: Ka Ka (footsteps)
184.1 FX: Ka (footstep)
184.2 FX: Zoku ("Brr!")
185.1 FX: Ba ("yank," "shove," "whoosh")

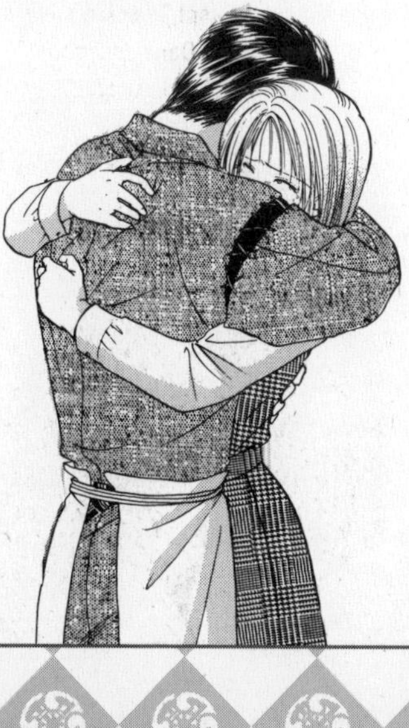

Yû Watase was born on March 5 in a town near Osaka, Japan, and she was raised there before moving to Tokyo to follow her dream of creating manga. In the decade since her debut short story, *PAJAMA DE OJAMA* ("An Intrusion in Pajamas"), she has produced more than 50 compiled volumes of short stories and continuing series. Her latest series, *ZETTAI KARESHI* ("He'll Be My Boyfriend"), is currently running in the anthology magazine *SHÔJO COMIC*. Watase's long-running fantasy/romance story *FUSHIGI YÛGI* and her most recent completed series, *ALICE 19TH*, are now available in North America, published by VIZ. She loves science fiction, fantasy and comedy.

If you enjoyed *CERES: CELESTIAL LEGEND,* here are some other titles VIZ recommends you read:

©2000 YUU WATASE/SHOGAKUKAN Inc.

THE ART OF CERES: CELESTIAL LEGEND gives Yû Watase fans another chance to drool over her art-work. The book contains full-color and black-and-white images from the series, plus character summaries, story background information and an interview with Ms. Watase.

©2001 YUMI TAMURA/SHOGAKUKAN Inc.

CHICAGO is an untradi-tional shôjo adventure by acclaimed artist Yumi Tamura. When their entire rescue team is wiped out, Rei, a tomboy heroine with brains and brawn, and her cool, handsome partner, Uozumi, begin uncovering the mystery that killed their squad. Their first clue is in the south-Shinjuku bar called Chicago.

VIDEO GIRL AI ©1989 by
MASAKAZU KATSURA/SHUEISHA Inc.

VIDEO GIRL AI is a twist on the traditional love triangle. Yota Moteuchi's heart is bro-ken when he finds out the girl he's in love with is in love with his friend. He wanders into a mysterious video store and picks up a rental starring cute, young Ai Amano. When he pops the tape into his bro-ken VCR, Ai jumps from the screen into Yota's arms.

COMPLETE OUR SURVEY AND LET US KNOW WHAT YOU THINK!

☐ Please do NOT send me information about VIZ products, news and events, special offers, or other information.

☐ Please do NOT send me information from VIZ's trusted business partners.

Name: _____

Address: _____

City: _____ **State:** _____ **Zip:** _____

E-mail: _____

☐ Male ☐ Female **Date of Birth** (mm/dd/yyyy): ___ / ___ / _____ (Under 13? Parental consent required)

What race/ethnicity do you consider yourself? (please check one)

☐ Asian/Pacific Islander ☐ Black/African American ☐ Hispanic/Latino

☐ Native American/Alaskan Native ☐ White/Caucasian ☐ Other: _____

What VIZ product did you purchase? (check all that apply and indicate title purchased)

☐ DVD/VHS _____

☐ Graphic Novel _____

☐ Magazines _____

☐ Merchandise _____

Reason for purchase: (check all that apply)

☐ Special offer ☐ Favorite title ☐ Gift

☐ Recommendation ☐ Other _____

Where did you make your purchase? (please check one)

☐ Comic store ☐ Bookstore ☐ Mass/Grocery Store

☐ Newsstand ☐ Video/Video Game Store ☐ Other: _____

☐ Online (site: _____)

What other VIZ properties have you purchased/own? _____
_____

How many anime and/or manga titles have you purchased in the last year? How many were VIZ titles? (please check one from each column)

ANIME	MANGA	VIZ
☐ None	☐ None	☐ None
☐ 1-4	☐ 1-4	☐ 1-4
☐ 5-10	☐ 5-10	☐ 5-10
☐ 11+	☐ 11+	☐ 11+

I find the pricing of VIZ products to be: (please check one)

☐ Cheap ☐ Reasonable ☐ Expensive

What genre of manga and anime would you like to see from VIZ? (please check two)

☐ Adventure ☐ Comic Strip ☐ Science Fiction ☐ Fighting

☐ Horror ☐ Romance ☐ Fantasy ☐ Sports

What do you think of VIZ's new look?

☐ Love It ☐ It's OK ☐ Hate It ☐ Didn't Notice ☐ No Opinion

Which do you prefer? (please check one)

☐ Reading right-to-left

☐ Reading left-to-right

Which do you prefer? (please check one)

☐ Sound effects in English

☐ Sound effects in Japanese with English captions

☐ Sound effects in Japanese only with a glossary at the back

THANK YOU! Please send the completed form to:

NJW Research
42 Catharine St.
Poughkeepsie, NY 12601

All information provided will be used for internal purposes only. We promise not to sell or otherwise divulge your information.